Super Imperialism

Super Imperialism

The Origin and Fundamentals of U.S. World Dominance

Second Edition

Michael Hudson

PLUTO PRESS
www.plutobooks.com

First published 1972 by Holt, Rinehart and Winston.
Second edition published 2003 by Pluto Press
345 Archway Road, London N6 5AA and
175 Fifth Avenue, New York, NY 10010

Distributed in the United States of America exclusively by
Palgrave Macmillan, a division of St. Martin's Press LLC,
175 Fifth Avenue, New York, NY 10010

www.plutobooks.com

British Library Cataloguing in Publication Data
A catalogue record for this book is available from the British Library

ISBN-13 978–0–7453–1989–6 paperback

Library of Congress Cataloging in Publication Data
Hudson, Michael, 1939–
    Super imperialism : the origin and fundamentals of U.S. world
dominance / Michael Hudson.— 2nd ed.
        p. cm.
Includes bibliographical references (p.) and index.
    1. United States—Foreign economic relations. 2. Imperialism. 3.
International finance. 4. United States—Foreign relations. I. Title:
Origin and fundamentals of U.S. world dominance. II. Title.
    HF1455 H782 2002
    337.73—dc21

                                                                    2002006489

This book is printed on paper suitable for recycling and made from fully managed
and sustained forest sources. Logging, pulping and manufacturing processes are
expected to conform to the environmental standards of the country of origin.
The paper may contain up to 70% post consumer waste.

10   9   8   7   6   5   4   3

Designed and produced for Pluto Press by
Chase Publishing Services, Fortescue, Sidmouth EX10 9QG, England
Typeset from disk by Stanford DTP Services, Northampton
Printed and bound in the European Union by
CPI Antony Rowe, Chippenham and Eastbourne

Contents

" . . . with fraternity on your lips, you declare war against mankind."

Jeremy Bentham, addressing France's National Convention
in 1793, urging it to "Emancipate Your Colonies:
Showing the Uselessness and Mischievousness
of distant Dependencies to an European State."

Preface to the Second Edition

As of summer 2002 the U.S. Treasury is pursuing the same strategy of "benign neglect" for its balance-of-payments deficit that it did thirty years ago. The deficit that caused a global crisis in 1971 when its $10 billion rate led to a 10 per cent dollar devaluation has now risen to hundreds of billions of dollars annually, and is still rising. Treasury Secretary O'Neill says he is not worried and that the situation does not call for any action, at least not on the part of the United States.

This confronts Europe and Asia with a dilemma. If they let the U.S. payments deficit drag the dollar down, this will give U.S. exporters a price advantage. To protect their own producers, central banks must support the dollar's exchange rate by recycling their surplus dollars back to the United States. This option obliges them to buy U.S. Government securities, as U.S. diplomats have made it clear that to buy control of U.S. companies or even to return to gold would be viewed as an unfriendly act.

As global investors move out of the sinking dollar, central banks hardly would want to buy American stocks in any event. Norway suffered such severe losses from recycling its North Sea oil earnings into the U.S. market that by October 2001 the government felt obliged to inform local municipalities that they would have to contribute extra sums to their pension funds. To make up for the U.S. market plunge, public support for Norwegian museums, orchestras and other cultural organizations was cut back.

Unfortunately for the world's central banks, buying U.S. Treasury IOUs also is a losing proposition. The falling dollar erodes their international value, causing Europe and Asia to lose over 10 per cent of the value of their U.S. dollar reserves in 2002. Japan and China each have lost over $35 billion on their dollar holdings. These losses are the equivalent of a negative interest rate.

The greatest loss, however, comes from the sterilized dollar balances themselves. What can central banks do with their dollar inflows except lend them back to the U.S. Treasury to help fund America's own domestic budget deficit? In fact, the larger the U.S. balance of payments grows, the more dollars mount up in the hands of foreign to be recycled to finance the U.S. budget deficit. These dollar holdings – in the form of Treasury bonds – have become a seignorage tax levied by America on the world's central banks.

The world has come to operate on a double standard as the U.S. payments deficit provides a free lunch in the form of compulsory foreign loans to finance U.S. Government policy. To make matters worse, the U.S. budget deficit is soaring as the Bush Administration slashes taxes on the wealthy and their inheritance legacies while increasing military spending.

Foreigners have no say over these policies. Americans fought a revolution over the principle of "no taxation without representation" two centuries ago, but Europe, Asia and Third World countries seem politically far from taking a similar step today. Their dollar claims do not give them the voting rights in U.S. policy formation, yet U.S. Government, IMF and World Bank officials use their dollar claims on debtor economies in Latin America, Africa and Asia to force them to follow the Washington Consensus.

Gold was the monetary medium that checked America's ability to run balance-of-payments deficits without limit. As the dollar ceased being "as good as gold" leading up to 1971, the U.S. Treasury put pressure on central banks to demonetize the metal and finally drove it out of the world monetary system – a geopolitical version of Gresham's Law that bad money drives out good. Removing gold convertibility of the dollar – or for that matter its convertibility into the purchase of U.S. companies or other hard assets – enabled the United States to pursue protectionist trade policies unilaterally. U.S. agricultural subsidies are now helping to drive foreign food production out of world markets, while illegal steel tariffs threaten to drive European and Asian steel out of U.S. and foreign markets alike.

It is significant that the most recent dollar decline started in late spring 2002, soon after President Bush announced steel tariffs that are illegal under international law while Alan Greenspan at the Federal Reserve Board lowered interest rates in an attempt to slow the U.S. stock market plunge. These acts recall the 1971–72 "Chicken War" between America and Europe, and the grain embargo that quadrupled wheat prices outside of the United States. It was this embargo that inspired OPEC to enact matching increases in oil prices to maintain terms-of-trade parity between oil and foodstuffs. The "oil shock" was simply a reverberation of the U.S. grain shock.

There always are two sides to every issue, of course. But as every lawyer and judge knows, rhetorical flourish and a massive ideological bombing in the press often sways public opinion. U.S. officials claim that their surplus dollars act as a "growth locomotive" for other countries by inflating their credit-creating powers, as if they needed dollars to do this. Another supposed silver lining to the dollar glut is that falling import prices for dollar-denominated commodities helps deter inflationary pressures in the industrialized European and Asian economies. The flip side of this coin, of course, is that the falling dollar once again is squeezing raw materials exporters who price their minerals, fuels and other commodities in dollars, throwing them into yet deeper financial dependency on the United States.

Credit creation for all countries is an inherently domestic affair. As long as national central banks rely on the dollar, their monetary backing must take the form of financing the U.S. budget deficit and balance-of-payments deficit simultaneously. This linkage promises to make the balance of payments as political an issue today as it was a generation ago in the days of General de Gaulle. But at least he was able to cash in France's surplus dollars for U.S. gold on a monthly basis. Today it would be necessary for Europe and Asia to design an artificial, politically created alternative to the dollar as an international store of value. This promises to become the crux of international political tensions for the next generation.

This book aims at providing the background for U.S.–European and U.S.–Asian financial relations by explaining how the U.S. Treasury bill standard came to provide America with a free lunch since gold was demonetized in 1971, and why the IMF and World Bank cannot be expected to help. Published thirty years ago, it was the first to criticize the World Bank and IMF for imposing destructive policies on the world's debtor economies, and to trace these policies to U.S. diplomatic pressure. It shows how Anglo-American maneuvering during the closing phases of World War II led the IMF to promote capital flight from debtor countries under the slogan of financial deregulation. Also documented is how the World Bank has aimed since the 1950s at promoting foreign trade dependency on U.S. farm exports, and accordingly has opposed land reform and agricultural self-sufficiency abroad. The seeds of the policies that created the disasters of Russian reform under the U.S.-sponsored kleptocrats after 1991 and the Asian-Russian crisis of 1997–98 may be traced back to the malstructuring of the World Bank and IMF at the insistence of U.S. economic diplomats at the inception of these two Bretton Woods institutions.

The new edition is an expanded version, as the dollar crisis was just breaking at the time I handed in the manuscript for this book to Holt, Rinehart and Winston early in 1972. By the time it was published in September, under the title *Super Imperialism: The Economic Strategy of American Empire*, the international financial system was being radically transformed by the currency upheavals that followed the closing of the London gold window in August 1971 and devaluation of the dollar by 10 per cent. America's balance-of-payments deficit continued to widen, but foreign central banks no longer were able to hold America to account by cashing in their surplus dollars for gold.

At the Smithsonian Conference in 1971 the world's major powers argued mightily over the U.S. demand that parity values should be changed in coordinated fashion with a view to permitting the U.S. to improve its external current account position by an annual amount of some $15–20 billion. Today that amount seems so small as to be merely marginal. A comparison of the 1971 dollar crisis with the situation that is now accepted as the norm shows the degree to which foreign nations have simply capitulated to the dollar's free lunch at their own expense.

The fact that running a balance-of-payments deficit forced foreign central banks to use their dollars to buy U.S. bonds to finance America's own domestic budget deficit came as somewhat of a surprise even to Washington officials. Politicians are notorious for lacking an economic perspective, preferring to confront worldly constraints with authoritarian commands. They simply overlooked the balance-of-payments constraint on U.S. overseas military spending.

In 1971 the Institute for Policy Studies obtained the Pentagon Papers, and invited me down to Washington for a series of meetings to review them. What struck me was that the absence of any discussion of the balance-of-payments costs of the war in Southeast Asia. Yet the war was single-handedly responsible for pushing the balance of payments into deficit, inspiring headlines each month when General de Gaulle cashed in his surplus dollars for gold. Rather than subordinate U.S. diplomacy to balance-of-payments constraints, the Pentagon mobilized a full-time desk to counter with the warnings about the war's balance-of-payments costs voiced by the "Columbia Group," composed of my mentor Terence McCarthy and Seymour Melman at Columbia University's School of Industrial Engineering, and myself.

No one anticipated that America's federal budget deficit during the 1990s would be financed by China, Japan and other East Asian countries rather than by American taxpayers and domestic investors. Yet this international exploitation was implicit in the U.S. Treasury bill standard. Since 1971 it has freed the U.S. economy from having to do what American diplomats insist that other debtor countries do when they run payments deficits: impose austerity to restore balance in its international payments. The United States alone has been free to pursue domestic expansion and foreign diplomacy with hardly a worry about the balance-of-payments consequences. Imposing austerity on debtor countries, America as the world's largest debtor economy acts uniquely without financial constraint. For that reason I originally wanted to entitle my book *Monetary Imperialism* so as to emphasize this new financial character of America's way of exploiting the world via the international monetary system itself.

I had published my analysis of the U.S. balance of payments (updated here in Chapter 8) in New York University's Institute of Finance *Bulletin* in March 1970. One of my students gave me an internal New York Federal Reserve review of my analysis that found it correct even while their economists publicly denounced my findings that the war alone was responsible for the crisis, not foreign aid or private investment. The balance of payments was becoming a highly political topic.

A few years ago I sought to update my breakdown of the balance of payments to update the impact of U.S. military spending and foreign aid. But the Commerce Department's Table 5 from its balance of payments data had been changed in such a way it no longer reveals the extent to which foreign aid generates a transfer of dollars from foreign countries *to* the United States, as it did in the 1960s and 1970s. I telephoned the statistical division responsible for collecting these statistics and in due course reached the technician responsible for the numbers. "We used to publish that data," he explained, "but some joker published a report showing that the United States actually made money off the countries we were aiding. It caused such a stir that we changed the accounting format so that nobody can embarrass us like that again." I realized that I was the joker who had been responsible for the present-day statistical concealment, and that it would take a Congressional request to get the Commerce and State Departments to replicate the analysis that still was being made public in the years in which I wrote *Super Imperialism*.

The book sold especially well in Washington. I was told that U.S. agencies were the main customers, using it in effect as a training manual on how to turn the payments deficit into an economically aggressive lever to exploit other countries via their central banks. It was translated into Spanish, Russian and Japanese almost immediately, but I was informed that U.S. diplomatic pressure on Japan led the publisher to withdraw the book (after having already paid for the translation rights) so as not to offend American sensibilities.

The book received a wider review in the business press than in academic journals. A few weeks after the U.S. publication I was invited to address the annual meeting of Drexel-Burnham to outline how the new Treasury bill standard of world finance had replaced the gold exchange standard. Herman Kahn was the meeting's other invited speaker. When I had finished, he got up and said, "You've shown how the United States has run rings around Britain and every other empire-building nation in history. We've pulled off the greatest rip-off ever achieved." He hired me on the spot to join him as the Hudson Institute's economist.

I was happy enough to leave my professorship in international economics at the New School for Social Research. My professional background had been on Wall Street as balance-of-payments economist for the Chase Manhattan Bank and Arthur Andersen. My research along these lines was too political to fit comfortably into the academic economics curriculum, but at the Hudson Institute I set to work tracing how America was turning its payments deficit into an unprecedented element of strength rather than weakness.

At the American Political Science Association's annual meeting in New Orleans in September 1972, the month the book was published, I gave a speech on "Intergovernmental Imperialism vs. Private-Sector Imperialism" outlining how the Treasury bill standard had turned the traditional rules of international finance on their head. This paper forms the new introduction to this book.

I also have expanded the first chapter into what now are three chapters in order put today's economic behavior in perspective to see the degree to which World War I was the watershed signaling the ascendancy of intergovernmental capital, that is, foreign official debt. This debt has a dynamic that overrides the usual political ideologies. Intergovernmental debts first were catalyzed in the 1920s by the breakdown of world payments and trade in the wake of Inter-Ally war debts and German reparations, a breakdown that resulted mainly from the absence of a responsible government policy on the part of the United States.

Had the U.S. Government been interested in dominating the world economy and its diplomacy at that time, as it sought to do after World War II, it could have done so while maintaining the semblance of business as usual. Instead, it pursued an essentially isolationist policy, looking within rather than involving itself directly in foreign affairs. America's major foreign policy was crudely to demand payment of its World War I arms loans to its allies, while erecting tariff barriers that prevented these debts from being paid in the form of higher exports to the United States. The parallel with today's Third World debts in the face of rising non-tariff barriers against Third World exports is clear enough.

U.S. private investment seemed prepared to pick up the slack, but could not bridge the payments gap imposed by the enormous weight of official debt service demanded by American nationalists. The U.S. Government refused to take the mantel of world financial leadership from Britain, and the result was a world economic breakdown whose fate was sealed in 1933 at the London Economic Conference. Modest attempts at internationalism gave way to renewed nationalist pressures which culminated in World War II.

In the years following the war the U.S. Government took a much more active role in directing the world economy. Espousing laissez-faire rhetoric, it moved deftly to shape the environment in which world market forces operated so as to promote international dependency on the United States.

I looked forward to adding these additional chapters to the paperback edition, but Holt Rinehart was not doing well enough to reprint much of anything as its owner, CBS, drastically cut its staff in an attempt to sell the company along with other CBS holdings. So I was given a reversion of the book's rights. In mid-1973 the Beacon Press in Boston offered to bring out a paperback version, but told me that their publication of *The Pentagon Papers* had brought down the wrathful power of government harassment, consuming their resources in heavy legal costs. They had no money to add any material to the book, as the additions that I had made to nearly every chapter would have entailed resetting the type. I chose to hold out until another offer was made that would include the expansions I had written.

In the meantime Harper & Row proposed that I write a sequel, *Global Fracture: The Economic Strategy of American Empire* (1977). That book's second chapter summarized the characteristics of the Treasury bill standard as an exploitative financial device enabling the United States to run cost-free payments deficits *ad infinitum.*

The rewritten manuscript of *Super Imperialism*'s second edition lay on my shelf for nearly thirty years. Periodically I discussed reprinting it, but the issue did not become pressing until 1999. Protest finally was arising against the failure of the World Bank and IMF, or more accurately – and what amounted to the same thing – their success at promoting an exploitative U.S.-centered diplomacy. It had begun to be acknowledged that the international financial system had been shunted onto a destructive path causing chronic balance-of-payments crises throughout the world. I found it appropriate to publish this revised edition of my book so as to relate present-day critiques to the fatal errors that were built into the World Bank and IMF at their inception. The new edition therefore is an augmented study of U.S. financial diplomacy, originally published when the character of America's response to its changing place in the world was just becoming apparent.

A number of trends that were merely implicit in 1972 have since become explicit. First has been the U.S. Treasury's ability to run up an international debt of over $600 billion, using the balance-of-payments deficit to finance not only its widening trade deficit but its federal budget deficit as well. To the extent that these Treasury IOUs are being built into the world's monetary base they will not have to be repaid, but are to be rolled over indefinitely. This feature is the essence of America's free financial ride, a tax imposed at the entire globe's expense.

U.S. economic interest lies supporting a world monetary order that permits it to run even more deeply into debt without foreign constraint. European and Asian attempts to create alternative regional currency clearing blocs accordingly are opposed. Foreign countries are to dollarize their economies, Argentina-style.

A second flowering of seeds planted in the early 1970s has been the use of the International Monetary Fund and World Bank to use Third World, Russian and East Asian debt as a lever to force debtor economies to pursue lines promoted by the Washington Consensus. To promote this objective U.S. diplomats oppose reform of these institutions and their replacement by new global institutions with an economic philosophy that would promote domestic or regional self-sufficiency rather than continued agricultural, financial and technological as well as political and military dependence on the United States.

A third dynamic has been an increasing domination of economic life by government, despite the recent wave of privatizations throughout the world. In fact, these privatizations reflect foreign government obedience to the Washington Consensus. The rhetoric is free enterprise, but the market is to be shaped and defined by bilateral diplomacy with U.S. planners. America would like to mobilize multilateral foreign aid through the IMF and World Bank to continue subsidizing client oligarchies and political parties whose policies serve U.S. interests rather than those of their own nationals. Landmarks in U.S. influence obliging foreign governments to warp their economies to serve U.S. designs include the Plaza Accord with Japan and Europe in 1985 and the ensuing Louvre Accord. These agreements triggered Japan's Bubble Economy and broke the "Japanese challenge." The most recent disaster has been the Russian reforms imposed by the U.S. client Yeltsin–Chubais families. They are the antithesis of weak government, acting as they do on behalf of the Washington Consensus. The government in question is simply that of the United States.

A fourth characteristic of U.S. diplomatic strong-arming has been the shift of world trade toward bilateral "orderly market-sharing agreements" in which foreign economies guarantee a fixed or rising market share to U.S. suppliers, regardless of growth in their own domestic production capacity. Dependency policies are to be pursued, not self-sufficiency in food, technology or other vital sectors.

Other tendencies that seemed likely to gain momentum in 1972 have passed their crest and are now being superseded. The New International

Economic Order aimed at resisting U.S. initiatives in the 1970s, but was successfully countered by American diplomats in the 1980s. Declining terms of trade for raw materials exporters were reversed temporarily following the 1973 Oil War, and negotiations to stabilize commodity prices favorable to Third World exporters began, but quickly collapsed. The fact that most commodities are now priced in dollars that are depreciating in value aggravates the terms of trade for Third World countries.

No serious alternative is now being proposed to the American-centered financial system and the debt deflation its monetarist policies are imposing on debtor economies outside of the United States. The euro has not been put forth as a political alternative to the dollar, nor has a Yen Area materialized in Asia.

Europe's tendency to buckle at each new U.S. diplomatic initiative was potentially stemmed by formation of the European Council and coordinated European Community foreign policy preparing for unification in the 1990s. But despite the euro's introduction there still is much opposition to a full-fledged United States of Europe. Britain is leading the opposition as usual, acting as America's Trojan horse as it did during and after World War II in reaching agreements with the U.S. Treasury that were adverse to its own interests. Lacking a common power to tax and create credit, the euro is no more on a par with the dollar than is the yen. The European Commission seems to be functioning virtually as an arm of U.S. diplomacy in curtailing the power of governments to take an independent monetary stance from the United States.

The upshot is that although the world seems to be consolidating into five major regions, each with its own north–south tensions, each region is heavily U.S.-centered: 1) a Western Hemisphere Dollar Bloc dominated by the United States, including Canada via NAFTA and Latin America; 2) a Japanese-dominated Yen Area, whose surplus are turned over to the U.S. as reserves kept in Treasury bills, while savings have been turned over to U.S. brokerage firms and money managers following Japan's Big Bang of 1998; 3) an emerging Mediterranean triangle including the European Community, the Near East and North Africa; 4) the former Soviet Union and associated COMECON economies, which have all but adopted the U.S. dollar as their currency as a result of adopting crippling U.S. economic recommendations; and 5) China, whose application to join the World Trade Organization does not yet indicate just what position it may end up taking.

I have analyzed the system that might have emerged out of these tendencies in *Global Fracture* (1977). The present book describes how the proposed New International Economic Order originated as a response to America's aggressive world economic diplomacy, and how U.S. strategy has provided other nations with a learning curve that they may follow in pressing their own national and regional interests.

Michael Hudson
2002

Introduction

It would be simplistic to view the United States' rise to world dominance as following the European model characterized by the drives of private finance capital. One must do more than merely read John Hobson and V. I. Lenin to perceive the dynamics of U.S. diplomacy over the past eight decades. The United States has achieved its global position through novel policies that were not anticipated by economists writing prior to World War I, or indeed prior to the 1970s.

One lesson of U.S. experience is that the national diplomacy, embodied in what now is called the Washington Consensus, is not simply an extension of business drives. It has been shaped by overriding concerns for world power (euphemized as national security) and economic advantage as perceived by American strategists quite apart from the profit motives of private investors. Although the roots of imperialism and its diplomatic rivalries always have been economic in character, these roots – and especially their tactics – are not the same for all nations in all periods.

To explain the principles and strategies at work, this book describes how the United States' ascent to world creditor status after World War I resulted from the unprecedented terms on which its government extended armaments and reconstruction loans to its wartime allies. In administering these Inter-Ally debts, U.S. Government aims and objectives were different from those of the private sector investment capital on which Hobson and Lenin had focused in their analysis of Europe's imperial conflicts. The United States had a unique perception of its place and role in the world, and hence of its self-interest.

The United States' isolationist and often messianic ethic can be traced back to the 1840s, although Republicans expressed it in a different way from Democrats. (I describe this social philosophy in my 1975 survey of *Economics and Technology in 19th-Century American Thought*.) Spokesmen for American industrialists prior to the Civil War – the American School of political economy led by Henry Carey, E. Peshine Smith and their followers – believed that their nation's rise to world power would be achieved by protecting their economy from that of Britain and other European nations. The objective was to create nothing less than a new civilization, one based on high wages as a precondition for achieving even higher productivity.

The result would be a society of abundance rather than one whose cultural and political principles were based on the phenomenon of scarcity.

The idea that America needed an ever-receding western frontier was voiced by Democrats motivated largely by the Slave Power's desire to expand cotton cultivation southward, while promoting westward territorial expansion to extend wheat-growing to provide food. The Democratic Party's agenda was to expand foreign trade by reducing tariffs and relying largely on food and raw materials exports to buy manufactures from abroad (mainly from Britain). By contrast, Republican protectionists sought to build up a domestic market for manufactures behind tariff walls. The party's industrial advocates focused on technological modernization in the eastern urban centers.

Whereas the Democratic Party was Anglophile, Republican strategists had a long history of Anglophobia, above all in their opposition to British free trade doctrines, which dominated the nation's religious colleges. It was largely to promote protectionist doctrines that state land-grant colleges and business schools were created after the Civil War. In contrast to the economic theories of David Ricardo and Thomas Malthus, these colleges described America as a new civilization, whose dynamics were those of increasing returns in agriculture as well as industry, and the perception that rising living standards would bring about a new social morality. The protectionist Simon Patten was typical in juxtaposing American civilization to European society wracked by class conflict, pauper labor and a struggle for foreign markets based on reducing wage levels. Teaching at the University of Pennsylvania from the 1890s through the 1910s, Patten's students included such future luminaries as Franklin Roosevelt's brainstruster Rex Tugwell and the socialist Scott Nearing.

Europe's imperial rivalries were viewed as stemming from its competing princely ambitions and an idle landed aristocracy, and from the fact that its home markets were too impoverished to purchase industrial manufactures of the type that were finding a ready market in the United States. To Republican nationalists the United States did not need colonies. Its tariff revenues would better be spent on internal improvements than on vainglorious foreign conquests.

This attitude helps explain America's belated commitment to World War I. The nation declared war in 1917 only when it became apparent that to stay out would entail at least an interim economic collapse as American bankers and exporters found themselves stuck with uncollectible loans to Britain and its allies. Reflecting the ideological and moral elements in America's entry, President Wilson viewed the nation's political and cultural heritage as stemming largely from England. He was a Democrat, and a southerner to boot, whereas most of the leading Republican intellectuals, including Patten, Thorstein Veblen and Charles Beard, felt a closer kinship to Germany. That nation was after all in much the same position as the United States in seeking to shape its social evolution by state policy to build a high-income, technologically innovative economy, marked by government leadership in social spending and the financing of heavy industry.

This social philosophy helps explain America's particular form of isolationism preceding and after World War I, and especially the government's demand to be repaid for its wartime loans to its allies. U.S. officials insisted that the nation was merely an associate in the war, not a full ally. Its $12 billion in armaments and reconstruction loans to Europe were more of a business character than a contribution to a common effort. America saw itself as economically and politically distinct.

The dilemma of U.S. economic diplomacy in the interwar years

The United States, and specifically its government, emerged from the war not only as the world's major creditor, but a creditor to foreign governments with which it felt little brotherhood. It did not see its dominant economic position as obliging it to take responsibility for stabilizing world finance and trade. If Europe wished to channel its labor and capital to produce armaments instead of paying its debts, and if it persisted in its historical antagonisms – as evidenced by the onerous Treaty of Versailles imposed on Germany – the United States need feel no obligation to accommodate it.

The government therefore did not seek to create a system capable of extending new loans to foreign countries to finance their payments to the United States, as it was to do after World War II. Nor did it lower its tariffs so as to open U.S. markets to foreign producers as a means of enabling them to pay their war debts to the U.S. Treasury. The United States rather wished to see Europe's empires dissolved, and did not mind seeing imperial governments stripped of their wealth, which tended to be used for military purposes with which few Americans sympathized. The resulting failure to take the lead in restructuring the world economy and to perceive the financial and commercial policy obligations inherent in the United States' new economic status rendered its war credits uncollectible.

Economically, the U.S. attitude was to urge European governments to reduce their military spending and/or living standards, to permit their money to flow out and their prices to fall. In this way, it was hoped, world payments equilibrium might be re-established even in the face of rising American protectionism and full payment of the Inter-Ally debts that were the legacy of the Great War.

This was not a clearly thought-out position or a realistic one, but many leading Europeans shared these attitudes. In trying to cope with the international financial breakdown of the 1920s, their governments were advised by anti-German writers such as Bertil Ohlin and Jacques Rueff, who insisted that Germany could repay its assessed reparations if only it would submit to sufficient austerity.

The parallel with monetarist Chicago School attitudes towards today's debtor economies is appallingly obvious. Its view of international payments adjustment was as self-defeating in the 1920s as are the IMF's austerity programs today. By insisting on repayment of its allies' war debts in full, and by simultaneously enacting increasingly protectionist tariffs at home, the U.S. Government made repayment of these debts impossible.

Private investors traditionally had been obliged to take losses when debtors defaulted, but it became apparent that the U.S. Government was not about to relinquish its creditor hold on the Allies. This intransigence obliged them to keep tightening the screws on Germany.

To review the 1920s from today's vantage point is to examine how nations were not acting in their enlightened self-interest but in an unquestioning reaction against obsolete economic attitudes. The orthodox ideology carried over from the prewar era was anachronistic in failing to recognize that the world economy emerged from World War I shackled with debts far beyond its ability to pay – or at least, beyond the ability to pay except on conditions in which debtor countries merely would borrow the funds from private lenders in the creditor nation to pay the creditor-nation government. U.S. bankers and investors lent money to German municipalities, which turned the dollars over to the central bank to pay reparations to the Allies, which in turn used the dollars to pay their war debts to the U.S. Treasury. The world financial system thus was kept afloat simply by intergovernmental debts being wound down by a proportional build-up in private sector and municipal debts.

The ensuing débâcle introduced a behavioral difference from the processes analyzed by Hobson, Lenin and other theorists of prewar world diplomacy. In the nineteenth century Britain took on the position of world banker in no small measure to provide its colonies and dependencies with the credit necessary to sustain the international specialization of production desired by British industry. After World War I, the U.S.

Government pursued no such policy. An enlightened imperialism would have sought to turn other countries into economic satellites of the United States. But the United States did not want European exports, nor were its investors particularly interested in Europe after its own stock market outperformed those of Europe.

The United States could have named the terms on which it would have supplied the world with dollars to enable foreign countries to repay their war debts. It could have specified what imports it wanted or was willing to take. But it did not ask, or even permit, debtor countries to pay their debts in the form of exports to the United States. Its investors could have named the foreign assets they wanted to buy, but private investors were overshadowed by intergovernmental financial agreements, or the lack of them, enforced by the U.S. Government. On both the trade and financial fronts the U.S. Government pursued policies that impelled European countries to withdraw from the world economy and turn within.

Even the United States' attempt to ameliorate matters backfired. To make it easier for the Bank of England to pay its war debts, the Federal Reserve held down interest rates so as not to draw money away from Britain. But low interest rates spurred a stock market boom, discouraging U.S. capital outflows to European financial markets.

America's failure to recycle the proceeds of its intergovernmental debt receipts into the purchase of European exports and assets was a failure to perceive the implicit strategy dictated by its unique position as world creditor. European diplomats spelled out the required strategy clearly enough in the 1920s, but the U.S. Government's economic isolationism precluded it from collecting its intergovernmental debts. Its status as world creditor proved ultimately worthless as the world economy broke into nationalist units, each striving to become independent of foreign trade and payments, and from the U.S. economy in particular. In this respect America forced its own inward-looking attitude on other nations.

The upshot was the breakdown of world payments, competitive devaluations, tariff wars and international autarchy that characterized the 1930s. This state of affairs was less an explicit attempt at imperialism than an inept result of narrowly legalistic and bureaucratic intransigence regarding the war debts, coupled with a parochial domestic tariff policy. It was just the opposite of a policy designed to establish the United States as the world's economic center based on a reciprocity of payments between creditor and periphery, a complementarity of imports and exports, production and payments. A viable U.S.-centered world economic system would have required some means of enabling Europe to repay its war debts.

What occurred instead was isolationism at home, prompting drives for national self-sufficiency abroad.

One can find cases throughout history in which seemingly logical paths of least resistance have not been followed. In most such cases the explanation is to be found in leadership looking backward rather than forward, or to narrow rather than broad economic and social interests. Although it certainly was logical in the 1920s for private U.S. investors to extend their power throughout the world, the financial policies pursued by the U.S. Government (and to a lesser extent by other governments) made this impossible. The Government narrowly construed America's national self-interest in terms of the Treasury's balance sheet, putting this above the cosmopolitan tendencies of private financial capital. This forced country after country to withdraw from the internationalism of the gold exchange standard and to abandon policies of currency stability and free trade.

The burden of Britain's war debts impelled it to convene the Ottawa Conference in 1932 to establish a system of Commonwealth tariff preferences. Germany turned its eyes inward to prepare for a war to seize by force the materials which it could not buy under existing world conditions. Japan, France and other countries were similarly stymied. Depression spread as the world financial crisis was internalized in one country after another. As world trade and payments broke down utterly, the national socialist governments of Italy and Germany became increasingly aggressive. Governments throughout the world responded to falling incomes and employment by vastly extending their role in economic affairs, prompting Keynes to proclaim the end of laissez-faire.

The Great Depression extinguished private capital throughout the world, just as intergovernmental capital had been extinguished by the short-sightedness of governments seeking to derive maximum economic benefit from their financial claims on other governments. This poses the question of why such debts were allowed to become so problematic in the first place.

Britain's agreement to begin paying its war debts to the United States no doubt was inspired largely by its world creditor ideology of maintaining the "sanctity of debt." Yet this policy no longer was appropriate in a situation where Britain, along with continental Europe, had become an international debtor rather than a creditor. There was little idea of adjusting the traditional ideology concerning the sanctity of debts to their realistic means of payment.

The Great Depression and World War II taught governments the folly of this attitude, although they were to lose it again with regard to Third World and Eastern Bloc debts within a few decades of the close of World War II.

American plans for a postwar "free trade imperialism"

Since 1945, U.S. foreign policy has sought to reverse foreign state control over economic policies generally, and attempts at economic self-reliance and independence from the United States in particular.

As U.S. diplomats and economists theorized during 1941–45 over the nation's imminent role as dominant power in the postwar world, they recognized that it would emerge from the war by far the strongest national economy, but would have to be a major exporter in order to maintain full employment during the transition back to peacetime life. This transition was expected to require about five years, 1946–50. Foreign markets would have to replace the War Department as a source of demand for the products of American industry and agriculture. This in turn required that foreign countries be able to earn or borrow dollars to pay the United States for these exports.

This time around it was clear that the United States could not impose war debts on its Allies similar to those that had followed World War I. For one thing, the Allies had been stripped of their marketable international assets. If they were obliged to pay war debts to the United States, they would have no remaining funds to buy American exports. The U.S. Government therefore would have to provide the world with dollars, by government loans, private investment or a combination of both. In exchange, it would be entitled to name the terms on which it would provide these dollars. The question was, what terms would U.S. economic diplomats stipulate?

In January 1944 the annual meeting of the American Economic Association was dominated by proposals for postwar U.S. economic policy. "For the first time in many decades," wrote J. B. Condliffe of the Carnegie Endowment for Peace, "– indeed for the first time since the very earliest years of the infant republic – attention is now being paid by soldiers and political scientists, but little as yet by economists, to the power position of the United States in the modern world. This attention is part of the re-examination of national policy made necessary by the fact that this war has shown the folly of complacent and self-centered isolationist theorist and attitudes."[1] Such an examination should not be thought of as Machiavellian or evil, Condliffe urged, but as a necessity if U.S. ideals were to carry real force behind them.

A central theme of the meeting was the relative roles that government and business would play in shaping the postwar world. In a symposium of former presidents of the American Economic Association on "What Should be the Relative Spheres of Private Business and Government in our Postwar American Economy?" most respondents held that the distinction between private business and government policy was becoming fuzzy, and that some degree of planning was needed to keep the economy working at relatively full employment.

This did not necessarily imply a nationalist economic policy, although that seemed to be an implicit long-term tendency. Speaking on "The Present Position of Economics," Arthur Salz observed that "government and economics have drawn close together and live in a real and, to a large extent, in a personal union. While formerly the economist made his reputation by constructive[ly] criticizing governments, he is now hand and glove with them and has become the friend and patron of the government machinery whose severest critic he once was."[2]

The problem of government/private sector relations was put in most rigorous form by Jacob Viner, the laissez-faire theoretician from the University of Chicago. His speech on "International Relations between State-Controlled National Economies" challenged the idea that private enterprise "is normally unpatriotic, while government is automatically patriotic." National economic planning was inherently belligerent, he warned, and the profit motive would be the best guarantee against the waste and destruction of international conflict. Corporations could not go to war, but governments found in war the ultimate expression of their drives for power and prestige. Viner concluded hopefully: "The pattern of international economic relations will be much less influenced by the operation of national power and national prestige considerations in a world of free-enterprise economies than in a world of state-operated national economies."[3]

This was just the opposite of socialist theory, which assumed that national governments were inherently peaceful, except when goaded by powerful business cartels. Hobson had insisted that "The apparent oppositions of interests between nations . . . are not oppositions between the people conceived as a whole; they are expositions of class interests within the nation. The interests of America and Great Britain and France and Germany are common,"[4] although those of their individual manufacturers and exporters were not.

The war debts and reparations after World War I had brought into question this generality. According to Viner's laissez-faire view, the tendency for conflict among nations – and hence the chances of war – would be greater rather than smaller in a world of state-controlled economies. Looking back on the experience of the 1930s in particular, he found that "The substitution of state control for private enterprise in the field of international economic relations would, with a certain degree of inevitability, have a series of undesirable consequences, to wit: the injection of a political element into all major international economic transactions; the conversion of international trade from a predominantly competitive to a predominantly monopolistic basis; a marked increase in the potentiality of business disputes to generate international friction," and so forth. From this perspective national rivalries as conceived and carried out by governments were inherently more belligerent than commercial rivalries among private exporters, bankers and investors.

Viner did not, however, cite the U.S. Government's own behavior in the 1920s. Inverting the Hobson–Lenin view of international commercial rivalries, his view had little room for such phenomena as IT&T's involvement in Chile in the early 1970s to oppose Allende's socialism, Lockheed's bribery scandals in Japan or other international bribery of foreign and domestic officials, or even presidential campaign promises to protectionist interests such as those made by Richard Nixon to America's dairy and textile industries in 1968 and again in 1972. Government planning was the problem as an autonomous force based on the inherently nationalistic ambitions of political leaders. No room was acknowledged for planning even of the kind that had led American industry to achieve world leadership from the end of the U.S. Civil War in 1865 to the end of World War I under a program of industrial protectionism and active internal improvements. "Insofar as, in the past, war has resulted from economic causes," Viner insisted,

> it has been to a very large extent the intervention of the national state into the economic process which has made the pattern of international economic relationships a pattern conducive to war . . . socialism on a national basis would not in any way be free from this ominous defect . . . economic factors can be prevented from breeding war if, and only if, private enterprise is freed from extensive state control other than state control intended to keep enterprise private and competitive . . . War, I believe, is essentially a political, not an economic phenomenon. It arises out of the organization of the world on the basis of sovereign nation-states . . . This will be true for a world of socialist states as for a world of capitalist states, and the more embracing the states are in their range of activities the more likely will be the serious friction between states. If states reduce to a minimum their involvement in economic matters, the role of economic factors in contributing to war will be likewise reduced.[5]

It seemed to many observers that U.S. officials were structuring the IMF and World Bank to enable countries to pursue laissez-faire policies by insuring adequate resources to finance the international payments imbalances that were anticipated to result from countries opening their markets to U.S. exporters after the return to peace. Special reconstruction lending would be made to war-torn Europe, followed by development loans to the colonies being freed, and balance-of-payments loans to countries in special straits so that they would not need to resort to currency depreciation and tariff barriers. It was believed that free trade and investment would settle into a state of balanced international trade and payments under the postwar conditions being created under U.S. leadership. Bilateral foreign aid would serve as a direct inducement to governments to acquiesce in the United States' postwar plans, while ensuring the balance-of-payments equilibrium that was a precondition for free trade and an Open Door to international investment.

When President Truman insisted, on March 23, 1946, that "World trade must be restored – and it must be restored to private enterprise," this was a way of saying that its regulation must be taken away from foreign governments that might be tempted to try to recover their prewar power at the expense of U.S. exporters and investors. America's laissez-faire stance promoted the United States as the center of a world system vastly more extensive and centralized, yet also more flexible, less costly and less bureaucratic than Europe's imperial systems had been.

Given the fact that only the United States possessed the foreign exchange necessary to undertake substantial overseas investment, and only the U.S. economy enjoyed the export potential to displace Britain and other European rivals, the ideal of laissez-faire was synonymous with the worldwide extension of U.S. national power. It was recognized that American commercial strength would achieve the government's underlying objective of turning foreign economies into satellites of the United States. The objectives of U.S. exporters and international investors thus were synonymous with those of the government in seeking to maximize U.S. world power, and this was best achieved by discouraging government planning and economic statism abroad.

The laissez-faire ideology that American industrialists had denounced in the nineteenth century, and that the U.S. Government would repudiate in practice in the 1970s and 1980s, served American ends after World War II. Europe's industrial nations would open their doors and permit U.S. investors to buy in to the extractive industries of their former colonies, especially into Near Eastern oil. These less developed regions would provide the United States with raw materials rather than working them up into their own manufactures to compete with U.S. industry. They would purchase a rising stream of American foodstuffs and manufactures, especially those produced by the industries whose productive capacity had expanded greatly during the war. The resulting U.S. trade surplus would provide the foreign exchange to enable American investors to buy up the most productive resources of the world's industry, mining and agriculture.

To the extent that America's export surplus exceeded its private sector investment outflows, the balance would have to be financed by growth in dollar lending via the World Bank, the Export-Import Bank and related intergovernmental aid-lending institutions. Under the aegis of the U.S. Government, American investors and creditors would accumulate a growing volume of claims on foreign economies, ultimately securing control over the non-Communist world's political as well as economic processes.

This idealized model never materialized for more than a brief period. The United States proved unwilling to lower its tariffs on commodities that foreigners could produce less expensively than American farmers and manufacturers, but only on those commodities that did not threaten vested U.S. interests. The International Trade Organization, which in principle was supposed to subject the U.S. economy to the same free trade principles that it demanded from foreign governments, was scuttled. Private U.S. investment abroad did not materialize to the degree needed to finance foreign purchases of U.S. exports, nor were IMF and World Bank loans anywhere near sufficient to buoy up the payments-deficit economies.

The result was that much of Europe's remaining gold was stripped by the United States, as was that of Latin America in the early postwar years. By 1949 foreign countries were all but faced with the need to revert to the protectionism of the 1930s to prevent an unconscionable loss of their economic independence. The U.S. Treasury accumulated three-fourths of the world's gold, denuding foreign markets of their ability to continue buying U.S. exports at their early postwar rates. Britain in particular floundered in a virtually bankrupt position with its overvalued pound sterling, having waived its right to devalue or protect its Sterling Area in exchange for receiving the 1946 British Loan from the U.S. Treasury. Other countries were falling into similar straits. America's payments surplus position thus was threatening its prospective export potential.

In these circumstances U.S. economic planners learned what European, Japanese and OPEC diplomats subsequently have learned. Beyond a point, a creditor and payments surplus status can be decidedly uncomfortable.

It was in America's enlightened self-interest to return some of Europe's gold. What private investors failed to recycle abroad, the government itself would have to do via an extended foreign aid program, perhaps under the emerging Cold War's military umbrella.

There were two potential obstacles to this strategy. First was the drive by foreign economies to regain a modicum of balance-of-payments equilibrium and to promote their own self-sufficiency through protectionism and other nationalist economic policies. This tendency was muted, however, as Britain led Europe's march into the U.S. orbit. This seemed to preempt any drives that continental Europe might have harbored toward achieving economic autonomy from America.

The other major obstacle to U.S. Government plans for the postwar world did not derive from foreign countries, but from Congress. Despite the overwhelming domestic benefits gained by foreign aid, Congress was unwilling to extend funds to impoverished countries as outright gifts, or even as loans beyond a point. The problem was not that it failed to perceive the benefits that would accrue from extending further aid, after the pattern of the British Loan and the subsequent Marshall Plan. It was just that Congress gave priority to domestic spending programs. What was at issue was not an abstract cost-benefit analysis for humanity at large, or even one of overall U.S. long-term interests, but one of parochial interests putting their local objectives ahead of foreign policy.

America embarks on a Cold War that pushes its balance of payments into deficit

As matters turned out, the line of least resistance to circumvent this domestic obstacle was to provide Congress with an anti-Communist national security hook on which to drape postwar foreign spending programs. Dollars were provided not simply to bribe foreign governments into enacting Open Door policies, but to help them fight Communism which might threaten the United States if not nipped in the bud. This red specter was what had turned the tide on the British Loan, and it carried Marshall Aid through Congress, along with most subsequent aid lending down through the present day. Congress would not appropriate funds to finance a quasi-idealistic worldwide transition to laissez-faire, but it would provide money to contain Communist expansion, conveniently defined as being virtually synonymous with spreading poverty nurturing seedbeds of anti-Americanism.

The U.S. Government hoped to keep its fellow capitalist countries solvent. U.S. diplomats remembered the 1930s well enough to recognize that economies threatened with balance-of-payments insolvency would move to insulate themselves, foreclosing U.S. trade and investment opportunities accordingly. As the Council of Foreign Relations observed in 1947:

> In public and Congressional debate, the Administration's case centered on two themes: the role of the [British] loan in world recovery, and the direct benefits to the country from this Agreement. American self-interest was established as the motivation . . . The Administration made a persuasive argument by pointing out what would happen without the loan. Britain would be forced to restrict imports, make bilateral trade bargains, and discriminate against American goods. . . . With the loan, things could be made to move in the other direction.[6]

Former U.S. Ambassador to Britain Joseph Kennedy was among the first to urge U.S. credits for that nation, "largely to combat communism." He even urged an outright gift, on the ground that Britain was for all practical purposes broke.

> Tension with Russia helped the loan, playing a considerable part in offsetting political objections and doubts of the loan's economic soundness. Anti-Soviet sentiment had risen throughout the country, since Winston Churchill, speaking at Fulton [Missouri] on March 5 [1946], had proposed a "fraternal association" of English-speaking nations to check Russia . . . Now . . . his idea seemed to be a decisive factor in determining many Congressmen to vote for the loan . . . Senator Barkely said, "I do not desire, for myself or for my country, to take a position that will drive our ally into arms into which we do not want her to be folded."

Speaker of the House Sam Rayburn endorsed this position. It was to become the political lever to extract U.S. foreign aid for the next two decades. International policies henceforth were dressed in anti-Communist garb in order to facilitate their acceptance by non-liberal congressmen whose sympathies hardly lay with the laissez-faire that had afforded the earlier window dressing for the government's postwar economic planning.

The problem from the government's point of view was that the U.S. balance of payments had reached a surplus level unattained by any other nation in history. It had an embarrassment of riches, and now required a payments deficit to promote foreign export markets and world currency stability. Foreigners could not buy American exports without a means of payment, and private creditors were not eager to extend further loans to countries that were not creditworthy.

The Korean War seemed to resolve this set of problems by shifting the U.S. balance of payments into deficit. Confrontation with Communism became a catalyst for U.S. military and aid programs abroad. Congress was much more willing to provide countries with dollars via anti-Communist or national defense programs than by outright gifts or loans, and after the Korean War U.S. military spending in the NATO and SEATO countries seemed to be a relatively bloodless form of international monetary support. In country after country, military spending and aid programs provided a reflux of some of the foreign gold that the United States had absorbed during the late 1940s.

Within a decade, however, what at first seemed to be a stabilizing economic dynamic became destabilizing. The United States, the only nation capable of financing a worldwide military program, began to sink into the mire that had bankrupted every European power that experimented with colonialism. America's Cold War strategists failed to perceive that whereas private investment tends to be flexible in cutting its losses, being committed to relatively autonomous projects on the basis of securing a satisfactory rate of return year after year, this is not the case with government spending programs, especially in the case of national security programs that created vested interests. Such programs are by no means as readily reversible as those of private industry, for military spending abroad, once initiated, tends to take on a momentum of its own. The government cannot simply say that national security programs have become economically disadvantageous and therefore must be curtailed. That would imply they were pursued in the first place only because they were economically remunerative – something involving the sacrifice of human lives for the narrow motives of economic gain, even if national gain. What began as pretense became a new reality.

The new characteristics of American financial imperialism

If the United States had continued to run payments surpluses, if it had absorbed more foreign gold and dollar balances, the world's monetary reserves would have been reduced. This would have constrained world trade, and especially imports from the United States. A US payments surplus thus was incompatible with continued growth in world liquidity and trade. The United States was obliged to buy more foreign goods, services and capital assets than it supplied to foreigners, unless they could augment monetary reserves with non-U.S. currencies.

What was not grasped was the corollary implication. Under the key-currency dollar standard the only way that the world financial system could become more liquid was for the United States to pump more dollars into it by running a payments deficit. The foreign dollar balances being built up as a result of foreign military and foreign aid spending in the 1950s and 1960s were, simultaneously, debts of the United States.

At first, foreign countries welcomed their surplus of dollar receipts. At the time there was no doubt that the United States was fully capable of redeeming these dollars with its enormous gold stock. But in autumn 1960 a run on the dollar temporarily pushed up the price of gold to $40 an ounce. This was a reminder that the U.S. balance of payments had been in continuing and growing deficit for a decade, since the Korean War. It became clear that just as the U.S. payments surplus had been destabilizing in the late 1940s, so in the early1960s a U.S. payments deficit beyond a point likewise would be incompatible with world financial stability.

The run on gold had followed John Kennedy's victory in the 1960 presidential election, waged largely over a rather demagogic debate over military preparedness. It seemed unlikely that the incoming Democratic administration would do much to change the Cold War policies responsible for the U.S. payments deficit.

Growing attention began to be paid to the difference between domestic and international money. Apart from metallic coinage, domestic currency is a form of debt, but one that nobody really expects to be paid. Attempts by governments to repay their debts beyond a point would extinguish their monetary base. Back in the 1890s high U.S. tariffs produced a federal budget surplus that obliged the Treasury to redeem its bonds, causing a painful monetary deflation. But in the sphere of international money and credit, most investors expect debts to be paid on schedule.

This expectation would seem to doom any attempt to create a key-currency standard. The problem is that international money (viewed as an asset) is simultaneously a debt of the key-currency nation. Growth in key-currency reserves accumulated by payments-surplus economies implies that the nation issuing the key currency acts in effect, and even in reality, as an international borrower. To provide other countries with key-currency assets involves running into debt, and to repay such debt is to extinguish an international monetary asset.

This debt character of the world's growing dollar reserves hardly had been noticed by foreign governments that needed them in the 1950s to finance their own foreign trade and payments. But by the early 1960s it became clear that the United States was approaching the point at which its debts to foreign central banks soon would exceed the value of the Treasury's gold stock. This point was reached and passed in 1964, by which time the U.S. payments deficit stemmed entirely from foreign military spending, mainly for the Vietnam War.

It would have required a change in national consciousness to reverse the military programs that had come to involve the United States in massive commitments abroad. America seemed to be succumbing to a European-style imperial syndrome, and was in danger of losing its dominant world position in much the way that Britain and other imperial powers had done, weighed down by the cost of maintaining its worldwide empire. And just as World Wars I and II had bankrupted Europe, so the Vietnam War threatened to bankrupt the United States.

If the United States had followed the creditor-oriented rules to which European governments had adhered after World Wars I and II, it would have sacrificed its world position. Its gold would have flowed out and Americans would have been obliged to sell off their international investments to pay for military activities abroad. This was what U.S. officials had demanded of their allies in World Wars I and II, but the United States was unwilling to abide by such rules itself. Unlike earlier nations in a similar position, it continued to spend abroad, and at home as well, without regard for the balance-of-payments consequences.

One result was a run on gold, whose momentum rose in keeping with sagging military fortunes in Vietnam. Foreign central banks, especially those of France and Germany, cashed in their surplus dollars for U.S. gold reserves almost on a monthly basis.

Official reserves were sold to meet private demand so as to hold down the price of gold. For a number of years the United States had joined other governments to finance the London Gold Pool. But by March 1968, after a six-month run, America's gold stock fell to the $10 billion floor beyond which the Treasury had let it be known that it would suspend further gold sales. The London Gold Pool was disbanded and informal agreement (*i.e.*, diplomatic arm-twisting) was reached among the world's central banks to stop converting their dollar inflows into gold.

This broke the link between the dollar and the market price of gold. Two prices for gold emerged, a rising open-market price and the lower "official" price of $35 an ounce at which the world's central banks continued to value their monetary reserves.

Three years later, in August 1971, President Nixon made the gold embargo official. The key-currency standard based on the dollar's convertibility into gold was dead. The U.S. Treasury bill standard – that is, the dollar-debt standard based on dollar inconvertibility – was inaugurated. Instead of being able to use their dollars to buy American gold, foreign governments found themselves able to purchase only U.S. Treasury obligations (and, to a much lesser extent, U.S. corporate stocks and bonds).

As foreign central banks received dollars from their exporters and commercial banks that preferred domestic currency, they had little choice but to lend these dollars to the U.S. Government. Running a dollar surplus in their balance of payments became synonymous with lending this surplus to the U.S. Treasury. The world's richest nation was enabled to borrow automatically from foreign central banks simply by running a payments deficit. The larger the U.S. payments deficit grew, the more dollars ended up in foreign central banks, which then lent them to the U.S. Government by investing them in Treasury obligations of varying degrees of liquidity and marketability.

The U.S. federal budget moved deeper into deficit in response to the guns-and-butter economy, inflating a domestic spending stream that spilled over to be spent on more imports and foreign investment and yet more foreign military spending to maintain the hegemonic system. But instead of U.S. citizens and companies being taxed or U.S. capital markets being obliged to finance the rising federal deficit, foreign economies were obliged to buy the new Treasury bonds being issued. America's Cold War spending thus became a tax on foreigners. It was their central banks who financed the costs of the war in Southeast Asia.

There was no real check to how far this circular flow could go. For understandable reasons foreign central banks did not wish to go into the U.S. stock market and buy Chrysler, Penn Central or other corporate securities. This would have posed the kind of risk that central bankers are not supposed to take. Nor was real estate any more attractive. What central banks need are liquidity and security for their official reserves. This is why they traditionally had held gold, as a means of settling their own deficits. To the extent that they began to accumulate surplus dollars, there was little alternative but to hold them in the form of U.S. Treasury bills and notes without limit.

This shift from asset money (gold) to debt money (U.S. Government bonds) inverted the traditional relationships between the balance of payments and domestic monetary adjustment. Conventional wisdom prior to 1968 held that countries that ran deficits were obliged to part with their gold until they stemmed their payments outflows by increasing interest rates so as to borrow more abroad, cutting back government spending and restricting domestic income growth. This is what Britain did in its stop–go policies of the 1960s. When its economy boomed, people bought more imports and spent more abroad. To save the value of sterling from declining, the Bank of England raised interest rates. This deterred new construction and other investment, slowing the economy down. At the government level, Britain was obliged to give up its dreams of empire, as it was unable to generate a large enough private sector trade and investment surplus to pay the costs of being a major world military and political power.

But now the world's major deficit nation, the United States, flouted this adjustment mechanism. It announced that it would not let its domestic policies be "dictated by foreigners." This go-it-alone policy had led it to refrain from joining the League of Nations after World War I, or to play the international economic game according to the rules that bound other nations. It had joined the World Bank and IMF only on the condition that it was granted unique veto power, which it also enjoyed as a member of the United Nations Security Council. This meant that no economic rules could be imposed that U.S. diplomats judged did not serve American interests.

These rules meant that, unlike Britain, the United States was able to pursue its Cold War spending in Asia and elsewhere in the world without constraint, as well as social welfare spending at home. This was just the reverse of Britain's stop–go policies or the austerity programs that the IMF imposed on Third World debtors when their balance of payments fell into deficit.

Thanks to the $50 billion cumulative U.S. payments deficit between April 1968 and March 1973, foreign central banks found themselves obliged to buy all of the $50 billion increase in U.S. federal debt during this period. In effect, the United States was financing its domestic budget deficit by running an international payments deficit. As the St. Louis Federal Reserve Bank described the situation, foreign central banks were obliged "to acquire increasing amounts of dollars as they attempted to maintain relatively fixed parities in exchange rates."[7] Failure to absorb these dollars would have led the dollar's value to fall vis-à-vis foreign currencies, as the supply of dollars greatly exceeded the demand. A depreciating dollar would have provided U.S. exporters with a competitive devaluation, and also would have reduced the domestic currency value of foreign dollar holdings.

Foreign governments had little desire to place their own exporters at a competitive disadvantage, so they kept on buying dollars to support the exchange rate – and hence, the export prices – of Dollar Area economies. "The greatly increased demand for short-term U.S. Government securities by these foreign institutions resulted in lower market yields on these securities relative to other marketable securities than had previously been the case," explained the St. Louis Federal Reserve Bank. "This development occurred in spite of the large U.S. Government deficits that prevailed in the period." Thanks to the extraordinary demand by central banks for government dollar-debt instruments, yields on U.S. Government bonds fell relative to those of corporate securities, which central banks did not buy.

This inverted the classical balance-of-payments adjustment mechanism, which for centuries had obliged nations to raise interest rates to attract foreign capital to finance their deficits. In America's case it was the balance-of-payments deficit that supplied the "foreign" capital, as foreign central banks recycled the dollar outflows – that is, their own dollar inflows – into Treasury securities. U.S. interest rates fell precisely because of the balance-of-payments deficit, not in spite of it. The larger the balance-of-payments deficit, the more dollars foreign governments were obliged to invest in U.S. Treasury securities, financing simultaneously the balance-of-payments deficit and the domestic federal budget deficit.

The stock and bond markets boomed as American banks and other investors moved out of government bonds into higher-yielding corporate bonds and mortgage loans, leaving the lower-yielding Treasury bonds for foreign governments to buy. U.S. companies also began to buy up lucrative foreign businesses. The dollars they spent were turned over to foreign governments, which had little option but to reinvest them in U.S. Treasury obligations at abnormally low interest rates. Foreign demand for these Treasury securities drove up their price, reducing their yields accordingly. This held down U.S. interest rates, spurring yet further capital outflows to Europe.

The U.S. Government had little motivation to stop this dollar-debt spiral. It recognized that foreign central banks hardly could refuse to accept further dollars, lest the world monetary system break down. Not even Germany or the Allies had thought of making this threat in the 1920s or after World War II, and they were not prepared to do it in the 1960s and 1970s. It was generally felt that such a breakdown would hurt foreign countries more than the United States, thanks to the larger role played by foreign trade in their own economic life. U.S. strategists recognized this, and insisted that the U.S. payments deficit was a foreign problem, not one for American citizens to worry about.

In the absence of the payments deficit, Americans themselves would have had to finance the growth in their federal debt. This would have had a deflationary effect, which in turn would have obliged the economy to live within its means. But under circumstances where growth in the national debt was financed by foreign central banks, a balance-of-payments deficit was in the U.S. national interest, for it became a means for the economy to tap the resources of other countries.

All the government had to do was to spend the money to push its domestic budget into deficit. This spending flowed abroad, both directly as military spending and indirectly via the overheated domestic economy's demand for foreign products, as well as for foreign assets. The excess dollars were recycled to their point of origin, the United States, spurring a worldwide inflation along the way. A large number of Americans felt they were getting rich from this inflation as incomes and property values rose.

Figure 1 shows that foreign governments financed the entire increase in publicly held U.S. federal debt between the end of World War II and March 1973, and were still doing this throughout the 1990s. (How the system ended up after that time is outlined in my sequel to this book, *Global Fracture*.) The process reached its first crisis during 1968–72, peaking in the inflationary blowout that culminated in the quadrupling of grain and oil prices in 1972–73. Of the $47 billion increase in net public debt the publicly held federal debt during this five-year period – the gross public debt, less that which the government owes to its own Social Security and other trust funds and the Federal Reserve System – foreign governments financed $42 billion.

This unique ability of the U.S. Government to borrow from foreign central banks rather than from its own citizens is one of the economic miracles of modern times. Without it the war-induced American prosperity of the 1960s and early 1970s would have ended quickly, as was threatened in 1973 when foreign central banks decided to cut their currencies loose from the dollar, letting them float upward rather than accepting a further flood of U.S. Treasury IOUs.

How America's payments deficit became a source of strength, not weakness

This Treasury bill standard was not at first a deliberate policy. Government officials tried to direct the private sector to run a balance-of-payments

Billion

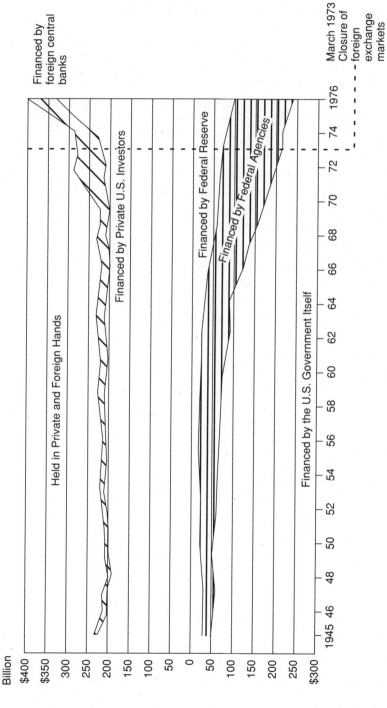

Figure 1   Ownership of U.S. Public Debt, 1945–76

Source: Hudson, *Global Fracture* New York: Harper & Row 1977

21

surplus capable of offsetting the deficit on overseas military spending. This was the stated objective of President Johnson's "voluntary" controls announced in February 1965. Banks and direct investors were limited as to how much they could lend or spend abroad. U.S. firms were obliged to finance their takeovers and other overseas investments by issuing foreign bonds so as to absorb foreign-held dollars and thereby keep them out of the hands of French, German and other central banks.

But it soon became apparent that the new situation possessed some unanticipated virtues. As long as the United States did not have to pay in gold to finance its payments deficits after 1971 (in practice, after 1968), foreign governments could use their dollars only to help the Nixon Administration roll over the mounting federal debt year after year.

This inspired a reckless attitude toward the balance of payments that U.S. officials smilingly called one of benign neglect. The economy enjoyed a free ride as the payments deficit obliged foreign governments to finance the domestic federal debt. When foreign governments finally stopped supporting the dollar in 1971, its exchange rate fell by 10 per cent. This reduced the foreign exchange value of foreign-held dollar debt accordingly, above and beyond the degree to which inflation was eroded its value. But American companies that had invested abroad saw the dollar value of their holdings rise by the degree to which the dollar depreciated.

What was so remarkable about dollar devaluation – that is, an upward revaluation of foreign currencies – is that far from signaling the end of American domination of its allies, it became the deliberate object of U.S. financial strategy, a means to enmesh foreign central banks further in the dollar-debt standard. What newspaper reports called a crisis actually was the successful culmination of U.S. monetary strategy. It might be a crisis of Europe's political and economic independence from the United States, but it was not perceived to be a crisis of domestic U.S. economic policy.

A financial crisis usually involves a shortage of funds resulting in a break in the chain of payments somewhere along the line. But what occurred in February and March 1973 was just the reverse, a plethora of dollars that inflated rather than deflated the world monetary system. In this respect that year's runs on the dollar were like the competitive devaluations of the 1930s, fed by U.S. official pronouncements of further devaluation to come. The Federal Reserve System expanded the money supply at a rapid pace and held down interest rates.

From the 1920s through the 1940s the United States had demanded concessions from foreign governments by virtue of its creditor position. It would not provide them with foreign aid and military support unless they opened their markets to American exports and investment capital. U.S. officials made similar demands in the 1960s and 1970s, but this time by virtue of their nation's payments-deficit status! They refused to stabilize the dollar in world markets or control U.S. deficit-spending policies unless foreign countries gave special treatment to favor American exports and investments. Europe was told to bend its agricultural policy to guarantee U.S. farmers a fixed share of Common Market food consumption, to relax its special trade ties with Africa, and to proffer special aid to Latin America with the intention that the latter region would pass on the money to U.S. creditors and exporters.

The United States thus achieved what no earlier imperial system had put in place: a flexible form of global exploitation that controlled debtor countries by imposing the Washington Consensus via the IMF and World Bank, while the Treasury bill standard obliged the payments-surplus nations of Europe and East Asia to extend forced loans to the U.S. Government. Against dollar-deficit regions the United States continued to apply the classical economic leverage that Europe and Japan were not able to use against it. Debtor economies were forced to impose economic austerity to block their own industrialization and agricultural modernization. Their designated role was to export raw materials and provide low-priced labor whose wages were denominated in depreciating currencies.

Against dollar-surplus nations the United States was learning to apply a new, unprecedented form of coercion. It dared the rest of the world to call its bluff and plunge the international economy into monetary crisis. That is what would have happened if creditor nations had not channeled their surplus savings to the United States by buying its Government securities.

Implications for the theory of imperialism

The thesis of this book is that it is not to the corporate sector that one must look to find the roots of modern international economic relations as much as to U.S. Government pressure on central banks and on multilateral organizations such as the IMF, World Bank and World Trade Organization. Already in the aftermath of World War I, but especially since the end of World War II, intergovernmental lending and debt relationships among the world's central banks have overshadowed the drives of private sector capital.

At the root of this new form of imperialism is the exploitation of governments by a single government, that of the United States, via the central banks and multilateral control institutions of intergovernmental capital rather than via the activities of private corporations seeking profits. What has turned the older forms of imperialism into a super imperialism is that whereas prior to the 1960s the U.S. Government dominated international organizations by virtue of its preeminent creditor status, since that time it has done so by virtue of its debtor position.

Confronted with this transformation of postwar economic relations, the non-Communist world seemed to have little choice but to move toward a defensive regulation of foreign trade, investment and payments. This objective became the crux of Third World demands for a New International Economic Order in the mid-1970s. But the United States defeated these attempts, in large part by a strengthening of its military power.

By the time the European Community and Japan began to assert their autonomy around 1990, the United States dropped all pretense of promoting the open world economy it had insisted on creating after World War II. Instead it demanded "orderly marketing agreements" to specify market shares on a country-by-country basis for textiles, steel, autos and food, regardless of "free market" developments and economic potential abroad. The European Common Market was told to set aside a fixed historical share of its grain market for U.S. farmers, except in conditions where U.S. shortages might develop, as occurred in summer 1973 when foreign countries were obliged to suffer the consequences of having U.S. export embargoes imposed. This abrogated private-sector contracts, destabilizing foreign economies in order to stabilize that of the United States.

In sum, U.S. diplomats pressed foreign governments to regulate their nations' trade and investment to serve U.S. national objectives. Foreign economies were to serve as residual markets for U.S. output over and above domestic U.S. needs, but not to impose upon these needs by buying U.S. commodities in times of scarcity. When world food and timber prices exceeded U.S. domestic prices in the early 1970s, American farmers were ordered to sell their output at home rather than export it.

The United States thus imposed export controls to keep down domestic prices while world prices rose. In order that prices retain the semblance of stability in the United States, foreign governments were asked to suffer shortages and inflate their own economies. The result was a divergence between U.S. domestic prices and wages on the one hand, and worldwide prices and incomes on the other. The greatest divergence emerged between the drives of the U.S. Government in its worldwide diplomacy and the objectives of other governments seeking to protect their own economic autonomy. Protectionist pressures abroad were quickly and deftly defeated by U.S. diplomacy as the double standard implicit in the Washington Consensus was put firmly in place.

When the prices of U.S. capital goods and other materials exceeded world prices, for instance, the World Bank was asked (unsuccessfully) to apportion its purchases of capital goods and materials in the United States so as to reflect the 25 per cent subscription share of its stock. Japan was asked to impose "voluntary controls" on its imports of U.S. timber, scrap metal and vegetable oils, while restricting its exports of textiles, iron and steel to the United States. U.S. Government agencies, states and municipalities also followed "buy American" rules.

All this was moving in just the opposite direction from what Jacob Viner, Cordell Hull and other early idealistic postwar planners had anticipated. In retrospect they look like "useful fools" who failed to perceive who actually benefits from ostensibly cosmopolitan liberalism. In this regard today's laissez-faire and monetarist orthodoxy may be said to play the academic role of useful foolishness as far as U.S. diplomacy has been concerned. Reviewing the 1945 rhetoric about how postwar society would be structured, one finds idealistic claims emanating from the United States with regard to how open world trade would promote economic development. But this has not materialized. Rather than increasing the ability of aid borrowers to earn the revenue to pay off the debts they have incurred, the Washington Consensus has made aid borrowers more dependent on their creditors, worsened their terms of trade by promoting raw materials exports and grain dependency, and forestalled needed social modernization such as land reform and progressive income and property taxation.

Even as U.S. diplomats were insisting that other nations open their doors to U.S. exports and investment after World War II, the government was extending its regulation of the nation's own markets. Early in the 1950s it tightened its dairy and farm quotas in contravention of GATT principles, providing the same kind of agricultural subsidies which U.S. negotiators subsequently criticized the Common Market for instituting. Today (2002) nearly half of U.S. agricultural income derives from government subsidy.

World commerce has been directed by an unprecedented intrusion of government planning, coordinated by the World Bank, IMF and what has come to be called the Washington Consensus. Its objective is to supply the United States with enough oil, copper and other raw materials to produce a chronic over-supply sufficient to hold down their world price. The exception to this rule is for grain and other agricultural products exported by the United States, in which case relatively high world prices are desired. If foreign countries still are able to run payments surpluses under these conditions, as have the oil-exporting countries, their governments are to use the proceeds to buy U.S. arms or invest in long-term illiquid, preferably non-marketable U.S. Treasury obligations. All economic initiative is to remain with Washington Consensus planners.

Having unhinged Britain's Sterling Area after World War II, U.S. officials created a Dollar Area more tightly controlled by their government than any prewar economy save for the fascist countries. As noted above, by the mid-1960s the financing of overseas expansion of U.S. companies was directed to be undertaken with foreign rather than U.S. funds, and their dividend remission policies likewise were controlled by U.S. Government regulations overriding the principles of foreign national sovereignty. Overseas affiliates were told to follow U.S. Government regulation of their head offices, not that of governments in the countries in which these affiliates were located and of which they were legal citizens.

The international trade of these affiliates likewise was regulated without regard either for the drives of the world marketplace or the policies of local governments. U.S. subsidiaries were prohibited from trading with Cuba or other countries whose economic philosophy did not follow the Washington Consensus. Protests by the governments of Canada and other countries were overridden by U.S. Government pressure on the head offices of U.S. multinational firms.

Matters were much the same in the financial sphere. Although foreign interest rates often exceeded those in the United States, foreign governments were obliged to invest their surplus dollars in U.S. Treasury securities. The effect was to hold down U.S. interest rates below those of foreign countries, enabling American capital investments to be financed at significantly lower cost (and at higher price/earnings ratios for their stocks) than could be matched by foreign companies.

The U.S. economy thus achieved a comparative advantage in capital-intensive products not through market competition but by government intrusion into the global marketplace, both directly and via the Bretton Woods institutions it controlled. This intrusion often aimed at promoting the interests of U.S. corporations, but the underlying motive was the perception that the regulated activities of these companies promoted U.S. national interests, above all the geopolitical interests of Cold War diplomacy with regard to the balance of payments.

Today's source of financial instability as compared to that of the 1920s

In the 1920s and 1930s the world suffered from a shortage of liquidity. Nations sought to export goods and services, not import them. The objective was to earn dollars. How different things had become by the early 1970s, when the great problem was how to cope from the surplus of world liquidity resulting from enormous dollar inflows into nearly every economy. The U.S. Government spent dollars without constraint, while private U.S. investors bought up foreign companies and the population bought more imports than was exported to other countries

Even Communist countries began to aim at running trade deficits in order to increase imports. Today, Europe and East Asia struggle to dispose of their surplus dollars with as little loss as possible as they recycle the U.S. balance-of-payments deficit into world capital markets, through which these dollars end up back in the United States. The result has been a global financial bubble.

America's shift from a creditor to a debtor strategy of world economic domination in the 1960s and 1970s reversed the kind of global relationships that had characterized the 1920s. At that time it was the U.S. balance-of-payments surplus on government account that untracked the world economy. Since the 1960s it has been the U.S. payments deficit that has done so, initially stemming from the government's overseas military spending. During the 1950s, 1960s and 1970s this military spending was responsible for the entire U.S. payments deficit.

Most economic models neglect the degree to which such spending and its consequent balance-of-payments deficits have played in the transformation of twentieth-century international finance. The world dollar surplus of initially was catalyzed by U.S. overseas military spending in Asia, starting with the Korean War in 1950–51. It was this spending that inverted America's balance-of-payments position from surplus to deficit, forced it off gold in 1971, and induced a debtor-oriented international financial policy vis-à-vis the rest of the world – the policy from which foreign economies have not been able to extricate themselves even today.

The new deficit strategy was accompanied by rising commercial protectionism and investment regulation – just the opposite of the philosophy that characterized early postwar U.S. policies, and continues in a vestigial manner to color much of today's anachronistic economic rhetoric. The shape of economic development in one economy after another has become a function of intergovernmental negotiation and diplomacy in ways not anticipated a half-century ago. Even Russia's privatizations were a product of U.S. diplomatic pressure, not a natural evolutionary development.

Rather than U.S. overseas military spending being designed simply to protect and extend private sector exports and investments, just the opposite set of priorities emerged in the 1960s and 1970s. U.S. foreign trade and investment were regulated increasingly to finance America's world military and diplomatic system. To finance the Cold War in Southeast Asia, U.S. banks and corporations were regulated in their foreign lending and investment activities, the IMF was all but broken up, GATT was gutted, and the system of free trade for which the United States ostensibly fought in World War II (and in its subsequent Cold War confrontation with Russia and China) was pushed aside.

The U.S. deficit is still disrupting the world, but its character has shifted from a military focus to one of insisting that foreign economies supply the consumer goods and investment goods that the domestic U.S. economy no longer is supplying as it postindustrializes and becomes a bubble economy, while buying American farm surpluses and other surplus output. In the financial sphere, the role of foreign economies is to sustain America's stock market and real estate bubble, producing capital gains and asset-price inflation even as the U.S. industrial economy is being hollowed out.

The United States' attempt to limit its payments surpluses in the 1920s by holding down its interest rates vis-à-vis those of Britain worked to inflate the stock market bubble that broke in 1929. Today, America's trade deficit is pumping dollars into the central banks of East Asia and Europe, to be recycled into the U.S. capital markets, creating a new form of financial bubble. The Plaza Accords of 1985, and the Louvre Accords the following year, obliged Japan's central bank to lower interest rates and inflate a bubble economy that burst in five years, leaving Japan a financial wreck, unable to challenge America as had been feared by U.S. strategists in the 1980s.

Both in the 1920s and today the U.S. payments imbalance grew so large as to split the world economy asunder, culminating in a statist reaction in one region after another. But today's government policies abroad ultimately are controlled by U.S. Government planners and the Washington Consensus they impose via the international organizations they dominate. The demand for free trade and dollarization of foreign debts is essentially a demand by the U.S. Government that other governments remain passive rather than adopting U.S.-style market regulation.

What is ironic is how short a period it took – just 25 years, from 1945 to 1970 – for the United States to invert its professed wartime idealism and build a double standard into the world "marketplace." By the 1970s the United States was insisting that West Germany revalue the Deutschmark and relend its dollar reserves to the U.S. Treasury as the price for keeping U.S. troops on German soil. Similar economic coercion occurred vis-à-vis Saudi Arabia, Kuwait and Iran to buy U.S. arms with the dollar proceeds of their oil exports, and between America and Japan. Even vis-à-vis the Soviet

Union the U.S. Government set out to negotiate bilateral agreements for the Soviet Union to spend the $10 billion anticipated proceeds from its natural gas exports to the United States exclusively on U.S. products. Such agreements recall the blocked-currency agreements developed by Hjalmar Schacht for Nazi Germany in the 1930s.

The drive to privatize public enterprises, ostensibly a move to get governments out of economic affairs, is a product of U.S. Government pressure (often wielded via the IMF and now increasingly by the World Bank) on debtor countries. The destruction of public sector initiative in countries selling off their public utilities and the rest of their public domain has not been matched by domestic U.S. policies, but is rather their mirror image. It is the kind of policy against which the U.S. Government itself protested in 1972–73 when Europe, OPEC and other creditors sought to use their creditor position to buy control of major American companies and key resources, and to dictate government policy at least to the extent of restraining international profligacy.

The public domains of debtor countries are passing into the hands of global finance capital, including that of Europe and Asia, plugged into an international system controlled and shaped by the Washington Consensus. American pension funds, mutual funds, vulture funds, hedge funds and other institutional investors and speculators have come to dominate Europe's stock markets and, since the 1997 Asian crash, have been appropriating those of the Far East. Stock markets in the former Communist economies and Third World are now dominated by the shares of the hitherto public domain that has been sold to institutional financial investors in the United States and other leading payments-surplus economies. The proceeds from these sales have been spent to pay interest accruals on debts taken on from consortia organized by the IMF and World Bank for projects that turn out not to be as self-amortizing as they were promised to be.

So we are brought back to the question of how conscious this system was. When did it became a deliberate policy rather than merely an *ad hoc* official opportunism in the game of international diplomacy?

To begin with, the United States paved the way by demanding that it be given veto power in any multilateral institution it might join. This power enabled it to block other countries from taking any collective measures to assert their interests as these might be distinct from U.S. economic drives and objectives.

I believe that at first the use of the U.S. payments deficit to get a free ride was a case of making a virtue out of necessity. But since 1972 it has been wielded as an increasingly conscious and deliberately exploitative financial lever.

What is novel about the new state capitalist form of imperialism is that it is the state itself that is siphoning off economic surpluses. Central banks are the vehicle for balance-of-payments exploitation via today's dollar standard, not private firms. What turns this financial key-currency imperialism into a veritable super imperialism is that the privilege of running free deficits belongs to one nation alone, not to every state. Only the credit-creating center's central bank (and the international monetary institutions its diplomats control) is able to create its own credit to buy up the assets and exports of foreign financial satellites.

On the other hand, there is nothing unique to capitalism about this mode of imperialism. Soviet Russia exerted control over the rule-making bodies of trade, investment and finance to exploit its fellow COMECON countries. Controlling the pricing and payments system of trade under conditions of rouble inconvertibility, Russia obtained the economic surpluses of Central Europe much as the United States had exploited its fellow capitalist economies by issuing unconvertible dollars. Russia established the terms of trade with its satellites in a way highly favorable to itself, as the United States has done vis-à-vis Third World countries, although Russia exported fuels and raw materials and the United States grain and high-technology manufactures. But viewed abstractly as a body of tactics, state capitalist and bureaucratic -socialist imperialism seemed to be approaching one another in their mutual resort to intergovernmental instrumentalities. Like the United States, the Soviet Union brandished a military sword at its allies.

As Jacob Burckhardt observed over a century ago, "the state incurs debts for politics, war, and other higher causes and 'progress'. . . . The assumption is that the future will honor this relationship in perpetuity. The state has learned from the merchants and industrialists how to exploit credit; it defies the nation ever to let it go into bankruptcy. Alongside all swindlers the state now stands there as swindler-in-chief."[8]

A century ago national states were permitted to exploit only their own citizens by creating money and credit. The unique feature of this new system is that governments in Europe and Asia, the Third World and the former Soviet sphere may now tap the wealth of their citizens, only to be tapped in turn by the imperial American center, which defies the world's creditor central banks to burst the international financial bubble and let the most open economies fall into bankruptcy. The U.S. economy remains the most self-reliant and hence readily able to insulate itself from any

European and Asian breakdown, but the financial sector remains most highly leveraged, as it was in the 1920s. Suppose that in the 1980s and 1990s, when Japan and continental Europe had built up hundreds of billions in dollar claims on the United States, they had behaved in the way that America acted as creditor in the 1920s vis-à-vis Britain and its other World War I Allies. Japan and Europe would have insisted that the United States sell off its major industrial companies at distress prices, and even the contents of its art museums. This is what America asked Britain to do. It was the classical prerogative of creditor powers. It was how General de Gaulle played his cards in the 1960s.

But neither Japan nor Europe outside of France played their creditor card. Japan behaved as if it were a debtor country, accepting a U.S. request that its government artificially lower interest rates in 1984 and 1986 as its contribution to the U.S. presidential and congressional campaigns. The result was to induce Japan's economy to run deeply into debt, creating a financial bubble that ended up obliging it to sell off its commanding heights to the Americans, even though the United States was itself a debtor to Japan. The United States thus played both sides of the creditor/debtor street.

The way to break such financial dependency is to do what America itself did as the world's major debtor: default. This is what Europe did in 1931. But rather than taking this path, Third World countries (following the lead of General Pinochet's Chile and Mrs. Thatcher's Britain) have agreed to sell off their public utilities, fuel and mineral rights and other parts of their public domain. They are playing by the classical creditor rules, while America itself plays by new debtor rules against Europe and Asia. The euro for its part has not been created as a political reserve currency, but only as a unit of account to function as a satellite currency to the dollar. Russia's rouble likewise has been dollarized.

The upshot has been to create a system in which the dollar is artificially supported by central bank capital flows offsetting those of the private sector. Capital movements in turn have become the byproduct of increasingly unstable, top-heavy stock and bond markets. It is these capital movements – mainly debt service for many countries – that determine currency values in today's world, not relative commodity prices for exports and imports. The classical adjustment mechanism of interest rate and price changes thus have been unplugged by the Washington Consensus.

The world's need for financial autonomy from dollarization

The Washington Consensus would not be so problematic if America used its free ride to invest in productive capital that yields future profits by putting capital in place. Unfortunately, it has pursued the less productive policy of maintaining an imperial military and bureaucratic superstructure that imposes dependency rather than self-sufficiency on its client countries. This is what makes the international system parasitic, in contrast to the implicitly productive and profitable private enterprise imperialism depicted prior to World War I by critics and advocates alike. Far from being the engine of development that Marx, Lenin and Rosa Luxemburg imagined the imperialism of Europe's colonialist powers to be in their day, the United States has drained the financial resources of its industrial Dollar Bloc allies while retarding the development of indebted Third World raw materials exporters and, most recently, the East Asian "Tiger Economies" and the formerly Soviet sphere. The fruits of this exploitation are not being invested in new capital formation, but dissipated in military and civilian consumption, and in a financial and real estate bubble.

The early system was supposed to grow stronger and stronger until it culminated in armed conflict, but economically developing the periphery in the process. But the tendency of today's Washington Consensus is to retard world development by loading down the economies of almost every country with dollar-denominated debt, and to require America's own dollar debts as the medium to settle payments imbalances in every region. The upshot is to exhaust the system until local economies assert their own sovereignty and let the chips fall where they may.

In today's world the form of breakdown is likely to be financial, not military. Vietnam showed that neither the United States nor any other democratic nation ever again can afford the foreign exchange costs of conventional warfare, although the periphery still is kept in line by American military initiatives, most recently in Yugoslavia and Afghanistan. The lesson is that peace will be maintained by governments refusing the finance the military and other excesses of the increasingly indebted imperial power.

Yet Europe, Japan and some Third World countries have made only feeble attempts to regain control of their economic destinies since 1972, and since 1991 even Russia has relinquished its fuels and minerals, public utilities and the rest of the public domain to private holders. Its overhead in acquiescing to the Washington Consensus has been to sustain a capital flight of about $25 billion annually for the past decade. Asian and Third World countries have permitted their domestic debts to be denominated in dollars, despite the fact that domestic revenues accrue in local currencies. This creates a permanent balance-of-payments outflow as a result of the privatization sell-offs that provided governments with enough hard currency to keep current on their otherwise bad dollarized debts, but demand future interest and dividend remittances, while the state must tax labor, not these enterprises.

This is a system that cannot last. But what is to take its place?

If foreign economies are to achieve financial independence, they must create their own regulatory mechanisms. Whether they will do so depends on how thoroughly America has succeeded in making irreversible the super imperialism implicit in the Washington Consensus and its ideology.

Financial independence presupposes a political and even cultural autonomy. The economics curriculum needs to be recast away from Chicago School monetarist lines on which IMF austerity programs are based and the Harvard-style economics that rationalized Russia's privatization disaster.

Money and credit always have been institutional products of national economic planning not objective and dictated by nature. The pretense that monetarist policies are technocratic masks the degree to which the financial austerity programs enforced by the IMF and World Bank serve U.S. trade and investment objectives, and incidentally those of Western Europe and East Asia with regard to the terms of trade between creditor and debtor economies.

A great help to promoting the Washington Consensus has been its control over the academic training of central bankers and diplomats so as to remove the dimension of political reality from the analysis of international trade, investment and finance. Economists assume, for instance, that the gains from trade are shared fully and equally. But in practice the U.S. Government has announced that its economy must get the best of any bargain, just the opposite of the situation portrayed by academic trade theorists and the idealistic assumptions of international law. Although the preambles to most international agreements contain promises of commercial reciprocity, the U.S. Government has pressed foreign countries to reduce their tariff barriers while increasing its own non-tariff barriers, getting by far the best of an unequal bargain.

The trade theory promoted by the monetarist Washington Consensus neglects the degree to which countries that have let their development programs be steered by the World Bank have fallen into chronic deficit status. Economics students seeking to explain this problem get little help from their textbooks, whose logic ignores the defining characteristics of global affairs over the past thirty years. This hardly is surprising, as the criterion by which the economics discipline calls theories scientific is simply whether their hypothetical and abstract assumptions are internally consistent, not whether they are realistic.[9]

The tactics by which global credit flows are controlled are a secret that U.S. financial diplomats are not interested in broadcasting. But without such a study being given a central place in the academic curriculum, the minds of central bankers and money managers throughout the world will be inculcated with a narrow-minded view of finance that misses the dimension of national geo-economic strategy, the failures of IMF austerity programs, the dangers of dollarizing foreign economies and the free-ride character of key-currency standards.

The required study would show that in place of the competing national imperialisms that existed before World War I, only one major imperial power now exists. And instead of disposing of financial surpluses abroad as in Hobson's and Lenin's day, the U.S. Treasury draws in foreign resources, even as its American investors buy up controlling shares of the recently privatized commanding heights of French, German, Japanese, Korean, Chilean, Bolivian, Argentinian, Canadian, Thai and other economies, capped by that of Russia.

The above view of U.S. financial imperialism differs not only from the traditional economic determinist view, but also from the anti-economic, idealistic (or "national security") rationale. Economic determinists have tended to neglect the full range of economic and political impulses in world diplomacy, and have limited themselves to those drives directly concerned with maximizing the profits of exporters and investors. This view by itself fails to note the drive for national military and overall economic power as a behavioral system that may conflict with the aim of promoting the wealth specifically of large international corporations.

On the other hand, "idealistic" writers (Samuel Flagg Bemis, A. A. Berle and so forth) have satisfied themselves simply with demonstrating the many non-economic motives underlying international diplomacy. They imagine that if they can show that the U.S. government often has been impelled by many non-economic motives, no economic imperialism or exploitation occurs.

But this is a *non sequitur*. It is precisely the United States' drive for world power to maximize its own economic autonomy (whether viewed simply as an expression of "national security" or something more expansionist in character) that led it to innovate its parasitic tapping of the world economy through such instrumentalities as the IMF and World Bank. Its military-induced payments deficit led it to flood the world with dollars and absorb foreign countries' material output, increasing its domestic consumption levels and ownership of foreign assets – the commanding heights of foreign economies, headed by privatized public enterprises, oil and minerals, public utilities and leading industrial companies. This again is just the opposite of the traditional view of imperialism, which asserts that imperialist economies seek to dispose of their domestic surpluses abroad.

The key to understanding today's dollar standard is to see that it has become a debt standard based on U.S. Treasury IOUs, not one of assets in the form of gold bullion. While applying creditor-oriented rules against Third World countries and other debtors, the IMF pursues a double standard with regard to the United States. It has established rules to monetize the deficits the United States runs up as the world's leading debtor, above all by the U.S. Government to foreign governments and their central banks. The World Bank pursues its own double standard by demanding privatization of foreign public sectors, while financing dependency rather than self-sufficiency, above all in the sphere of food production. While the U.S. Government runs up debts to the central banks of Europe and East Asia, U.S. investors buy up the privatized public enterprises of debtor economies. Yet while imposing financial austerity on these hapless countries, the Washington Consensus promotes domestic U.S. credit expansion – indeed, a real estate and stock market bubble – untrammeled by America's own deepening trade deficit.

The early twenty-first century is witnessing the emergence of a new kind of centralized global planning. It is not by governments generally, as anticipated in the aftermath of World War II, but is mainly by the U.S. Government. Its focus and control mechanisms are financial, not industrial. Unlike the International Trade Organization envisioned in the closing days of World War II, today's WTO is promoting the interests of financial investors in ways that transfer foreign gains from trade to the United States, not uplift world labor.

Part I

Birth of the American World Order: 1914–46

1 Origins of Intergovernmental Debt, 1917–21

One great change . . . – probably, in the end, a fatal change – has been effected by our generation. During the war individuals threw their little stocks into the national melting-pots. Wars have sometimes served to disperse gold, as when Alexander scattered the temple hoards of Persia or Pizarro those of the Incas. But on this occasion war concentrated gold in the vaults of the Central Banks; and these banks have not released it.

John Maynard Keynes, *Treatise on Money*,
Vol. II (London 1930), p. 291

During World War I and its aftermath debts among governments came to overshadow the private investments that had characterized prewar economic relations. Even more important than their size, however, was the geographic concentration of credit in the hands of a single nation, the United States. No prewar economist had anticipated how the behavior of this government would differ from that of earlier creditor nations, or how the new system of intergovernmental debt might differ from that of private international investment.

Before World War I, claims on foreign assets were held mainly by private investors in the form of equity interests or mortgage bonds secured by income-producing assets in railroads, mining companies, banks and other foreign-based corporations. Large government debts were common, but were held principally by private investors, not other governments.

International lending and investment was assumed to be self-amortizing. As foreign wealth increased, investors in mines, factories and other such enterprises would be repaid out of their profits, and in the case of government debts, by growth in the national tax base. Governments borrowed to finance projects designed in principle to increase income, and hence their ability to levy higher taxes out of which their borrowings could be repaid.

The war changed all that. It gave birth to massive claims by governments on other governments far exceeding the value of international private investments, and based on altogether different principles.

Paramount among the postwar claims were the Inter-Ally armaments debts, which stood at $28 billion in 1923, plus Germany's reparations bill, set at $60 billion in 1921. These obligations, totaling some $88 billion – excluding future interest charges that accumulated and magnified the sum – did not find any counterpart in productive resources or in visibly expanding taxing capacity. Postwar claims for payment were to finance the war's destruction of resources, not their creation. Credits to finance Allied arms purchases, and Germany's devastation of other countries for which it was now told to pay, were incapable of generating any earnings to amortize the postwar debts. Unlike private investments, they were not secured by productive assets as collateral, nor was their size at all related to the Allies' or Germany's capacity to pay out of current national income and foreign trade.

World War I had cost its participants some $209 billion in direct expenditures,[1] a consumption of resources that Europe was unable to finance by itself. Prior to April 7, 1917, when the United States joined them, the Allies purchased U.S. arms on credit, running up a $3.5 billion debt in the form of European government obligations held by private U.S. investors. The belligerents also paid for U.S. arms by selling back to American residents nearly $4 billion of U.S. railroad bonds, common stocks and other securities.[2] The result was a $7.5 billion net shift in America's investment position.

This represented Europe's financial limit in terms of normal commercial standards. By the time the United States entered the war, the continent was close to the end of its financial tether. It lacked the means to purchase American arms for cash in the amounts required, or even adequate collateral on which to borrow further sums through U.S. banks. One of the first acts of Congress following declaration of war by the United States therefore was to vote government funds to finance arms loans to the Allies.

It would be almost a year before U.S. troops could be enlisted, trained and ready for battle in Europe. President Wilson not only had kept the country out of the war until 1917, he had left it militarily unprepared for conflict on the European scale. What the nation did have was money, labor power and plant capacity for arms productions. In a matter of weeks, Congress authorized a $3 billion loan to the Allies. A Treasury bulletin explained that "the loans were being made to the Allies to enable them to do the fighting which otherwise the American army would have to do at much expense, not only of men, but of money – money which would never be returned to America, and lives that never could be restored." Representative A. Piatt Andrew drew the parallel that the United States was "virtually placed in a situation like that voluntarily assumed by many men in the North during the Civil War, who, having been drafted for the Union armies, hired substitutes to take their places."[3]

Congress had a rationale for extending funds to Europe in the form of loans rather than freely sharing American resources for the common Allied cause. "The general principle underlying these obligations," observed the Council on Foreign Relations a decade later, "was that the Allies should not pay less for accommodation than the United States had incurred in raising the funds from American citizens. Thus, as the Ways and Means Committee said in reporting on the first Liberty loan bill, the loan 'will take care of itself and will not have to be met by taxation in the future.'"[4] Not weighed in the bargain was the cost sustained by Europe in lives lost and property destroyed.

On the one hand, private international claims were being wound down by European governments requisitioning and reselling their citizens' U.S. investments to pay for American arms. But in short order liabilities of governments to one another were built up as Europe owed a growing arms debt to the U.S. Treasury. Including postwar Victory Loans, obligations of the Allies to the U.S. Government grew to $12 billion by 1921, starting with a $3 billion credit granted in 1917. Philip Snowden, Chancellor of the Exchequer in Britain's first Labour government, observed that the United States had levied about $3 billion in excess profits taxes on its armaments and related industries. Pointing out that this just happened to correspond in value to America's first official loan package to Europe, he concluded: "The sums loaned by America from 1917 to help the Allies to fight her battle were but a part of the profits she made out of the Allies before her entry into the war."[5]

Secretary of the Treasury Andrew Mellon acknowledged that U.S. profits on some war transactions ran as high as 80 per cent.[6] Still, the die had been cast for loans, not subsidies: As one banker later observed: "Little did anyone realize, whether in or out of official life, what this decision was to cost. It meant that within the next three years the United States Government would supply the Allied Powers with which it had now become associated, in exchange for their unsecured promises of payment at indefinite dates in the future, with munitions of war valued at over $9,500,000,000."[7]

Earlier wars had been conducted largely on a subsidy basis, with one nation – Britain in particular – financing the military costs of its allies. This practice had been employed as early as the fourteenth century, "when Edward III paid French and Flemish princelings to win French territory.

When the modern system of European states evolved every contender for European dominance found himself opposed by a combination financed by an implacable Britain." Subsidies "insured loyalty and effort. Being granted monthly, they could be stopped promptly if any ally showed slackness . . . When loans were granted in place of subsidies, they invited unfortunate consequences," as occurred with the Austrian loans of 1795–97.[8] Exorbitant brokerage fees, followed by economic problems in the debtor countries, tended to become sore spots of international diplomacy, creating almost as much antagonism as gratitude toward the lending government.

France had followed a subsidy policy when it helped finance the American War of Independence.

French financial assistance, expressed in consignments of munitions and supplies, contributed greatly to the success of the revolting North American colonies leading up to Yorktown, and for this last victory the revolutionists were indebted in equal measure to French military and naval support, which is estimated to have cost France $700,000,000 and for which she asked no recompense. France's help was expressed in outright gifts amounting to nearly $2,000,000 and in post-alliance loans to the extent of some $6,000,000. In making funding arrangements with Benjamin Franklin, the government of Louis XVI remitted wartime interest charges, a course that the United States was to pursue after the World War [only] in her funding agreement with Belgium.

However, the United States was lax in paying the loan portion of French assistance. "Between 1786, when the first repayment fell due, and 1790, no contribution on the debt either of principal or interest could be made by either the Confederation or the infant Republic, and repeated calls for a settlement by the new-born French republic in 1793 fell on ears attuned only to the needs of an impoverished people struggling to nationhood. It was left to Alexander Hamilton eventually to apply his financial genius to a tardy liquidation of this indebtedness, which was converted into domestic bonds and retired in 1815."[9]

Most of the wars fought during the century spanning the Napoleonic Wars and World War I were of a confined, bilateral character, such as the Franco-Prussian War, the Boer War, the Spanish-American War and the Russo-Japanese War. With the exception of the Crimean War, they did not involve large groups of nations, and hence there were neither Inter-Ally debts nor subsidies. World War I, however, was a conflagration of unprecedented scope, in both its direct costs and its economic aftermath. Unlike most of the wars of the preceding century, it was fought on the European mainland itself, with great destruction of lives and property.

As the war began to engulf the world, it seemed at first that the subsidy system would have to be pursued if the Allies were not simply to drop out of the fighting once they exhausted their economic strength. Toward the beginning of the war, in February 1915, representatives of the British, French and Russian governments met and agreed to pool their financial as well as military resources. Three years later Britain and France (Russia having dropped out of the war) induced Greece to join forces on the Allied side by promising that payment for the munitions supplied to Greece "was to be decided after the war in accordance with the financial and economic situation of Greece. Reimbursement could hardly have been contemplated here; as a matter of fact, it was subordinated to the need of securing allegiance and thus was a harking back to eighteenth century methods."[10]

U.S. Government representatives likewise had originally told their allies not to worry about conditions of repayment, which were to be settled after victory had been won, implicitly on nominal terms. For instance, at a time when there was broad public support for a $1 billion gift to France to help it wage the war in gratitude for its aid during the American Revolution, the French Government was officially encouraged to do all its arms financing through U.S. Government channels. The implication was that this financing ultimately would be equivalent to a gift. Senator Kenyon of Iowa announced: "I want to say this for myself, Mr. President, that I hope one of the loans, if we make it, will never be paid and that we will never ask that it be paid. We owe more to the Republic of France for what it has done for U.S. than we can ever repay. France came to us with money, with a part of her army and navy in the hour of our sore distress. And without the aid of France it is doubtful if we would have had this nation of ours . . . I never want to see this government ask France to return the loan which we may make to them."[11]

Typical of the overall U.S. tone at the time of its European loan negotiations was the statement of Representative Kitchin, chairman of the House Ways and Means Committee: "The fact is that if we ever get this money back at all when the war is won we shall get off cheap."[12] A later writer observed: "When America joined the partnership in April 1917, it was her effort to get the men and munitions to the line at the earliest date possible. The munitions got there about a year before the men. If the men had reached there as soon as the munitions, they could have fired the shells. In that case we would have paid for the shells and also for the white crosses and war-risk insurance of the men who were destroyed while shooting them. But our men did not get there so soon, and to our partners fell the job of repelling the enemy and of paying for the ammunition with which they did that job."[13]

The United States, however, entered the war on special terms. As the Council on Foreign Relations put matters, it was not an Ally but merely an Associate. Instead of subsidies it offered only loans, on the ground that it was not entering the war with territorial or colonialist ambitions.

> If her loans had had a relation to subsidy, she would naturally have been interested in the apportionment of the spoils of victory, for it is of the essence of subsidy that the subsidizer shall be the principal artificer of the rearrangement. Pitt guided the coalition against Napoleon; his interest lay in the new map of Europe. America's interest in the war in Europe was to secure her sovereign rights from an aggressor, and these secured, the apportionment of the spoils became a matter for the Allies to settle, while the United States negotiated a separate treaty of peace with Germany. The Treaty of Berlin is the final evidence of the lack of alliance of the United States with her former associates in war.[14]

The result of this unique military policy was that American credits became the war's distinguishing economic feature. It insured that once the war was over the nominal loans made among the European Allies themselves would harden into intergovernmental claims in an attempt to service American requests for repayment, in full, of all arms and rehabilitation assistance granted during the war and reconstruction years.

The foundation of Europe's official indebtedness was nothing more than the narrow, legalistic and ultimately bureaucratic assumption that debt, because it was debt, was somehow sacrosanct. "But the debt system is fragile," observed John Maynard Keynes soon after the Versailles Treaty was signed, "and it has only survived because this burden is represented by real assets and is bound up with the property system generally, and because the sums already lent are not unduly large in relation to those which it is still hoped to borrow."[15] He predicted that neither Germany nor the Allied Powers would be able to repay the official debts out of their current output and incomes, much less translate their domestic taxing capacity into foreign exchange. The result would be a breakdown of world investment and trade. A new era of world hostility would then be aggravated by defaults on international investments, specifically on intergovernmental claims.

America's motives for making post-Armistice loans

The fighting ended with the Armistice in November 1918. U.S. officials immediately sought to provide Europe with relief and reconstruction loans, but Congress refused to allocate the funds. This posed the threat of an agricultural and industrial price collapse in the United States since Europe could not continue to purchase food from the United States at inflated wartime prices. In January 1919, when Britain canceled its monthly food orders, fear spread among U.S. farming interests that a price collapse was imminent. Already the government had been "scrapping thousands of automobiles and motor trucks in order not to bring the automobile industry into ruin."[16]

The same practice seemed in store for agriculture. Herbert Hoover, then head of the U.S. Food Administration, wrote to President Wilson:

Our manufacturers have enormous stocks . . . in hand ready for delivery. While we can protect our assurances given producers in many commodities, the most acute situation is in pork products which are perishable and must be exported . . . If there should be no remedy to this situation we shall have a debacle in the American markets and with the advances of several hundred million dollars now outstanding from the banks to the pork products industry, we shall not only be precipitated into a financial crisis but shall betray the American farmer who has engaged himself to these ends. The surplus is so large that there can be no absorption of it in the United States, and, being perishable, it will go to waste.[17]

The government therefore sought to bypass Congress's refusal to grant reconstruction credits. "The Administration decided to act as if war were still in process. Technically this was so, for the loan acts provided that the legal ending of the war was to be determined by proclamation of the President."[18] In fact, one report to the U.S. Government on the problems of demobilization suggested a plan anticipating that of the World Bank after World War II: "In lieu of government demands, there are many uses to which men and materials could be devoted during the transition period, and from which they could very gradually be withdrawn. In the first place, there is a great need for replacing machinery, equipment, and other capital goods worn out and made obsolete by the war. In the second place, men, materials, and plants can be used in the rehabilitation of territory devastated in the war. There is abundant use in France, in Belgium, and in

Russia for men and materials, and a large part of the industrial equipment to be used there might well be manufactured in this country."[19] Some of these reconstruction resources were transferred to Germany and Austria, with official U.S. sanction, in order to help stave off revolution there.[20]

The first Victory Liberty Loan was made in March 1918, "for the purpose only of providing for purchases of any property owned directly or indirectly by the United States, not needed by the United States, or of any wheat the price of which has been or may be guaranteed by the United States." These post-Armistice loans were made to cover a three-year interim, until 1921. Congress refused to sign the Treaty of Versailles, and the United States did not make its own peace with Germany until the Treaty of Berlin in August 1921. Not until November 4 of that year did President Harding declare World War I legally over, retroactive to July 2, 1921, the date of the Senate's resolution ending the state of war with Germany, Austria and Hungary.

The war finally being ended, the United States turned to the problem of collecting payment for the arms with which it had enabled its Allies to secure victory. Even prior to the Armistice ending military hostilities, "many suggestions were bruited among the European chancelleries for the readjustment of intergovernmental war indebtedness. Communicated informally to the American delegates to the Peace Conference, they eventually became the subject of direct overtures." But the United States demurred. Mr Rathbone of the U.S. Treasury declared to the French Deputy High Commissioner in March 1919 that the Treasury Department would "not assent to any discussion at the Peace Conference, or elsewhere, of any plan or arrangement for the release, consolidation, or reapportionment of the obligations of foreign governments held by the United States." He further warned France that American post-Armistice credits could not be continued "to any Allied Government which is lending its support to any plan which would create uncertainty as to its due payment of advances."[21]

By 1921 the United States had grown antagonistic to the seeming indifference with which France and Italy viewed their war debts, and even more to the direct pressure from Britain to wipe all liabilities off the books, including reparations, in an attempt to reestablish commercial normalcy. In February 1922, Congress acted to bring matters to a head by establishing the Foreign War Debt Commission. It was headed by Secretary of the Treasury Andrew Mellon, who invited the nation's foreign debtors to reach an agreement as to how to repay the funds they had borrowed during the war. "In drawing up the terms of reference of the Commission, Congress made two stipulations: first, that the debts should be refunded within twenty-five years and that 4½ per cent should be the lowest limit of the rate of interest; and, secondly, it was laid down, in a very complicated legal form, that no connection with any debts arising out of the war could possibly be created by the agreements which were to be concluded between America and her debtors."[22] In other words, America's Inter-Ally debts were to be kept on the books and normal commercial interest rates charged on them. No contextual relationship between Allied arms debts and German reparations was ever acknowledged.

The link between German reparations and Inter-Ally war debts

It later was suggested that this refusal to acknowledge this seemingly obvious relationship between the Inter-Ally debts and German reparations stemmed from President Wilson's desire to see a fair settlement reached with Germany.

When, at the close of the war, the Allies suggested to President Wilson that their war debts should be forgiven, the suggestion amounted to a proposal that the United States surrender its claims in order that their net collection from Germany might be greater. The idea was that if the United States would not compel the Allies to pay, the Allies would not need to compel Germany to pay so much. Thus by moderating their claims against Germany, they would have stronger assurance of collecting their claims. It was this proposition that President Wilson rejected with some heat in his letter of August 5, 1920, to Lloyd George. "The United States," he said, "fails to perceive the logic in a suggestion in effect either that the United States shall pay part of Germany's reparation obligation or that it shall make a gratuity to the Allied Governments to induce them to fix such obligations at an amount within Germany's capacity to pay."[23]

On November 3, Wilson further elaborated this policy: "It is highly improbable that either the Congress or popular opinion in this country will ever permit a cancellation of any part of the debt of the British Government to the United States in order to induce the British Government to remit, in whole or in part, the debt to Great Britain of France or any other of the Allied Governments, or that it would consent to a cancellation or reduction in the debts of any of the Allied Governments as an inducement towards a practical settlement of the reparations claims." These remarks were made in response to the May 16 Hythe

Conference, where Great Britain and France joined to urge a parallel liquidation of Inter-Ally debts and German reparations, the principle later embodied in Britain's Belfour Note of August 1923.

The United States' best and most equitable judgment was brought out in regard to the German reparations problem. Having severed the link between German reparations and Inter-Ally debts, the United States had no direct financial interest in reparations and therefore could be virtuous at no visible cost to itself. By contrast, the issue of Inter-Ally debts brought out all of its most shortsighted, greedy and blindly bureaucratic qualities, apparently because of the nation's more direct financial interest in this matter. The U.S. Government advised its Allies to be moderate with Germany, but was itself immoderate with them. It urged them not to expect restitution of their war costs and war damage, but wished to be repaid in full for the cost of its own arms contribution to victory, on the above-noted technical ground that it was not an Ally but merely an Associate, unconcerned with dividing German spoils.

The motivation underlying U.S. Government policy was highly economic, but not a function simply of U.S. private sector drives. The only way Germany could have made reparations payments in the form of hard currencies would have been to export more goods by underselling U.S. and other Allied producers. In a similar manner U.S. insistence on Inter-Ally debt payments beyond Europe's ability to pay soon wrecked the financial and commercial price stability that was a precondition for profitable international trade and investment.

American economists were by no means blind to the fact that "the amount of reparation was the measure of service that the world was willing that Germany should render to it."[24] They pointed out that if Allied governments imposed heavy reparations on Germany, they must be prepared to enable Germany to make payment by exporting its products to the Allied Powers. How else, after all, could Germany earn the funds to make reparations now that its foreign investments had been stripped away? Unfortunately, and tragically, the U.S. Government turned a deaf ear to the corollary principle that the amount of Inter-Ally debts to be collected represented the amount of imports it was willing to purchase from its Allies and Germany. Instead of lowering its tariffs, it increased them steadily during 1921–33 to protect its own producers from foreign competition, especially from debtor countries whose depreciating currencies rendered their products cheaper as they tried to service their war obligations.

Meanwhile, the Federal Reserve System acted to insulate America's economy from the monetary effect of gold inflows, so as to prevent normal inflationary developments from helping to restore balance-of-payments equilibrium with Europe. The result was that despite the nation's major share of the world's gold, the U.S. Treasury and Federal Reserve System refrained from taking over from Britain the lead in maintaining a stable system of international finance. As George Auld put matters: "At the time of the Dawes Plan (in 1924), the world system was out of gear. Sterling had passed or seemed to have passed, but the dollar had not yet arrived. The day when the dollar would be the determining factor in the operation of the world machine had not begun. The machinery of foreign exchange was trying to function without its partner, the machinery of credit. No genuine creditor role was being played by any nation in the world system."[25]

The result of this attitude was that Germany was bled white after all, because the European Allies fixed its reparations at far above the sum that it could conceivably pay. Germany's only hope was that it could somehow obtain from U.S. lenders the funds to meet its reparations payments. And for a time, it did.

The hard line regarding Inter-Ally indebtedness led the State Department to intrude into the foreign loan process of its private investors. It often had served the interests of private finance capital prior to the war, but now this finance capital was constrained to serve the ends of national diplomacy. This was clearly perceived by the Council on Foreign Relations in 1928: "Whereas in 1914 we owed foreigners about $4,500,000,000, we are now creditors to the extent of $25,000,000,000, inclusive of war debt. The metamorphosis in our financial relation to the world is the occasion for the intervention of the Federal Government. True, this relation, save for the war debt, is a private one between the American investor and the foreign borrower, but the lender is also a citizen of the United States, and his overseas undertakings affect his citizenship and might run counter to the conduct of our foreign relations."[26]

The United States thus joined Britain, Switzerland, France and other nations that subsumed their international capital exports to diplomatic ends. A State Department memorandum dated March 3, 1922, announced its hope "that American concerns that contemplate making foreign loans will inform the Department of State in due time of the essential facts and of subsequent developments of importance." (The memorandum acknowledged that the State Department could not require such consultation.)

The government's first concern was to prevent loans to nations that had not yet made arrangements to fund and begin paying their war debts to the United States. The U.S. Treasury report for 1925 describes how "after much consideration, it was decided that it was contrary to the best interests of the United States to permit foreign governments which refused to adjust or make a reasonable effort to adjust their debts to the United States to finance any portion of their requirements in this country. States, municipalities, and private enterprises within the country concerned were included in the prohibition. Bankers consulting the State Department were notified that the government objected to such financing."[27]

This objection blocked loans to at least one country in 1925, and it opened the way for the State Department to assert its influence over other types of loans. For instance, it objected to a loan to Brazil's coffee cartel on the ground that the proceeds would be used to support world coffee prices at the expense of U.S. consumers. It also announced its objection in principle to loans made for non-productive purposes on the ground that foreign difficulties in repaying these loans might complicate further diplomacy. But no comment was made on the lack of productiveness that characterized the Inter-Ally arms debts, or on the intergovernmental antagonisms created by America's hard-line policy to enforce their timely repayment. The Allies' war debts could be deemed economically remunerative only if they could wring from Germany sufficient funds to repay their own wartime borrowings.

The question no longer remains open why the United States refused to acknowledge the tie between German reparations and the Inter-Ally debts after the reparations were fixed. The Allies did indeed need German funds to pay their armaments debts to America. Failure of the United States to adjust their debts in keeping with their receipt of German reparations and their general ability to pay bled the Allies as the Allies bled Germany.

U.S. Government intransigence over the war debts

U.S. Government finance capital would not even make the accommodation to its debtors that commercial creditors often are prepared to make. As soon as the war ended the government asked its allies to begin paying, with interest, for the arms and related support that had been financed by U.S. Government credits. In the history of warfare no ally had requested such payment for its military support. The provision of arms to allies, by universal custom, had been written off as a war cost. This time the credits were kept on the books. The eagle had unsheathed its claws.

Indeed, U.S. refusal to negotiate the Inter-Ally debts represented a more intransigent position than that taken by the Allies collectively vis-à-vis Germany in the Treaty of Versailles. The treaty itself imposed no fixed sum of reparations upon Germany, large or small, leaving this matter to the Reparations Commission. Article 234 specifically provided that "The Reparation Commission shall after May 1, 1921, from time to time, consider the resources and capacity of Germany, and after giving her representatives a just opportunity to be heard, shall have discretion to extend the date, and to modify the form of payments, such as are to be provided for in accordance with Article 233; but not to cancel any part, except with the specific authority of the several Governments represented upon the Commission." Thus, although Germany's reparation payments might be appealed, and even – by unanimous agreement – canceled, no such accommodation was made to America's wartime Allies. This provision enabled Germany's annual payments to be scaled down from an annual rate of 7 billion gold marks in 1920 to 2 billion marks in 1929 (about $426 million, at 4.2 gold marks to the dollar).[28] But the Allies were granted no such provision. This made it inevitable that they would follow in Germany's ultimate bankruptcy.

When General Pershing marched into Paris at the head of the Allied troops, he saluted Lafayette's tomb and announced, "Lafayette, we are here." A cartoon of the early 1920s depicted him as having approached the monument and saying, "Lafayette, we are here. And now we want to be paid." Of the nominal $28 billion of total Inter-Ally debts, the U.S. Government was owed $12 billion, some $4.7 billion by Britain, which in turn was owed $11 billion by its European allies. Much of this was owed by Russia and became uncollectible after the Bolshevik Revolution of November 1917. The size of this official indebtedness overwhelmed the private international investments existing prior to the war. Furthermore, whereas "America's war debts were extended in commodities, the United States asks their repayment in dollars or in United States Government securities at par. The face value of these debts is $2,000,000,000 more than the world's gold holdings. The completion of the syllogism is that *nolens volens* the United States must accept remittances in commodities or services in order to provide Europe with dollar exchange."[29] But instead, its tariffs were increased and the Federal Reserve System pursued anti-inflationary policies. The result was to drain European gold to the United States.

The only visible way the Allies could obtain the funds to pay the United States was to insist upon German reparations. "Without the payments of the Allies to the United States," a British official commented in 1929, "the reparation problem would be perfectly simple. It would be quite easy to fix a figure which Germany could pay, and which the Allies would accept; but once Europe has to pay these huge sums to the United States it becomes very difficult not to put the German debt too high."[30] Germany was burdened with a sum calculated to reimburse the Allies for most of the damage wrought during the war, a sum that exceeded the total value of Germany's corporate assets. It simply lacked the resources to provide the Allies with the funds necessary to amortize their debts to the United States and to each other. As Snowden noted:

> When the funding arrangements which America had made with her European debtors fully mature she will be receiving approximately £120,000,000 [$600 million] a year on account of these debts. The most sanguine expectation of the yield of German reparations is not more than £50,000,000 [$250 million] a year, though the Dawes scheme provides for an eventual payment of £125,000,000 [$625 million] a year. But no authority believes that Germany will ever be able to pay a sum approaching the latter figure. Therefore, what all this amounts to is that America is going to take the whole of the German reparations and probably an equal sum in addition. This is not a bad arrangement for a country that entered the war with "No indemnities, and no material gain" emblazoned upon its banners.[31]

Snowden's reference was to President Wilson's address to Congress of April 2, 1917, in which he stated: "We have no selfish ends to serve, we desire no conquest, no dominion, we seek no indemnities for ourselves, no material compensation for the sacrifices we shall freely make." Wilson had also promised Belgium that it would never be asked to repay the $171 million it had borrowed. But his promise was not honored, although the U.S. Government did agreed to waive the interest on this loan. Britain and France, by contrast, waived the principal as well as the interest on their much larger loans to Belgium.[32] As Keynes put matters, France could "barely secure from Germany the full measure of the destruction of her countryside. Yet victorious France must pay her friends and Allies more than four times the indemnity which in the defeat of 1870 she paid Germany. The hand of Bismarck was light compared with that of an Ally or of an Associate."[33] The result, he warned, would be that "the war will have ended with a network of heavy tribute payable from one Ally to another. The total amount of this tribute is even likely to exceed the amount obtainable from the enemy; and the war will have ended with the intolerable result of the Allies paying indemnities to one another instead of receiving them from the enemy."

Despite these facts, the U.S. Treasury persistently refused to consider its scheduled repayments and interest as being in any way contingent upon the receipt of German reparations by the Allied Powers. Britain therefore had to turn to France and Germany to raise the funds with which to pay its war debts to the United States. France had only Germany to turn to, and marched into the Saar in 1921 to take in kind what it could not obtain in cash. It was a period in which the most extortionate of nationalistic acts were inspired by frustration at the economic situation imposed upon the world by the United States.

Super imperialism

The emergence of the United States as the overwhelming world creditor was at its very origin a governmental function. It was not the product of private investment abroad of surpluses earned through foreign trade, nor the result of self-expansion of private overseas investment through reemployment in foreign ventures of earnings and internally generated cash flow. Although such reinvestment of private funds did occur, it was small in comparison with the advances made by the U.S. Government during the war to its allies and, after the war, for relief and reconstruction.

In the case of other nations, government intervention in foreign lands generally had followed growth of private investments, especially in areas rich in undeveloped natural resources. Governments either seized territories to secure expansion of the private interests of their nationals in these areas and to exclude the capitalists of other nations from them, or they entered into special agreements with the rulers of such areas to produce identical results. In either case private capital took the initiative; government action was subsequent. This may not have been the invariable order of events but it was the usual order. There had been unquestioned emphasis upon the nurturing of private interests abroad, such interests being identified with those of the nation as a whole.

Attainment of world creditor status by the United States did not follow this historic path, nor was it identically motivated. The great surge of U.S. investments overseas was by government, not by private investors, although this did occur, of course. It was not directed principally toward undeveloped areas rich in raw materials, but to a Europe whose industrial output was larger than that of the United States, but visibly deficient in raw materials within its borders. Motivation for massive U.S. Government financial claims on Europe was political in its emphasis; economics played a smaller role.

The argument is valid, in fact, that private industrial and financial interests in the United States would have been best served by government nonintervention, financial or military, in the European war and in Europe's reconstruction. An exhausted Europe, prostrated by an indefinitely prolonged war, would have exposed the whole continent to domination by U.S. finance capital, whose resources would have been generated in part by continued sales of arms on commercial terms to the belligerents. From the viewpoint of the generality of U.S. private finance capital, intervention therefore was an error. A totally exhausted Europe could not have continued its hold on its raw materials-producing colonies, as the end of World War II demonstrated. In these respects intervention by the U.S. Government limited the potential spheres of expansion of private U.S. finance capital in both Europe and its colonial areas.

This aspect of the evolution of American international finance capital, politically motivated and initiated and dominated by government, was unique in history. This is not to say that other governments had not in the past financed one or another side in foreign wars, as suited their political aims. But on no previous occasion had any nation employed government capital to become unquestioned creditor vis-à-vis the world. It was something new in international finance. It represented the accumulation and concentration of international assets in the hands of a government, not in the diverse holdings of private capital accretions, however concentrated these might be.

This unique development of U.S. international finance capital departed from the norms of finance, certainly from what had been foreseen by Hobson, Kautsky and Lenin. It not only was unforeseen, it was unforeseeable in the evolving economic and international relations of the period in which their thinking was formed. What had been anticipated was that the growth and concentration of finance capital in the international sphere was an unavoidable stage of the general accumulation and concentration of capital. Kautsky and Lenin shared this view with Hobson, as did Hilferding. Kautsky reasoned that this could lead to war, or to peace if adequate and binding agreements were reached among the international cartels of finance capital.

Lenin disagreed. War not only could, but must result from internationalization of the role of private finance capital. Governments in a capitalist world were the executive committees of the national bourgeoisies. The conflicts of interest among competing national groupings of finance capital must, *ipso facto*, become international disputes involving governments. It followed that war must ensue, and the wider the industrial and geographic range of the conflicts of interests, the wider the war would be.

Neither Kautsky nor Lenin anticipated or analyzed the unique aspects of emergence of the United States as the one great creditor nation. Not only were they both in error on this account, but so were the people of the United States, including the majority of its scholars. Attention was riveted on the transfer problems inherent in the massive intergovernmental debts and on technical adjustments in the transfer mechanism. But the real question that called for examination by scholars, and was not examined, was what it portended for the world that a leading government would subordinate the interests of its national bourgeoisie to the autonomous interests of the national government. Under such a condition the resources of the nation's private capitalists would be regulated to serve the ends considered appropriate by government. Not only would international financial resources of overwhelming magnitude accrue to such government, but obligations would be levied, as borrowings and taxes, by foreign governments upon their own citizens, including their bourgeoisies.

In 1925 a European theorist of imperialism, Gerhart von Schulze-Gaevernitz, wrote: "When the history of our time someday is written, what will be deemed the most important upshot of the Great War? The destruction of the royal dynasties that ruled Germany, Russia, Austria and Italy? The rise of France, destroying the balance of power which Great Britain promoted to preserve its own security?" No, he answered. The key effect was not to be found in Europe at all, for all these experiences were overshadowed by a single fact: the shift in the world's center of gravity "from Europe, where it had existed since the days of Marathon, to America."[34] He concluded that a new era of world politics was opened, which one could call Super Imperialism (*Überimperialismus*). "In order not to be misunderstood," he explained, "I turn the concept of imperialism upside down. I understand by Super Imperialism that stage of the capitalist epoch in which finance capital mediates political power internationally, to acquire monopolistic control – and monopoly profits – from natural resources, raw materials and the power of labor, with the tendency towards autarky by controlling all regions, the entire world's raw materials."[35]

Schulze-Gaevernitz saw that something was new, and that it was finance, but he missed the point that it was more in the hands of governments than in those of private investors. Nor did he follow up the implications of the fact that it was based on collecting money by selling arms, yet went beyond warfare, being based on the financial power of a single government as the antithesis of territorial military strategy and private interests alike.

No clear economic ends for the collectivity of private U.S. interests could be gained by the policy that was pursued by the U.S. Government. This distinguished its arrival on the world scene as the dominant creditor from, for example, the more gradual and military initiatives of Britain toward its earlier attainment of such status. Britain's economic and territorial objectives had been as obvious as their clash with comparable aims in Germany was inevitable. But the United States occupied no such position. Territorial gain was neither a purpose nor a result of U.S. intervention in World War I. When the war was won, no clash of imperialist ambitions followed in the traditional colonial sense.

Instead, the U.S. Government undertook further capital issues to Europe, to recent foe as well as friend. The overwhelmingly governmental nature of U.S. international finance capital, initiated during the war, was further emphasized when the war ended. What was being experienced was the earliest manifestation of what was to evolve in other countries, though in far cruder form, into National Socialism. Germany under Hitler, Italy under Mussolini and Spain under Franco subordinated the individual interests of their separate capitalist groupings to a national political purpose without injuring these interests, but subjecting them to more or less effective regulation depending upon the character of the regime. Precisely this, but in far more benign fashion, was implicit in assumption of the role of the nation's and the world's main credit functions by the government of the United States.

There was no resistance to this usurpation of power by even the most formidable of domestic or international finance capital aggregations. On the contrary, the world financial order came to rest on the dominant role in world finance not only able to be played but actually played by the government of the United States.

In the world of capitalism this assumption of lending power by a single national government proved as revolutionary as the Bolshevik Revolution. The United States became all-powerful in the capitalist world; the more so since, immediately after World War I, it reduced the rate of dissipation of its assets by reducing its military budget. The ability of the U.S. Government to pursue political objectives abroad by impassive lending to other countries was reinforced by the government's decision not to burden itself with the cost of attempting to attain these same objectives by the more traditional military means.

From the outset, therefore, the role of government in U.S. overseas investments was decisive. It was government that, however circuitously, determined the growth and direction of U.S. investments abroad, not the investment of private finance capital that determined the foreign policies of the United States. Without this perception one cannot comprehend the seemingly contradictory and apparently self-defeating policies pursued by the United States toward its World War I allies and during the years that followed. Nor can a foundation be laid for understanding the financial-imperial policies of the United States after World War II until one has grasped the power-seeking context within which the United States conducted itself in the interwar period with respect to German reparations and the Inter-Ally war debts.

2 Breakdown of World Balance, 1921–33

Nearly 80 per cent of bond flotations in the United States, and 60 per cent in Britain, during 1921–25, were by government entities: $3.6 billion in New York, nearly $2 billion in London (Table 2.1). These sums reflect the magnitude of the postwar shift from private to governmental borrowings. Although these bond issues were vast for the period, they were insufficient to enable the European Allies to pay their war debts to the U.S. Government, as repayment out of German reparations was not guaranteed.

Foreign government borrowings in London of almost $2 billion (at a parity of $5 to the pound) were a mere 7 per cent of the Inter-Ally war debts, and little more than 2 per cent of the total Inter-Ally war debts plus German reparations obligations. Yet they overwhelmed private sector issues of $1.1 billion on London during 1921–25.

These years of postwar recovery were of comparative prosperity for most of Europe. Yet the burden of Inter-Ally debt imposed by the United States compelled the governments of Europe, Allies of the United States in World War I, to impoverish their national treasuries, to run deeper and deeper into debt, to deprive their industries of needed credits, to limit their export potentials and to leave a clear field for the United States to grow as a world power to any extent and in any direction its government desired. These were the years when the United States was given – and earned – the name Uncle Shylock. The policy of compelling the European Allies – ultimately Britain – to continue after the war to meet capital and interest charges on war debts to the United States was a political aggression of first magnitude, in violation of the implied promises made during the war by the United States to its allies.

Keynes proved correct in his judgment that German society would buckle in its attempt to meet its reparations schedule. Germany succumbed to hyperinflation during 1921–22. To prevent this type of breakdown, an international economic conference had been convened in Brussels in 1920, and another was held in Genoa in 1922. In spirit, these two conferences were precursors of the 1945 Bretton Woods meetings, for they proposed many of the aims and principles endorsed after World War II by the

Table 2.1   New Capital Issues in London and New York, 1921–30

(a) **New Bond Flotations in the United States, 1921–30**

	Total	Government	Corporate	Percentage Composition Government	Corporate
		(millions of dollars)			
1921	692.4	554.4	138.0	80.1	19.9
1922	863.0	711.6	151.4	82.5	17.5
1923	497.6	377.2	120.4	75.8	24.2
1924	1,217.2	1,035.3	181.9	85.1	14.9
1925	1,316.2	939.7	376.5	71.4	28.6
1926	1,288.5	715.0	573.5	55.5	44.5
1927	1,577.4	1,074.5	502.9	68.1	31.9
1928	1,489.4	900.5	588.9	60.5	39.5
1929	705.8	262.3	443.4	37.2	62.8
1930	1,087.5	735.5	352.0	67.6	32.4
1921–25	4,586.4	3,618.2	968.3	78.9	21.1
1926–30	6,148.6	3,687.9	2,460.7	60.0	40.0

(b) **New Capital Applications in London, 1921–25**

	Total	Government	Corporate	Percentage Composition Government	Corporate
		(millions of pounds sterling)			
1921	110.6	80.5	30.0	72.8	27.2
1922	139.4	86.0	53.4	61.7	38.3
1923	135.3	95.1	40.2	70.2	29.8
1924	134.7	99.1	35.6	77.6	22.4
1925	91.0	35.7	55.3	39.2	60.8
1921–25	611.0	396.4	214.1	60.5	39.5

Source: Council on Foreign Relations, *The United States in World Affairs: 1932* (New York: 1933), p. 74 for the U.S. figures; and William Adams Brown, *The Gold Standard Reinterpreted: 1914–1934* (New York: 1940), Vol. I, p. 328 for the London figures.

International Monetary Fund and the World Bank. They were followed by the Dawes Plan in 1924 and the Young Plan in 1929 to coordinate the payment of intergovernmental debts by Germany to the Allied Powers. But they could not paper over the fundamentally untenable situation. Under the burden of reparations, Germany's economy was bankrupted by the greatest inflation in history. The German middle class was wiped out, sowing the seeds for fascism.

Shortly after Andrew Bonar Law became Conservative Prime Minister of Britain in January 1923, he sent Stanley Baldwin and Montagu Norman to Washington to negotiate the funding of Britain's war debt with US Treasury Secretary Andrew Mellon. Former Liberal Prime Minister Lloyd George, just displaced by Bonar Law, described the business transaction between Mellon and Baldwin as being

> in the nature of a negotiation between a weasel and its quarry. The result was a bargain which has brought international debt collection into disrepute . . . The Treasury officials were not exactly bluffing, but they put forward their full demand as a start in the conversations, and to their surprise Dir. Baldwin said he thought the terms were fair, and accepted them. If all business was as easy as that there would be no joy in its pursuit. But this crude job, jocularly called a "settlement," was to have a disastrous effect upon the whole further course of negotiations on international war-debts. The United States could not easily let off other countries with more favourable terms than she had exacted from us, and as a consequence the settlement of their American debts by our European allies hung fire for years, provoking continual friction and bitterness. Equally the exorbitant figure we had promised to pay raised by so much the amounts which under the policy of the Balfour Note we were compelled to demand from our own debtors.[1]

As matters worked out, "the United States agreed to fund the debts to her of our Continental Allies on terms markedly more favourable than she had granted to Britain." The sums funded over time stood as shown in the table.

Country-Funded Debt ($)		Total Payments in 62 Years ($)	Rate of Interest (%)
Britain	4,600,000,000	11,105,965,000	3.3
Belgium	417,780,000	727,830,500	1.8
France	4,025,000,000	6, 847, 674, 104	1.6
Yugoslavia	62,850,000	95,177,635	1.0
Italy	2,042,000,000	2,407,677,500	0.4

The total sum due from Britain, including interest, amounted to over twice its original debt, having been settled at nearly twice the interest rate agreed to by Belgium, France, Yugoslavia and Italy (although identical to the 3.3 per cent charged to Poland, Czechoslovakia, Romania, Estonia, Finland, Lithuania, Latvia and Hungary). This was the price paid for being the first country to break European ranks and sign its "separate peace" with the U.S. Government – all in the name of preserving the sanctity of debt, as if Britain and its fellow Europeans were still world creditors. Here was certainly a case of economic ideology failing to keep pace with the evolution of national self-interest. "Probably," the Council on Foreign Relations remarked, "the pact had more significance as a determinant of war debt policy than any other factor. It bound the other debtors by example to the principle of war debt acquittance; it put the American policy in a groove of formalism; it set the pace of treatment of other debtors by allowing of no other deviation than 'capacity to pay.'" Even so, "opposition developed in the Senate against any ratification of the agreement. Not that it was felt to be too onerous; it was felt to be too lenient."[2]

Mellon was clearly overjoyed. In the *Combined Annual Reports of the World War Foreign Debt Commission* he concluded: "We have, I believe, made for the United States the most favorable settlements that could be obtained short of force . . . The only other alternative which they [*i.e.,* critics of the settlements] might urge is that the United States go to war to collect." Another observer, Newton Baker, called the American principle of debt collection "the amount thought possible of collection without causing revolutions in the paying countries."[3]

Perhaps the worst psychological consequence of the war debts, observed the Council on Foreign Relations, was to keep alive the question "Who won the war?" with its implicitly self-righteous answer. "It would seem that general bankruptcy should have attended the long-deferred day of reckoning for some of the Allied states. This was the outcome predicted by many observers who in prewar days had freely proclaimed the economic impossibility of waging a world war such as overtook mankind in 1914."[4]

But unlike the situation with private debtors, there was to be no bankruptcy among national states. The U.S. Government refused to relax its unsustainable demands upon its European Allies. A 1929 observer remarked: "An American banker whom I saw today held the extreme view that ultimately Europe would declare war on the United States to repudiate her debts." A contemporary asked: "[can] we be perfectly certain that Germany will go on cooperating, helping and pursuing a policy of peace and reconciliation, and turning her back on the policy of militarism and reaction?" He believed that a victory for Germany's right wing was imminent as pressure built up to stop its reparations payments. "It will not mean a return to immediate armament by Germany, it will not mean an immediate outbreak of war; but it will mean the reversal of the present German policy of constructive cooperation in the building up of world peace."[5]

The burdens imposed by international governmental finance thus prepared the ground for future war, as Lenin had anticipated that private capital and its growing concentration must do. In fact, to many observers, the hope for peace seemed to lie precisely in a restoration of international claims and investments to private hands. "At the end of 1927," wrote the Council on Foreign Relations,

> it was the hope in Europe that the United States would join in a scheme of readjustment of both debts and reparations by transplanting from the political bed of intergovernmental relationships to a wider field where they would be absorbed by private investors in the world markets of international finance. The idea was gaining ground in the United States, but the approach of responsible opinion, while recognizing the advisability of taking debts and reparations but of international politics, was lukewarm to European suggestions of a conference. It was felt that such a conference would seek to disturb settlements that are considered inviolable.

Perhaps, the Council speculated, Germany might deliver negotiable securities to the Allies, who would then market them for cash and ask the U.S. Treasury to make a once-and-for-all cash settlement for the proceeds. Intergovernmental claims thus would be limited to the private sector's ability to finance and transfer them. Garrard Winston suggested at a University of Chicago Round Table Conference that "War debtors could very well approach the United States Treasury and suggest canceling future installments of the debt settlements by discount for cash. At reasonable current interest rates the discount would reduce payments for the later years of the term to quite attainable figures, and the menace of a continuing burden on generations not yet born would end."[6] Furthermore, American investors would probably be the major purchasers of the Allied bond issues, just as Germans subscribed to a great indemnity following the Franco-Prussian fear in 1871–72 and Englishmen did the same in 1816–17. To be sure, this would displace private corporate borrowing for productive purposes, but it seemed unlikely in any event that business expansion could persist without resolving the problem of intergovernmental debt service.

In short, whereas the hope for world peace prior to World War I, as voiced by Kautsky and others, lay in the prospects for intergovernmental cooperation, this now seemed dashed. Lenin had rejected Kautsky's prescription, which he called ultra-imperialism, on the ground that it was an unattainable ideal: cartels, and the governments they influenced, could not cooperate because of the constantly shifting relative power among firms and nations, even at the monopoly level. Governments would tend to break any agreement as their actual economic strength outgrew the constraints of past international agreements.

However, what was now occurring was the concentration of world power in American hands, despite the desire by other governments to shift this power from the United States towards a more balanced and multi-centric world. World balance was prevented largely by U.S. intransigence regarding the Inter-Ally debts and its insistence that this problem had nothing to do with that of reparations. Foreign governments acquiesced, at least for the time being.

Whatever the new system was, it was no longer dominated by private sector finance capital, unless one insists on viewing the breakdown of world finance created by the Inter-Ally debts, the stock market crash of 1929 and the Great Depression as policies supported by finance capital. To be sure, the disenfranchisement of private capital was in large part the result of a war whose motivations stemmed largely from competition of international finance capital. However, the consequence of this war was to disenfranchise it, to supplant it by a system overburdened by intergovernmental claims and debts. Individualist laissez-faire in the international monetary sphere was shortsighted in advocating that their governments carve up the world and its markets even at the risk of war. The results were not what any prewar observers had anticipated, including those in the socialist camp.

The destructive effect of the postwar intergovernmental debt system was aggravated by the fact that its financial claims had no counterpart in productive capital resources, and hence no real means by which it might be paid. It was, instead, a claim for payment of the cost of destroying Europe's resources. Keynes was quick to dispute the false analogy between the sanctity of private productive investments and the more tenuous postwar intergovernmental claims, and to deride the typical bankers' view "that a comparable system between Governments, on a far vaster and definitely oppressive scale, represented by no real assets, and less closely associated with the property system, is natural and reasonable and in conformity with human nature." An old country could develop a young country by private investment to bring productive resources into being, so that "the arrangement may be mutually advantageous, and out of abundant profits the lender may hope to be repaid. But the position cannot be reversed." A young country such as the United States could not expect the older countries of Europe to be capable of out-producing her to the extent of generating a saleable export surplus sufficient to amortize the heavy Inter-Ally debts and at the same time meet internal needs. "If European bonds are issued in America on the analogy of the American bonds issued in Europe during the nineteenth century, the analogy will be a false one; because, taken in the aggregate, there is no natural increase, no *real* sinking fund, out of which they can be repaid. The interest will be furnished out of new loans, so long as these are obtainable, and the financial structure will mount always higher, until it is not worth while to maintain any longer the illusion that it has foundations. The unwillingness of American investors to buy European bonds is based on common sense."[7]

Europe could directly raise the funds necessary to amortize its Inter-Ally debts by generating a payments surplus with the United States in two ways: by expanding imports into this country – that is, by making incursions into U.S. markets – and by borrowing from U.S. investors. As Frank Taussig emphasized: "Certain lines of American industry will experience additional competition from their European rivals. Consequences of this sort, even though less in quantitative importance than is commonly supposed, must be faced as a probable result of the debt payments."[8] Commerce Department theoreticians suggested that the United States would have to evolve into a trade deficit nation in order to finance its receipt of debt service from Europe: "If the European Governments that have not yet started to pay their debts to the United States Government should do so, there can be little doubt that imports of merchandise would regularly equal or exceed exports, as is usually the case with creditor countries."[9]

These theoreticians accepted as axiomatic that debt repayments to the U.S. Government must take precedence over other concerns, including some shift in trading patterns between the United States and other countries. The primacy in finance of government over private interests was made nakedly obvious. Yet private U.S. interests could not go unconsidered. The dilemma of the United States lay in the contradiction between the role of world usurer played by the U.S. Government as an autonomous economic institution and the injury this must inflict upon domestic industrial interests – and hence, upon the nation – if European imports into the United States were to grow large enough to permit payment of the war debts.

The government attempted to resolve this contradiction by insisting that this was the problem of Europe, not of the United States. Europe must not be made more able to compete in U.S. markets. By inference, therefore, Europe must meet its debt obligations not by expansion of overseas commerce, but by reduction of consumption. The obvious means to this end was to limit European imports into the United States by raising tariffs. Europe, then, must limit consumption in order to raise a surplus out of which to meet its debts. To monetize this surplus, Europe must sell abroad what it saved out of reduced consumption – but not in U.S. markets.

The government of the United States after World War I thus established the precedent that, through government international finance capital, the United States would influence the direction of growth in world commerce and, simultaneously, the consumption functions of other nations. U.S. tariffs served the double purpose of sheltering domestic industries and influencing the direction of world trade, each within the context of the paramount needs of intergovernmental debt service. Minimizing consumption in Europe increased both the margin out of which debt payments could be made and the creditworthiness of Europe, so that Europe could borrow in U.S. capital markets, further facilitating principal and interest payments on the intergovernmental debt.

However, the United States refused to permit Europe to pay off its World War I debt by exporting more goods to the United States. The country's tariffs were raised in 1921 specifically to defend U.S. producers against the prospect of Germany and other countries depreciating their currencies under pressure of their foreign debts.[10] In May of that year prices began their collapse in the United States, following the drying up of European markets that had been supported by U.S. War and Victory loans. An emergency tariff on agricultural imports was levied, followed in 1922 by the Fordney Tariff which restored the high level of import duties set by the Payne-Aldrich Act of 1909. Tariffs on dutiable imports were raised to an average 38 per cent, compared to 16 per cent in 1920.

Even more devastating to international trade, the American Selling Price features of the 1909 Act were also restored as the "equalized cost of production" principle and applied to a number of commodity categories. This meant that tariffs were levied not according to the value of imports as charged by foreign suppliers, but according to the value of similar goods produced in the United States. This legislation made it virtually impossible for other economies to undersell American producers in their home market. The President was authorized to raise tariffs wherever existing duties were insufficient to neutralize the comparative advantage of production costs enjoyed by other countries.

The economic principle of international comparative advantage thus was denied in law. Neither Germany nor the Allies could obtain the dollars necessary to pay their intergovernmental debt by running a trade surplus with the United States and displacing American labor. Their alternative was to raise the funds by new private sector borrowings in the United States.

Labor spokesmen endorsed this policy of European borrowing in the U.S. private sector instead of selling more products to the United States.

Matthew Wohl, vice-president of the American Federation of Labor, recognized that the U.S. Government was only "going through the motions of collecting these debts. Europe is going to pay with one hand and borrow back with the other, and go on using the capital just the same . . . it is better for us that it shall be so, instead of actually receiving payment in goods that would interrupt our own industries. I think it is a safe guess that fifty years from now the United States will have more loans and investments abroad than it has today, including these debts, and this will mean that we will not have received actual payment of these debts. They will only have changed their forms."[11]

The transformation of intergovernmental debts to private debts took the form of a triangular flow of payments. Funds flowed from the United States to Germany, from Germany back to the European Allies, and from these back to the United States. During 1924–31, U.S. private investors lent $1.2 billion to German municipalities and industries, and other countries lent an additional $1.1 billion.[12] The Reichsbank used these dollars to pay reparations to the Allied Powers. Some went directly to Britain, others to France to be used by France to pay Britain on its wartime loans. Britain and the other European Allies then paid the funds to the U.S. Government to service their war debt. Intergovernmental claims thus became partially supplanted by and integrated with private investment capital. Europe's debt repayments tended to inflate the American credit base, making accessible to U.S. investors still more funds to lend to Germany and other European countries.

This circular flow of payments was maintained precariously, but with no realistic hope of its functioning perpetually. The assets required to underwrite the debt simply did not exist. As Keynes wryly described the situation: "the European Allies, having stripped Germany of her last vestige of working capital, in opposition to the arguments and appeals of the American financial representatives at Paris . . . then turn to the United States for funds to rehabilitate the victim in sufficient measure to allow the spoliation to recommence in a year or two."[13] For Germany and the Allies, wrote another economist, the "only incentive to agree to pay is the opportunity to get new private loans not otherwise obtainable." The U.S. stake "from the beginning was represented by the sum we could persuade our debtors to pay us, while not permitting our demands to rise so high as to prevent settlement and delay the restoration of international trade and commerce. We had nicely to appraise the relative values of old debts and new business."[14]

During 1928–29 the circular flow of payments between the United States and Europe began to break down, first by a slowing down in U.S. private purchases of foreign bonds when investments increased domestically in response to the stock market boom; then by the market collapse which erased lendable assets; and finally by the Great Depression, itself the product of the impossibility of pyramiding debt to infinity. The first great swelling of intergovernmental claims came to an end in bankruptcy on a world scale.

First came the problems associated with sterling, toward whose stability the British Government sacrificed the nation's living standards in a deflationary process in 1926. On the one hand, a higher value for sterling meant that a given number of British pounds would exchange for a greater number of dollars and thus pay off a larger value of dollar-denominated debt. On the other, this worked to price British exports out of world markets, reducing Britain's ability to earn dollars and other foreign exchange. Internal deflation thus was accompanied by loss of export markets, high interest rates which deterred investment, and a wave of strikes culminating in the General Strike of 1926.

Meanwhile, the attempt by the U.S. Government to help foreign governments maintain their Inter-Ally debt service set in motion responses that prevented this process from continuing. After 1926 the Federal Reserve System helped Britain hold the pound sterling at its (overvalued) prewar level by promoting low interest rates in the United States via a policy of monetary ease. As long as British interest rates exceeded those of the United States, Britain was able to borrow the funds needed to sustain its Inter-Ally debt transfer. Thus "American support for the pound sterling in 1927 implied low rates of interest in New York in order to avert big movements of capital from London to New York . . . but presently America herself was in need of high rates as her own price system began to be perilously inflated (this fact was obscured by the existence of a stable price level, maintained in spite of tremendously diminished costs)."[15]

The United States could not raise its interest rates without depriving Britain of the ability to borrow the money (mainly from U.S. lenders) to pay its war debt. "As long as America lends freely to the world, and thus gives the nations greater buying power than otherwise they would have," George Paish wrote in 1927, "Great Britain will be able to continue to buy from America and to sell to other nations. But should anything occur to cause American investors and bankers to stop their loans to foreign countries, Great Britain's position would become most precarious. . . . If a time should come when [Britain's] credit is exhausted and she is forced to reduce her purchases to the limit of her selling power, less her reparation and interest payments, then the full consequences of the impoverishment of the German people will be experienced by other nations."[16] The U.S. financial sector thus became responsible not only for its own prosperity, but also for that of its debtors including, indirectly, Germany. The government could collect on its Inter-Ally debts only so long as its own investment bankers and other investors would provide the funds. To be sure, the longer this process continued, the longer it seemed that it could go on forever. Economists even began to speak of a new era of world prosperity rather than examine the shaky foundations on which the world's growing debt pyramid rested.

U.S. interest rates were held down in part by the inflationary money creation facilitated by the Treasury's receipt of foreign debt payments. As is normal in such situations, the credit inflation made its first appearance in the money and capital markets: the price of stocks and bonds was bid up considerably before commodity prices began to rise. By 1928 nearly 30 per cent of bank assets were devoted to broker loans to finance stock market speculation (requiring only 20 per cent down payment, with favored customers putting up as little as 10 per cent of the price of their stocks). "As rates on call loans ran above other market rates by wide margins, funds were drawn into the New York stock market from all over the country and from financial centers abroad," much of it in the form of short-term funds. This became a major factor curtailing new American loans to Europe – and to Germany in particular – loans without which U.S. export trade could not be financed. And without exports there could be no American prosperity, at least not without a sharp economic readjustment. Stocks and bonds soared even as earning power was threatened by the situation developing. "An extraordinary volume of new issues of common stock was floated toward the end of the boom – $2.1 billion in 1928 and $5.1 billion in 1929, as compared with a total of $3.3 billion in 1921–27 and the later postwar peak of $4.5 billion ($2.65 billion 'net change') in 1961."[17]

America's speculative prosperity undercut world equilibrium as "investors turned from foreign bonds to American stocks since that was where the greatest gains were to be made. The rise in stocks brought European funds into the American market. The cessation of lending drew gold to balance the accounts. The combined effect was to force a contraction of credit in the outer world which undermined gold prices. A year later international prices fell so rapidly that they impaired the position of the debtors. This in turn forced a further contraction of credit and set prices and credits spinning in a vicious spiral of deflation. The depression which had begun in the far corners of the world in 1928 reached the United States and Europe in 1929–30."[18]

Private funds flowed increasingly from foreign stock markets to the U.S. market. This explains why Europe's stock markets peaked before the U.S. market. "Abroad, stock markets had peaked in Berlin in the spring of 1927, in London and Brussels in April and May 1928, in Tokyo in midsummer 1928, in Switzerland in September 1928, and in Paris an Amsterdam early in 1929." Not until September 1929 did the U.S. stock market turn down; and following Black Friday, on October 24, the New York market collapse accelerated further declines abroad. The London *Economist* reported in December that "Wall Street speculation ceased to be a national and became an international problem, and one that affected London, the world's financial center, most of all."[19]

In point of fact the U.S. economy and its financial markets were most seriously affected by the stock market crash and its aftermath. Despite the fact that the U.S. economy was much less exposed to the vicissitudes of international financial and trade movements than other countries relative to the size of its national income and wealth, its financial practices were much more highly pyramided. Checking accounts were used more in the United States than abroad. Furthermore, the years of monetary ease in the United States had spurred a tripling of consumer debt and security loans, mortgage debt and nearly all forms of credit during 1921–29. This pyramiding was now called in by the banks – at a time when most home and farm mortgages came up for renewal every three years – contributing to a wave of foreclosures in the wake of stock market margin calls.

The United States thus became a major victim of its own intransigence with regard to the Inter-Ally debt problem. Its national income fell by $20 billion in 1931 (from a $90 billion level in 1929), losing "in a single year three times as much as the whole capital value of the war-debts due to her, and nearly eighty times as much as the total of one year's annuities."[20] Its exports and domestic tax revenues fell correspondingly. The illusion that Europe could settle its war debts and reparations on a workable basis by borrowing the funds from U.S. investors *ad infinitum* was shattered. "What had actually happened was that they were supported by an increasingly dizzy structure of private debt. It was a structure which could stand only so long as it was raised higher and higher. By June of 1931 the whole structure was in collapse, threatening to bring down with it in one smash all the public and private debts of Germany."[21]

President Hoover declares a moratorium on Inter-Ally debts

On June 5, 1931, Germany appealed to the world to forgo demand for reparations payments. Andrew Mellon, still Secretary of the Treasury, met with President Hoover on June 18 and convinced him that Germany could not possibly meet its scheduled payment. A number of leading financial houses and banks in New York were heavily involved in the German bond market and "were threatened with bankruptcy in the event of a wholesale default by Germany."[22] The President held a series of Cabinet meetings and met with Republican and Democratic congressional leaders to obtain general endorsement of a one-year postponement of all payments on intergovernmental debts.

This became his moratorium plan of June 20, which froze all private as well as governmental short-term German liabilities. He emphasized, however, that he did not approve "in any remote sense, the cancellation of debts to the United States of America." True, he acknowledged, the basis of debt settlement was finally to become "the capacity, under normal conditions, of the debtor to pay . . . I am sure that the American people have no desire to attempt to extract any ounce beyond the capacity to pay . . ." But every ounce up to that point would be expected. Yet to Europe the term "capacity" meant capacity to pay put of reparations receipts; to America it meant the capacity to pay out of ordinary budgets, assisted preferably by cuts in arms expenditures.[23]

Nonetheless, Hoover's announcements made stock markets jump throughout the world, and improvements in foreign exchange conditions more than repaid the United States for the loss of the nominal $250 million sum of funds forgone.[24] The winding down of intergovernmental claims thus had a salutary initial effect on the network of private international finance capital.

However, letting Germany off the hook shifted the focus of world anxiety to London. Publication of the Macmillan Report in July 1931 disclosed that Britain's foreign short-term credits amounted to over £400 million as against her realizable short-term foreign claims of only about £50 million after deducting the uncollectible Central European claims. On July 13, the day the Macmillan Report was made public, the Danat Bank closed its doors. A run on sterling dislodged its exchange parity, and Europan exchange rates began to collapse under the accumulated debt burdens of the preceding decade.[25] The Hoover Moratorium had come too late.

As in a Greek tragedy, inexorable forces were set in motion. To begin with, Britain's devaluation impaired Germany's export potential. British coal, for instance, became cheaper than German coal, so that German ships took on British coal at Rotterdam rather than buying domestic coal in Bremen and Hamburg. To make matters worse, many German firms had carried on their business in sterling, and suffered considerable loss when its exchange rate fell.[26]

These events triggered a worldwide tariff and devaluation war. Britain's abandonment of the gold exchange standard was followed by similar moves by the Scandinavian countries (Sweden, Denmark Norway and Finland) and by Portugal, Greece, Egypt, Japan, several South American states with major trading ties to Britain, and by the British Commonwealth generally. These nations formed a *de facto* Sterling Area capable, in principle of, turning the tables of international economic power against the gold standard countries, led by the United States and France, which between themselves were left with 80 per cent of the world's monetary gold. But what good was this bullion if an alternative instrument, paper sterling, were to become acceptable by most of the world in preference to continued subservience to gold? This potential contributed to Anglo-French and Anglo-American economic tensions, And fear of a new world trading system based on devalued sterling underlay much of President Roosevelt's subsequent hard line towards Britain.

How could this deterioration of the world economy have been avoided? The German Government scarcely could have worked harder to meet its reparations obligations. Throughout the 1920s there was little talk of suspending these payments, and Germany's political parties vied to devise ways in which the payments schedule might be met.[27] The European Allies also tried their best to service their debts to the United States. This is not to say that they were blameless in their relations with Germany. The Poincaré Government in France was especially vindictive and, after occupying the Ruhr in 1923, replied in the following words to Britain's protest over this act:

An eye for an eye, a tooth for a tooth. In strict accordance with the precedent established by Germany in 1871, the Ruhr District will be released only when Germany pays. The Reich must be brought to such a state of distress that it will prefer the execution of the Treaty of Versailles to the conditions created by the occupation. German resistance must cease unconditionally, without any compensation. Germany's capacity to pay cannot be established at all in presence of the present confusion in her economy. Furthermore it is absurd to fix it definitely, as it is continually changing. The German Government will never recognize any amount as just and reasonable, and, if it does, it will deny it on the f following day. In 1871 nobody in the world cared whether France considered the Treaty of Frankfort just and possible of execution. And what about the investigation of Germany's capacity to pay by impartial experts? What does impartial mean? Who has to select the experts?[28]

The Allies were extortionate in their ways of exacting tribute from Germany, but they were acting under the *force majeure* imposed by the United States' insistence that their war debts be paid to the last cent, including interest. Because the U.S. Government was the ultimate claimant on all war debts, the failure to achieve a realistic solution to the transfer problem cannot but be attributed to U.S. policy.

With regard to world indebtedness, the United States had adopted a double standard. Under the Dawes Plan, Germany was protected against enlargement of the real burden of her reparations payments by a fall in world commodity prices relative to the dollar, or more properly, relative to gold. The Dawes Plan stipulated that "the German government and the Reparation Commission each have the right in any future year, in case of a claim that the general purchasing power of gold as compared with 1928 had altered by not less than 10 per cent, to ask for a revision on the sole and single ground of such altered gold value," and that "after revision, the altered basis should stand for each succeeding year until a claim be made by either party that there has again been a change, since the year to which the alteration applied, of not less than 10 per cent."[29]

This provision recognized that the sum of reparations payments by Germany, as fixed under the Dawes Plan, was the maximum the Allies could extort. In fact, it was beyond the capacity of Germany to pay, as any increase in the real value of the reparations debt must impoverish Germany to the point of national exhaustion. Hence, the protection extended to Germany against the terms of trade turning against her as between the changing values of commodity exports and fixed gold-mark reparations payments.

Similar treatment was not accorded to the Allies with respect to their debts to the United States. America refused even to contemplate that given a fall in world prices – a rise in the value of gold as measured in commodities – the Inter-Ally debts, which amounted in practice to Britain's and France's debts to the United States, no more could be paid by Britain than reparations could be paid by Germany. U.S. policy was to treat Germany, the recent enemy, as a country in need of protection against the effects of a fall in prices, but to treat Britain, the recent ally, as a nation to be trodden down if a fall in world prices should occur. The recent enemy was to become a ward of the U.S. Government; the recent ally to be punished.

Because this ally was the world's great imperial power and Germany its recent challenger for imperial supremacy, the suspicion is warranted that the United States had set its eyes lustfully on the British Empire. To swallow the Empire, the United States must first dislodge it. Britain must be forbidden the fruits of victory and Germany established again as its rival. The same policy was to recur after World War II.

World debt had become, and was used as, an instrument of power by the United States against its only serious rival, the British Empire. Britain was held responsible for payment to the United States of Germany's reparations equivalents to Belgium, France and Britain, whether or not Germany could and did make such payment. The British debt was to be increased in real value if commodity prices should fall, but Germany's debt obligations to Britain, both direct and indirect, were to be substantially protected in terms of its commodity price equivalent.

The derailing of international debt service prompts controversy

For a decade the world's debt overhang had been kept afloat by the expedient of yet more debt. Private U.S. lending provided dollars that followed a triangular route to German municipal and private borrowers, via the German central bank to the governments of Britain, France and other Allied Powers, who recycled the dollars back to the United States. But the Great Crash of 1929 extinguished vast pools of paper capital, drying up sources of international borrowings. In 1931 international short-term debt was reduced between 33 and 40 per cent, withdrawing about $6 billion from commercial use in the debtor countries.[30] The reduction of credit would have been much greater had it not been for the standstill agreements that froze short-term loans to Germany. The effect in any case was violently deflationary, collapsing world prices and trade. Foreign governments were unable to raise the dollars needed to pay their scheduled debt service, either by increasing their exports or by borrowing new private funds.

Almost unable to borrow abroad, Germany reduced its reparations payments. In 1932 it cut back its debt-service transfer first by half, then by

70 per cent. Meanwhile, Britain's attempt to continue paying its share of the Inter-Ally debts, despite the slowing reparations receipts from Germany, forcing down the value of sterling at the same time that British prices were tumbling.

The decline in world prices increased the real burden of debt service because the transfer requirements, measured in commodities, increased as the dollar price of these commodities fell. "Since the various installments of that debt were negotiated and spent in this country, our price level has fallen by perhaps 50 per cent, thereby approximately doubling the actual payments demanded."[31] Yet the U.S. Congress was adamant that the Hoover Moratorium was merely a one-year postponement, not a cancellation of foreign indebtedness to the U.S. Treasury and certainly not contingent on Europe's success in extracting further reparations from Germany. On December 10, 1931, President Hoover reassured Congress that "Reparations are a wholly European problem with which we have no relations." And when the Brookings Institution published Harold Moulton's analysis of the French war debt problem, leading the Foreign Debt Commission to scale down the U.S. claims on France, Hoover told a press conference that Moulton "represented a liability to the United States to the extent of $10 million a year in perpetuity."[32] He subsequently asked Congress to reestablish the Foreign Debt Commission with a possible eye to scaling down the debts, but his request was in vain, despite support by Senator Borah, Chairman of the Committee on Foreign Relations.

The representative U.S. view was epitomized in ex-President Calvin Coolidge's terse comment, "We hired them the money, didn't we?"[33] On December 17 the House Ways and Means Committee reported that "It is hereby expressly declared to be against the policy of Congress that any indebtedness by foreign countries to the United States should be in any manner canceled or reduced." A minority report went so far as to criticize President Hoover for proposing the reparations-and-debt moratorium in the first place, without first having consulted the full Congress. But on December 22, 1931, the Hoover Moratorium finally was ratified, although Congress charged the nation's debtors 4 per cent on their outstanding balances, on the ground that this was the rate at which U.S. Treasury bonds were then selling. This somewhat awkwardly obliged the Allies to renegotiate their waiver of German reparations under the Hoover plan, increasing the rate of interest charged on Germany's postponed payments and on their mutual indebtedness from 3 per cent to 4 per cent.

Meanwhile, Britain was forced to abandon the gold exchange standard in September 1931. Its attempt to service its debt to the United States had resulted first in a deflation of its domestic prices stemming largely from the government's budgetary needs to raise the sterling equivalent of its debts to the U.S. Government; and then, despite this deflation, a collapse of its currency against those of other nations as it converted sterling into dollars. This transfer aspect of the debt problem disturbed Europe's economies even more than their domestic budgetary problems.

The Lausanne Conference proposes to settle the debt tangle

At the Lausanne Conference in summer 1932, six months after the Hoover Moratorium, it was clear that the Allied Powers could not extract any more funds from Germany, and they turned to save themselves from their own debts to the United States. When Germany proposed a lump-sum final settlement of its reparations, Premier Herriot of France pointed out that "cancellation of reparations without a corresponding readjustment of allied war debts would place Germany in a privileged position."[34] Italy's foreign minister proposed on July 4 that war debts and reparations be wiped off the books altogether. At the end of the conference the European Allies agreed to waive German reparations to the extent that the U.S. Government would waive its war claims against them. Herriot announced in an interview with the newspaper *L'Intransigeant*: "What must be clearly understood is that the link is now clearly established between the settlement of reparations and the solution of the debt problems with relation to the United States. Everything is now subordinated to an agreement with America."[35]

The European Allies reasoned that they hardly could afford to give up German reparations if the price would be a stripping of their own gold stocks to continue paying for a war whose economic aftermath they now wanted to end. They agreed to cut German reparations by nearly 98 per cent, from $30 billion to about $700 million under a gentlemen's agreement that the write-off was conditional on the United States' reducing its own claims on the Allies. With a motto sanctified by the Lord's Prayer, "Forgive us our debts, as we forgive our debtors," Britain and France signed an addendum to their agreement with Germany stipulating that "if a satisfactory settlement about their own debts is reached, the aforesaid creditor Governments will ratify and the agreement with Germany will come into full effect. But if no such settlement can be obtained, the agreement with Germany will not be ratified; a new situation will have arisen and the Governments interested will have to consult together as to what should be done."[36]

U.S. politicians accused Europe of forming a united front against the United States. (It was an election year, after all.) The Lausanne Conference disbanded in some disarray as American anxiety began to be awakened with regard to the prospect of British and French trade resurgence. U.S. officials began to worry that they had pressed their creditor position too far in forcing Britain and its Empire off the gold standard, for this freed Britain, its Commonwealth and associated Sterling Area countries to create their own commercial bloc if they so chose. Almost immediately they did exactly this at the Ottawa Conference convened by Britain to establish a generalized system of Commonwealth tariff preferences, with the potential of extending their trade and currency system to any nation choosing to adhere to the Sterling Bloc.

Even before the Ottawa Conference, American economic antagonism toward the British Empire was apparent. In the Senate debate on the Hoover Moratorium, Senator Reed of Pennsylvania dismissed as "silly" the idea that payment of war debts could present any great difficulty to a country like Great Britain, "owning far-flung colonies, holding funds all round the circle of the globe, with museums stuffed with art treasures worth millions and millions."[37] The implication was that Britain should sell these art works, along with its colonies, to pay what remained of its war debt. The drive to break up the British Empire had thus begun in embryonic form. But so reluctant was Europe to recognize this ultimate policy intent – still only in its germinal stage – that the only response was an angry editorial in *The Times* of London denouncing the suggestion that Britain ship its National Gallery and the British Museum to New York in partial satisfaction of its debts.

The Hoover Moratorium expired on June 30. The first payment due was that of Greece on July 1. It "notified the Treasury Department that it would take advantage of a clause in its agreement with the United States permitting it to postpone payment for two and a half years, with interest to accrue on postponed amount at $4\frac{1}{4}$ per cent." Smaller debtors followed suit.

The Hoover Administration recognized the need to negotiate some longer-term resolution, toward which a Preparatory Commission of Experts met at Geneva in autumn 1932. The U.S. representatives were John H. Williams, a respected Harvard economist specializing in balance-of-payments analysis who had worked for some years as a consultant to the New York Federal Reserve Bank, and Edmund E. Day. "One important development in the intergovernmental situation is indispensable," their report stated: "a definitive settlement of the war debts must be clearly in prospect, if not already attained, before the Commission comes together again . . . With a satisfactory debt settlement in hand, or in the making, and with a willingness on the part of two or three of the principal powers to assume initiative in working out a program of normalization of the world's economic order, the next meeting of the Preparatory Commission may be expected to yield highly important results."[38]

The report was not made public in view of the nationalistic views of most voters, but Hoover and his Cabinet saw the writing on the wall and planned to implement its recommendations. Their stance was shaped by the fact that the balance of forces dealing with the Inter-Ally debts did not involve only the European and U.S. Governments. Private bankers also had an interest in alleviating the burden. Enlightened and compassionate as their internationalist position may have been, it was not entirely altruistic, for intergovernmental debt service had thoroughly crowded out private lending. Whereas private loans had played a facilitating role prior to 1929, the Crash had destroyed capital and debt-paying power from one economy to the next, forcing a choice to be made between Europe paying either the U.S. Government or, potentially, American bankers.

The bankers favored international debt leniency on the part of governments for much the same reason they did in 2000 when they urged that governments, the World Bank and IMF forgive the official debts owed by the poorest Third World countries. Their objective was not so much to let Third World debtors off the hook as simply to remove governments from their senior status as first claimants on the export revenues and foreign exchange generated by debtor countries selling off their public domain to pay foreigners. Government forgiveness meant that all the available revenues of the poorest countries would be "freed" to be paid to large private global creditors.

Farm interests also had an interest in alleviating Europe's debts, for the more it had to pay in debt service, the fewer dollars it could raise to buy U.S. farm output. However, notes Raymond Moley, Roosevelt's advisor on the debt issue, "the debt payments are relatively unimportant in comparison with the interest on the private debts (foreign bonds, etc.) and payments on short-term bank paper of which eight hundred millions (about) are in New York."[39] The issue of the primacy of intergovernmental or private finance capital thus was the determining issue. One or the other had to give.

The question was whether it would be intergovernmental debts or private loans that would suffer. Favoring private creditors, Hoover and his Republican Cabinet were amenable to seeing the government relinquish its claims on Europe. Roosevelt and his economic nationalists put the public sector's interest first, that of private creditors last. To Moley and Rex Tugwell, two of the leading members of Roosevelt's Brains Trust, that was the essence of the New Deal's political philosophy. Tugwell pointed out that one reason why the Eastern establishment's bankers favored cancellation or at least a major reduction of the debts was that it would help in the revival of their own international loan business. That was the essence of their internationalist position. Even though "the debtor countries were able to pay their installments, the international bankers wanted the government debts out of the way to help the revival of their own business abroad."[40]

The prospect of negotiating a settlement of European debts a was disrupted when Franklin Delano Roosevelt defeated Hoover by a heavy plurality in the presidential election held on Tuesday, November 8, 1932. The Democrats also captured the Senate and House of Representatives, giving the White House control over policy. No mention of the war debt issue had been made at the Republican National Convention held in June 1932, but the Democratic Convention formulated a plank registering opposition to their cancellation.

Allied debt payments were scheduled to begin falling due just two days after the election, starting with Greece's November 10 payment on its non-postponable payment of $444,920. It defaulted. This was not unexpected in view of its June request for a postponement. More unsettling that day was the fact that "the British and French ambassadors had called on the Secretary of State Henry L. Stimson to ask for a review of the entire question of debts and, pending such a review, for a postponement of the installments due on December 15th." Their notes demanded "not only that the debt payments due on December 15 be deferred but that we review the whole debt situation with debtor nations." Stimson described this demand as a "bombshell," but urged Hoover to take a lenient line toward the debts, hoping to avoid the outright break with Britain and other debtors that defaults would cause. In fact, reports Moley, Stimson "was not happy about Hoover's determination not to cancel the debts without an adequate *quid pro quo* or about the President's refusal to link the debts with reparations."[41]

Roosevelt, Moley and Tugwell took a much less "internationalist" position, reflected in Moley's complaint that Stimson's professional life "had been that of a New York lawyer in close contact with the great international financial and cultural community that centered in that city . . . he leaned heavily upon advice from New York, especially from the partners of the Morgan company." In fact, "Stimson's sympathies for any relationship with the New York banking community were greater than Hoover's and [Treasury Secretary] Mills's."[42] Roosevelt's supporters, especially from the silver states, were soft-money populists sympathetic to debtor-oriented inflationists, as it was the West that owed money to the East Coast bankers.

America's leaders thus looked first to the domestic economy, not anticipating the scope of the world's financial problems or grasping the extent to which the nation's hard line toward European war debts would provide new impetus urging the continent toward a renewed nationalism and autarchy that would culminate in World War II.

America's reasoning was neither devilish nor incorrect, as far as it went. But it did not go far enough. Europe did everything it could to avoid default on the tangle of reparations and Inter-Ally debt payments in the absence of U.S. permission to stop payment. This permission was not given. America therefore left Europe virtually no alternative but to pursue creditor-oriented deflationary policies at first, and protectionist and nationalistic policies after dollar devaluation in 1933–34. Domestically, the U.S. economy adhered to a much more populist, debtor-oriented economic philosophy than did Europe, but internationally it held to a hard creditor line.

3 America Spurns World Leadership

> I shall spare no effort to restore world trade by international economic readjustment, but the emergency at home cannot wait on that accomplishment.
>
> Franklin Delano Roosevelt
> Inauguration Speech, March 4, 1933

It is not the job of political leaders to adopt economic policies based on broad principles that appear to best serve the world as a whole. Voters expect heads of state to pursue the national interest. Far-sighted leaders may look to the long run rather than pursuing merely transitory advantages, and the long-term position no doubt is helped by growth in the world economy. But the means to such growth along the way must reflect a composite of calculated pursuits of national interest, not its subordination by some to the advantage of other economies.

No nation has shown itself more aware of this distinction between national self-interest and cosmopolitan ideals than the United States. This is partly because of congressional veto power over international policies. It is hard enough for the Executive Branch to mobilize U.S. policy even at the national level, answerable as it is to congressmen and senators representing their local interests. Politicians since the Civil War have set aside protectionist policies to pursue the goals of more open trade and markets, currency stability and the responsibilities of world leadership only when these policies have been calculated to support America's own prosperity. When economic expansion at home has called for federal budget deficits, monetary inflation, competitive devaluation of the dollar, agricultural protectionism, industrial trade quotas and other abandonments of internationalist principles, the United States has been much quicker to adopt nationalist policies than have other industrial nations.

Also important in understanding U.S. international relations is the sheer size of its home market. U.S. economic policy traditionally has looked to this market as the mainspring of economic growth rather than depending on foreign markets for its major stimulus. This policy of self-reliance was what John Hobson had urged upon Europe as an alternative to its attempts to monopolize foreign markets through the colonialism that helped bring on World War I. In this respect American isolationism contained an element of idealism and even anti-militarism, at least as expressed by the American School's economic theory. The Economics of Abundance of Rex Tugwell's mentor Simon Patten went hand in hand with his distinction between private and national interest.[1]

European countries historically have been more internationally oriented. This has led them to formulate their policies in terms of symmetrical economic rights so as to provide a basis for nations voluntarily trading, lending and investing with each other in order to widen the overall market. To be sure, there has been a recognition that free trade favors the lead nations, just as free capital movements favor creditor powers. Taken in conjunction with the inflationary excesses of the debt-burdened 1920s, The shift of world economic momentum from trade to finance during the 1920s and early 1930s, prompted France, Britain and other countries to view currency stability as a precondition for stable trade and prosperity. Europe's internationalist emphasis followed from the fact that trade represented a much higher proportion of its national income than that of the United States – 20 to 25 per cent, compared to just 3 to 4 per cent for the United States. Europe sought to achieve stability as a precondition for business revival.

The resolution of the Inter-Ally debt and its related trade problems was by no means implicit, although it seemed so to economists. There were strong party differences in the United States, reflecting regional as well as ideological differences about what position the nation should take. In fact, Roosevelt's election signified an about-face in U.S. policy which had been on the way to making the economic accommodation with Europe that most economists – and certainly most Europeans – had believed was inevitable. To the incoming Democratic Administration nothing was inevitable, least of all a relinquishing of America's creditor hold over Britain, France and the rest of Europe. Yet Roosevelt's advisors were soon shown financial facts that indeed seemed to speak for themselves: "Up to June 15, 1931, we had received $750,000,000 on principal and $1,900,000,000 in interest."[2]

Interest charges thus were nearly two and a half times as large as principal payments. Europe seemed to be on a financial treadmill as its debts mounted up, unpaid and indeed unpayable without access to U.S. markets and elsewhere to displace American exports, or a large-scale government intrusion into property relations by sequestering private European holdings to pay the U.S. Government. In fact, throughout Roosevelt's twelve-year administration the United States put itself in precisely this "socialist" position of urging nationalization of the properties held by large corporations in order to turn them over to the U.S. Government. To be sure, the United States intended to sell off these enterprises to private-sector U.S. buyers. But the financial process was threatening to transform the world's major property relations, shifting ownership from debtor to creditor economy. This was a structural change which Hoover and his Cabinet were not prepared to initiate.

An indication of Roosevelt's willingness to break sharply from the traditional worldview is reflected in Moley's sarcastic remark that "the collapse of the system of international economics which had, up to that time, prevailed" hardly meant the end of civilization.

> Those to whom the gold-standard and free-trade ideals were the twin deities of an unshakable orthodoxy – the international bankers, the majority of our economists, and almost every graduate at every Eastern university who had dipped into the fields of foreign relations or economics – had undertaken to discover a remedy for it. By common consent they had settled upon the reparations and the war debts. If these were canceled (these particular debts among all debts – public and private) or traded for general European disarmament or British resumption of the gold standard or what not, we would root out the cause of our troubles, they had announced. And so ponderous were the arguments that buttressed this formula in the Atlantic states – in academic and presumably "intellectual" circles, at any rate – that it was actually unrespectable not to accept them. . . . Only their prospective dupes, the majority of American citizens, stubbornly refused to swallow them.[3]

Roosevelt and Moley certainly had no intention of being so duped!

Although Roosevelt was elected president on November 8, 1932, he would not take office for nearly four months, on March 4, 1933. This interregnum reflected one of the American political system's distinguishing features, a survival from an epoch when rapid transportation had not yet developed to carry newly elected officials to Washington from as far away as California. (Even though air transport has become the norm today, it still takes nearly two months for the new president to take office after being elected.) This interregnum left the Hoover Administration in the position of being a "lame duck." Not only European governments were concerned over what the change of party control would mean for U.S. attitudes toward the World War I debts, so was the Hoover Administration. An interregnum was at hand that threatened to disrupt the diplomatic negotiations in process. European diplomats and Hoover himself wanted to know how much of this was merely public posturing and what the intentions of the incoming administration really were.

The problem was so pressing in view of the British and French notes of November 10 that two days later, on Saturday, November 12, Hoover sent a telegram to President-elect Roosevelt asking for a meeting to discuss the foreign debt issue. The Moratorium to which Congress had agreed a year earlier had expired, and major payments were scheduled to due on December 15, headed by $95.5 million from Britain and $19.3 million from France.

Roosevelt and his advisors were surprised to receive Hoover's telegram, as such joint meetings between the outgoing and incoming presidents seemed unprecedented. It was apparent that Hoover wanted to commit Roosevelt to a debt settlement that the Republicans had been negotiating out of sight of the voters. Roosevelt for his part did everything he could to avoid being saddled with responsibility for "the December 15th problem," that is, the problem of what to do when Europe refrained from paying its scheduled resumption of Inter-Ally debts. He could not very well refuse to meet with Hoover, but he did not want to commit himself to being a part of the solution toward which Hoover seemed to be moving vis-à-vis Europe.

"We were profoundly certain that the foreign protestations of inability to pay were in large part untrue," writes Raymond Moley, whom Roosevelt had invited to the meeting with Hoover.* "Even if they were not, we knew of no trade for the war debts which seemed advisable – as advisable, at least, as keeping the debts alive to remind our debtors that they were going to find it pretty difficult to finance another war in this country."[4] The position of Moley, Tugwell and other advisors set the tone for U.S. policy over the remainder of the 1930s. One constant theme was that the U.S.

---

* The most extensive reports on the tumultuous first six months of the Roosevelt administration's financial negotiations with Europe have been written by Raymond Moley: *After Seven Years* (1939), followed by *The First New Deal* (1966), an elaborated second edition of the former, taking into account sources published during the intervening generation and discussing in a more philosophical light the day-to-day politics of how America handled the Inter-Ally debt problems.

Raymond Moley, a Professor of Public Law at Columbia University, was appointed Assistant Secretary of State to serve as a personal advisor to Roosevelt. His designated duties were to include the handling of "the foreign debts, the world economic conference, supervision of the economic adviser's office and such additional duties as the President may direct in the general field of foreign and domestic government" (Moley, *After Seven Years* (1939, pp. 81 and 116), and *The First New Deal* (1966, p. 60)). As an isolationist he did not want to serve under the internationalist Secretary of State Cordell Hull, a single-minded free trader from Tennessee who gave up what was in effect a lifetime Senate seat to serve in Roosevelt's Cabinet. But Roosevelt picked him precisely for his "to hell with Europe" attitude and kept him independent of Hull.

Government should not give up its claims just so that Europe could use the money to re-arm. The idea was that if Europe would stop arming, it would have the money to pay its debts. It also could raise the money if chose to requisition private holdings.

What makes these U.S. attitudes so fascinating today is that almost no European (with the exception of Charles de Gaulle) made such demands on the U.S. in the 1960s, even though most Europeans disagreed with its military activities in Southeast Asia and were accumulating dollars that they found unusable for buying out U.S. industrial companies, even their European holdings. Just the opposite, as later chapters will describe; despite America's shift into debtor position vis-à-vis Europe, American private investors continued to buy out European companies. This contrast between the 1930s and 1960s and 1970s should be borne in mind while reviewing the American diplomacy leading up to World War II. It shows how difficult it is to gain international acquiescence in a change in underlying financial and property structures.

Roosevelt meets with Hoover to discuss the debt problem

Roosevelt was well aware of the ideological gulf between himself and Hoover when, on Monday, November 14, he sent a telegram accepting Hoover's invitation for a "wholly informal and personal" meeting on November 22. He asked Moley to accompany him; Hoover was joined by Treasury Secretary Ogden Mills, but not Stimson.

Moley describes Hoover as plunging "into a long recital on the debt question. He spoke without interruption for nearly an hour . . . Before he had finished, it was clear that we were in the presence of the best-informed individual in the country on the question of the debts. His story showed a mastery of detail and a clarity of arrangement that compelled admiration." He started by explaining that "our government is now confronted with a world problem of major importance to this nation." While he did not favor debt revision in itself, "he was willing to bargain if, in compensation for some readjustments on our part, we should receive benefits in an expansion of markets for the products of our labor and our farms."[5] The question was, what trade concessions did foreign countries really have to give America?

Roosevelt's team complained that Britain had failed to include provision for the debt payment in her budget. Why had the Hoover Administration made no attempt to bring up the issue? The debt agreements provided "that questions concerning adjustment of the debt should be brought up ninety days before payment was due," but this period had passed, as Britain and France had not sent notes to the State Department until November 10. Had Hoover promised these countries that if he were re-elected, he would pressure Congress to forgive the debts? If so, how had he planned to get Congress to approve of any such settlement? "Finally – and this was the core of our doubts and misgivings – we wondered if there was any truth in the rumor that the President had promised [French Premier] Laval or [Prime Minister] MacDonald, when these gentlemen visited him, that he would attempt to bring about a complete readjustment of the debt situation. Men close to Laval openly made this claim . . . the British seemed to believe it. (I was later flatly told by three of the highest British officials that such had been the import of President Hoover's conversations.)"[6] Just what unpublicized agreements had been made?

Laying out the common ground between his views and Roosevelt's, Hoover described the Inter-Ally debts as normal business obligations, not political debts. But the way the United States could best negotiate them was indeed political, on a country-by-country (that is, divide-and-conquer) basis, treating each country individually and bargaining for trade concessions or other benefits in exchange for relinquishing the debt stranglehold. Hoover even agreed that the Allied debts were not related to reparations receipts from Germany, a link that would have let the Allies off the hook from paying the United States once Germany stopped paying them. America had not played a role in setting reparations, but entered the picture simply as an arms creditor and provider of postwar aid. On the other hand, Hoover pointed out, the fact was that the debtors simply could not meet their scheduled December 15 payment. Britain had only $78 million available. If it threw more sterling onto the market to buy dollars, the pound would decline, forcing the dollar up and, with it, U.S. export prices relative to those of Commonwealth producers.

Then, describes Moley, "Mr. Hoover moved to one of those plausible generalizations into which he so frequently fell. Either cancellation *or* default, he said, would shake international credit. And that would cause economic shivers to pass through this country."[7] Thus, "while *both* cancellation and default ought to be avoided at all costs, we could not insist upon payment without extending some hope of revision or reexamination unless we wanted to force the European nations to establish a united front against us on economic questions. The price of this policy would be 'grave repercussions' both here and abroad." Hoover therefore wanted to revive the Debt Commission called for at Lausanne the preceding summer, for which his administration had been preparing.

Roosevelt rejected Hoover's emphasis upon restoring financial normalcy. It was business as usual, he believed, that had brought on the depression, which was the result of structural problems such as monopoly power, especially the concentration of financial power. Roosevelt's solution was to regulate business, whereas Hoover took for granted the political, legal and public regulatory structure. And Hoover hardly was amenable to Roosevelt's intention of using public regulation to shift power into the hands of government agencies, and incidentally to the hands of the Executive Branch. But precisely because Roosevelt saw economies as being controlled by their governments, he played down the role of foreign relations, even for Europe's more open and trade-dependent economies. Quite simply, Roosevelt and Congress viewed international debts as a marginal consideration as compared to national planning.

Hoover reports that he concluded the meeting by inviting Roosevelt to join him in calling for "a meeting with Congressional leaders of both parties, which I would call for the next day at the White House, where we would jointly urge the reactivation of a War Debt Commission. This would at once display our united front in the foreign field."[8] In fact, he recognized, without Roosevelt's support he could not get the Congressional assent that was needed to wind up the debt issue. He therefore invited Roosevelt to join with him in naming a bipartisan government commission to negotiate with Europe.

This was just what Roosevelt did not want. He said that he could not be a party to giving up the December 15 payments, although he granted that if these were made as a show of good faith, he would agree to discuss future adjustments "through action of the Executive" at such time as his own administration took office. The problem was complex, and a settlement would take considerable time to work out – the kind of stall people use when they are not prepared to let an issue be brought to a head. "Hoover and Mills were visibly annoyed," Moley reports. "They had hoped that Roosevelt would prove receptive to Hoover's general conclusions about the dreadful urgency of the problem. They had hoped that he would go along on the Debt Commission proposal." The atmosphere became tense as their attitude toward Moley turned from contempt "into cold anger as the afternoon passed."[9] They could not understand Roosevelt's refusal to see what to them was obvious regarding the debt problem, that America hardly could expect to restore trade while the international financial system remained deranged by debts far in excess of the ability of countries to pay.

The press was informed that Roosevelt had accepted "the idea of continuing diplomatic negotiation on debt revision," but not "the Hoover proposal to revive the Debt Commission." The East Coast papers denounced his rejection of Hoover's internationalism as if "he didn't quite know what the meeting with Hoover was all about." Much of the blame was put on Moley, whom Roosevelt had chosen precisely for his rejection of internationalist principles. Indeed, six years later, even as war was breaking out, Moley still believed that the refusal to accept Hoover's proposal "was the first spectacular step Roosevelt took to differentiate his foreign policy from that of the internationalists . . . It was a warning that the New Deal rejected the point of view of those who would make us parties to a political and economic alliance with England and France – policing the world, maintaining the international *status quo*, and seeking to enforce peace through threats of war."[10]

Having failed to win Roosevelt's support, Hoover felt obliged to reject European requests that its debt payments be postponed. On November 23, the day after he met with Roosevelt, Stimson replied to the French and German notes of November 10, explaining that only Congress, not the President, had authority suspend the December 15 payments, and that "reparations are solely a European question in which the United States is not involved." The notes reminded the European Allies that their debts "must be treated as entirely separate from reparation claims arising out of the war."

As the U.S. Council on Foreign Relations summed up the situation, "in Great Britain, Yugoslavia, Finland, Greece, and other debtor nations, an additional increase has occurred in consequence of currency depreciation. With the pound sterling at par, the British Treasury needed £20,000,000 to purchase the dollars required to pay principal and interest falling due in December, 1932. With the pound sterling at $3.22, it needed nearly £30,000,000."[11] In sterling, Britain's debt to the United States increased as it threw sterling onto foreign exchange markets for dollars, forcing down the value of its currency. The effect was to make Britain's debt transfer an infinite function, much as Germany's had been a decade earlier.

To such arguments U.S. diplomats replied coldly that if the debtor countries only would reduce their armaments expenditures, they would have that much more money to honor their international obligations. The debtors replied that they could not take steps to stabilize their currencies until their war debts had been reduced to workable levels. On December 1, a week after receiving Stimson's reply, Britain informed U.S. officials that it deplored their demand to be paid in full, and "and concluded with the veiled threat that if war-debt payments were to be resumed the United Kingdom would have to strengthen its exchange position through measures further restricting British purchases of American goods."[12] The effect of this warning was much like that of Third World countries arguing today that if the United States insists on payment of dollar loans, it must open its agricultural, textile and steel markets to debtor countries and let debtor countries protect their markets from U.S. suppliers.

On December 11 a follow-up note from Britain said that it would make the scheduled payment due on December 15, but would view it "as a capital payment of which account should be taken in any final settlement." Stimson replied that the United States could not accept conditions imposed outside of the original payment agreement. Britain paid anyway, but insisted on the right to bring up at a future conference the idea of counting its debt payment as reducing the principal. This would have converted the debt effectively into an interest-free obligation. This is what friends traditionally do amongst themselves, so the idea hardly was out of the question anthropologically speaking. But what was at issue was power politics, not friendship.

France defaults and Britain pays only a token amount

Britain paid in full on December 15, but France defaulted, claiming that suspension of its payment was "the normal, equitable and necessary sequel" to the Hoover Moratorium. What infuriated U.S. officials was that, unlike Britain, France had the money and could have paid in their view, but chose not to as a matter of policy. Britain had never made the debt issue so categorical. It had asked politely hat in hand for debt forgiveness, not insisted on this imperiously as if it were a matter of obvious common sense. The Chamber of Deputies "authorized payment only if the United States would join an international conference designed to adjust all international obligations."[13] Britain, with its "good behavior" which had been so pleasing to the Americans, exemplified precisely what the French wanted to avoid. Yet Premier Herriot paid a steep price as his government fell when he failed to persuade the Chamber of Deputies to follow the British course. Yet another step was being taken on the path leading toward World War II.

On December 16, Moley and Tugwell were presented with the Williams-Day Report which had been prepared for Hoover's intended follow-up to Lausanne. Moley was "alarmed" to see that it took just the opposite position from the priority Roosevelt and Congress wanted to give to the domestic market. It "indicated that out of the meetings of experts was going to come an internationalists' agenda – a program for a return to an international gold standard, for the sharp writing-down of international debts, and for measures of international 'cooperation' wholly incompatible with the inauguration of the New Deal's domestic program."[14] Roosevelt believed that domestic recovery must take precedence over international concerns. It was not a revival of foreign trade that would cure the depression, but economic restructuring at home – the restructuring that the New Deal promised to bring about.

Moley was made "sick at heart" by hearing from Geneva that "Professor Williams had said that he personally believed that a debt settlement was the chief contribution that the United States could make to the Conference." This attitude made him worry that Europe might succeed in bamboozling America at any such international meeting. "The more we'd considered what might come of the Conference, as a matter of fact, the less importance it seemed to have to the United States." For the agenda for the conference "offered no real prospect of substantial benefits to this country." Why, then, bother with it at all? Why not simply demand continued payment? "In the winter of 1932–33 our problem was to make them understand plainly that we saw what was up and refused to be out-traded. And our immediate task was to resist the efforts of their sympathizers in this country to persuade us that there was an inseverable relation between debts, world economic recovery and disarmament."[15]

On December 17, Hoover sent a lengthy telegram to Roosevelt pointing out "that the debts could not be dissociated from the other problems that would come before the Economic Conference, and that the conference should be assembled as soon as possible." Picking up the arguments he had made at their November meeting, he once again urged Roosevelt to join with him to select a delegation to make progress in reducing the level of intergovernmental debt.[16]

But Roosevelt would not go along, so two days later, on December 19, Hoover found himself obliged to announce in a special message to Congress that the government had declined to grant Europe the requested postponements, "as we considered that such action world amount to practical breakdown of the integrity of the agreements; would impose an abandonment of the national policies of dealing with these obligations separately with each nation; would create a situation where debts would have been regarded as being a counterpart of German reparations and indemnities and thus not only destroy their individual character and obligation but become an effective transfer of German reparations to the American taxpayer; would be no relief to the world situation without consideration of the destructive forces militating against economic recovery;

would not be a proper call upon the American people to further sacrifices unless there were definite compensations."[17]

Roosevelt replied to Hoover's message that day, reiterating that he "looked upon the three questions of disarmament, debts, and economic relations as requiring selective treatment," and that there was no reason to submerge the Economic Conference "in conversations relating to disarmament or debts. There was a 'relationship, but not an identity.'" As Moley put matters, the British "wanted to establish, if possible, the theory that unless debts were settled there could be no possibility of agreement on other economic questions. But we could take in good part this natural attempt of the British to out-trade us without falling for it. And what was there to be gained by rushing into a conference with people who had championed the substance of the British proposals even before the British had made them?" All negotiations should be put on hold until after March 4, when a strongly Democratic Congress would be put in place, immune to such internationalist Anglophilia.[18]

Hoover recognized that affairs were surging ahead in Europe regardless for America's political schedule, and on December 20 suggested that Roosevelt pick as an advisor someone knowledgeable about international affairs, such as Owen Young, Colonel House or, presumably, nearly anyone other than Moley. Roosevelt granted that "the British were probably entitled to special consideration because we had been less lenient with them than with any of our other debtors in the debt settlement." But he insisted that any debt negotiations would have to be conducted by officials appointed by himself, after March 4. And as for the Economic Conference, the topic of debts should not be brought up, as it was an annoying side-issue. Creditors never want to hear about why debtors can't pay, after all, preferring to focus single-mindedly on the debt that is owed. Roosevelt's main concern was the U.S. economy in any event, and he decided that no further meetings with Hoover, Stimson or others were necessary regarding the debt issue prior to his taking office in March.

Led by the Morgan partner Russell Leffingwell, the internationalists tried to promote Norman Davis, a State Department Democrat, to a position of influence. Moley "was sure he wanted to get the debts out of the way to facilitate reviving private lending to Europe." His fate was sealed when Roosevelt let him tag along with Moley and Tugwell on January 20 to meet at the State Department with Stimson to compose a reply to the British regarding the agenda for the Economic Conference planned for London in the summer. After Davis sided with Stimson's position, Roosevelt henceforth chose to dispense with his advice.

With regard to the prospects of negotiating a *quid pro quo* with Europe at the January 20 meeting, Tugwell repeated Roosevelt's argument that U.S. economic recovery did not really need tariff concessions from Britain or France. What was needed was a revival of confidence at home. To concede that German reparations could not be paid would open the door for the Allies to claim that this would deprive them of the money to pay their World War I debts. They would demand U.S. concessions on their own debts in return so that their debt service should be brought within their ability to pay. (In fact, Stimson's diary for that day reveals that in a talk with Owen Young in New York, Britain hoped "for an independent settlement of the debt question without any concession in return.")

Deliberate blindness as to the financial dynamics at work was thus the position dictated by U.S. self-interest – that is to say, the interest of its government as creditor, which the Eastern banking interests had come to realize was antithetical to their own private ambitions. Tugwell and Moley refused to authorize a statement acknowledging that America would address the debt problem at the London conference. They also insisted that Stimson's reply to the British note would have to reject the idea that concessions on the debt issue might form the basis for currency stabilization. The major internationalist U.S. newspapers might agree with public opinion in Europe not to pay the war debts, but Congress was not about to let Europe off the hook. On the other hand, tariff and trade matters affecting the local interests with which voters and Congressmen were concerned might be dealt with at an international conference. Roosevelt's advisors wanted to narrow the agenda to this area alone.

In a huff, Stimson accused Tugwell of "trying to tear down everything I have been working for in my whole term," and said he would "leave a memorandum in the State Department files registering his mature judgment that another course would have been preferable."[19] Moley records that he didn't give a hoot. The liberal internationalist wing of the Democrats was shunted onto a political siding. Hull's position as Secretary of State served as little more than protective coloration for the New Dealers.

On January 24, having been apprised of the stalemated State Department meeting, Chancellor of the Exchequer Neville Chamberlain gave a speech taking "the position that the settlement of the debt to the United States must be both small and final." This time Britain did not seek a *quid pro quo*. A showdown was clearly in the making, and Roosevelt's team for its part did not intend to give an inch.

When Britain's ambassador Ronald Lindsay was called back to London for consultation, Roosevelt suggested to Stimson that it might clarify matters if Sir Ronald first came to have a talk with him in Warm Springs where he was resting up. On January 28, Lindsay arrived and was treated to a discussion outlining the U.S. logic that Europe could pay if it would cut back its military spending, and that in any event "the nationals of both England and France owned vast amounts of securities and other property in this country which could have been utilized, within limits, in making the transfer."[20] As the next chapter will show, U.S. diplomats were still making the latter point in 1940–41 when they were negotiating Lend-Lease and U.S. support of Britain and the rest of Europe against the Nazi aggression that ultimately drew the nation into World War II.

Moley brusquely dismissed the fact that selling sterling on the foreign exchange market to buy dollars to pay foreign debts was quite a different matter from buying arms for domestic currency. In the former case sterling's exchange rate would fall, but this would be the response to domestic arms spending only if 100 per cent spilled over to buy foreign products – something unlikely given Britain's large-scale unemployment. This Transfer Problem had been the basic point Keynes had made in the 1920s, but neither Moley nor the President was well versed in economic theory. "I doubt that either Roosevelt or I could have passed an examination such as is required of college students in elementary economics," he reminisced. "Both of us were bored and confused by long, learned memoranda with which so many people had inundated us over the year since the campaign started in 1932." Perhaps "the limitation of our economic expertise was an advantage," for at least they had not been indoctrinated by the internationalist orthodoxy "that things would automatically right themselves in the fairly short run." The problem with Republican policy was that "the advice sought by Stimson and Mills came mostly from the New York banking community and . . . these gentlemen not only were grossly ignorant of causes and effect in agriculture and industry, but in the crisis they could not supply a remedy for their own derelictions."[21]

Moley recognized that "future payments on the debts would be small and far between," but nonetheless believed that "they should remain on the books. So long as they were alive, their presence would be a warning, however slight, that the European debtors should not look upon the United States as a source of new help." He later sought to justify his actions in 1933 by depicting Lausanne as "a minor Munich," as "the cut in German reparations had been nothing less than an invitation to the Germans, who looked upon France and England as 'paper tigers,' to dedicate themselves to rearmament in anticipation of another war." It followed that "To make what Tugwell called 'the grand gesture' of reducing or canceling the debts would seem ironical to the people of the country, who were themselves sorely burdened with private indebtedness – impoverished and mortgage-laden farmers, small businesses that could barely borrow enough from the banks to stay alive, big businesses that were depressed for lack of customers. For a Presidential candidate who had so seriously planned to attack the problem of debt on the home front to make international concessions after election would be resented."[22] Left out of account was a recognition that foreign economies no more could pay their international debts than American farmers, consumers and businesses could pay their domestic debts.

The European delegates hoped that the Allies, Germans and Americans might settle among themselves what had been left unresolved at Lausanne. Matters moved toward a head on the eve of Roosevelt's inauguration when Britain presented a seven-point memorandum on "British Policy on Economic Problems."[23] "The depression cannot be effectively remedied by isolated action," it stated, hoping to ward off U.S. isolationism. Hence, solutions must be sought through "international action on a very broad front," toward which the Preparatory Commission of Experts established at Lausanne provided a useful basis for discussion.

In keeping with Roosevelt's own ideas, the note's first objective endorsed "a rise in the general level of prices, especially of farm commodities." It also endorsed a coordinated monetary policy in both Britain and the United States "to ensure the provision of cheap and abundant short-term money." The implication was that debtor countries should be freed from having to pay their debts to the United States, and to keep their interest rates high so as to attract foreign loans to provide the dollars to make these payments.

A third objective was currency stabilization – something that could not be done without alleviating the debt burden, for the major factor destabilizing currencies was debt service. And only an alleviation of this debt service would promote the fourth objective endorsed by the British note: abolition of the exchange controls that were threatening to restrict world trade. A related fifth objective was to relax trade barriers such as quotas, as well as a general agreement to reduce tariffs. This ran counter to the agricultural protectionism advocated by U.S. farm interests and soon written into law by the New Deal's Agricultural Adjustment Act of 1933.

Hopes by Western U.S. senators for bimetallism – that is, inclusion of silver alongside gold in world central bank reserves – was dismissed as being "impossible of adoption," a verdict that the Preparatory Commission also had reached. The problem of low silver prices would be solved "not by a rise in the price of silver as such," but through "a rise in the general level of commodity prices, which would bring up the value of silver at the same time."

Finally, the British listed their most important objective: U.S. assurance that the debt issue would soon be settled at an international conference. "The existence of these debts constitutes, as the Preparatory Commission have said, an insuperable barrier to economic and financial reconstruction, and there is no prospect of the World Economic Conference making progress if this barrier cannot be removed."

This British agenda was about to be countered by Roosevelt's New Deal. His program did indeed endorse higher price levels and lower interest rates. But as far as currency stabilization was concerned, Roosevelt was about to take America off gold, while his agricultural program and related policies would require protectionist trade quotas. As to settlement of the war debts, Roosevelt wasn't prepared even to begin discussing a resolution of this problem.

MacDonald and Herriot visit Washington

After taking office on March 4, 1933, just five weeks after Hitler became Chancellor of Germany, President Roosevelt declared a bank holiday, repealed prohibition, provided unemployment relief and endorsed agricultural price supports. The last presupposed import quotas for the crops whose prices were being supported. On April 17, Senator Elmer Thomas of Oklahoma added an amendment authorizing the President to issue greenbacks, fix the ratio of the value of silver to gold and provide for free silver coinage, and fix the weight of the gold dollar by proclamation. Three days later, on April 20, Roosevelt cut the dollar loose from gold to find its own level. His objective was to reflate prices according to the theory of Cornell economics professor George F. Warren that domestic prices would rise in proportion to the dollar's depreciation against gold. Rising prices would alleviate the depression by making it easier for farmers, workers and businesses to pay their debts. Both the House of Representatives and Senate backed the inflationary policies deemed necessary to reduce the debt burden and speed economic recovery.

Dollar depreciation had the incidental effect of increasing U.S. export competitiveness vis-à-vis Europe, wiping out much of the trade advantage that Britain had gained by going off gold the previous year and generally aggravating Europe's already debt-ridden balance-of-payments position.

But for the United States, Walter Lippman wrote, "national policies were bound to prevail. In such a conflict they always do prevail in any powerful nation." The basic problem with such a policy was that "In spite of the underlying conception of the AAA [Agricultural Adjustment Act] and of NRA [National Recovery Act], that competition in the domestic market must be limited and controlled, the Administration continued to advocate freer trade in the world."[24] The erroneous assumption was that foreign countries could open their markets in the face of increasing U.S. payments surpluses and still pay their dollar-denominated war debts.

Britain began to prepare for the worst. In May it negotiated trade preferences with Argentina, extending the Imperial Preference system whose foundation had been laid at Ottawa a year earlier. Roosevelt approved an increase in U.S. cotton tariffs, and the trade wars of the 1930s began to gain momentum.

Hoping that the conflict could be resolved without a break, the British Prime Minister, Ramsay MacDonald, planned to visit Washington to seek U.S. commitment for the London Economic Conference. His Cabinet warned him not to make the trip "without advance assurance from us that the June 15th debt payment could be postponed." Otherwise, it was feared, he would be embarrassed by a failure in what had become Britain's major economic concern. The United States refused to provide any such advance commitment, but MacDonald came anyway, accompanied by Sir Frederick Leith-Ross, Chief Economic Advisor to His Majesty's Government, and Sir Robert Vansittart, Permanent Under-Secretary of State for Foreign Affairs.[25]

Roosevelt invited former Prime Minister Herriot to the meeting in recognition of his having risked his political career attempting to get France to pay its December debt installment. Herriot was flanked by the economic advisor Charles Rist and Jean J. Bizot, Advisor to the French Treasury, as well as Robert Coulondre of the French Foreign Office and Paul Elbel of the Ministry of Commerce. Italy sent Guido Jung and a staff. Germany sent Hjalmar Schacht.

With the London Conference less than three months away, the world's financial system was thrown into turmoil as Roosevelt cut the dollar free of gold while these visitors were crossing the Atlantic. Meanwhile, the State Department drafted a reply to the British proposals for a joint statement of principles that would guide the London negotiations. The task initially fell to Norman Davis, the suspect internationalist, but Moley quickly eliminated him from further involvement in the negotiations and set about preparing a reply himself, rejecting the idea "that the maintenance of the debts, whether the installments were paid or not paid, would in any way hinder recovery here or abroad."[26]

James Warburg, an official formerly with the Bank of New York, worked out a formula to settle the debt issue. Nicknamed "the Bunny," it proposed to cancel all interest charges and substantially reduce the remaining principal "in the light of the depressed conditions that had arisen since the last agreements had been made in the 1920s. The debtors would reaffirm their obligations by depositing a note for the new amounts with the Bank for International Settlements. These notes were to be secured by a deposit of 25 per cent of the principal amount in gold bullion plus another 5 per cent in gold or silver. The remainder of the debts would be dealt with by a sinking-fund agreement under which each debtor would make certain annual payments to the Bank for International Settlements," which would use the payments to buy U.S. Government debt. This proposal would have turned the Bank for International Settlements from an instrument designed to collect German reparations into one in charge of transferring European payments to the United States. European tribute would finance America's budget deficit, leaving its revenue to be spent on goods and services to help pull the country out of depression.[27]

Upon their arrival Roosevelt informed the European leaders that this was as far as the United States would go toward resolving the debt issue. As for the dollar's falling value, he assured them that he did not want speculation to push it down "unnaturally," but wanted it to find a "natural" level, defined as one that would restore prosperity for America. This certainly meant a much lower exchange rate against gold, as there is little point to devaluation unless one devalues to excess, that is, by enough to change existing trade patterns in one's favor. This meant that the dollar's fall would win export trade from countries that sought to keep their currencies on the gold standard at the existing gold price.[28]

Roosevelt left the Europeans with the impression that he was eager to resolve the problem, however, and they left Washington in the belief that a final solution would be reached at the London Economic Conference. To a large extent they were merely reading in their hopes, for the joint statement Roosevelt issued with MacDonald was carefully written to be noncommittal, providing the United States with the escape clause that an improved gold standard should operate "without depressing prices," "when circumstances permit," and containing the qualification that its policy commitments would aim at "ultimate reestablishment of equilibrium in the international exchanges."[29] Just what did all this mean about stabilizing exchange rates and opening markets in the near future was not clear.

Wheeler-Bennett noted how urgent this had become in January: "The flagging hopes and expectations of the world are centered on the Economic Conference . . . It may be the last upward effort that brings the world from the brink of disaster on to firm ground; it may be the last despairing struggle before the final plunge. By the date of the opening of the Conference, President Roosevelt will have been inaugurated, and the world will know whether or not he will use the reduction of war debts to bargain for the reduction of tariffs."[30] Europe's financial cohesion was at stake, and its leaders dared not look into the abyss that the Americans seemed to be welcoming without much care.

Part of the problem was similar to that which Americans found in dealing with the Japanese in the 1980s. When MacDonald, Herriot and other statesmen spoke with Roosevelt he would nod his head and might reply "fine," which they took as an indication of agreement. It merely meant that he understood what they were saying, not that he was agreeing with them. He also adopted a tactic that would be typical of U.S. negotiating policy over many decades. "When an agreement became uncomfortable he was adept at contriving an escape, and when that failed he would simply repudiate it."

But for the time being, Roosevelt appeared to many Americans as well as to Europeans as an internationalist, and even as the chief sponsor of the London Conference in view of America's dominant role in the world economy. But people were reading in their wishes, not the reality. Roosevelt was being praised for taking on a position of world leadership that he had no intention of assuming, for it would have entailed the burden of making Europe happy, above all with regard to the debt issue. His objective was to help America recover, and only Americans formed his electorate. Internationalists such as Secretary of State Hull seemed to have little understanding "that in any actual conflict between his domestic program and a program of international economics the President would decide in favor of his domestic program."[31] The New Deal was taking a go-it-alone position such as no major nation outside of the new fascist powers had done, and Germany and France were acting under *force majeure*.

This, then, was the U.S.-European opposition at the time the London Economic Conference was set to open on June 12, "because, as F.D.R. pointed out, the Conference ought not to meet earlier, when Congress would still be in session, and because, as MacDonald pointed out, the Conference ought not to meet later, or it would run on into the grouse season and all the British statesmen would walk out on it. What with Congress on the one side and grouse on the other, agreement on June 12th was a triumph of diplomacy."[32] That having been decided, MacDonald sailed away, followed by Herriot three days later.

Preparing for London

What was so fateful about London's opening date of June 12 was that June 15 was the day on which quarterly Inter-Ally debt service was due. Probably the Europeans expected debt payments to be held in suspension during the negotiations.

Leith-Ross was asked to stay behind in Washington in early May to prepare for the London meeting. The U.S. team worried that he and the other Europeans were likely to outsmart them by crying poverty. "In negotiating with the British," wrote Moley about the Washington meetings, "we were confronting a relatively small country that by the sophistication of its trading methods had spread its power over the whole world. The advantage of the United States in this instance was almost solely due to its economic might, certainly not to the talent it had developed to represent the government in trade affairs. Our trump cards were the debts and the freedom of action permitted by the terms of the Thomas amendment. We had already made it clear that Congress had spoken the final word about compromising the debts. The reluctance of Roosevelt about stabilization was wholly in the interest of our own recovery."[33]

When confronted with "the Bunny," the British diplomat explained

that economic and political conditions in England made payment in June exceedingly unlikely. Financially it would be a very great hardship on the British to make the payment. Politically it would be dangerous for the Government to ignore the strong public opinion that Britain could not and should not be expected to make full payment. And yet the British did not like the idea of default. The very word was offensive to their moral sensibilities. It ran counter to every precept of that system of financial ethics they had grown great by observing. Might President Roosevelt not persuade congress to agree to a temporary suspension of the June 15th payment on the ground, say, that nonpayment would interrupt the negotiations for a final settlement, or perhaps on the ground that it would jeopardize the Economic Conference?

Lew Douglas and Moley gave a flat no. Public opinion in Britain might favor annulling the debts, but "there existed a public opinion here as well as in Great Britain, that public opinion would not permit the President to make such a move. Congress was in no mood to do anything but exact payment." Leith-Ross pressed on, asking whether, to avoid an outright breakdown of negotiations, Britain might refrain from paying, but call it a "suspension" rather than default. "We thought not," writes Moley, adding, "Of all this Secretary Hull knew nothing – by F.D.R.'s express orders."[34]

The problem from Roosevelt's view (shared by Moley) was that Hull recognized what they did not want to see: "if something agreeable to the British could not be worked out on the June 15th matter failure would threaten the Economic Conference itself." Hull wanted Roosevelt "to 'save' the British and the Conference." But to Roosevelt, saving America meant disappointing Britain and other European debtor countries. While he was all for alleviating domestic debt, he was not for lifting the burden of foreign indebtedness to the United States.

So a showdown seemed inevitable. Ramsay MacDonald wrote a letter upholding the position taken by Leith-Ross, that Britain was in no position to make the June 15 payment. Was there perhaps a nice public relations way of handling this so as to make it all appear perfectly natural, with a show of American understanding to keep the internationalist spirit alive (if not indeed to revivify it)? "Default would cause hostility in both countries: the American man on the street would blame the British for defaulting, and the British man on the street would blame the United States for forcing Britain into the position of defaulting. Couldn't a request be made to Congress for general powers to deal with the debt situation pending negotiations for a final settlement?"[35]

It was evident that Britain and the rest of Europe still were hoping for the scenario that had seemed likely under the debt commission set up after Lausanne and endorsed by Hoover's team, at best a debt annulment, perhaps in exchange for some trade concessions to U.S. exporters, and at worst a kind of Young Plan for the Allied powers. But this was just what Roosevelt and his advisors had been turning down since November. Roosevelt replied to MacDonald on May 22, that he "was determined not to let any aspect of the debt question get mixed up with the issues before the Conference." He asked Britain if it could "pay a *part* of what it owed." Later that week he decided not to send to Congress the Reciprocal Tariff Treaty bill on which Hull and the internationalists had set their hearts.[36]

It was not yet clear just how destabilizing the floating (that is, sinking) dollar would prove to be. Treasury Secretary William Woodin, Warburg, Douglas and most experts believed that "the dollar, if left to itself, would not sink more than eighteen or twenty per cent, which, in relation to sterling at the moment, would mean about $4.00 a pound as compared with the current quotation of around $3.50 and the old par of $4.87." The pound had fallen severely, and the U.S. devaluation would not even make up half the difference under this scenario. But by May 20 the dollar was depreciating so rapidly that it looked like the pound would be lifted back above the $4.00 level. U.S. officials blamed the dollar's plunge on large speculators, but did nothing, explaining that in due course economic "fundamentals" would correct the decline.

Roosevelt proved to be more astute in taking "the position (in private, of course) that the dollar might sink to lows that the experts hadn't conceived of. He was in no hurry to stabilize until he was sure he was going to get the best bargain there was to be got. With the dollar falling as it was in the exchange markets, our stock and bond prices were leaping upward and our commodity prices soaring. New purchasing power was being created in this country, he held. This stimulating movement must not be stopped. This was recovery – not a dangerous speculative spree!" The British warned that no progress could be made at the Conference without knowing "just how far the United States intended to let the dollar plummet." But Roosevelt told the U.S. delegation to London "to shun the subject [of stabilization] like the plague."[37]

Trying to soften the U.S. position, Ambassador Lindsay explained why "Britain deserved some sympathy from us. They had never once failed to make their payments. The total they had paid, to date, was $1,447,270,000, whereas the French, who originally had owed us almost as much as the British, had paid us only $200,000,000. Furthermore . . . a very considerable debt was owed them by European nations. How could they forgive their debtors if we were unwilling to forgive ours? (This curious use of the sacred mandate of the Lord's Prayer was not lost upon us . . .)" Moley did not have an answer that addressed the issue, but reverted to blaming Congress. The Executive Branch would not take responsibility for resolving the debt issue. Roosevelt explained that he "could not seek power to postpone payments without a tremendous uproar in an already rebellious Congress." On this ground the United States rejected Britain's request to make only a token payment of $5 million, "to be lumped with the payment of December and considered as a payment on account toward an amount to be determined in the final settlement." In the first place, Moley explained, "the word 'token' in the United States conveyed a wholly different idea than it did in England: 'token,' to us, meant a small worthless coin." And $5 million looked like just such a paltry token.

"So we dickered, like traders in an Eastern bazaar," he describes the proceedings. "In the end the British came through with the offer of a

$10,000,000 payment. This was to constitute 'an acknowledgement of the debt pending a final settlement,' their note said . . . we accepted the offer. The way was now open to an amicable adjustment of the whole matter – an adjustment which was never achieved."[38] In fact, Feis observed: "It is more probable that the default washed away the remnants of Roosevelt's tolerance for the French effort to cause us to return to the international gold standard at a fixed rate to the franc, and made him more determined not to let the British authorities ease him into an agreement about the relative pound-dollar value which might be to Britain's advantage."[39]

Negotiations with the French were more unpleasant. They sent a note announcing that they would defer the June payment, adding "the droll touch that France by no means intended 'to break unilaterally engagements entered into.'" The curt U.S. reply remarked that France had missed the December 15 payment and had not shown "any desire even to discuss the problem." What annoyed the U.S. team was that unlike Britain, France had a relatively large supply of gold and appeared to have been able to pay its December installment, but "neither confessed inability to pay nor offered payment of even a small amount on account, which seemed to us completely faithless." Likewise when Italy's Ambassador offered to pay $1 million on account, "We reminded him that the payment of $1,000,000 on a total due of $13,545,438.00 would 'be regarded in the United States as insubstantial' – that, in fact, it looked to us like the kind of a tip which one gave in a very unfashionable restaurant. But it was impossible to force them up."[40] A bazaar indeed!

Roosevelt's "Bombshell" breaks up the London Economic Conference

On May 20, just before the U.S. delegation was to sail for London, Moley gave a speech in which he urged international delegates to the conference to "recognize that world trade, after all, is only a small percentage of the trade of the United States. This means that our domestic policy is of paramount importance."[41] It also meant that the United States was in a position to do pretty much what it wanted. The Roosevelt Administration felt that by the time the London Conference convened on Monday, June 12, the dollar had depreciated 20 per cent against the Gold Bloc currencies. Foreign countries were coming to recognize that whereas they were seeking to stabilize their currencies, the United States "believed that its stabilization at too early a date would jeopardize the gains made during the preceding two months."[42] Next to the debt issue, currency stabilization would become the area that broke up the conference in disarray and inaugurated the competitive depreciations that became so corrosive a characteristic of the 1930s.

The American delegation was led by Secretary of State Hull, whose internationalist hopes would be severely undercut by Roosevelt during the conference. Former Governor James M. Cox of Ohio, the Democratic presidential candidate in 1920, was named Vice Chairman. He was a newspaper publisher with conservative monetary views, mildly low-tariff. Among the technicians were Herbert Feis, a State Department economic advisor held over from the Hoover Administration, and Warburg. The leading politician was Key Pittman, Chairman of the Senate Foreign Relations Committee, a high-tariff, pro-inflationary advocate from the silver-producing state of Nevada, chairman of the Senate Committee on Foreign Relations, of whom Feis commented: "He was mean . . . he cared little, or nothing, about any foreign country. His interest in monetary policies was centered on improving the prices and prospects of silver mined in Nevada and neighboring states." Eager to "do something for silver," he was more sympathetic than any other member of the delegation to the increasingly unorthodox monetary views of Roosevelt.[43] The man who would prove to be most influential, Raymond Moley, was sent over to London when the meetings already were underway. "I didn't think much of the Conference's prospects," he wrote in his memoirs. "I didn't think we could obtain from it anything of substantial value to this country." He was interested almost exclusively "in the domestic picture [rather] than in the foreign."[44]

Signs *en route* hardly were auspicious for an agreement between the United States and Europe. Roosevelt had been considering legislation that ultimately would become the Trade Expansion Act of 1934 authorizing him to negotiate tariff cuts, but "midway across the Atlantic, Hull heard from the President that he had decided not to ask Congress to pass the new law affecting the tariff. Hull realized that unless it did, other governments would be dubious of our intention to reverse the trend to higher and more comprehensive restrictions."[45] He warned Roosevelt that this might reduce the delegation to a passive role in the Conference, as the United States already had ruled out negotiations on the debt issue and exchange rate stability. Without an agreement to halt the dollar devaluation vis-à-vis other currencies, and without negotiated tariff reductions and a waiving of intergovernmental debt, the United States had little to offer. Foreign governments had little opportunity to do much beside defaulting on their Inter-Ally debts and trying to devalue their own currencies against the dollar in an attempt to make their exports competitive.

In his welcoming speech MacDonald brought up the forbidden subject of Inter-Ally debts, which U.S. representatives accused of being a breach of promise. The Europeans for their part were disturbed by events on the currency front as the pound rose to $4.18 against the dollar, just the opposite direction from the rumored British and French hope to stabilize at $3.50.

On Tuesday a fight developed over who would become chairman of the Conference's Monetary Committee, France's Foreign Minister Georges Bonnet or the American James Cox. "Bonnet addressed himself directly to Cox, saying that 'France would not look with favor upon the selection of someone to head the monetary committee who comes from a country that has recently gone off the gold standard.' Cox rejoined, 'Nor will the United States look with favor upon the election of a man presented by a country which has repudiated its debts.' This crackling exchange was a sign of the thunderclaps in the atmosphere that hovered over the conference even as it was convening."[46] MacDonald did not help matters by promising both parties the chairmanship, which was awarded to Cox when Bonnet agreed to become the committee's rapporteur.

When Secretary Hull failed to appear later that day at the hour appointed for his speech, the Europeans suspected that this was a rebuke for MacDonald's mention of the war debts, but the reason was simply that he had not finished writing his speech. In fact, that day saw Warburg work with the New York Federal Reserve Bank and the Bank of England to devise a plan to maintain exchange rates within a 3 per cent spread against the franc and to earmark up to $60 million for each institution to spend on maintaining a dollar–pound ratio of about $4.00. On Thursday, June 15, the dollar rose as sterling fell to $4.02. Stock and bond prices swooped and soared to reflect the dollar's gyrations. $4.05 appeared to be a likely stabilization level, perhaps even $4.00. Montagu Norman of the Bank of England and Clément Moret of the Bank of France made a virtually peremptory demand for currency stabilization in this range, but the American delegation said this was impossible. The essence of Roosevelt's plan, after all, was to devalue the dollar so as to raise U.S. prices. Back at the White House a war council was summoned of Woodin, Under Secretary of the Treasury Dean Acheson, and Moley. "It was decided that while agreement on the $4.00 middle rate would have seemed like a good trade in late April, in mid-June it was preposterous: $4.20 would have been nearer the mark."[47] Moley thought that $4.25 was about the upper limit the pound should reach, but he didn't put this in writing, thinking it wise to give the Europeans a good fright to show them who really was in control. The dollar continued to fall as Roosevelt made it clear that he would not approve "close" stabilization.

On June 17, with Congress adjourned, Roosevelt asked Moley to go to London to make sure the U.S. delegation adhered to the hard line he had committed them to. He was to go as "liaison officer" reporting directly to Roosevelt, not formally as part of the delegation itself, which would have made him subject to Hull's authority. His instructions were that America might reach some ameliorative stabilization agreement, perhaps with a high and low of $4.25 and $4.05, for a midpoint of $4.15, "if that could be contrived without the shipment of gold from this country and without checking the magnificent advance of American prices which had followed our departure from gold in April."

But by the time Moley landed at Plymouth on June 27 the pound had risen to $4.30, the lowest exchange rate for the dollar since the Civil War. The next day sterling reached a high of $4.43, closing at $4.37½. "F.D.R.'s bargaining tactics had succeeded beyond his wildest imagining between June 17th and June 20th," describes Moley. "The foreign nations now believed that he would not stabilize. They accepted this as a fact. They asked only that he make some gesture – some small gesture – that would in no way limit his freedom of action on the dollar and that would, nevertheless, tend to discourage the mad exchange speculation of the preceding three weeks."[48]

Britain and France could have maintained parity with the dollar by devaluing their own currencies against gold, of course. But whereas Roosevelt welcomed inflation, they feared it. MacDonald took an emotional approach, warning about Europe's phobia about inflation and the panic this was creating in the Netherlands, Switzerland and France. But this anti-inflationary attitude was precisely what led Roosevelt to dismiss the idea of stabilization. He had come to recognize that his domestic policies were at odds with his stated international policies and was not willing to stabilize the dollar even for the duration of the conference. It continued to fall, and by June 28 was down to 76.3 per cent of its pre-devaluation value. France, Belgium, Switzerland and the Netherlands announced that unless it stabilized, they too would have to abandon gold.

A speculative panic ensued, and even Moley came to favor a message that would serve at least as a symbolic gesture, however innocuous, that the United States wanted to help stabilize the world's financial system. It seemed that at least the appearance of cooperation might be given, based on a resolution introduced by Senator Pittman on June 19 to the effect "that gold would ultimately be reestablished as a measure of international exchange value, but that each nation reserved the right to decide when it would return to a gold standard and undertake stabilization."[49] The aim of this statement was not to constrain the dollar's response to the "fundamentals" that Roosevelt sought to bring about, but simply to deter speculation.

Neville Chamberlain sought to appease the Americans by proposing a "harmless" declaration that "would commit Roosevelt to absolutely nothing except to ask the Federal Reserve to cooperate in limiting fluctuations due to speculation . . . *It did not mean stabilization*." Moley "suggested, informally, one or two minor changes of phraseology further devitalizing the limp document, so that it could not conceivably be interpreted as a promise, however vague, that the United States would forswear price raising by monetary action."[50] The Big Three representatives drafted a message to calm world markets, but "with characteristic subtlety, the French had twisted some phrases ever so slightly to make the declaration possibly capable of interpretation as stabilization." Moley insisted that their version be brought in line with the Anglo-American draft before submitting it to Roosevelt for his approval.

Roosevelt had chosen precisely this time to go on vacation, however. He was on Campobello Island, and unreachable by telephone. The U.S. delegation called Woodin's home in New York, where the advisor Bernard Baruch, Acheson and George L. Harrison of the New York Federal Reserve Bank were at his bedside, as he was sick. But they still hadn't received the draft, which was going through the laborious process of being coded at both ends of the transmission. Moley and Swope returned the call to assure them that the draft statement "couldn't possibly obligate us to ship gold. It would not check the steady rise of American prices in so far as that rise was based upon the sound revival of business. At most it would check only the ultra-speculative aspects of that rise . . . it would be a better bargain than any Roosevelt had in mind when I last saw him, since it expressed no more than a detached, though sympathetic interest in the gold standard; and it would keep the Conference from breaking up as it threatened to do."[51] But Roosevelt could not be reached, as he was sailing back down to Washington on the *Indianapolis*, accompanied by Henry Morgenthau, Jr. and Louis Howe, cut off from advice from the U.S. delegation in London. Moley's assistant believed that he "deliberately designed his vacation to avoid responsibility for what might happen. As it did happen, however, he emerged as the man who wrecked the whole affair."[52] He had implicitly assumed sponsorship of the conference with

MacDonald and Herriot, but was not prepared to commit America internationally until the monetary situation was put in order at home.

Finally, on Saturday, July 2, as "practically everyone connected with the delegation was starting out for Cliveden to attend a garden party given by Lady Astor," the coded message from the President began to come through. It came as a bombshell, being a tirade "against rigid and arbitrary stabilization."[53] Regarding statements that the United States would join with other central banks in fighting inflation, Roosevelt "did not know how governments could check speculation." How could one distinguish between shifts in the exchange rate that were justified from those which were unjustified? His message repudiated currency stabilization entirely.

I would regard it as a catastrophe, amounting to a world tragedy, if the great Conference of Nations called to bring about a more real and permanent financial stability and a greater prosperity to the masses of all nations should, in advance of any serious effort to consider these broader problems, allow itself to be diverted by the proposal of a purely artificial and temporary experiment affecting the monetary exchange of a few nations only. . . . The sound internal economic situation of a nation is a greater factor in the well-being than the price of its currency in changing terms of the currencies of other nations . . . old fetishes of so-called international bankers are being replaced by efforts to plan national currencies . . . Gold or gold and silver can well continue to be a metallic reserve behind currencies, but this is not the time to dissipate gold reserves,

that is, not the time to spend them on stabilizing foreign exchange rates. "The sound internal economic system of a nation is a greater factor in its well-being than the price of its currency in changing terms of the currencies of other nations."[54]

"It was less the substance of this message that shocked us as we read it in Claridge's than its tone of belligerence," Moley remembers. Roosevelt could have made his points without rejecting the declaration two days before. What the Europeans wanted was simply an idea of cooperation from America. What they got instead was to be told to get lost. Roosevelt wanted to raise the price level and was not going to let foreign complaints about the dollar's value stand in the way. As the world's major creditor and largest economy, America really did not have to listen to anyone else. He seemed to be sending a message to the world that the U.S. Government would not be available to help extricate it from a financial tangle that it itself had caused largely by taking a narrow-minded position with regard to the Inter-Ally debts. In Lippman's words, stabilizing the exchange value of the dollar would have "meant that the Administration must surrender its independence of action in monetary matters and fasten the American price level to the gold price level in the outer world. The gold price level was, however, too low to permit the restoration of the equilibrium in America . . . There was nothing further for the London Conference to do once the American government had decided it must have a free hand in monetary policy."[55]

The message effectively killed the Conference. It shocked even the American delegates, because they had been careful to phrase the proposed statement in a way that did not bind Roosevelt to stabilize the dollar. They felt there had been a misunderstanding, and saw that it would wreck the Conference. "The reading of 'The Bombshell' completely demoralized Hull and all the rest of the delegation but Pittman. They were frank to say that they didn't know what it meant." Three days later, on July 6, Warburg resigned "because he neither felt that he could interpret the President's new objective – which seemed to be a currency based on commodity prices – nor believed that the President's ideas had crystallized sufficiently to enable the Conference to proceed."[56] Lippman helped prepare a press release, but little remained for the delegates to talk about. A 10 per cent, across-the-board reduction in tariffs was suggested, but was deemed "not consistent with recent legislation in the United States authorizing the imposition of new tariffs in connection with a national effort to raise prices, and it did not remain long before the conference."[57] What soon was to become the Agricultural Adjustment Act imposed quotas on all foreign farm products competing with those produced by American farmers. The United States claimed special exceptions to free trade by imposing these restrictive agricultural quotas, and was not averse to devaluing the dollar in order to obtain export price advantages.

The Conference adjourned on July 27. Professor William Brown observed, it "split apart as the result of four great negatives. The countries applying the new protection refused to modify their systems of trade restriction unless currency stability was assured. The countries on the gold standard, many of which had had bitter experience of currency inflation, refused to accept a policy of price raising as the major instrument of economic reconstruction. Great Britain, though favorable to price raising, refused to unbalance her budget to achieve it or to embark upon a great program of public works with that end in view. The United States refused to allow her own program of price raising and of public works to be interfered with by currency stabilization."[58]

It was indeed wise for President Roosevelt to use the monetary means of dollar devaluation to hasten reflation of prices in the United States, and shortsighted of the Gold Bloc countries to cling rigidly to their gold parities, a policy that bankrupted them in short order. What was not forgivable was his use of dollar devaluation specifically as a means of economic warfare against an already impoverished Europe. Simultaneous with devaluing the dollar, which made it impossible for Europe to repay its Inter-Ally debts by means of running a trade surplus with the United States, Roosevelt insisted that these debts be honored regardless of whether the Allies were receiving reparations funds from Germany. It was this insistence, not dollar devaluation, that fragmented the world economy during 1931–33.

It showed that Roosevelt's focus was "domestic prices in American money regardless of what foreign exchange rates might be."[59] The reality was that only the United States seemed to perceive the need for government to take the lead in abandoning the creditor-oriented monetary philosophy to which Europe continued to adhere, even in the face of its own debtor position vis-à-vis the United States. Foreign experts simply couldn't imagine what Roosevelt meant. Despite their debtor position internationally, their concern was to prevent inflation, not deflation. America was playing the debtor card at home, even while using its creditor leverage vis-à-vis Europe.

At home, Roosevelt favored debtor interests. It was this position that led him to reject Europe's hope for stabilizing currencies. Lowering the dollar's gold value was a key to his almost populist attempt to inflate prices so as to reduce the debt burden. At the same time, he saw that a pillar of America's international strength lay in the fact that its European Allies owed heavy war debts. European governments pointed out that these debts were beyond their ability to carry without suffering a fall in their exchange rates and thereby destabilizing world trade, as prices would not reflect relative economic efficiency but currency values dominated by capital transfers to pay intergovernmental debts. Members of Roosevelt's Cabinet such as Hull recognized that a precondition for stable trade was currency stability. But as far as domestic price levels were concerned, what Europe wanted was incompatible with U.S. aims at the time. This helps explain why Roosevelt acted the way he did. His primary focus on raising U.S. prices led him to reject the joint international declaration on monetary policy proposed by his own delegation. However, Moley points out: "This policy was reversed in September, 1936, when the Treasury completed a stabilization agreement with France and England, prompted by the wholly orthodox desire to prevent France's forced abandonment of gold from ushering in a wild currency warfare."

Roosevelt's refusal to stabilize the American price level vis-à-vis gold in 1933 was not a hostile act in itself. John Maynard Keynes defended him in a July 4 article for the London *Daily Mail* entitled "President Roosevelt is Magnificently Right." Winston Churchill also supported him and criticized the gold standard countries.

When Moley visited Roosevelt in Washington on July 14 he found the President in a state of "egregious satisfaction and good humor." He felt business was improving and so was his political popularity, for the rejection of Europe always has played well in America. Louis Howe said that "'Franklin hasn't done anything so popular as his rejection of the declaration since the bank crisis.' There were no regrets about the way things had gone in London."[60]

Europe could have joined in the U.S. populist anti-creditor stance, of course, but the French and most British sought to protect small savers. Keynes rightly saw that deflation would be the cause of its downfall, but he was one of the few monetary theorists not to take a pro-creditor side regarding the purchasing power of debt-claims over the economy's property, goods and labor.

To most Europeans – and to American economic historians as well – America had rejected the role of world leadership. It had acted unilaterally in pursuit of an isolationist economic policy based on its domestic needs, leaving the international situation to be settled only later. In practice, its policies made economic depression inevitable for Europe and contributed mightily to World War II. That was not the intent of Roosevelt and his diplomats, but it was the unavoidable result of their going their own way and – as would happen again after 1971 – virtually daring Europe and Asia to create an alternative international system, one that in principle could work only as a bloc thoroughly independent of the United States.

Roosevelt had thrown down the gauntlet. For a generation Europeans would remember the message as the one that fractured European hopes for recovery. Yet to Roosevelt it seemed simply to be an announcement of how America was going about its own economic recovery.

France and all other Allied debtors to the United States, with the sole exception of Finland, failed to pay anything at all as their installments fell due on June 15.

Later on, in July, still hoping against hope that we might induce our debtors to take something out of their armament appropriations to pay part of what they owed us, F.D.R. decided to ask Finland to come in first to discuss the possible adjustment of the debt. He felt that the popularity of Finland with the American people would assure a favorable reception in Congress of a proposal offering Finland a substantial reduction. This might enable us to follow up such a reduction to Finland with considerable debt scalings to other countries. Much to our surprise, Finland notified [William] Philips, who was then Acting Secretary, that she had no desire to carry on negotiations with regard to a readjustment of her debt. She was content to pay in full. This amazing news polished off the scheme. It probably would have got us nowhere anyhow.[61]

All the other Allies suspended their debt payments, and after December 1933 no serious attempt ever again was made to collect these debts. "However," concluded Feis, "remembrance of them later warped American foreign policy. The American government, thinking it had once been singed, refused financial support to our former allies during the nineteen-thirties, when it might have enabled and encouraged them to stand against Hitler and Mussolini. It also nurtured sentiment for neutrality laws which included a ban on loans to belligerents."[62]

European countries found themselves with little choice but to resort to the autarchic practices that became the characteristic of the 1930s. They were forced either to devalue or to raise tariffs to prevent importing American unemployment into their own countries. Having just emerged from racking inflations, most countries chose to raise their tariffs. "The final rejection of exchange stabilization by the United States," concluded Brown, "was immediately followed by the definite joining together of the gold standard countries under the leadership of France in a group known as the gold bloc."[63] This blocism became the principal feature of the remainder of the 1930s. But it did not include defeated Germany, nor did it reach out to Japan. The military implications of the breakdown of the London Conference, Feis concluded, "brought about only greater confusion in international affairs and had marred the friendship between the United States and its former allies. The only beneficiaries were Germany and Japan, who were losing all fear of concerted opposition to their plans for expansion."[64]

Roosevelt had declared in 1932 that the United States would not have to cancel the Inter-Ally debts if America opened its trade doors and let foreigners earn the funds to repay the U.S. Government. But then he devalued, while keeping the nation's trade closed until June 1934, by which time Germany had ceased paying reparations. Arthur M. Schlesinger's *Coming of the New Deal* called Roosevelt's role in the Conference "deplorable," and another historian pointed out that his decision to reject cooperation with Europe "spurred nationalism in Britain, France, and the United States, with each of them searching out new devices for the waging of economic warfare."[65] In his memoirs Hull wrote that the collapse of the London Economic Conference "played into the hands of such dictator nations as Germany, Japan, and Italy. At London the bitterest recrimination occurred among the United States, Britain, and France." Henceforth, wrote William F. Leuchtenburg: "international trade would be directed by national governments as a form of bloodless warfare . . . Roosevelt, declared Hjalmar Schacht, had the same idea as Hitler and Mussolini: 'Take your economic fate in your own hands.'"[66]

As the Great Depression spread, countries supported their currencies by an array of trade controls that included tariffs, import quotas, export embargoes, bilateral clearing systems and barter deals. As Karl Polanyi has remarked of this period: "The frantic efforts to protect the external value of the currency as a medium of foreign trade drove the peoples, against their will, into an autarchized economy. The whole arsenal of restrictive measures, which formed a radical departure from traditional economics, was actually the outcome of conservative free trade purposes,"[67] at least the outcome of a rigid philosophy of currency stability and the sanctity of international debts, come what may.

European countries fought among themselves to export more goods to support foreign rather than domestic living standards and to stabilize their currencies while sacrificing their domestic economies to repay the international debts to which they had committed themselves. How different this was from America's behavior four decades later, when the U.S. Treasury insisted that its own $80–$85 billion in debts owed to foreign central banks be effectively wiped off the books by being "funded" into the world monetary system as "paper gold."

The more Europe armed and resorted to blocked currency practices, tariff wars and the other paraphernalia of nationalism in the 1930s, the more antagonistic became American public opinion and foreign policy, and the more self-righteous its refusal to involve itself with Europe's debt and trade problems. If Europe would not follow the U.S. example, that was its own cross to bear. Having devalued the dollar and thus given U.S. exporters a price advantage in world markets, the Roosevelt Administration enacted the Trade Agreements Act of 1934, designed to modify existing duties and import restrictions "within carefully guarded limits" and "in such a way as will benefit American agriculture and industry." A House rider stipulated that nothing in the measure should "be construed to give any authority to cancel or reduce, in any manner, any of the indebtedness of any foreign country to the United States."[68]

This Act, widely heralded by its supporters as a movement away from the high protectionism of the Hawley–Smoot tariff, underlies all subsequent U.S. tariff legislation. It did not simply reduce U.S. tariff barriers, but provided authority for the President and his representatives to negotiate reciprocal tariff concessions with other countries, in which American exports would be the anticipated net beneficiary. "The Hull policy was not a free trade policy, nor did it seek to eliminate all government control of foreign trade," describes William Diebold, Jr. "This 'adjusted protectionism' differed from past American protectionist policy more in technique than in fundamental concept. However, the primary importance of the Hull policy lay in the fact that in 1934, for the first time since the Underwood Act of 1913, United States tariff rates started moving downward, and the apparently irresistible drive toward increased protection was checked."[69]

The reduction in tariffs from an average 54 per cent in 1933 to 36 per cent in 1940 did increase U.S. imports in specific areas, but it also stemmed protectionist retaliation abroad, so its effect was to provide the United States with a more than proportional trade advantage. U.S. tariff cuts were nullified by the Agricultural Adjustment Act of 1933, which gave absolute protectionism to U.S. farmers by providing for quota restrictions on U.S. farm imports. The U.S. trade surplus, which had been declining since 1929 largely because of foreign emulation of U.S. protectionism, increased from $225 million in 1933 to $1.4 billion in 1940. The strategy of negotiated tariff reductions was by no means one of laying open the U.S. market to foreign exporters, nor did it enable them to earn more dollars to repay their debts to the United States.

It would be false to say that the United States provoked World War II out of malice or out of knowledge of the results of insisting on repayment of its war debts by a world utterly unable to repay them. It is true, however, that no Act contributed more to the genesis of World War II than the intolerable burdens that the United States imposed on its allies of World War I and, through them, on Germany. Every U.S. administration from 1917 through the Roosevelt era employed the strategy of compelling repayment of these war debts, above all by Britain. The effect was to splinter Europe so that the continent was laid open politically as a possible province of the United States.

Private finance capital could not have achieved that end, especially as the United States disarmed after World War I. The division and immiserization of Europe could achieve it, had the world not tumbled into a depression. Not only did the United States not escape the Great Depression, it became the principal sufferer from a collapse of its own creating, as a result of its highly debt-leveraged economy. It came to recognize that it needed export markets to maintain full employment and prosperity, and that bleeding Europe dry by over-indebting it was counter-productive.

The first great foray of U.S. governmental finance capital into world power politics thus ended in ignominious failure, and ultimately in a war of dimensions vaster even than World War I. It was a war that the United States had no desire to bring about, but had no deep feeling that it must prevent. Despite the disaster that followed its first great venture into governmental financial imperialism, America had learned a basic lesson in power politics. Between Treasury and Treasury, and between central bank and central bank, decisions could be reached of far greater and more enduring significance than those reached in the normal course of diplomacy. Money was the lifeblood of nations. A creditor overwhelming on international account could control the pulse of nations. A powerful nation, as usurer, could dominate the actions of equally powerful nations as debtors.

There were many paths the United States might have followed to safeguard the integrity of its financial claims on Europe without rupturing the world economy. It could have pursued policies similar to those which it implemented after World War II. Sentiments to this end existed in some quarters of Congress. On July 24, 1932, Senator Borah asserted:

There can be no reason for urging a reduction or cancellation of these debts other than that it would be in the interest of the people of the United States to do so. Upon that theory, and that alone, it seems to me, is the subject open to discussion. Will reduction or cancellation bring to the people of the United States an equal or a greater benefit than the amount which they may collect from the debts? Will such a course open foreign markets for the products of the farm and the factory, cause the price level to rise, put an end to unemployment, and thaw out the frozen credits of the banks? I entertain the belief that the cancellation of the debts in connection with, and as part of, a program including the settlement of the other war problems, would have the effect above indicated.[70]

Had the United States relinquished its creditor position vis-à-vis foreign governments, less austerity would have been imposed on Europe's home markets in a futile attempt to transfer intergovernmental debt service, and world trade could have developed in more normal circumstances. American capital would have been devoted more to financing industry at home and abroad than to financing the German government's international payments and those of the European Allies to the U.S. Government. This would have helped pave the way for American industrial supremacy to acquire foreign markets in the 1920s and 1930s, while U.S. direct investors might have used their profits on this export trade to buy control of European industry, as occurred in the 1960s. But this policy was beyond the reference points of government officials at the time. There was little enlightened self-interest in U.S. policy during the 1930s, only the crudest of power games.

Even so, the government could have used its Inter-Ally claims as a diplomatic lever, offering to waive them or relend their debt service payments to Europe's governments in exchange for their acquiescence in policies favorable to U.S. interests, including the opening of their markets to U.S. exports. This was essentially Hoover's plan, rejected by Roosevelt. The U.S. Government did not yet want to see its economy linked inextricably with those of foreign nations, and did not yet feel secure or powerful enough to endorse free trade. If it were to take responsibility for stabilizing the world economy, it would not do so in any way that would yield its domestic autonomy as to how it should manage its economic affairs. That was why it had refused to join the League of Nations, after all. America would accept world responsibility only to the extent that it was a paying proposition, financially and commercially.

Ironically, the eventual effect of the financial breakdown of 1933 was to increase the U.S. Government's accumulation of international financial assets, precisely by catalyzing the movement toward war in Europe. Devaluation of the dollar in 1934 raised the price of gold from $20 to $35 an ounce, increasing the stated value of the country's gold stock and attracting further gold inflows. The U.S. gold stock rose to $7.4 billion, about one-third of the world's monetary gold reserves at that time. By the end of 1937, as war loomed in Europe, U.S. gold holdings had increased to $11.3 billion, more than half the world monetary reserves. This gain resulted neither from trade and investment surpluses nor from other normal economic conditions, but from Europeans and Asians responding to the threat of war by transferring their funds into U.S. securities and bank deposits. Their capital flight was accompanied by a corresponding inflow of gold from Europe's central banks, mainly from Britain, France and the Netherlands.

So extraordinary was this receipt of gold that, in December 1937, the U.S. Treasury acted to sterilize it in order to counteract its inflationary potential. Normally the gold inflow would have increased the U.S. monetary supply. The Treasury, however, borrowed enough funds each month to purchase for itself the Federal Reserve System's newly acquired gold, adding it to its own account so that the gold inflow would not swell the banking system's credit base. By segregating the gold inflow from the amount needed by the money and credit system, the normal adjustment process that would have inflated domestic U.S. currency and credit was negated – precisely the policy that the U.S. Government was to denounce when European central banks resorted to it defensively in the 1960s in response to the overwhelming and inflationary series of U.S. payments deficits.

Gold inflows accelerated as Europe once again became dependent on America for its armaments after Hitler's invasion of Czechoslovakia and the *Anschluss* with Austria. The financial effects of World War I between Europe and America thus repeated themselves. After the September 1938 Four Power settlement in Munich, "the movement of refugee funds from European centers to the United States assumed panic proportions as the pressure upon Czechoslovakia to cede territory to Germany brought Europe to the brink of war."[71] Nearly $1 billion flowed into the United States during September and October alone. By the time the United States was forced into the war in 1941, its gold stock had grown to $22.7 billion, three times the 1934 amount.

World War II erupted not because of strains created by private finance capital, but because of a world bankruptcy in which intergovernmental financial claims played the major role. The debt and reparations tangle rendered nationalism the path of least resistance, and made pan-European internationalism impossible. Europe tried to accommodate itself to the shift of world power to the United States without struggle. But America's creditor leverage proved of no avail as long as it refused to take from Britain the role of stabilizing the international financial system, or to take payment in the form of imports. Business simply could not operate "as usual" without the cooperation of the world's major governments, and that of the United States in particular. The presumably automatic adjustment mechanisms regulating private sector international trade and finance could not operate beyond rather narrow limits that were far exceeded by the burden of intergovernmental debts.

Debt is inherently destabilizing, and the mathematics of compound interest, typically unleashed by national war borrowings, lead debts to grow inexorably without regard to the ability to pay. Something must give, and the harshness of debt terms usually ended up forcing at break in the chain of payments. The resulting international rivalry did not take the form of a new scramble for territory or colonies, but increasingly belligerent attempts just to maintain economic self-sufficiency and international payments balance. As Polanyi has observed, whereas World War I was "a simple conflict of powers, released by the lapse of the balance-of-power system," World War II was "part of the world upheaval," whose origins "lay in the utopian endeavor of economic liberalism to set up a self-regulating market system."[72]

By 1933 the world economic environment was dominated by intergovernmental debts requiring currency transfers far beyond the surplus-generating capacities of the private sectors in debtor countries to finance. This rendered laissez-faire principles anachronistic. Governments henceforth would have to accept responsibility for balancing international trade and payments by negotiating overall agreements and systems rather than via "free" markets. World War II's fusion of business and government planning to serve military ends established this perception on a permanent, irreversible basis, for the industrial nations.

Prior to World War II, America spurned internationalism because this connoted a form of world responsibility that did not seem to pay. For starters, it would have entailed writing off U.S. claims to the Inter-Ally war debts. Even in the 1970s the U.S. Government insisted on keeping these debts on its books. In its 1974 annual report, for instance, the National Advisory council on International Monetary and Financial Policies announced that:

As of December 31, 1973, the outstanding World War I debt owed to the United States, including unmatured principal and interest, amounted to $25.2 billion, of which $20.8 billion was delinquent. The largest due and unpaid accounts are with the United Kingdom ($9.1 billion), France ($6.4 billion), Germany ($1.6 billion), and Italy ($1.5 billion).

The countries with large World War I obligations to the U.S. have never denied the juridical validity of these debts. They have, however, linked payment to the U.S. to the condition of simultaneous payment of World War I reparations by Germany to them in amounts which roughly offset their war debts to the United States. Resolution of the problem of governmental claims against Germany arising out of World War I was deferred "until a final general settlement of this matter" by the London Agreement on German external debts, to which the United States is a party, concluded in 1953. This agreement was ratified by the United States Senate and has the status of a treaty.

While the United States Government has never recognized any legal connection between World War I obligations owed U.S. and reparations claims on Germany, there is a linkage in reality, which makes this issue sensitive politically as well as economically. A National Advisory Council Working Group is studying the matter and is expected to make concrete proposals in the near future.[73]

Similar paragraphs have concluded the National Advisory Council's annual reports throughout the 1970s. But no new proposal ever has been made, and the debts remain outstanding.

As America entered World War II the idea of economic gain broadened to become more enlightened and long-term – and for that reason, more powerful. America's overwhelming creditor position enabled it to gain a controlling interest in the International Monetary Fund and World Bank, which it used to transform international finance to serve its interests when it moved into an almost unbroken series of deficits after the Korean War.

By 1971 the United States was virtually daring Europe and Asia to cash in their surplus dollars. Doing so would have forced up the exchange rates for their own currencies against the dollar. Foreign countries were no more able to develop a countervailing strategy than they had been able to do in 1934, even though this time it was they that stood in the creditor position. Neither Europe nor East Asia was prepared to take an integrated region-wide approach to achieve the scale needed to provide an alternative to following the U.S. lead.

In 1933, European countries did not even attempt to develop a strategy to make a virtue of their debtor position. They could not threaten that their default would bring down the U.S. economy, as America would threaten Europe and Asia after 1971. They did not owe money to America's banking and monetary system, but to the U.S. Government, which did not really need the money at the time.

An even deeper problem was Europe's worldview regarding debt, in thrall to a creditor-oriented mentality that led its governments to pay the United States even at the cost of deranging national exchange rates and imposing monetary austerity.

America was different. Roosevelt spoke for the rural areas whose debts threatened to result in widespread mortgage default. His palliative was to revalue gold in the hope that this would reflate farm prices and incomes to their 1926 levels, that is, to where they had stood when many of the mortgages originally were taken out.

The idea of a financial system being debtor-oriented and pro-inflationary was so alien that, except for Keynes, few Europeans were able to understand Roosevelt's scuttling of the London Economic Conference. Europe's policy-makers still failed to grasp the debtor-oriented logic in the 1960s and 1970s, when the United States used its debtor leverage to conclusive advantage. Europeans expected debtors to acquiesce in whatever their creditors demanded. This is why both the Allies and Germany in the 1920s sacrificed their economies trying to pay their war debts. No such logic led the United States to abandon its global, even imperial military spending in the 1960s or subsequently. Rather than sequestering the private investments of American companies, the government encouraged them to go on acquiring European firms, while erecting unilateral trade barriers without regard for international law and its principles of symmetrical economic practice.

The debtor's power lies in the ability to threaten the system, bringing down the creditors by their default. Once this wrecking power is recognized, the debtor is able to lay down the law. America has used this strategy for the past thirty years, but the Third World, the former Soviet Union and other debtor economies still have not grasped it. European nations had not a hint of this potential power in the 1930s. Much like Third World countries in modern times, they subjected themselves to an economic depression from which they were rescued only by war spending. It proved easier to go to war than to join together to create an alternative financial system.

4 Lend-Lease and Fracturing of the British Empire, 1941–45

Along with its immediate purpose, lend-lease had from the beginning an important postwar aspect. . . . Lend-lease was a successful case of postwar planning in wartime.

Council on Foreign Relations,
The United States in World Affairs,
1945–47 (New York: 1947), p. 344

They [the U.S. negotiators] mean us no harm – but their minds are so small, their prospect so restricted, their knowledge so inadequate, their obstinacy so boundless and their legal pedantries so infuriating.

Keynes to his mother, November 21, 1945,
in Robert Skidelsky, *John Maynard Keynes*, Vol. III:
Fighting For Freedom, 1937–46 (New York: 2001), p. 438.

Postwar economic relations were shaped in the conditions of World War II, starting with the negotiations between the United States and Britain prior to U.S. entry into the war. Britain was near the end of its financial tether. Its gold and dollar reserves, which had exceeded $4 billion in 1938, had fallen to just over $1 billion by September 1940, when it nationalized the overseas investments of its large companies and put them for sale abroad. This created a $4.5 billion war chest, out of which Britain would spend some $3.6 billion to buy arms from the United States over the next two years. Yet by December 1940 the British "had little more than enough dollar assets left to pay for the materials they had already ordered here."[1]

Although the United States did not join the war until Pearl Harbor was attacked a year later, in December 1941, it already had associated itself with the Allied Powers. Treasury Secretary Henry Morgenthau Jr and his staff negotiated with Britain the terms on which America would provide support. Their aim was to help Britain against Germany, but not to help it recover its position as world banker, for it was seen not only as a friendly belligerent in need of arms credit but as a potential rival.

The American negotiators proved more single-minded and unyielding. Morgenthau acted as if he worried that the British might get the better of his country. Perhaps his insecurity stemmed from the fact that he owed his position mainly to his father, a neighbor of Roosevelt in rural Dutchess County and party fund-raiser whose ambition had been to see his son become Secretary of Agriculture. Roosevelt made Morgenthau Jr governor of the Farm Credit Administration, from which he was promoted to the Treasury after William Woodin became ill and had to step down. By this time Morgenthau had become thoroughly imbued with the New Deal's political philosophy. One of his biographers describes him as sharing with his aide Harry Dexter White a "reflexive distrust of Great Britain," and of the motives and effects of international finance generally. "His aim was to shift financial power from New York and London to Washington," Skidelsky summarizes. "The dollar would become the instrument of a global 'New Deal,'" permitting more socially enlightened management. This would require "American financial hegemony" not only to provide adequate export credit but also to fund the kinds of social welfare planning toward which private creditors traditionally had been cool.[2]

To U.S. officials, what was being decided were the terms for just how the dollar would end up replacing sterling as the world's leading currency. When Britain's negotiator Frederick Phillips reached Washington in December 1940, he found that Morgenthau "insisted that the British should turn their pockets 'inside out' and give him full details of their assets in the United States and Latin America, and what they were willing to take for them." Morgenthau "started putting pressure on the British to sell off their big American companies – Shell Oil, Lever Brothers and Brown & Williamson Tobacco," and on January 28, 1941, promised the Senate Foreign Relations Committee that "If Lord and Lady Astor own real estate in New York their assets will be on the auction block with the rest." The assets that Roosevelt's officials had been unable to get the British Government to requisition from its citizens and sell off to pay U.S. buyers to settle its World War I debts now would be sold to pay for arming itself and fighting World War II. This was the attitude that drove Keynes "to remark that the Americans believed the British owned their empire 'lock, stock, and barrel.'"[3]

"Asked by Cordell Hull why Britain could not put up collateral as security for orders," the best that Phillips could do was to stall by claiming not to have much data to provide "about the size of Britain's 'war chest'. Did it, for example, include the stocks of refugee gold deposited in London for safekeeping by Britain's defeated allies? The Americans thought it did. The British said it did not. These stocks were debts to foreign governments." In vain, Churchill tried to insert a protective phrase about "pre-existing commitments" in the Anglo-American agreements so as to keep as much as possible from being yielded to the United States. "Then there was South African gold. South Africa was in the British Empire; Washington seemed to believe that Britain could simply seize the production of the South African mines. Even while the Lend-Lease weapon was being forged, Roosevelt 'helpfully' insisted, over Churchill's objection, on sending a cruiser to South Africa to ship to Washington £42m. of gold held there."[4]

Not being at war, the United States could not provide arms *gratis*, but it did not repeat the practice of outright loans. To supply Britain with munitions and related war support the Treasury Department devised the system of Lend-Lease in December 1940. "The Treasury lawyers found that under an old statute of 1892, the Secretary of War, 'when in his discretion it will be for the public good,' could lease Army property 'not required for public use,' for a period of not longer than five years. Under this statute, tractors, lathes, cranes, barges, and other such Army items had been leased from time to time."[5]

An ordinary lease drawn up on commercial terms was deemed clearly unsatisfactory. "When a man rents a house, for instance, he ordinarily fixes a definite price and a length of time for the lease to run. This was plainly impossible when we sent weapons to Britain or to China," explained Edward R. Stettinius, Jr, who became head of the Lend-Lease Administration in June 1941. "The lease would have to be open-ended, with a gentlemen's agreement for a fair and workable settlement in the best interests of all of U.S. after the Axis had been defeated." The U.S. Government would purchase all the munitions being turned out by its factories, and if it thought that these could be best used for the defense of the United States by Britain, France, and the other Allies, including Russia, then it would "either lease or sell the materials, subject to mortgage, to the people on the other side."

The symbolically numbered H.R. 1776 was introduced in January 1941, entitled an "Act to Promote the Defense of the United States." Any country would qualify for Lend-Lease aid "whose defense the President deems vital to the defense of the United States." The benefit received by the United States in return for these Lend-Lease transfers "may be payment or repayment in kind or property, or any other direct or indirect benefit which the President deems satisfactory." According to Stettinius, "This provision was purposely broad."[6]

"From the very beginning," summarizes Richard Gardner in *Sterling–Dollar Diplomacy*, "the price of Congressional co-operation in appropriating Lend-Lease funds was the assurance that the President would require some 'benefit' in return for Lend-Lease beyond the defense of the United States by the military action of other countries. Accordingly, the President and his advisers had to find a 'benefit' which they could hold out as the consideration' for Lend-Lease assistance. What they hit upon was the promise by Britain and other aid recipients to co-operate in the post-war reconstruction of multilateral trade."[7]

This became Article VII of the Lend-Lease agreement with Britain, extending the multilateral provisions already called for in the Atlantic Charter. In this earlier document Churchill had begged that the nondiscrimination clause opening up Europe's colonial raw materials resources and import markets to all comers (naturally led by the United States) be qualified by the phrase "with all due respect to our existing obligations." This phrase would have preserved Imperial Preference as well as Britain's monopoly over the raw-materials resources of its colonies. But no such qualification appeared in the Lend-Lease agreements.

In fact, during the two months that it took for Lend-lease to pass through Congress, U.S. negotiators tightened the screws on Britain. On March 11, the day Lend-Lease became law, Keynes complained to a fellow diplomat that Morgenthau

"has been aiming, partly perhaps . . . to placate opposition in Congress, and partly . . . connected with his future power to impose his will on us, at stripping us of our liquid assets to the greatest extent possible *before* the Lend Lease Bill comes into operation, so as to leave us with the minimum in hand to meet during the rest of the war the numerous obligations which will not be covered by the Lend Lease Bill." He was aiming to reduce Britain's gold reserves to nil, "treat[ing] us worse than we have ever ourselves thought it proper to treat the humblest and least responsible Balkan country." The main British objective must be "the retention by us of enough assets to leave us capable of independent action." While exempting the President from ill-intent, Keynes never forgave the US Treasury – and later the State Department – for taking advantage of Britain's weakness, incurred in a joint cause.[8]

Even after the Lend-Lease Act became law, Congress still had to approve the Appropriation Bill of $7 billion before credit actually could begin to flow. Furthermore, the Americans insisted that none of this money should be used for materials ordered before March 11. Britain naturally asked that Lend-Lease be made retroactive, which would have helped it recoup the heavy expenditures it had made in the United States before the Lend-Lease program had begun, but this request was rejected, leaving substantial sums still owed for the military and economic support Britain had obtained prior to that date.

Britain did its best to try to raise the money rather than deferring payment and arguing about it later. Morgenthau suggested that Britain sequester and sell, or at least pledge as collateral, the U.S. and other overseas direct investments assets of its nationals as the price for aid in exchange for a $900 million loan to Britain. Federal Reserve Chairman Marriner Eccles treated it much as if it were a bankrupt corporation, seeking to place the United States ahead of its Sterling Area members in securing first claim on its assets. Britain began to cave in. "On 15 March, Lord Halifax, the new ambassador, and Sir Edward Peacock of the Bank of England agreed to sell Courtauld's Viscose Corporation to an American banking group for $54 million, about half its real value." The money was duly raised, and became known as the "Jesse Jones Loan," after the Texan businessman who headed Roosevelt's Reconstruction Finance Corporation.[9]

By the time Congress signed the Lend-Lease Act into law, a financially exhausted Britain was left with only $12 million in uncommitted reserves.[10] This set the stage for the British controversy that immediately broke out concerning Article VII of the Lend-Lease Master Agreements, which provided for "(1) the expansion, by appropriate international and domestic measures, of production, employment, and the exchange and consumption of goods, which are the material foundations of the liberty and welfare of all peoples; (2) the elimination of all forms of discriminatory treatment in international commerce; and (3) the reduction of tariff and other trade barriers."[11]

Opening up Britain's Empire to U.S. trade

On July 28, 1941, Keynes was handed a draft of Article VII calling for a strict commitment to nondiscriminatory foreign trade and the end of British Empire Preference, saying "nothing at all about the essential counterparts in American policy – the lowering of tariffs and the avoidance of a serious post-war depression."[12] Keynes called these the "lunatic proposals of Mr. Hull," and hinted that Britain would have to impose even tighter financial and trade controls after the war.

"What particularly concerned the members of the British Cabinet," writes Gardner, "was the commitment to eliminate 'discriminatory treatment'. This, the American negotiators had explained in unmistakable terms, definitely meant the elimination of Imperial Preference." Both the British Cabinet and Churchill "shrank from approving any agreement which seemed to make the dismantling of Commonwealth economic arrangements the 'price' of Lend-Lease aid."[13] An arrangement of this kind, Churchill warned, "would provoke unpleasant debates in Parliament and enable enemy propagandists to say that the United States was capitalizing on British adversity to seize control of the British Empire." Keynes accordingly insisted that Britain could not sign Article VII "without a full-fledged imperial conference, since the dominions were not bound by British decisions."[14] In the end, Britain's acquiescence to this article required President Roosevelt's personal assurances to Churchill that Britain was "no more committed to the abolition of Imperial Preference, than the American Government were committed to the abolition of their high protective tariff."[15]

The Imperial Preference system of relatively low tariffs among British Commonwealth members had been developed in 1932 at the Ottawa Conference in an attempt to maintain some degree of payments stability within the British Empire in the face of the Inter-Ally debt disruptions. This British initiative was now to be broken up at the behest of the State Department's promotion of free trade, although this made it even more difficult for Britain to agree to the Treasury Department's demands that Britain make sterling freely convertible into dollars after the war's end. Final British acquiescence in these two-pronged American terms came only with Britain's loss of Singapore to Japan in February 1942, the low point of its war in the Far East.

Congress had passed the Act as Lend-Lease, the British Parliament had ratified it as a Mutual Aid agreement, and popular usage in both countries followed these two quite different terms. To the U.S. Congress the Act was an investment whose rewards would accrue after the war had ended in both tangible and intangible forms, pending later negotiation. To the British leaders, most of whom seemed to have become smitten with the concept of harmony of the English-speaking peoples, U.S. national interests formed only a part of the broader English-speaking self-interest which transcended national boundaries. In any event, final settlement of the Lend-Lease account was never spelled out, even in the closing days of the war.

In early 1945, as the war was ending, the Council on Foreign Relations published a study, *The United States in a Multi-National Economy*, in which Arthur Gayer, writing the chapter on the economic aspects of Lend-Lease, reminded his readers that "we have yet to learn what terms the President has in mind and whether a settlement on those terms will be acceptable to public opinion and to the Congress."[16] It might prove necessary, he warned,

> because of political pressures in the United States, to ask foreign countries for concessions along political and other lines as compensation for fixed installations which we cannot bring home. A preferable arrangement would link the lend-lease settlement with agreements on the part of the debtors to pursue economic policies beneficial to all nations, along the lines of Article VII of the Master Agreements. There is, however, reason to question whether Article VII provides warrant or power for such bargaining. It is also questionable whether the suggestion could be implemented in practice. Are we prepared to say, for example, that we would cancel lend-lease obligations only if the debtor countries agreed to some international pact? Or reduced their tariffs? Would we be prepared to reduce our own correspondingly, as Article VII seems to require? If we did not, would the debtors feel any moral obligation to make one-way trade concessions? In any event, care should be exercised to avert a situation in which countries we have aided could claim that we had wrung unilateral concessions from them under pressure.[17]

But of course the United States had indeed sought to gain concessions, and would continue to do so after the war had ended. Although Britain's objective clearly was to restore its 1938 position in the world, it was a measure of British desperation that just the reverse occurred.

The 1943 renewal of Lend-Lease arrangements

The first Lend-Lease Act had been passed by Congress for a two-year period, and was set to expire in March 1943. With the United States at war, the option was open for it to make the transition to outright grants to its allies. Secretary of War Henry L. Stimson reminded Congress that Britain had, in its long history, "never rendered financial assistance in the form of loans to her allies, but always in the form of subsidy."[18] But U.S. arms support for its allies was continued under Lend-Lease subject to repayment, not as a pooling of Allied resources.

President Roosevelt, in the *Fifth Report on Lend-Lease Operations* (June 15, 1942), endorsed the principle "that no nation will grow rich from the war effort of its allies. The money costs of the war will fall according to the rule of equality in sacrifice, as in effort."[19] It was apparent, however, that the principle of "equality in sacrifice" was to be, as it had been in World War I, more for the other Allied Powers than for the United States. Roosevelt toyed with the principle, but rejected it.

In his letter transmitting to Congress the *Eleventh Report on Lend-Lease Operations*, filed on August 25, 1943, Roosevelt defined the terms of a liberal settlement: "The Congress in passing and extending the Lend-Lease Act made it plain that the United States wants no new war debts to jeopardize the coming peace. Victory and a secure peace are the only coin in which we can be repaid." On September 7, however, he repudiated these sentiments, asserting that he had never in fact seen the letter, that he had been in Quebec at the time, and that the wrong letter had been filed with the Lend-Lease Report. "There was truth in those words [of the letter], the President said, but it was a condensation of the truth which might lead to misunderstanding. It was only about a quarter of the truth. It said no debt, but what is debt? the President asked. Is it to be paid in goods? As stated in the letter, he added, it did not do the situation justice." It was his thought "and that of most of the other countries that they would repay all that they possibly could."[20]

Under the provisions for Reverse Lend-Lease, in summer 1943 when Britain was still in the process of paying out its dollar reserves for the $3.6 billion of pre-Lend-Lease contracts placed in the United States, it made available to U.S. military authorities the fifty over-aged destroyers it had obtained in 1940 in exchange for its Western Hemisphere naval base rights. It also provided massive raw materials and foodstuffs to the United States from its colonies, including rubber, hemp, chrome, asbestos, tea, coconut oil, cocoa, and many other materials that previously had been bought by U.S. Government agencies. Britain's payment to its colonies for these commodities became part of the sterling balances accumulating in London. In addition, Britain "furnished 31 per cent of all the supplies and equipment currently required by the United States Army in the European theater of operations between June 1, 1942, and June 30, 1944 . . . Almost one-third of Great Britain's total building and construction workers were employed in this program."[21] Clearly, Britain was bearing the brunt of the "equality of sacrifice" principle that nominally underlay Lend-Lease.

U.S. net benefits from its Lend-Lease program were not gleaned exclusively from Britain. "The Chinese turned back to us as a gift all the P-40 pursuits which remained of those they had bought from us," as well as providing gasoline from their scarce reserve stocks to the U.S. 14th Air Force in China.[22]

In July 1943 the Foreign Economic Administration replaced the Office of Lend-Lease Administration, headed by Leo Crowley, "an anti-British American of Irish extraction, close to business interests in Congress. But

Harry White was the real author of the policy of manipulating the Lend-lease Agreement to limit the growth of British reserves. He was the chairman of an interdepartmental committee which recommended in December 1942 that they be kept within the range of $600m. to $1bn, a policy endorsed by Roosevelt on 11 January 1943."[23]

The Treasury wanted to unblock Britain's sterling balances, while the State Department's free traders wanted to open up Britain's system of Imperial Trade Preferences. By December 1943, Morgenthau and White were insisting that Britain's reserves "had grown too high and that Britain would now have to pay in cash for some of the goods being supplied on Lend-Lease account. When British officials pleaded the need to maintain adequate reserves for the post-war period, Morgenthau assured them that Britain's post-war needs would be met by special measures at a later date."[24]

Congressional leaders were equally hard on Britain, if not harder. Senator George, chairman of the Senate Foreign Relations Committee, attempted to amend the Lend-Lease Act to require Britain to provide the United States with a lien on the British Empire's rubber and tin resources. Harry Truman, then head of the Senate's War Investigating Committee, demanded in November 1943 "that lend-lease be 'thrown into reverse' following the war. Asserting that 'lend-lease was never intended as a device to shift Allied war costs to the United States,' the Committee proposed that if the benefitted nations could not repay in dollars they might transfer some of their internationally held assets to this country, such as oil reserves and metal deposits."

> For example, if Britain cannot pay us dollars for petroleum needed by her and cannot, by reason of a shipping shortage or other situation, procure the petroleum she needs from the petroleum resources she controls in Asia, South America, and the Dutch East Indies, consideration should be given as to whether she might not pay for the petroleum obtained from us by transferring to us her ownership of an equivalent value of foreign petroleum reserves or of the English-held securities of the corporations having title to such reserves . . .
>
> Attention should also be given to the possibility of acquiring rights in the deposits of British-owned resources of nickel, copper, tin and iron in countries outside Britain, and the right to receive manganese from Russia after the war in return for lend-lease articles furnished to it now.[25]

Lend-Lease thus was to become a means by which the United States might gain control of the British Empire's most economically productive assets, its raw materials resources.

Recognizing Britain's need to enter the postwar period with some modicum of financial viability, Roosevelt promised Churchill at the Quebec Conference in September 1944 to provide Britain with some $6 billion in special Lend-Lease aid for the first year of what he called Phase II, the period between the defeat of Germany and that of Japan. Roosevelt's agreement, however, coupled with Britain's formal proposals for reconstruction aid presented by Keynes in Washington the following month, "set off a storm of opposition that would force the president to retreat . . . The lend-lease agreement especially outraged Hull. He protested that by promising to help the British without requiring trade concessions in return, Roosevelt had 'given away the bait' and destroyed Hull's life-long hopes of liberalizing trade . . . In the face of this opposition, Roosevelt backed down, and the program finally emerging from the Anglo-American negotiations in late November bore only slight resemblance to the Quebec promises."[26]

The United States demurred from binding itself to any set aid figure during Phase II. And as matters turned out,

> The sudden end of the war against Japan delivered the final blow. The British had counted upon the war lasting at least a year: "The Japanese will not let us down" was a common expression in Whitehall offices during 1945. But the atomic bomb dashed these hopes. With the first signs of Japanese capitulation, the Truman administration began preparations to liquidate lend-lease. On August 13, without waiting for advice from the president, the Army terminated shipments of munitions to the United Kingdom. Four days later . . . without first consulting the British, Truman ordered the termination of all lend-lease on V-J Day, "in order that the best faith may be observed toward Congress" and the administration protect itself against any charge of misuse of Congressional authorization. "After practically no time of transition," British historians have written, "no time to restore neglected plant or build up reserves or expand export production, the United Kingdom was plunged straight into the grim difficulties of Stage III."[27]

The principle of "equality of sacrifice," which nominally underlay U.S. economic and military aid to its Allies after America entered the war, had been left ambiguous, except that it should not "burden commerce." Europe was left with hopes that this meant the United States would lower its tariffs and provide its allies with resources to help them recover and, in the process, help them become prosperous markets for U.S. exports. However, all initiative lay with the United States. It had begun to lend Britain and its other allies funds at a time when their foreign reserves were exhausted, and it interpreted any improvement in their financial position over and above the point of exhaustion as gaining funds from the war at the expense of the American people. "If the philosophy of 'equality of sacrifice' had been literally applied, there should have been no objection to a moderate increase in these reserves," observes Gardner.

> In fact, a grant-in-aid might have been positively required in order to make such "equality" effective. Yet until the very last months of the war the American Government exerted continuous pressure to keep British reserves to a figure not greatly in excess of $1 billion. This principle of "scraping the barrel" as a condition of eligibility for Lend-Lease materials was prompted in part by the same concern with "bargaining power" that we have already noted on the part of some Administration officials. For the lower the level at which British war-time reserves were kept, the greater would be the British dependence on American postwar assistance. And the greater that dependence, it was argued, the greater would be the chances of gaining acceptance for American views on multilateral trade.[28]

The 1945 wind-up of Lend-Lease

America's success in this strategy is reflected in the following exchange that occurred in the 1945 House Hearings on the Trade Agreements Act:

> MR KNUDSON: My attention has been called to a statement made by Mr. Churchill that they would no more change the Imperial Preferences than we would abolish the tariff. How about that?
> MR CLAYTON: Well, wise men often change their minds.[29]

So much for the assurances that President Roosevelt gave Churchill in February 1942. This, however, was only the beginning.

Particularly worrisome to Britain was the fact that the Lend-Lease agreements provided that upon the end of hostilities, cash must be paid by the Allies for all U.S. resources still in the pipeline. Lend-Lease goods used up or destroyed in the war would be written off, but payment for remaining assets and war-surplus materials would be made on the agreed postwar value of civilian goods. Fixed installations, such as airfields and airports, would be kept by the governments in whose territories they were located, but would be paid for according to their value for postwar civilian use. Even so, there were further ties. "Disposal of surplus airfields was geared to the negotiation of bilateral agreements for reciprocal air rights. Service agreements assuring American airlines the nondiscriminatory use of American-installed navigational aids, communications and weather reporting facilities were negotiated as part of surplus property sales."[30]

The $20 billion Lend-Lease account between the United States and Britain was not simply cancelled at the end of the war. The $6 billion in surplus property and Lend-Lease remaining in Britain was transferred for the sum of $532 million, with an additional $118 million levied upon Britain for Lend-Lease still in the pipeline. This raised the residual Lend-Lease for which Britain had to pay to $650 million, a sum that obviously would have to be funded.

"From the point of view of the American Government," Gardner claims, "this was a settlement of unprecedented generosity."[31] It was, however, more than the totality of British foreign currency reserves, and was therefore a burden upon Britain's future at a particularly uncomfortable moment.

> British foreign investments worth $4.5 billion were sold or repatriated from September 1939 to June 1945; meanwhile, foreigners accumulated $14 billion worth of blocked sterling balances in London. Net shipping losses were almost one-third of the prewar British tonnage. Clearly, the British balance of payments would never be the same again. To pay for imports at prewar levels exports would have to rise 50 to 75 per cent, by volume . . . With the end of lend-lease, the British were faced with what Lord Keynes called "the prospect of just that interregnum which we had hoped to avoid." . . . The British opened the negotiations by requesting a gift or grant-in-aid, which was at once rejected. Whatever the American officials may have thought of the idea, they judged that Congress would not accept it.[32]

As Gayer evaluated the program: "Lend-lease under the political circumstances which prevailed in March 1941 was a brilliant expedient for defeating the Axis powers, but it threatens to leave behind it highly complex problems of settlement, which, unless they are satisfactorily solved, may leave the world a more bitter legacy than the Inter-Ally debts of the last war."[33] In fact, Britain's sterling debts owed to its colonies were war debts, which had the same sanctity of commercial obligation that had characterized the Inter-Ally debts after World War I. These debts represented the Sterling Area's receipts from the export to Britain of raw materials and foodstuffs. They also represented Britain's troop support costs of its armies in Egypt and India, as well as the costs of financing the Indian Army in its campaigns on foreign soil. They even represented America's own dollar expenditures in India, Egypt and other British colonies. "Having been debtors of Britain for so long, the Indians were determined to take advantage of the change in their country's external economic fortunes and demand repayment in full from the United Kingdom."[34] Britain once again became a war debtor through victory.

This general European attitude enabled America's new postwar strategy which sought and secured foreign markets for U.S. exports, and new fields for American investment capital in Europe's raw materials-producing colonial areas. Despite Roosevelt's assurances to the contrary, the Lend-Lease agreements and the terms of the first postwar U.S. loan to Britain compelled it to relinquish Empire Preference and open its markets to U.S. competition, at a time when Britain desperately needed these markets as a means by which to fund its sterling debt.

Behind Hull, the State Department sought to promote a free trade agenda, realizing the United States would easily dominate in a free contest. Britain's Treasury "wanted to retain the right to use exchange and import controls to deal with Britain's postwar balance of payments problem; the imperialist wing of the conservative Party wanted to retain imperial preference as a means to Empire unity."[35]

Critical to Britain was the fact that the U.S. Government insisted that wartime Lend-Lease support would stop abruptly with the end of hostilities. In an April 1945 amendment to the Lend-Lease Act, Congress prohibited the President from promising "postwar relief, post-war rehabilitation or postwar reconstruction." Rehabilitation was emphatically not considered part of the cost of World War II. Yet this was necessary if the U.S. Government was to be absolved from liability under the "equality of sacrifice" principle to share with Britain the cost of amortizing the sterling balances built up during the war. What actually occurred was that Britain and other countries became hopelessly indebted to the United States once again. The American principle of "safeguarding U.S. interests" turned out to extend these interests extraordinarily.

How Lend-Lease paved the way for America's postwar trade and payments strategy

What Britain feared more than U.S. financial domination was the prospect of America relapsing into commercial and financial isolation. In the discussions of postwar policy that took place during 1944 and 1945 it was acknowledged that the U.S. Government had bankrupted its allies following World War I by demanding repayment of the Inter-Ally debts and raising its tariff barriers. This, the consensus held, must not be repeated. "We have profited by our past mistakes," announced Roosevelt in a speech delivered on September 3, 1942. "This time we shall know how to make full use of victory." Now the U.S. Government would conquer its allies in a more enlightened manner, by demanding economic concessions of a legal and political nature instead of futilely seeking repayment of its wartime loans.

To start with, Britain was forced to unblock the sterling balances built up by its colonies and other Sterling Area countries during the wartime years. Instead of the Allied Powers as a whole bearing the costs of these wartime credits to the British Empire's war effort, they would be borne by Britain itself. Instead of blocking these balances for use only to buy British or other Sterling Area exports, the savings were to be made available for spending on the exports of any nation. Under postwar conditions this meant that they would be used in large part to purchase U.S. products.

The largest holder of these balances was India as a result of its wartime exports to Britain and from dollar expenditures by the American military forces in India and Burma. Egypt also was a major holder as a result of Allied military spending in the Near East. "Despite much pressure from the British side," observes Skidelsky, the Americans steadfastly resisted the principle of "pooling" the financial resources of both countries. At the time America entered the war it "had agreed to finance most of Britain's purchases of war materials in the United States, but had left Britain to pay for the local expenditure of its armies in the Middle and Far East out of its own resources."[36]

The dollars that the American forces had spent in the Near and Far East had been turned over to the Bank of England's Foreign Exchange Pool, and sterling credits issued to India, Egypt and other recipients of this spending. The British Loan of December 1945 – signed just before the IMF and World Bank articles of agreement came into effect – provided that dollar spending in Sterling Area countries "will no longer be impounded into the London Foreign Exchange Pool," but could be spent freely on American exports. As Chapter 10 will describe in greater detail, the terms on which Britain joined the International Monetary Fund precluded it from devaluing the pound sterling so as to dissipate the foreign exchange value of these balances.

Britain's promise to maintain the value of sterling prevented it from devaluing until 1949, at which time holders of sterling had spent their money at a high exchange rate. It was as if Britain continued to think of herself egoistically as a creditor, not as a debtor.

Britain could have avoided many of sterling's problems through more skilful negotiation. Indeed, notes Skidelsky, "expectation of a British devaluation was one reason Harry White gave to the Senate Banking Committee in the summer of 1945 for denying that Britain would need extensive transitional assistance."[37] But Keynes opposed devaluation on the ground that it would lower the international price of British exports to a greater degree than it would have increased their sales volume, given Britain's productivity and supply constraints. Therefore, he believed, this "elasticities problem" would have meant lower overall foreign revenue.

Britain's liability thus was maximized – and so was America's gain from the pool of liquidity that the sterling balances now represented. "If no international monetary arrangements are set up," warned Alvin H. Hansen, one of the major theoreticians of the postwar intergovernmental banking institutions, "friction growing out of nationalist policies will be intensified . . . A partial international monetary union under British leadership could provide multilateral clearing among its members. But such a British union would necessarily seek to bring its payments into balance vis-à-vis the United States. Multilateral trade between the members of the sterling-area union would grow at the expense of American trade. This, in turn, would provoke the United States to build up its own dollar area, using foreign lending as a potent means to bring this about."[38]

By relinquishing its right to block these balances, Britain gave up its option, while enabling the United States to make full use of its gold stock as the basis for postwar lending to purchased generalized (primarily U.S.) exports. At a stroke, Britain's economic power was broken. What Germany as foe had been unable to accomplish in two wars against Britain, the United States accomplished with ease as its Ally.

When war ended on August 17, 1945, President Truman terminated Lend-Lease immediately, on the advice of Leo Crowley, whom Skidelsky describes as an Irish anglophobe. Vinson "had advised a taper," and Skidelsky notes that "Vinson and Clayton were both furious at being 'double-crossed' by Crowley. The British plight was worsened by the fact that it lacked a 3(c) agreement – the section in the Lend-Lease Act of March 1945 which enabled other Allies – the newly liberated ones – to borrow for

Lend-Lease supplies, by this time mainly civilian, in the pipeline."[39] Only after urgent scrambling was Britain able to keep the flow of deliveries going.

As had occurred after World War I and again in 1933 at the London Economic Conference, U.S. officials expected other nations to negotiate their own self-interest as actively as the Americans themselves did. When British economic diplomats failed to bargain equally hard, the United States got a one-sided deal once again. And the Anglo-American agreement set a precedent that it was hard for the rest of Europe not to follow. In effect, Britain paved the way for a bad European deal all round.

What U.S. diplomats aimed at was always to maximize U.S. freedom of action, without foreign constraint. Evaluating Anglo-American diplomacy during the wartime years in his recent biography of Keynes, Robert Skidelsky believes that the United States did not set out deliberately to ruin Britain, but simply sought to protect its own interests and behaved somewhat recklessly, a bull in the china shop of international finance. The U.S. negotiators reflected the widespread Congressional view of Britain as reflecting financial drives operating autonomously in ways that threatened America's own freedom of action.

Skidelsky blames the British for negotiating poorly, and cites interference from the Bank of England and Labour Party academics whose broad general principles often missed the small print where the most constraining clauses on Britain's freedom of economic action tended to be buried. But most of all, Keynes and his fellow negotiators felt that they had to reach a mutually amicable resolution with the United States. The British team was willing to go to any length to avoid a breakdown of negotiations, almost without regard for the ultimate cost to Britain. "Vinson and Clayton were no match for Keynes in argument," Skidelsky summarizes the state of negotiations in autumn 1945. "But they always held the whip-hand." "It was a case of brains pitted against power."[40]

The alternative would have been simply to walk out, to announce that no resolution of the Lend-Lease debts could be reached and hence to shelve them, treating them in effect in a manner similar to the World War I debts. This would have confronted the United States with being last in line rather than first, as Britain would have turned to its Sterling Area countries to negotiate how to pay off its sterling balances in the form of rising industrial exports. Under such conditions the United States would have been chasing after Britain, not the other way round. Skidelsky cites approvingly Richard Clarke's *Anglo-American Economic Collaboration in War and Peace 1942–49* (1982):

We could easily have said "We are willing to sign the Bretton Woods Agreement and participate in the International Commercial Policy conference; but we are not willing to accept any prior commitments at all until we see how the new world develops: we would be willing to negotiate in 1947." . . . After the abrupt end of the war and the cessation of Lend-Lease, the Americans could not have refused or tried to impose strings. In fact events by 1947 showed that the multilateral theologians' concepts of the course of events had been utterly wrong, and that the doctrines of the 1945 negotiations had fallen into the background of US policy, and that the combination of the Communist threat to Europe together with the world dollar shortage had pursuaded the Americans to grant millions of dollars in pursuit of European discrimination against the USA! So the idea of postponing the "Grand Design" negotiation, and borrowing relatively small amounts, if necessarily expensively, would have been well justified by events.

"This is not just hindsight," affirms Skidelsky. At the British Treasury, Robert Brand (Treasury representative in Washington 1944–46 and a Director of Lazard Bros.) and Wilfred Eady, as well as Ernest Bevin (Foreign Secretary under the incoming Labour Government in 1945) and the Bank of England suggested this course, "though often in passing. Had Keynes advocated it, there wouldn't have been much opposition."[41] But Keynes had wanted to reach an agreement at any cost in order to guarantee acceptance of his own grand design of postwar international financial policy, the plan that would be negotiated at Bretton Woods and Savannah. And of course an immediate cause leading Britain to fear overplaying its hand was the fact that it was truly broke.

The problem was that under the agreements it had signed, Britain continued to be broke. The nineteenth-century's classical free trade theorizing that underlay Hull's State Department position, Keynes argued, "contemplated the impossible and hopeless task of returning to a gold standard where international trade was controlled by mechanical monetary devices. It banned exchange controls, which were the only way to maintain economies in balance." This was what he had meant by "the end of laissez faire." He meant that it should end – yet under American aegis it was to take a new, almost unprecedented form. Britons learned to eat whale as the wartime consumer rationing was about to intensify rather than alleviate upon the return to peace and its New World economy.

What Keynes realized – but which he was unable to do anything about – was the fact that an open international economy along the lines American planned, "sacrificed domestic employment to free trade and the gold standard *and* the nineteenth-century reactions against it in the form of protectionism and imperialism." He wanted to stabilize the international economy with "exchange controls and import licensing," but this ran against American academic economic ideas and, most of all, its immediate economic interests.[42]

5 Bretton Woods: The Triumph of U.S. Government Finance Capital, 1944–45

[Under a properly regulated system of colonial trade, England,] standing like the Sun in the midst of its Plantations would not only refresh them, but also draw Profits from them; and indeed it's a matter of exact Justice that it should be so, for from hence its Fleets of Ships and Regiments of Soldiers are frequently sent for their Defence, at the charge of the Inhabitants of this Kingdom, besides the equal Benefit the Inhabitants there receive with us from the Advantages expected by the Issue of this War, the Security of Religion, Liberty, and Property, towards the Charge whereof they contribute little though a way may and ought to be found out to make them pay more, by such insensible Methods as are both rational and practicable.

John Cary, *An Essay on the State of England*
(Bristol: 1695), pp. 70f

As the arena of conflict shifted from the battlefield to diplomatic meeting rooms, the world's economic evolution after World War II was steered by the Inter-Allied financial negotiations that settled Europe's reconstruction debts to the United States. What had been a contest between the Allied and the Axis Powers gave way to one among the Allies themselves, with the United States emerging victorious.

In the closing days of World War II the Allies' collective self-interest was at first enlightened. With the exception of the Soviet Union, no Ally wished to burden the Axis Powers with reparations debts. The problem facing U.S. diplomats was how to enable their Allies and former enemies to maintain their imports of U.S. goods and services in the absence of German reparations. What was enlightened about U.S. policy was its recognition that this time the Allies could not be left without international institutions capable of organizing and administering the anticipated growth in postwar debt needed to finance these purchases.

It was primarily to solve this problem that the United States took the lead in creating the International Monetary Fund and the World Bank to supplant German reparations as the vehicle through which to provide the Allies with institutionalized means to sustain their demand for U.S. products while maintaining the discipline of gold in international relations. Formal mechanisms were established to organize borrowing from the United States on much sounder bases than had occurred after World War I. The foundation of U.S. lending capacity was its enlarged stock of monetary gold, which had soared during the prewar and wartime years.

The United States had learned the folly of overplaying its position as world creditor. It could not pursue commercial policies that were so aggressively successful that they would bankrupt foreign nations, as this would only force them into retaliatory trade and investment policies that might foreclose long-term U.S. penetration of the world economy. For U.S. firms and exporters to be able to trade and invest in desired product lines, some payments reciprocity had to be guaranteed. Failure to provide this on private sector account by a rising level of foreign investment and/or by rising U.S. imports would require its provision on U.S. Government account, either as foreign aid or as military spending. The latter might be easier from a political point of view in light of Congress's traditionally narrow self-interest in most matters, except those of national security.

The origins and international setting for the great increase in U.S. intergovernmental lending after World War II thus were quite different from those of the previous postwar period. Not only were there no major arms debts or reparations to be paid, but the U.S. Government made substantial outright grants via the United Nations Relief and Rehabilitation Administration (UNRRA) during 1946–48, and through Marshall Plan aid during 1948–51. It took the initiative in forming the United Nations and the Bretton Woods institutions to ward off a renewal of the economic warfare of the interwar period. It pressed for international laissez-faire under controls, and for a return to the gold exchange standard, which it itself had abandoned in 1934.

During the war its diplomats had come to recognize that given America's economic supremacy, a more open international economy would not threaten the U.S. economy but would link the economic activity of other countries into a satellite relationship with the United States. It was unlikely that in the foreseeable future countries dependent on U.S. resources for their reconstruction would seriously interfere with U.S. domestic policies. But the reverse, an extension of U.S. influence over other countries, was visibly possible. Thus, whereas America had boycotted the League of Nations after World War I as a threat to its domestic sovereignty, it no longer feared multilateralism. The more open and interlinked the postwar international economy became, the greater would be the force of U.S. diplomacy throughout the world.

The U.S. Government did not extend unilateral credits to Europe and other nations without forming new institutions to facilitate their repayment, and specifically their repayment in convertible foreign exchange. In 1944 the IMF and World Bank were established at Bretton Woods, New Hampshire, as permanent financial and debt-management consortia. Foreign governments held some shares in these institutions, but not enough to match the dominating veto share held by the U.S. Government. They thus could do little to control the use of the capital of these bodies, save to facilitate the servicing of their own indebtedness. The U.S. economy was enabled to draw the finances of other governments into an international cartel directed by its own policy-makers, dominated by U.S. officials and their appointees.

Assuming that the United States wanted its loans to be repaid this time, this was the proper way to go about things. Europe's postwar borrowing was mainly to finance reconstruction, and hence was self-amortizing to the extent that the projects it financed helped restore the continent's earnings base and gradually permitted an export surplus to be produced over and above rising domestic consumption standards. Because the loans were for productive purposes, and because the organizations designed to insure smooth handling of foreign debt service were multinational, the feasibility of U.S.-centered intergovernmental lending was enormously enhanced, promoting its influence over foreign economic policies and political attitudes.

Instead of giving the United States a continuing diplomatic advantage after World War I, its Inter-Ally claims had placed it in awkward possession of questionable debt instruments which it treated as immutable sums, never open to bilateral negotiation. By contrast, U.S. lending to European governments after World War II was accompanied by what resembled a gigantic multilateral Dawes Plan. The IMF and World Bank were put in a position to recommend specific policies to be followed by their member governments in the interest of world financial stability. This stability was conceived of as an expansion in foreign economic life and its adjustment to the needs and capacities of America. U.S. Government claims thus were formalized into an institutional edifice of world economic domination.

The system seemed to be working as U.S. Government claims on Europe and other foreign regions grew as rapidly after World War II as they had during World War I and its aftermath, without a threat of world financial breakdown. U.S. claims on foreigners during 1914–24 had increased by

$19.1 billion, of which $11.7 billion represented claims by the U.S. Government on other governments as its share of the Inter-Ally debts. During 1945–52, U.S. foreign claims and investments again rose by $19 billion, and once more most of this increase – some $11 billion – represented U.S. Government claims on foreign governments, in the form of bilateral lending plus U.S. capital subscriptions to the International Monetary Fund and the World Bank.[1] This time, however, European repayments were managed in such a way that they did not exhaust international liquidity. Instead of simply being poured into the U.S. economy, thereby reducing capital available to foreign economies, loan repayments to the World Bank and IMF were recycled to replenish these organizations' loanable funds. The new arrangement maintained a pool of intergovernmental capital administered by an international consortium that quickly became a vital institution of world diplomacy, used by the U.S. Government to finance a worldwide Open Door policy and to facilitate the breaking up of the colonial spheres of influence. In this way the IMF, World Bank, GATT and the U.S. foreign aid program became a formal system for the political implementation of American economic strength.

Even before war was declared on the United States in 1941, the nation's economic and political strategy for the postwar period had been debated by spokesmen for its special interest groups. After Pearl Harbor the discussion was elaborated in congressional hearings, policy pamphlets, public conferences, official speeches, and a myriad of periodical articles and books.[2] The result was to create a broad agreement as to the aims and strategy of postwar American policy.

One aim common to all groups in the United States was to avoid a postwar depression caused by a reduction in public spending. The consensus in 1945 was that 60 million jobs were needed for full employment. In the absence of effective demand sufficient to create these jobs, and of finances to underwrite their related corporate investment, a leftward shift might occur in American politics. This explains the national interest in full employment, despite its effects on unit labor costs and competitive pricing of U.S. products in the world economy.

It was agreed that American access to foreign markets was a precondition for full employment in the United States. The most obvious market was devastated Europe in its reconstruction phase. In 1944 the National Planning Association estimated that $10 billion in annual U.S. exports would be necessary to ensure full employment, particularly agricultural and heavy industry products whose output had increased greatly during the war. This round figure was generally accepted by discussants. It represented the market demand which the U.S. private sector, serving only the domestic economy, would fall short of providing, given the existing forms and purposes of U.S. fixed capital investment. There was no serious suggestion that the federal government supply this demand, either by military or civilian spending. The days of WPA were long past, and military spending as a stabilization device still lay some years in the future.

U.S. export production would be constrained if foreign countries insulated their economies. The greatest potential obstacle to American expansionism was the British Empire, whose Tariff Preference system would have to be dismantled. Political pressures also existed in Europe and Japan to establish commercial autonomy. Then there were the less developed countries, which in general had been obliged to industrialize during the wartime disruption of trade and were likely to seek to protect the industries that had come into being during the more than five years of enforced economic isolation. As the Department of Commerce summarized the situation: "During the interwar period, particularly during and after the great depression, foreign countries energetically pursued policies of industrialization and self-sufficiency. This development has been strongly accentuated by the enforced expansion of national productive efforts and capacities during the present war and may lead to the permanent loss of some of this country's export outlets for specific commodities."[3] This must not be permitted to occur if U.S. exports were to be built up.

It seemed probable that agricultural exports would be the first to be cut back if foreign countries' financial resources were exhausted in the postwar world and if new funds were not made available by U.S. imports of raw materials and other commodities or by new U.S. private investment or intergovernmental loans.

A low level of transactions between the United States and other countries would inevitably mean perpetuation of restrictive trade and financial controls abroad and further development of bilateral arrangements among foreign countries to the exclusion of the United States. Foreign demand will not be evenly spread over all our export goods but will be directed first toward types essential for carrying out programs of economic reconstruction and development. In the absence of a relatively plentiful supply of dollars permitting a greater measure of freedom, foreign governments will insist on exercising selective control over the uses to which the available amounts are put.

. . .

Although various branches of industry, such as machinery and machine tools, automotive products, and aircraft, will be dependent on foreign markets to absorb their expanded output, the interests of agriculture are special. It is not as easy to establish for farm products technical superiority, such as that which marks our manufactured goods, and in general farm products are subject to intense competition in foreign markets from other sources of supply . . . American agriculture cannot hope to recover and maintain large foreign outlets, beyond the obvious requirements of postwar relief, except within the framework of a large volume of international transactions.[4]

"There are two principal ways by which this result may be attained," the study added, "and these are not mutually exclusive but rather are naturally complementary. One way is by a renewed outflow of American capital, and the other is by positive measures to permit a larger volume of imports." Direct U.S. investment abroad was recommended as "the most promising outlet for private American capital," particularly as the profit motive underlying the establishment of U.S. enterprises abroad tended "to insure their productivity, whereas loans floated by foreign governments were not subject to this test." Joint ownership of foreign affiliates with foreign nationals also was recommended. "This expedient serves to 'nationalize' enterprises financed by alien capital, to reduce the friction commonly generated by absentee ownership, and, thus, to deter movements toward expropriation and various forms of tax and other discrimination."[5]

Indeed, given the fact of congressional protectionism, especially where special regional interests were concerned, the ideal way to supply dollars to the world seemed to be by direct U.S. investment abroad. As Stacy May of the National Planning Association pointed out to the House of Representatives in 1943: "We will have this big accumulation during the war in funds and War bonds and savings accounts and so forth. I think then there will be tremendous investment funds in the United States."[6]

It was recognized that some U.S. Government funds would be required to satisfy those situations in which private U.S. investment capital had little interest. "Sure, we are going to rehabilitate them," announced President Roosevelt at a press conference in November 1942, speaking of his postwar plans for foreign countries. "Why? . . . Not only from the humanitarian point of view – you needn't stress that unless you want to – there's something in it – but from the point of view of our own pocketbooks, and our safety from future war."[7]

In the sphere of international trade an Open Door policy was required in both Europe and Asia in order that American producers might enjoy freedom to expand abroad. To deter protectionist measures from being implemented, U.S. diplomats would provide foreign assistance to induce other countries to adhere to free trade, stable currency parities, general dependence on American food and industrial exports, and to open their investment markets to private capital. Neither protective tariffs, nor quotas, nor financial barriers such as competitive devaluation, multiple exchange rates, bilateral clearing agreements or blocked currency practices could be permitted beyond a brief transition period. The postwar world would have to move toward rules of fixed parities and open access to national markets in order for American producers to be able to adapt their activities to peacetime production of exports, and foreign countries to adjust themselves to American production and export capacity.

Europe and Asia specifically would have to relinquish their traditional ideas of economic self-sufficiency and foreclose a return to such policies by joining appropriate international organizations. Two sets of institutions were needed to implement these designs: one to ward off possible reversion to Europe's and America's nationalistic trade and financial practices of the 1930s, the other to provide foreign countries with loans and other economic incentives sufficient to make tariff reductions positively attractive to them. American industry and agriculture would provide the physical resources for postwar European reconstruction and growth, the U.S. Government the funding. For "unless dollars are made available with greater regularity than in the past it would be both unjust and unwise to demand the removal of restraints and controls largely designed to protect the internal economies of other countries against external shock and pressure."[8] In return, foreign countries would expose their economies to dependence on U.S. producers, recognizing that autarchy would entail protracted poverty, unemployment and most likely a political move to the left in most countries.

The postwar dynamic of U.S.–European financial relations stood in sharp contrast to the situation that had existed after World War I, when the circular flow had been from the private sector through the governments of Europe back to the U.S. Government. After World War II, Europe's payments to the United States were principally for actual goods and services, not for reparations or Inter-Ally debts. A circular investment and trade relationship once again was established, but this time European governments were lent funds directly by U.S. official agencies and the World Bank rather than by private investors. These funds were used to pay private sector exporters, not the U.S. Treasury. The U.S. Government for its part ultimately obtained its resources from the private sector, via taxation and the sale of government bonds. The net flow of funds through the world economy thus ran from the U.S. Government to U.S. exporters.

The guiding logic was that the full employment that was required to ensure postwar political stability in the United States would need growing foreign markets for American exports. Foreign countries, whose industry and agriculture were less productive than those of the United States, could not be permitted to offset their adverse productivity differentials by tariffs or currency manipulations. To prevent that kind of response the United States took the lead in forming the International Monetary Fund to ensure a postwar system of fixed currency parities, and the World Bank as an economic incentive for countries to join the Fund. Any nation wishing to join the World Bank had to agree to join the IMF and to service all its outstanding and future official government and government-guaranteed debt to foreigners, buttressing the intergovernmental loan system. Having accomplished this end, U.S. diplomats then took the lead in drawing up the charter for an International Trade Organization (ITO), later dropped in favor of the General Agreement on Tariffs and Trade (GATT) to sponsor a reduction in world tariffs and to coordinate commodity agreements.

Europe gladly borrowed funds from the U.S. Government and the new international lending agencies to purchase a rising flow of American exports. The result was an average $3.5 billion annual U.S. trade surplus during 1945–50. By the latter year the United States had achieved its $10 billion gross export target.

Dividing and conquering at Bretton Woods

The IMF and the World Bank were conceived during 1941–45 as the product of joint U.S. and British diplomatic plans for the postwar world. Their articles of agreement were designed to avoid a resumption of the financial problems that had plagued the interwar period, in particular monetary and fiscal protectionism, by meeting Europe's immediate postwar reconstruction needs within the context of American self-interest.

Still, the interests of the two nations were essentially different. Britain had become the world's major debtor on short-term capital account and major deficit nation on current trade account. Its position in fact was analogous to that of Germany after World War I. The parallel to German reparations lay in Britain's chronic deficit on military and trade account, its unmanageably high sterling balances and its impending postwar reconstruction debts.

Britain owed nearly $10 billion in sterling balances at the end of 1944, mainly to India, Egypt and Argentina. These deposits were effectively frozen because Britain could not provide a commercial export surplus out of current production. Nor did it have a current account surplus out of which to amortize its longer-term debts, owed mainly to the United States. The costs associated with its desire to maintain an imperial world status threatened to drain it of whatever net international receipts its private sector might generate. To amortize its foreign debts and sustain the military costs of its empire, some external source of funding had to be found. Otherwise these debts would remain blocked credits restricted to the purchase British exports at the expense of American products.

In the face of this problem Britain's representatives to Bretton Woods sought domestic autonomy to pursue expansionary postwar employment policies despite the constraints imposed by its fragile position. It was even more reluctant to give up its privileged status as international banker than to relinquish its imperial role, for its banking status had made it the repository of a massive inflow of short-term liquid funds. Its private investors traditionally had reinvested these deposits abroad on long term at higher rates of return. Billions of dollars of these investments already had been sold to finance Britain's war effort.

Understandably, Britain did not wish to liquidate its remaining long-term investments to satisfy short-term creditors, although in later years Prime Minister Harold Wilson suggested that he might do this if the run on sterling continued. Nor did Britain wish to impose deflationary income policies on its citizens. Quite simply, it wished to enjoy the benefits without the responsibilities of being a banker – namely, to receive deposits without having to pay them out on demand.

This attitude caused Britain's representatives at Bretton Woods to portray their nation's choice as one of either satisfying its creditors or of imposing domestic austerity, omitting all reference to selling off its still massive remaining foreign investments or cutting back on overseas spending. "We are determined," announced Keynes to the House of Lords on May 23, 1944, "that in the future the external value of sterling shall conform to its internal value as set by our own domestic policies, and not the other way around." The implication was that foreign countries, especially those in the Sterling Area but also the United States itself, would have to adjust their economic policies to those of deficit Britain. "A proper share of responsibility for maintaining equilibrium in the balance of payments," Keynes continued, "is squarely placed on the creditor countries" by the IMF's articles of agreement, specifically the Scarce Currency Clause (Article VII).

In its original formulation this clause called for chronic surplus nations, most obviously the United States, to let their credit balances accumulate indefinitely with the proposed clearing union. These credits might be canceled altogether at the point where they became unmanageably high, or the deficit countries might be freed of their obligations in some other way.

In view of Britain's seemingly permanent payments deficit, its government wished to make large drawings from the planned IMF without incurring indebtedness to specific countries. This would have enabled it to remain free of the political strictures that indebtedness to specific countries would be likely to entail. The United States, however, insisted that because currency drawings would be made at the cost of individual countries – most notably themselves – these credits should be denominated in the actual currencies drawn down, not some nebulous "bancor" credit. This constraint meant that dollar credits should be made available to foreign countries only up to the limit of the U.S. subscription tranche. "It was never reasonable," observed John H. Williams of the New York Federal Reserve Bank, "to suppose that the United States could assent to a scheme under which its liability, in the event of a concentration of world demand upon the dollar, would be limited only by the aggregate size of the clearing union."[9]

U.S. representatives to Bretton Woods therefore insisted on a literal fund of currencies rather than Keynes's "bank" in the form of a blanket overdraft facility. As Professor Williams explained the contrast between the original American (White) and British (Keynes) plans of 1943: "The White plan provides for an international stabilization fund. The member countries would deposit their currencies with the fund, which would then undertake to provide the currencies needed by each country to settle its international account. The Keynes plan provides for an international clearing union in which no funds are deposited. Instead, international payment would be effected by debiting the paying country and crediting the receiving country on the books of the union." The difference, in short, was between the U.S. bank deposit principle and the British overdraft practice. By the latter, "the clearing union would engage in no exchange operations itself, but merely keep books."[10] Ironically, but clearly reflecting the self-interest of payments-deficit countries, once the United States moved into chronic deficit on its own current account in the 1960s, it would set to work transforming the IMF so as to create Special Drawing Rights whose principle harked back to Keynes's proposals.

U.S. representatives at the Bretton Woods meetings were concerned with the problem of how to foster postwar trade while maintaining gold as the basis of the world monetary order, not with lightening the rigors of stabilization that so troubled Britain. They presented the IMF and World Bank to Congress essentially on the ground that it was necessary to provide Europe with resources to purchase the targeted $10 billion of U.S. exports. As Assistant Secretary of State Dean Acheson testified before Congress:

> We have the greatest productive plant in the world. While the rest of the world has been undergoing destruction we have been building up this plant in order to carry the great burden of the war.
>
> One of the problems in the future will be to keep that great plant employed and to keep the people employed who are now working in it or who come back from the armed forces.
>
> Very well. We all profit by enabling these countries which have been destroyed, or which need development, to make purchases from those who can produce the goods they need.[11]

In this respect the Bretton Woods Act was a complement to the Employment Act of 1946. In the words of one expert, "I think what we put into the fund will represent for all practical purposes an export subsidy."[12] Without the financial resources of the Bretton Woods institutions, the United States would find itself obliged to supply these exports to Europe as outright grants. "We want our exports to increase," testified Harry Dexter White, "but we want other countries to be in a position to pay."[13]

They also must not be given the peg of anti-Americanism on which to hang any default. Indeed, a major function of the Bank and IMF would be to channel postwar debt payments to the United States without stirring up anti-American resentment over these payments. This concern had been a major factor leading U.S. officials to propose the Inter-American Development Bank in 1939–40, whose example was used by Alvin Hansen in 1942 when the State Department sent him to London to discuss plans for a more worldwide International Development Corporation to be established upon the return to peace. "Shares in the Inter-American Bank were to be held by governments; each country was to have a member on the board of directors; and voting was to be in proportion to stock holding,"[14] the same principle that would be adopted for the World Bank and IMF. The United States would be the major financier, but funds would be raised from other countries to promote Latin America's demand for imports, primarily from the United States.

Hansen explained that international consultation and cooperation was becoming increasingly necessary in world affairs as a means of dissipating bilateral national antagonisms. "From this standpoint a very good case could be made out to change over the American Export-Import Bank into an Inter-American Bank."[15] This would not change the fact that the U.S. Government would still have to furnish the funds for other countries to borrow. "It would, however, remove any possible argument that the United States was playing Shylock. An Inter-American Bank would promote self-discipline among the members and would relieve the United States from alone carrying the onus of securing enforcement of contract. We know from past experience that countries have not hesitated to default on bonds issued in the American private capital market. To be sure, they are likely to be more reluctant to default on loans made by the American Export-Import Bank. And, indeed, the record of these loans is incontestable. They would be still more reluctant to default on bonds that they and their neighbors help to underwrite."

In addition to providing countries with purchasing power to buy U.S. exports, the Bretton Woods meetings laid the groundwork for freer trade. The IMF's articles of agreement required signatories not to enter into bilateral monetary agreements or other forms of protectionism, save for the Sterling Area, which was to be left intact. This principle established the foundations for what was to become the General Agreement on Tariffs and Trade. In the words of Treasury Secretary Morgenthau, who acted as chairman of the U.S. delegation to Bretton Woods: "Because it offers a method for stabilizing currencies, the monetary fund . . . removes the excuse for the tangle of import quotas, discriminatory tariffs and other disparate measures which added so many difficulties to the friendly economic relations between nations in the thirties."[16]

Supplying Europe with credit to buy American exports would enable it to reconstruct its economies within the context of political stability. "Unless something is done," one banker testified, "it is my belief that you are going to have a continuing chaotic condition in those countries and that they will inevitably go on to some form of totalitarian government, simply because it will be the only way that their people can get food to eat. And I think that if such a thing happened, apart from the destruction of any possibility of increase in foreign trade, it would increase military and naval expenditures on the part of the United States that would cost us far more than any possible risk that is involved in our contribution to the fund . . . chaotic economic conditions in a country produce civil wars and civil wars are apt to produce wars between nations." As Senator

Millikin paraphrased this thought, "as you have an increase in totalitarianism our own military risks increase; therefore, we have to spend more for armament, and so forth." Yes, the banker responded. Without currency stabilization, "you won't have any great volume of foreign trade, and you will have very heavily increased military expenditures."[17] America's IMF subscription thus represented a political subsidy to help dampen the hyperinflation and related dislocations that had disrupted Europe in the 1920s.

A related consideration was that utilization of the IMF's resources would enable Britain to maintain its high level of overseas military spending, including its counterinsurgency warfare in Burma and Malaya for example, without destabilizing its currency and domestic economy.

This assertion of imperial power did not come without a political price. Britain came to depend on America in the vague and unspecified "special relationship with the United States" that its politicians so often have voiced. The foundation of this special relationship lay in America's veto power in the IMF. The understanding was that the veto power would not be exercised against Britain for undertaking acts that adversely affected its balance of payments, but which the United States otherwise might have to take to stamp out threats from what President Kennedy later described as "so-called wars of national liberation," whose suppression was in accord with U.S. military policy.

The outcome for Britain was an increased dependence on the United States, so great as to represent effective surrender of its national economic autonomy. The balance-of-payments costs of its presence east of Suez compelled it to borrow continuously, and to rely on America not to exercise its veto power against its IMF borrowing. U.S. domination thus effectively was extended over Britain.

The financial resources provided by the Bretton Woods institutions also enabled continental Europe to service its growing debts to the United States. In the absence of such resources a moratorium on these debts would have been required at some point, in the same way that the gold exchange standard earlier had led to a suspension of the Inter-Ally debts and widespread default on securities held by private investors. By providing Europe with the means to continue its debt-service payments, the U.S. Government was able to maintain its creditor hold on Britain and the Continent.

Perhaps the most basic advantage of Bretton Woods to America was that providing international resources to supplement Europe's depleted gold reserves enabled gold to be maintained as the basis of international finance instead of a managed paper or commodity standard. In 1945 the United

States held 59 per cent of world gold reserves, and was to increase its share to 72 per cent by 1948. "Unless that gold can be used as the foundation for international trade," observed Senator Downey, "it really has no actual value at all, more than its value for commerce. In putting up a few billions of gold in this great enterprise we are merely attempting to salvage the value of that gold itself . . . that gold just isn't worth anything unless it becomes the foundation of international trade."[18] Many economists had recognized this fact by the late 1920s. "Nobody could know better than [the Federal Reserve]," wrote the Council on Foreign Relations in 1928, "that America's gold derived its value from its universal validity as money, and that, since the gold standard was an international convention, the United States, as the holder of half the world's gold, must assume some role of guardianship of that standard."[19]

U.S. authorities acknowledged that a maldistribution of gold had occurred during the 1930s and wartime years, and that an inordinate amount was concentrated in America. But their first desire was to conserve the economic and diplomatic power embodied in this gold, to retain it as the basis of international finance and to lay the foundation of postwar economic evolution upon it while moving toward freer trade policies that were jeopardized by the maldistribution of international gold holdings and their excessive concentration in one national Treasury. By mitigating the effects of this concentration of gold, IMF and World Bank operations enabled the rigor of the gold exchange standard to be preserved, and with it freedom of trade and investment to expand American hegemony.

Like Britain, the United States understandably desired domestic economic autonomy. Toward this end it organized the IMF and World Bank along the lines of private stock corporations. The U.S. capital subscription of just under $3 billion entitled it to 27 per cent of the voting power in the two institutions. This share would rise to a maximum of 33 per cent as its currency was drawn down by other nations. Because an 80 per cent majority vote was required for most rulings, the United States thus maintained veto power in both organizations. The British Empire as a whole controlled 25 per cent of the voting power, also representing a veto capacity, but one that could not be exercised autonomously in light of Britain's growing dependence on the United States and, indeed, the uncertainty of its ability to unite the separate voting rights of the Dominions in IMF decisions. Practically speaking, therefore, the U.S. veto power was unique.

Being both the world's major creditor and the major surplus power on current account, the United States wished to moderate the Scarce Currency Clause, as its diplomats had come to term Article VII. At U.S. insistence the clause was rewritten so that chronically surplus economies were obligated merely to listen to IMF recommendations, not necessarily to act upon them. Treasury Under-Secretary Harry White's 1945 testimony on the subject is illuminating:

In some of the proposals that were submitted by experts of foreign countries they wanted to impose a penalty on the country whose currency became scarce, having in mind, of course, chiefly the United States . . .

The American technicians took this position: We would not consider any such penalty and we would not accept such a conclusion. The causes for countries buying more than they are selling differ from time to time and from country to country, and the chief fault may not at all be ours. It might be ours in part, but it might also be the fault of the other countries. The mere fact that a particular country wants to sell us fish oil although we don't want to buy it, perhaps we don't like so much fish oil, is no reason why they should force us to buy more fish oil. In other words, countries may be living beyond their means. They may think there is an unlimited amount of foreign goods they can buy from the United States irrespective of what they can sell. What they have to sell may not be sufficiently desirable to other countries.

Countries may get into a position where there is a scarcity of foreign currency not because of the fault of the country from which they are buying but due to their own extravagant policies. We said we could accept no such assumption, either implicit or explicit, that if dollars become scarce in the fund, that the fault is necessarily ours. We finally agreed that if any currency becomes scarce a report will be prepared and a member of the committee which prepares that report shall be a representative of the country whose currency is becoming scarce. We want to make certain any report made is a competent one, and places the responsibility for the scarcity where it belongs and gives proper weight to each of the various causes. We said we would agree to have the fund make a report. More than that if the fund declares a currency scarce we would agree that the fund be required to make public the report. That, we think, is highly desirable, because if there are causes for that scarcity which are in part due to politics pursued by the United States, then we think that Congress ought to know it. The report of the fund would have prestige, if the fund earns prestige. If the fund conducts itself in such a way that it wins the confidence of the various countries, Congress or a committee – your committee would have it – would have before it the report of the fund for you to examine for what it was worth. If the reason stated in the report seemed sound it might influence your policy, you would take that fact into consideration. You are not required to do anything about it. All that you are called upon to do is to give the report of the fund consideration.

. . . The only thing that the fund can do – and we were quite agreeable to include that, and I think it is an excellent thing – is to make a report. . . . If you thought the arguments that were given were sound and that they did indicate and called for some modification of Government policy, I am sure you would be glad to adopt it. If, on the other hand, you felt that they were in error, if you felt they were distorting the facts, I am sure you would likewise give the report the consideration which it deserves. You would in that case throw it in the basket.[20]

These, then, were the U.S. objectives: to increase U.S. exports on commercial terms by extending dollar loans through the IMF and World Bank and by establishing a worldwide trend toward free trade; to curtail potential political and possible military dislocations in Europe; to receive payment on its postwar loans to Europe; to maintain the gold stock as the basis of postwar financial power; and to retain full domestic autonomy to follow whatever policies the United States might desire, while holding veto power over possible actions the other IMF member nations might wish to initiate. These objectives were attained by the United States at the cost of a mere $3 billion capital subscription to the IMF and World Bank.

U.S. self-interest in seeking these ends was enlightened to the extent that Europe was provided with resources that it could not otherwise have obtained. But the limits of U.S. enlightenment were defined by the directions in which it did not push the IMF and Bank. As documents of political-economic intent, the articles of agreement establishing the two organizations must be viewed as alternatives to other possible resolutions of the period's financial strains. America's postwar plans, for instance, did not absolve Europe of its World War II-related debt, an action that would have freed some $300 million annually for Europe to spend on imported goods and services. On the contrary, by providing Europe with the resources to meet its debt service, the Bretton Woods institutions enabled the World War II debts to be retained on the books.

Nor did the agreements help redistribute the world's gold stock. In fact, they served to concentrate more gold in the United States throughout the remainder of the 1940s. America's strategy of postwar economic development called for Europe to add some of the world's newly mined gold to its reserves, and somehow to obtain for itself a substantial portion of the gold balances that had been built up by the South American republics during the war, but not for Europe to draw gold from the United States. In this respect there was a radical departure from the U.S. policies that followed World War I. Then it was Europe toward which the United States had been extortionate. Henceforth it would be the less developed countries that were squeezed for the benefit of Europe and the U.S. gold stock. As Commerce Department economists explained this policy:

> Service charges on loans have to be transferred by the new debtors [*i.e.*, the European countries] primarily through increased exports of manufactured goods or through the rendering of services, such as shipping or tourist services. Exports of these goods and services direct to the creditor countries, particularly the United States, may not be sufficient to meet all the debt obligations in addition to making payments for current transactions. It is necessary that these debtor countries have an export surplus on current account with the countries producing and exporting primary products, and that the United States and all other creditor countries which supply most of their requirements for manufactured products from domestic production have an equivalent import surplus from the countries producing primary materials.[21]

One interested congressional witness asserted that "We can keep triangular trade alive and promote its further growth. This kind of trade is important to us because it lets us sell to Europe hundreds of millions of dollars worth of goods more than we buy from Europe – and most of these sales are normally agricultural products, including wheat, pork, lard, etc., from our Northwest. This is possible because we buy from countries other than Europe hundreds of millions of dollars worth of goods more than we sell to them; we buy goods we need for our economy, particularly tie world's great noncompetitive raw materials. It is through these purchases that our dollars are made available for these other countries to buy from Europe, so providing Europe with the dollars necessary to pay for our agricultural exports."[22]

The Latin American gold reserve was to drift to Europe as the continent increased its exports to Latin America. Europe used this gold to buy U.S. farm surpluses and industrial exports. The resulting triangular trade flow led Latin American's gold reserves to become virtually a U.S. possession, stripping Latin America of its monetary reserves and indeed, increasingly indebting it to the United States.

In this respect the Bretton Woods institutions did not succeed in establishing true multilateralism the arena of international finance. Originally they were held up as an alternative to the key-currency standard advocated by Professor Williams and others, which would have been effectively a dollar standard tying the rest of the world into a Dollar Bloc. As August Maffry, a division chief of the Bureau of Commerce, observed in 1944 while the plans still were being discussed:

> The key-currency approach as set forth by its principal advocates envisages an initial agreement between the United States and the United Kingdom on the sterling-dollar rate. Other currencies would be linked to either the dollar or the pound. There would be consultation and collaboration between the United States and the United Kingdom and other major financial powers and between such powers and their respective satellites. This approach is frequently accompanied by a proposal for a loan or gift of large amount (say $5,000,000,000) by the United States to the United Kingdom and similar aid to other countries requiring it, as a means of assisting them in liquidating debts incurred during the war and in rehabilitating their international positions generally. For strictly stabilization purposes, however, a relatively small revolving fund of perhaps a few hundred millions of dollars would be considered adequate by its proponents.
>
> Now, there are many common elements in this approach to the problem of currency stabilization and the approach embodied in the proposed Monetary Fund. The fixing of the dollar–sterling rate would be a prerequisite under either approach to the establishment of a general system of exchange rates. Both would give chief responsibility and authority to the major powers. Both provide for stabilization credits, and both are conditioned upon a substantial reduction of trade barriers generally and upon sound internal financial and economic policies. Indeed, it is a fair guess that a full development of the key-currency approach would result in a plan not dissimilar to the Monetary Fund proposal.
>
> There are, however, crucial differences between the proposed Monetary Fund and the key-currency scheme in its present stage of development. Smaller nations have an important voice in the fund which would be denied them under arrangements between key currencies only. The multilateral provisions of the fund plan discourage, while the, other approach would seem to encourage, the perpetuation

and formation of economic blocs, with all of the trade preferences and restrictive bilateral deals which go with them.[23]

In the words of one reporter: "The difference between the key-currency approach and that of Bretton Woods might be illustrated by observing the difference, in the political sphere, between an Anglo-American alliance and the wider plan for world security drafted at San Francisco. The key-currency plan is a plan for a currency alliance. It would not be an exclusive one, to be sure, since other nations would be encouraged to tie their currencies to the standard set up by Anglo-American cooperation. But it would mean that other countries, to get into the alliance, would have to meet Anglo-American terms."[24]

This is what indeed materialized after 1952. In a situation where Fund and Bank resources were inadequate to meet the various needs of international finance, the dollar filled the breach. By providing dollars to the world through the mechanism of its balance-of-payments deficits, the United States ended up obtaining foreign resources through the U.S. printing press instead of parting with its own real resources. In this sense any reserve currency enjoys a privileged position. Beneath the rhetorical trappings of multilateralism, the Bretton Woods institutions cloaked the Anglo-American key-currency system.

Why Britain and other countries supported the U.S. plans

The question naturally arises as to why, if these factors were recognized at the time, Europe elected to join the IMF and World Bank. The answer is to be found in the fact that these two organizations provided something in place of nothing. As General Ayres of the American Bankers Association testified, "I fully expected that the people of the other nations would agree with whatever we agreed to, because they knew that this was going to deal with money, and we have the money and they need the money."[25] In the words of Leon Fraser of First National City Bank (and former president of the Bank for International Settlements during 1933–35):

We are told that 44 nations agreed to this. I think a more exact statement would be that 3 or 4 groups of very expert chaps got together and wrote a plan, and then took it up with 44 other technicians, stating that "this is what the United States and Great Britain are willing to stand for with you."

Of course, in the condition of the world as it was at the time of those negotiations, these fellows said, "Sure, why not?" They had nothing whatever to lose. They looked to us for their military salvation and for their economic salvation, and any proposal within human reason put forward by representatives of the United States would in the nature of things be acceptable.[26]

Britain was the first to agree to the U.S. proposals, followed by Continental Europe and finally the less developed countries. By the end of 1946, U.S. governmental finance capital had achieved a secure linkage between all foreign non-socialist economies and its own. The financial and aid-lending institutions created by the United States funded what then seemed to be a permanent postwar U.S. balance-of-payments surplus by means of increased indebtedness of foreign governments to that of the United States.

This policy pleased most free trade ideologists by its apparently liberal ideals and methods. Many had viewed the war as being fought primarily over whether the postwar world would be run by state-controlled and nationalist societies or by approximately free enterprise systems. The laissez-faire relations assured by the postwar economic institutions were financed by a large flow of U.S. loans, investments and resources. Foreign countries tended to become economic satellites of the United States, but liberal theoreticians did not anticipate that this dictatorship of the marketplace might prove to be nonbenevolent. Its purpose appeared simply to be the assurance of more peaceful international relations, as no capitalist country would find its economic or political, much less its military interest to lie in withdrawing from the Free World community.

With the exception of cases where urgent military and political considerations overwhelmed the required adherence to the U.S. concept of modified free trade, withdrawal from any one of the three crucial international economic organizations would, *de facto*, involve withdrawal from the others as well. Failure to join any one of the three (the IMF, World Bank and GATT), or membership in the IMF and the World Bank without adherence to the principles of GATT, were plainly incompatible, except in very special cases. Yugoslavia was among these special exceptions. As a Communist, state-directed economy it could not subscribe to GATT's free trade principles, as these were in violation of its concepts as to national economic planning, even though it encouraged a certain degree of competition between its socialized industrial enterprises. On politico-strategic grounds Yugoslavia was admitted to the IMF and the World Bank without membership in GATT.

However, withdrawal from the World Bank would involve withdrawal from the IMF, and vice versa. With the exceptions noted, the same was true of GATT. *De jure*, the non-exception member nations of the IMF and World Bank might not be required to join GATT, but *de facto*, U.S. veto power in the IMF could cut off any nation that repudiated GATT principles from recourse to the IMF and the World Bank, blocking their access to Western markets and investment resources. The price for any country seeking full economic autonomy thus was exile. Faced with this choice, it is not surprising that most non-Communist countries chose to adhere to the U.S. plan.

The assumed virtues of this seeming harmony of interests rested on the concept that the commercial norms of dollar diplomacy worked to maximize international welfare. Free trade and international investment were not viewed as being at odds with the freedom of foreign countries to shape their destinies. Attempts in fact were made to reconcile the aims of foreign governments with those of the United States. America's postwar strategy thus appeared to its liberal formulators as a dynamic plan to satisfy the collective and separate economic and political interests not only of the United States and its allies – including originally the Soviet Union – but even of the defeated fascist powers. It aimed at securing a politically and economically stable, full employment and therefore peaceful postwar world.

The resulting economic system was held to be expansive, not static. U.S. investors and exporters would share in the growing wealth of foreign countries. This growth in wealth would foster these countries' political evolution toward more equitable forms of society. In a phrase reminiscent of eighteenth-century British empire-builders, Cordell Hull baptized this system the Interdependence of Mutual Parts. As long as these parts remained elements of a system involved with and revolving about the U.S. economy, no conflicts of interest were foreseen, nor any economic and political rigidification of the world economy, much less the abject dependency so widespread today.

The model worked well enough for Point Four and World Bank lending extended to Europe to aid in its postwar reconstruction. U.S. assistance helped quieten discontent and forestalled concerted political attempts to reconstruct the Continent along socialist, regionalist or nationalistic lines which would have limited the expansion of U.S. trade and investment. As Europe began to recover, it was able to finance an increasing share of the NATO policing efforts believed necessary to thwart a potential military threat from the Soviet Bloc. Political and military ends thus were achieved through economic means.

From the U.S. point of view, growth in Europe's military power helped safeguard America's foreign markets from Soviet penetration and from internal upheavals. To its liberal progenitors this arrangement promised to usher in an era of enlightened dollar diplomacy, enlightened in recognizing America's stake in international economic expansion and the amelioration of world poverty. But it remained dollar diplomacy in seeking to maximize America's commercial and strategic gains from the thriving new international economy.

How the U.S. balance of payments became the pivot of the Bretton Woods system

The problem as seen in its early years was that gains in net U.S. exports seemed to be too large for the new international system to support. Foreign gold continued to flow into the U.S. Treasury. America's gold stock stabilized after it granted Lend-Lease credits to its allies for the duration of World War II, and actually fell slightly as a result of payments to Latin American countries for their raw materials. When the war ended in 1945, U.S. gold holdings stood at about $20 billion. During the next three years, however, U.S. gold holdings increased by $4.3 billion. Neither the World Bank's reconstruction loans nor the IMF's balance-of-payments stabilization loans proved adequate to meet the financial needs of European recovery, as evidenced by the continued flow of gold to the United States. During 1946–47, France lost 60 per cent of its gold and foreign exchange reserves, while Sweden's reserves fell by 75 per cent. Meanwhile, the United States continued to accumulate gold. In 1949 its gold stock reached an all-time high of $24.8 billion, reflecting an inflow of nearly $5 billion since the end of the war.

This was too much. Far from constituting an advantage to the United States, this maldistribution of gold became a matter of serious concern to U.S. strategists. Not only did it threaten to reduce Europe's vitality as a market for U.S. exports, it threatened to aggravate inflation at home. U.S. diplomats therefore redesigned the nation's foreign aid and investment programs in such a way as to repatriate gold to Europe. What greatly assisted in this endeavor were the Korean War's inflationary consequences for the U.S. economy in 1950–51.

Nonetheless, following a modest decline to $22 billion in 1953, the U.S. gold stock remained fairly stable until 1958, despite the nation's payments deficits during these years. This was because Europe's central banks chose to build up their depleted dollar reserves instead of cashing in dollars for gold. The dollar, after all, was freely convertible into gold by foreign official holders, and in some countries by private citizens. Moreover, holding gold involved losing the interest yield on dollar deposits, in addition to the positive costs of storage and insurance. Why hold gold under these conditions, even in the form of earmarked deposits in the United States?

The willingness of foreigners to hold dollars helps explain why, beginning in 1950, the United States was able to sustain a nearly unbroken twenty-two-year series of payments deficits until the late 1960s without the nation or the rest of the world growing alarmed. During the 1950s these payments deficits were welcomed abroad, as they helped alleviate Europe's liquidity pressures. European economic activity thrived, spurring the Continent's demand for U.S. exports and allaying still further whatever postwar fears remained of economic depression and left-wing political ascendancy in Europe.

The various elements of postwar U.S. foreign policy, despite the emergence of U.S. balance-of-payments deficits in 1950, were based on the premise that the United States was in a unique and permanent position of payments strength. Its first decade of deficits supplied other countries with monetary reserves without impairing the functioning of the Bretton Woods and GATT systems, and without inspiring fear that the United States would be driven off gold. U.S. foreign policy thus was carried out without initial concern for its costs to U.S. monetary reserves. So great was the nation's domestic productive power as compared to that of Europe and the less developed countries, and so large was its gold stock even though declining, that U.S. strategists did not anticipate that the balance of payments eventually might move into a chronic and incurable deficit that would threaten to reverse the flow of world financial, military and diplomatic power.

It had seemed logical after the war to assume that economic growth and stability in the United States would result in a comfortable balance-of-payments position, and consequently would support continued growth of U.S. intergovernmental capital claims. The policy implication was that if any country contemplated insulating its economy from the United States by withdrawing from the dollar area, it might be bought off with U.S. aid loans recycled out of America's chronic payments surplus. In any case the United States somehow would have to recycle its international receipts, and how better to do this than by loans to induce foreign governments to remain politically and economically friendly?

In this manner the economic polarization implicit in the postwar system that the United States imposed upon the world could be offset by rising U.S. investment and productivity, while U.S. gold, debt service and other income from foreign investments would finance U.S. military spending abroad to any desired level. Its increase to a level beyond the ability of the U.S. public and private sectors to sustain was not anticipated.

What Britain gave up

Despite the fact that America's post-World War II lending was more enlightened than that of the 1920s, this does not mean that acceptance of these loans was the only option open to Europe. U.S. reconstruction lending to Europe after 1945 was channeled through the World Bank and IMF, stretching out the debt-service burden so that the U.S. Government would not have to make Europe an outright gift. There can be little doubt that if Britain had taken the lead in refusing to commit itself to direct financial borrowing from the U.S. Government, it and the rest of Europe would have been offered outright grants-in-aid. European economic and political stability was the prime aim of U.S. foreign policy, taking precedence even over the question of whether the United States would be repaid. Britain's Labour Government capitulated, however, and was quite willing to pay for what the U.S. Government ultimately would have donated had the need arisen.

U.S. diplomats simply took the best repayment terms they could negotiate. If they could in fact secure repayment for their costs of maintaining a viable non-Communist Free World, so much the better. The institutionalization of U.S. governmental finance capital was thus established with Britain as midwife at its birth.

The political effect was to concentrate in U.S. Government hands most of the major decisions as to how much, to which countries and on what conditions international loans would be extended. Much of the World Bank's lending was financed by bonds sold in the U.S. capital market, but all specific loan decisions rested with the Bank, which was dominated by U.S. officials. In this respect the U.S. Government obtained far greater power over the restructuring of Europe's political and economic systems than it had enjoyed after World War I.

This was apparent in the negotiations that established the IMF, the World Bank, and GATT. U.S. diplomats used bilateral aid, along with the promise of multilateral lending via the World Bank, as economic pressure to secure the adherence of foreign governments to laissez-faire. As a prelude to the $3.75 billion British Loan of 1946, for example, the U.S. Government terminated Lend-Lease to Britain, posing the threat of insolvency. Britain was granted the loan explicitly in return for its agreement to join the United States in a united front to negotiate vis-à-vis Continental Europe regarding the operational philosophy of the Bretton Woods institutions and the International Trade Organization. Having obtained British support, the State Department elicited Continental Europe's adherence in the same manner, its power position being that Europe was losing gold rapidly to the U.S. Treasury. The developed nations as a group, having thus reached agreement among themselves, confronted the less developed countries with a *fait accompli*, establishing the postwar order for most of the world on laissez-faire principles under U.S. leadership and domination.

6   Isolating the Communist Bloc, 1945–46

Externally, by being severed from the *British* Empire, you will be excluded from cutting Logwood in the Bays *Campeache* and *Honduras*, from fishing on the Banks of Newfoundland, on the Coast of *Labrador*, or in the Bay of *St. Lawrence*, from trading (except by Stealth) with the Sugar Islands, or with the *British* Colonies in any Part of the Globe. You will also lose all the Bounties upon the Importation of your Goods into *Great Britain*: You will not dare to seduce a single Manufacturer or Mechanic from us under Pain of Death; because you will then be considered in the Eye of the Law as mere Foreigners, against whom these Laws were made.

> Rev. Josiah Tucker, "A Letter from a Merchant
> in London to his Nephew in America" (1766),
> in *Four Tracts on Political and Commercial Subjects*
> (Gloucester: 1776), p. 145

America's Cold War policy is to be explained largely by its attitude toward Russian participation in the postwar world economy. What is ironic is that the Cold War was designed specifically by liberals to defend their concepts of commercial and political freedom. Unhappily for its formulators, the method by which the United States pursued its goal of an open world economy served instead to close it.

How did it come about that America's ideal of implementing laissez-faire economic institutions, political democracy and a dismantling of formal empires and colonial systems ended up with Cold War spending, above all overseas military spending, subverting free trade and payments among the Western nations, splitting the Dollar Area from the Common Market, supporting paramilitary oligarchies in the less developed countries, and orienting the Western economies toward preparation for possible armed conflict with the Communist Bloc countries?

At the beginning, the intention had been to include Soviet Russia in the Bretton Woods system. In June 1943 the U.S. Treasury tentatively ascribed to the USSR an IMF quota of $763 million, which was increased some months later to give Russia 10 per cent of the quota and voting rights in the new organization. The Russian quota subsequently negotiated at Bretton Woods amounted to $1.2 billion.[1]

Substantial bilateral loans also were discussed, on even more favorable terms than the British Loan. On New Year's Day, 1945, Morgenthau wrote to Roosevelt that during the past year "I have discussed several times with [U.S. Ambassador to Moscow] Harriman a plan which we in the Treasury have been formulating for comprehensive aid to Russia during her reconstruction period . . . that will have definite and long range benefits for the United States and for Russia."[2] Two days later, "a Soviet Foreign Minister Molotov asked Harriman for $6bn repayable over thirty years at 2.5 per cent." The following week two of the Treasury's most pro-Soviet officials, Harry Dexter White assisted by Harold Glasser (whom Robert Skidelsky reports as being a Soviet agent), wrote a memorandum sent by Morgenthau to Roosevelt suggesting a $10 billion 35-year loan at 2 per cent interest to buy U.S. construction goods.[3]

White had a staff member produce a formula based on estimated national income that "should yield a quota of $2.5 billion for the USA, about half that for Britain and its colonies, with the Soviet Union and China assured third and fourth places." These were the quotas announced at Bretton Woods. "Russia, which wanted quotas to reflect military as well as economic prowess, said it would not accept a quota smaller than Britain's," and most other countries also viewed their quota sizes as matters of national pride, and also of course as potential lines of credit in the postwar years.[4] (It was a reflection of these negotiations, Skidelsky observes, that "the largest quota holders, the USA, Britain, the USSR, China and France, became permanent members of the Security Council of the United Nations a year later, affirming the world's political as well as financial pecking order.")

"From the purely economic view," summarizes John Gaddis in reviewing this period, prospects for postwar Soviet–American cooperation seemed encouraging. During World War II the United States had built up a massive industrial plant to produce war materials not only for itself, but also for its allies.

Reconversion to the production of consumer goods would be at best a painful process, and could be disastrous, for no one knew whether the American economy could maintain full employment in peacetime. The Soviet Union needed heavy industrial equipment, partly to rebuild its war-devastated economy and partly to satisfy its people's long-denied desire for more consumer goods. Moscow could solve its reconstruction problems, it appeared, by placing massive orders for industrial equipment with American firms. Filling these orders would help the United States deal with its own postwar reconversion problems and, in the process, would begin to integrate the Soviet Union into the multi-lateral system of world trade to which Washington attached such great importance. Both countries, it seemed, had a strong interest in promoting this most promising of economic partnerships.[5]

For, unlike the case with Britain and the nations tied into its Sterling Area through the Imperial Preference trading system, Russia was not viewed as an industrial or agricultural rival to the United States, much less a rival as foreign investor. Like China, it appeared as a market, not as a competitor.

Russia's attitude toward the IMF and the World Bank was enunciated by Professor Z. Y. Atlas in the August 1944 issue of *Bolshevik*:

The USSR is interested in such postwar cooperation because this cooperation will enable us to expedite and facilitate the process of restoring our national economy and to proceed quickly along the road to further social-economic progress. At the same time our allies and neutral countries are in no lesser degree interested in the development of their trade turnover with our country, because the USSR can buy and consume large quantities of surplus manufactures from these countries. It is well known that the USSR has always strictly observed its obligations. It will be the same in the near future.[6]

Also representative is Josef A. Trakhtenberg's statement in a 1944 issue of *Planned Economy*:

Our country is importing merchandise from abroad and exporting articles of our production. After the war, our trade with foreign countries will greatly increase. Therefore the USSR is interested in the stability of the capitalistic currency and in the restoration of the economic life of foreign countries.

. . .

Short-term credit by the Monetary Fund and the stimulation of long-term credit by the Bank for Reconstruction will contribute to the development of trade relations between the USSR and other countries. The USSR is interested in this as much as foreign countries.[7]

Although the postwar system was designed by the United States mainly to implement laissez-faire (at least abroad), and by means of this policy to effect a concentric world economy revolving around the United States, there appeared to be no major obstacles to Soviet membership in the IMF and the World Bank. Most of the problems concerning economic relations between the state-controlled Soviet economy and the Western nations seemed to be secondary and technical in character. One frequently cited problem, for instance, was the fact that Article V of the IMF Charter required nations to report their gold holdings, and Russia had not published statistics on its gold production since 1936. Russia, however, did not raise this point as constituting an obstacle.[8]

Given Russia's reconstruction needs, it was apparent that its proposed $1.2 billion quota in the Fund would serve as the basis for a long-term revolving credit, and therefore would reduce "the potential dollar supply to England, Australia, or any other country, and does to some extent permanently impair the ability of the fund to fulfill its functions. It is not desirable to freeze up the fund like that."[9] Edward E. Brown, chairman of the board of the First National City Bank of Chicago, anticipated that the USSR would "probably use up her quota in the first few years of the fund's existence to pay for imported capital goods necessary for her economic construction."[10] So too, however, would most of the war-torn European nations, which were expected to be chronic borrowers in the early postwar years. This certainly was no blanket objection to Russian membership.

The USSR, one may conjecture, desired long-term credits from the World Bank and bilateral credits from the United States in the form of Lend-Lease. It was Lend-Lease, in fact, in which Russia was mainly interested; in long- and short-term credit, on favorable terms, by which to accelerate its own postwar reconstruction and expansion. "Soviet Russia's interest in the fund," concluded Charles Prince in the *Harvard Business Review*, "is likely to be in some measure a reflection of Lend-Lease arrangements effected subsequently to the United Nations Conference at San Francisco and the Conference of the Council of Foreign Ministers in London, Paris, and Moscow and of the extent, scope, and nature of long-term credits that the Soviet Government may receive in the United States. In the last analysis, securing this credit might be *the* determining factor apropos of Soviet Russia's ultimate participation in the Bank and Fund."[11]

Inasmuch as European countries also viewed the World Bank with its long-term credits as being the main inducement for joining the Fund, Russia's position in this respect was not exceptional. Roosevelt's Cabinet for its part generally supported credits to the Soviets, and in summer 1944 there was much talk of a $3.5 billion loan to Russia.[12] The following year Treasury Secretary Morgenthau advocated a $6 billion credit, equal to that offered to Britain. Before the end of the war it was understood that Russia would be offered substantial reconstruction credits.

Another technicality was that "Russia doesn't have fluctuations in its balance of payments for the same reasons that we do. Russia doesn't have free exchange, doesn't have a free economy, and any condition that obtains in her balance of payments is presumably deliberate."[13] For this very reason, however, Western commercial relations with the Soviets promised to have a number of positive technical advantages. Because government credit was intrinsically superior to private credit, Russia's trading institutions assured Western exporters of relatively risk-free transactions. Furthermore, because Russia's state monopoly of foreign trade enabled it freely to administer its export prices, and because it had no foreign investments, "the projected mechanism affecting exchange rates is not of urgent interest to them . . ."[14] Russia therefore was prepared to concur in whatever proposal the Anglo-American Bloc supported for exchange rate adjustment, as this would have no direct bearing on its own internal monetary policies.

U.S. strategists originally believed that Soviet membership in the Bretton Woods institutions necessary to guarantee postwar political and economic stability. "It is difficult to see how any scheme for international stabilization of currencies could work with Russia not cooperating," testified the banker Brown. "Her exports and imports in a few years will be very large. Russia borders, in eastern Europe, in the Near East, and in Asia, the very countries whose currency-stabilization problems will be the most difficult. To give her a credit of $1,200,000,000 with the realization that it will be used to buy foreign capital goods and not for strictly stabilization purposes is not too high a price to pay for her cooperation, even, if we forget, which the representatives of the United Nations at Bretton Woods did not, her tremendous losses in human lives and in property destroyed and the great part she has played and is playing in the war."[15] He elaborated that

> the countries which are going to have, perhaps, the most difficult currency problems in stabilizing their currencies when peace comes are going to be the countries of eastern Europe, the countries of the Middle East, and probably China.
>
> All of those countries are contiguous to Russia. If Russia did not want to cooperate, if it thought it would be to Russia's political advantage to produce political chaos in those countries in the hope that they might

go communistic – I do not say that Russia would have such purposes now – but the easiest way it could do it would be by upsetting the currencies of those countries and the agreement of Russia to refrain from doing that, and from my contact with the Russians, both at Atlantic City and at Bretton Woods, I am firmly convinced that they do want to cooperate because they believe that a peaceful world offers the greatest chance for the future development of Russia, and I think the greatest achievement on the part of our Government and our experts – Treasury, State, and so forth – was to get Russia to adhere to the statement of principles and to get them to agree to this, because if Russia was morally free to go out and undermine the currency systems of neighboring states it could do so with great ease, and I mean by entering into this agreement it agrees not to do that.[16]

Morgenthau viewed long-term credits as guaranteeing U.S. access to Russia's rich raw materials resources as well as developing a market for U.S. consumer goods. Harry Dexter White placed great emphasis on the United States' need for raw materials. As its stocks had seriously diminished during the war,

the United States was now dependent upon foreign supplies. The nation's dire need for manganese, tungsten, graphite, zinc, lead, chrome, mercury, petroleum, platinum, vanadium, and mica could be met in substantial part by Russian production of these materials. [White] stated bluntly that "the necessity of growing U.S. dependence on foreign sources of supply in order to satisfy anticipated post-war industrial requirements and to maintain security reserves, is inescapable." Russia could export these items to America only if it were provided with developmental funds. Therefore, White proposed a loan of five billion dollars to be repaid in full over a thirty-year period in the form of raw materials. He brushed aside the notion that postwar trade with Russia would return to the low prewar levels and argued that both economies "have been fundamentally restructured by the war," which indicated to him "the new and larger dimensions which foreign trade can assume, in both economies in the postwar period."[17]

During the war Russia had taken some 20 per cent of U.S. exports, and as late as 1947 the United States was acquiring one-third of its manganese ore, half its chrome ore and more than half its platinum from the Soviet Union.[18]

Secretary of Commerce Henry Wallace wanted to initiate air travel to and via Russia, and thereby open Asian commerce on a permanent basis.[19]

There were several ways in which Soviet and U.S. policies were similar. Each nation wished to maximize its voice in the Fund's management, as well as in the Bank; a tripartite Anglo-American-Soviet alliance was mooted. "Neither the Soviet Government nor the American financiers want to be beholden to any of the small nations in Europe and the Far East, since both forces operate on a global-wide basis. Moreover, both are reluctant to underwrite the credit risks and to stabilize the currency of the small nations affected."[20] On these grounds, "the underlying philosophy and methodology expressed in the statement published by the American Bankers Association in February, 1945, are parallel to those outlined by Soviet monetary experts."[21] The similarity in views was explained by the fact that "the views expressed by American financiers stem from the 'key-countries approach,' whereas the Soviets' views emanate from the 'major powers' thesis which they have been advocating consistently during the past decade."[22]

Alvin Hansen envisioned a joint Soviet–American domination of Europe which anticipated Henry Kissinger's subsequent "Partnership of Strength." Hansen observed in 1945, at the outset of his study of *America's Role in the World Economy*, that the great new postwar fact would be "the rise of Russia on the one side of the globe and the economic and military power of the United States on the other. A happy geographical accident – two great powers occupying vast continents and controlling vast resources in areas that are noncompetitive – this fact must be set down as a dominating and directing force in the future course of history. We are confronted here with a completely new constellation of forces. Within this framework the role of France, Germany and England of necessity must be something very different from that set by the European patterns of past generations . . . Confronted with this giant [Russia] in terms of both population and of industrial development Germany cannot again challenge the peace of the world."[23]

The United States and USSR each could transact business through their mutual global monopolies and cartels. Each preferred multilateral to bilateral trade agreements, and "both the Soviet Government and American financiers have an abiding interest in maintaining a managed gold standard . . . This is the more so because the United States and the Soviet Union allegedly have the largest gold reserves and are potentially the largest gold producers." Finally, although Russia was a state-controlled economy, it was not an expansionist one and in no way threatened U.S.

export and international investment plans to the extent that Britain did. Its massive internal needs would keep its resources employed mainly to satisfy home demand, not economic penetration of other countries.

Russia itself, however, had some major fears with regard to U.S. plans for the postwar world order. Its primary concern was that laissez-faire domination over the marketplace – which in practice meant dictatorship of world commerce by the U.S. economy – might threaten Russian security itself. "In the preliminary discussions bearing on the Bretton Woods Agreements, the Soviets expressed apprehension about the White Plan, which allegedly proposed in the near future to abolish all restrictions on trade, currency, and the like. It seemed quite clear to them that under conditions of contemporary capitalism, especially after the war, such a course would be impossible for many countries since their economic independence would be seriously threatened by refraining from state regulatory measures."[24] Soviet spokesmen made it clear that "they did not fight the deadliest war in history in order to make the world safe for British merchants and American exporters. This is perhaps one of the basic reasons why they refused the American invitation to participate in the projected International Conference on Trade and Employment."[25] As Professor A. F. Voskresenski, writing in the February 1944 issue of *War and the Working Class*, observed:

> Authors do not conceal the fact that this version of "free trade" would force European agriculture to switch from grain production to the production of dairy products and the raising of vegetables, thus creating the prerequisites for a monopolization of the European market for transoceanic grain export . . . It is useless to hide the fact that certain groups will aspire to a "free trade" which will trample the interests of economically feeble countries ruined by the Fascists. The democratic powers must decisively overcome these tendencies. The trade policy of the democratic nations after the war must assist in bringing about a sound economic development for all the countries of the world.[26]

Russia was particularly concerned that open commercial intercourse along the principles of comparative advantage would transfer to the United States economic control of the Eastern European security areas captured from the Axis Powers. Equal U.S. and ultimately German access to Poland and the rest of Eastern Europe would threaten Russia's strategy of making this a buffer area against possible future German or other Western aggression. As Foreign Minister Molotov put the matter in 1946:

The principle of so-called equal opportunity has become a favorite topic of late. What, it is argued, could be better than this principle, which would establish equal opportunity for all states without discrimination? . . . Let us discuss the principle of equality seriously and honestly . . . [Take] Rumania, enfeebled by the war, or Yugoslavia, ruined by the German and Italian fascists, and the United States of America, whose wealth has grown immensely during the war, and you will clearly see what the implementation of the principle of "equal opportunity" would mean in practice. Imagine, under these circumstances, that in this same Rumania or Yugoslavia, or in some other war-weakened state, you have this so-called equal opportunity for, let U.S. say, American capital – that is, the opportunity for it to penetrate unhindered into Rumanian industry, or Yugoslav industry and so forth: what, then, will remain of Rumania's national industry, or of Yugoslavia's national industry?[27]

At the close of World War II, Stalin emphasized to Ambassador Harriman that he would not tolerate a new *cordon sanitaire* around the Soviet Union. The U.S. pressure toward free trade threatened to be a move in that direction. Article 31 of the proposed Charter for an International Trade Organization stipulated, in Feis's words,

that no member shall seek exclusive or preferential advantages for its trade in the territory of any nonmember which would result, directly or indirectly, in discrimination against the trade of any other member. Construed by standards defined in other sections of the text, this stipulation would mean that members could not enter into agreement with the USSR which provided for specific exchanges of goods unless the exchanges fitted into quotas allotted by reference to a previous representative period. This would require modification of most, if not all, the agreements to which the USSR is now a party. It was quite possibly this provision of the Charter that the Deputy Minister of Finance of Czechoslovakia had in mind when he remarked that the chief obstacle to a new trade understanding with the United States was our desire to include a clause providing for membership in a world trade body. He explained that Czechoslovakia could not pledge itself to join a trade arrangement that might in effect exclude the Soviet Union and the eastern bloc of states with which Czechoslovakia is closely linked economically. Article 31 of the Charter further provides that no member shall be a party to any agreement with a non-member under which the latter becomes contractually entitled to any of the benefits under this

Charter. And also that members shall not, except with the concurrence of the Organization, apply tariff reductions made in pursuance of the Charter to the trade of non-members.[28]

A serious attempt to apply this group of provisions, Feis concluded, "would result either in the demoralization of the International Trade Organization, or open economic warfare between members on one side and the USSR and its allies on the other." It certainly would threaten Russia's planned role in Eastern Europe.

Russia thus had the same fears as had most of the less developed areas, that a dismantling of world economic barriers would enable the most developed nations, in particular the United States, to impair their political-economic autonomy, *i.e.*, to dictate the directions and rates of growth of, in this instance, the Soviet Union. U.S. strategists anticipated that the less developed countries eventually would acquiesce in exchange for a sufficient amount of foreign aid, but that for political reasons Russia would not. "Barring unforeseen events," observed Prince, "the Stalin regime will not be prone to sacrifice basic Soviet principles and policies in its eagerness to reconstruct the devastated areas within the shortest possible time and to expand the developments in Central Soviet Asia and in the Soviet Far East."[29] Soviet spokesmen, he concluded, "have repeatedly emphasized that although the USSR is in immediate dire need of vast quantities of consumers' goods and means of production, Soviet leaders are determined *not* to deviate one iota from their set objectives – to strengthen Sovietism within the boundaries of the Soviet Union and to expand Sovietism into the Soviet 'security zones' in Europe and especially the Far East; and to be regarded as the second great power. These goals do not, however, preclude the Stalin regime from participating in international economic cooperation."[30]

To some extent, therefore, "the irony of fate apparently has willed it that the proponents of free international trade, free markets, free competition, and private enterprise will soon find themselves strengthening a global-wide collectivist system of society and rigorous planned economies in many countries in Europe and the Far East . . . Obviously, makers of American foreign policy will of necessity have to reorient their course of action in effecting a *modus vivendi* with the Soviet Government, perhaps in the form of a realistic commercial treaty."[31] Thus, U.S. aid would to some extent underwrite the extension of Soviet power into Eastern Europe and the Far East.

Even at the time Churchill made his famous "Iron Curtain" speech at Fulton, Missouri in March, 1946, just before the meetings to structure the World Bank and IMF were held in Savannah, Georgia, White "noted that the future of the world would depend much more on friendly relations between the USA and the Soviet Union than between the USA and Britain." However, White already had been placed under FBI surveillance as a pro-Russian security risk, and was blocked from being nominated as executive director of the IMF, despite the fact that the Senate already had approved his nomination to the post.[32]

The question was whether the political and economic costs of reconstructing Russia and building up its postwar power justified its inclusion in the postwar world economy revolving around the United States. "Every time the Soviet Union extends its power over another area or state," wrote William C. Bullitt, America's first ambassador to the Soviet Union, "the United States and Great Britain lose another normal market."[33] The question was whether long-term credits to Russia ultimately would aid or impair U.S. commercial designs for the postwar world. The final decision was that it would impair them.

Direct loans of the type and amount the United States supplied to Britain were not offered to Russia or its satellites, leaving them no incentive to join the IMF, World Bank or the ITO, but major economic and political incentives to refrain from doing so. Russia did not refuse to join the IMF, but "merely stated to U.S. officials that Moscow needed more time to consider the terms of the Agreement," holding open the path of monetary cooperation in the hope that aid would be forthcoming.[34] Russia did in fact get $249 million in economic assistance from the United Nations Relief and Rehabilitation Administration, but the United States withheld post-UNRRA aid from Russia and its sphere of influence.

The problem was that America could not trust Russia to put short-term economic interests above long-term political and military interests. True, Russia seemed as ready as Europe to accept increased indebtedness to the United States, some U.S. penetration of its home market – at least in the capital goods sector – and U.S. purchase of Russian raw materials in exchange for U.S. aid in reconstruction and industrialization. But all this, U.S. officials reasoned, was for the purpose of becoming a world rival to America. Europe, to be sure, also might someday recover to rival the United States, but it could be depended upon to play the game according to U.S. rules. But whereas Europe was committed, Russia promised to become a center for increasing other countries' opposition to laissez-faire, and probably would transform the planned international organizations into forums to denounce the political implications of the ostensibly objective and altruistic free trade and investment policies endorsed by U.S. planners.

Of more immediate concern was the fact that with its system of administered prices, the Soviet Union could displace U.S. exporters in some foreign markets, yet claim that it was not resorting to the kind of currency manipulation barred by IMF regulations. The thought that Russia might conduct its economy to achieve essentially non-economic goals was anathema to American liberals who based their foreign policy precepts on the premise that all social intercourse should reflect Economic Man – a hypothetical man living only in the present, only to consume, and without political motives or presuppositions. This thought for its part was not only anathema, but plainly absurd to Russian planners.

American strategists acted as if Russia would exclude the United States from economic intercourse with Russia's Eastern European satellites, and as if the Soviet Union's major goal were not to reconstruct its own economy but to destabilize the non-Communist economies bordering its satellites. In this respect, the U.S.–British fight against Nazi economics evolved easily into a fight against state-controlled economies in general, and those of the Communist Bloc in particular. In increasingly convoluted reasoning the attempt to isolate Russia from economic relations with the West was expressed as an attempt to defend the Four Freedoms. U.S. planners compelled their allies to choose between Russia and the United States as their major trading and investment partner. Countries chose the United States largely because it was by far the richer power, and more capable of advancing aid to them.

Soviet Russia and its satellites not only were excluded from the system, they were denied Most Favored Nation tariff rights. And to ensure that U.S. laissez-faire expansionism would not be threatened by Russian military conquest, a network of mutual security treaties was drawn up that evolved into the Cold War as a worldwide economic and military system. This view is now accepted among most American historians. "American leaders did not want a Cold War," states Gaddis, "but they wanted insecurity even less." Gaddis adds that

> Moscow's refusal to participate in the Bretton Woods monetary system or to relax trade barriers in the areas under its control was an effect rather than a cause of the Cold War. Once the Grand Alliance had collapsed in mutual recrimination over the fate of Eastern Europe, economic cooperation became impossible. Washington chose to withhold the one instrument which might have influenced Soviet economic behavior – a

postwar reconstruction loan – in hopes of extracting political concessions. Moscow responded by taking what it needed for reconstruction
from the Soviet zone of Germany. The American belief that Stalin might
agree to integrate the Soviet economy with those of the world's leading
capitalist nations reflected a fundamental lack of sophistication which
pervaded much of Washington's wartime economic planning.[35]

The United States, seeking its own spheres of influence, was unwilling
to permit any other nation to secure such spheres. Having obtained
Britain's agreement that it would dissolve its Imperial Preference system,
U.S. officials demanded the same of Soviet Russia. In the words of William
Bullitt, Russia wanted "the great globe itself." Henceforth it and all other
co-aspirants to some or any part of the globe were defined as the enemy.

The upshot was that U.S. strategists adopted a military stance whose
costs would become so heavy as to undercut America's commercial
supremacy and to render the institutions of laissez-faire inconsistent with
continued global domination of the Dollar Bloc. This is the irony of
America's postwar diplomacy: its pursuit of military security, to ensure that
Russia would not destabilize the system from without, has itself eroded the
system's economy from within. Today the Dollar Bloc and its economic
system are dissolving, not by Russian or Chinese initiative, but as a result
of the United States' military and financial burdens which it undertook
with no real comprehension of their critical scale of costs.

When the United States set out to dominate the postwar world economy,
it did not wish Russia or any other nation to be a second power of near-
equal magnitude. If countries showed themselves unwilling to join the
U.S.-led Complementarity of Parts, they had to be isolated so that they
could not threaten the economic interrelationships on which U.S. plans
for the postwar world economy were based. It was deemed better to
suspend trade and investment relations with such countries than to permit
the threat of state-controlled export monopolies and their uneconomic
pricing policies to impair the U.S. world system.

The drive to avoid potential interference from without lapsed into fear
that Russia would use its trade and monetary organizations for just this
end. Russia, so the thinking ran, would seek to capture selected U.S.
satellites by dominating their foreign trade, so foreclosing key portions of
the world economy to American access. It would upset matters just to upset
matters, imparting to international relations a high-risk element that could
thwart U.S. plans. This fear appears to have been overstated, in view of
Tibor Varga's judgment that American capitalism would not break down
even in the absence of foreign markets. As long as Russia held this view it

could not anticipate achieving any great and permanent gain from disrupting international trade relations.

But in view of U.S. intransigence with regard to breaking down all state controls and protectionist institutions abroad, the Russians were led to conclude that the Leninist view of imperialism was indeed being borne out. "At a meeting of the General Assembly of the United Nations in 1947 the Soviet representative charged that the Bretton Woods institutions were merely 'branches of Wall Street' and that the Bank was 'subordinated to political purposes which make it the instrument of one great power,'" the United States.[36]

If indeed there was a chance to have obtained grudging and at least partial but generally peaceful Russian acquiescence in the Bretton Woods system, then U.S. policy must be adjudged to have been shortsighted and fraught with internal contradictions from the beginning. Vietnam finally made it clear that the costs of pursuing a global policy of isolating the Soviet Bloc was self-defeating. By economically isolating Russia, American planners brought about precisely the drive for Soviet self-sufficiency it had hoped to thwart. And within its own Dollar Area, the balance-of-payments costs of Cold War policies became so large as to negate the once unquestioned U.S. hegemony. Russia's movement toward becoming an independent national economy was accelerated, not retarded. It was the U.S. economy that became terribly retarded by the costs of the Cold War, although Russia was to follow suit after 1991.

All the same, the costs to the United States of overseeing a world order designed to serve its Cold War strategy have grown to exceed the economic and political benefits that might have accrued had it not been for the U.S. all-or-nothing view of Communist membership in the world economy. Originally liberal, economic and political ideals ended in a plan for U.S. autarchy. Free trade gave way to blocism and protectionism, open investment policies to controls over the international movements of capital and to price-and-wage controls within the United States after the costs of war in Southeast Asia became unsupportable from 1964 onward.

Part of today's difficulties can be traced to the peculiarly nationalistic U.S. concept of free economic intercourse following World War II. It was a one-sided freedom for U.S. producers to enter the markets of foreign producers. From the outset it connoted loss of economic freedom by foreign countries, and impairment of their freedom to reach independent decisions. Withdrawal from the system eventually became impossible. The economic goal of the United States to isolate Russia from the world was attained, but having been attained, it proved valueless.

Part II

The Institutions of the American Empire

7 American Strategy within the World Bank

"I went to Savannah to meet the world and all I met was a tyrant."
Keynes, cited in Robert Skidelsky, *John Maynard Keynes*,
Vol. III (2001), p. 468, referring to the U.S. officials at
the IMF–World Bank meetings in Savannah

The creation of the World Bank saw Britain jockey in vain to minimize the organization's domination by U.S. Government interests. It had argued at Bretton Woods that the Bank's and Fund's head offices should be located in Europe, preferably in London. Britain recognized that their location in the United States, where the Bank obviously would be raising most of its funds, instead of on the continent where it would be lending most of them during its early years of operation, would tend to make it more creditor-oriented. But America's nearly 40 per cent investment in the Bank's stock had bought the decisive voice in its lending and borrowing operations, and inevitably the creditor called the tune. The Bank was situated in the United States.

Britain's hope was at least to make the Bank as independent from national politics as possible. Having seen U.S. officials tie American loans to a sharply reduced British role in postwar world affairs, Britain preferred to take its chances with more business-oriented creditors to whom a loan was simply a loan, not a lever to extract British capitulation to U.S. diplomacy.

When a debate arose as to just where in the United States the Bank should be located, therefore, Britain – joined by France and India – favored New York. As the Committee on Site summarized their logic, the Bank and Fund "should not be associated too closely with the capital of any nation, and the staff and officials should be in an atmosphere conducive to allegiance to the [Bank and] Fund. New York, in addition to being a financial and economic world center, would afford a good opportunity for cooperation with the Social and Economic Councils of the United Nations Organization. The selection of New York would minimize the technical difficulties of operation; transportation facilities would be better."[1]

The U.S. delegation, however, insisted that the IMF and World Bank offices be situated in Washington, confirming control by government rather than by private financial interests. As intergovernmental institutions, it was argued, the Bank and Fund "should be free of any possible influence from economic, financial, or commercial private-interests." Calling a spade a spade, the U.S. delegates pointed out that recent years had seen a shift from New York to Washington of international financial policy-making. "The judgment of the government of the country in which the Fund [and thus the World Bank, which shared the IMF's offices in the early years] is to be located should be given substantial weight. Washington, D.C., affords a better opportunity for the members to communicate with the representatives of their respective governments." So while the United Nations ended up in New York, the Bank and Fund were placed in Washington, close to U.S. officials from the Treasury and State Departments and to planners from the Executive Branch.

The Americans saw the distinction between private and governmental interests to be of central importance. The function of governments in the postwar world was to insure world peace by taking economic decisions out of private hands, a position that was endorsed by many members of Congress. Senator Pepper of Florida, for instance, told a labor group in March 1945 that large banks were seeking to dominate international finance against the interests of the nation and the world, a view which was endorsed by the Teamsters Union. More to the point for international diplomats, he added that "Congress made it clear, if it had not been clear already, that the executive directors of the Bank and the Fund were not to be international civil servants, but would be, at least so far as the United States was concerned, answerable to their own governments."[2] The United States would not let other countries force it to finance policies not deemed to be in the national interest.

A year later, in March 1946, at the close of the World Bank–IMF meetings in Savannah, Georgia, former Treasury Secretary Morgenthau explained that "Bretton Woods tried to get away from the concept of control of international finance by private financiers who were not accountable to the people." He pointed out that "Under the leadership of President Roosevelt, I sought for a period of 12 years . . . to move the financial center of the world from London and Wall Street to the United States Treasury and to create a new concept between nations in international finance." Urging that a government-oriented diplomat rather than a representative of private banking interests be appointed first president of the Bank, Morgenthau warned: "I feel very deeply that if at the insistence of the United States Lewis Douglas [president of the Mutual Life Insurance Company, a major prospective buyer of World Bank bonds] is elected the head of the World Bank, the Truman administration will be regarded, and justly so, as having by the stroke of a pen handed back control of international finance to Wall Street."[3] Rather, he insisted, the International Monetary Fund and World Bank should be "instrumentalities of sovereign governments and not of private financial interests."

The National Advisory Council on International Monetary and Financial Problems (NAC) was created within the U.S. Government to oversee the operations of the World Bank, IMF and other intergovernmental lending institutions. It was headed by the Secretary of the Treasury, and included the Secretaries of State and Commerce, the Chairman of the Board of Governors of the Federal Reserve System and the Chairman of the Board of Directors of the Export-Import Bank. The U.S. Executive Directors of the Bank and Fund were responsible directly to the NAC for their votes in these organizations.

The new Treasury Secretary, Fred M. Vinson, headed the U.S. delegation to Savannah. He made it clear that more than just "convenience" was at stake in locating the Bank's offices in Washington rather than New York. The World Bank and IMF, he asserted, "are cooperative enterprises of governments and their chief business is with governments. Their location in Washington would have the great merit of making it easy for all the members to carry on their business with them, since all members have adequate representation in that city. But more than merely this convenience is at stake. The Fund and the Bank are not business institutions in the ordinary sense. While they must be operated so as to conserve their assets and allow the most fruitful use of their facilities, they are not profit-making institutions. The business of the Fund and Bank involves matters of high economic policy. They should not become just two more financial institutions."[4] Control of international finance was being wrested from Wall Street by Washington (as if Wall Street, not Washington had been responsible for the breakdown of world payments in the 1920s and 1930s).

The U.S. position was strongly opposed by Keynes, who argued that the World Bank and IMF should be located in New York to keep them clear of "the politics of Congress and the nationalistic whispering gallery of the Embassies and Legations." He concluded his speech at the Savannah meeting by making an allusion to Tchaikovsky's *Sleeping Beauty* ballet, warning "that the fairy Carabosse had not been forgotten, lest coming uninvited she should curse the children. 'You two brats,' he visualized her saying, 'shall grow up politicians; your every thought and act shall have an *arrière-pensée*; everything you determine shall not be for its own sake or on its own merits but because of something else.'" Upon losing the location issue he remarked: "In the light of the unyielding attitude taken up by the American representative, we are . . . prepared to accept the proposal of the United States, but I am afraid that the arguments employed here have not persuaded U.S. that a mistake is not being made."[5] Skidelsky's biography cites letters Keynes wrote to the effect that the Americans "had no idea of international co-operation: 'since they are the biggest partners they think they have the right to call the tune on practically every point.' . . . The Latin Americans could be depended on to read, in broken English, speeches prepared for them by the State Department."[6]

The *Manchester Guardian* echoed Keynes's views in writing that "The American Treasury, which in these matters seems at present to take the lead over the State Department, massed its voting powers and ran the conference in a rigidly domineering manner. Every proposal put forward by the American delegation was pressed through with steam-roller tactics, and the delegation seems to have made no secret of its belief that the United States, which pays the piper, has a right to call the tune. In fact, the worst fears of those who had always warned U.S. that this was what the United States meant by international economic co-operation were borne out at Savannah."[7]

Conflict between ordinary business principles and those of power politics also caused a clash at the Savannah meetings over the status of the Bank's and Fund's executive directors, who were to be placed in charge of the Bank's day-to-day transactions as well as governing its long-term operations. The United States insisted that they be full-time officials, working at the Bank and Fund on a day-to-day basis at high salaries, not part-time functionaries with other, more primary appointments in their own countries and hence in tune with the needs of these countries, most of whom would be debtors to the United States. "Since the Executive Directors are directly responsible to their respective governments, this again would insure strong government control over the World Bank – particularly U.S. government control, since the U.S. Executive Director would have 40% of the vote on all matters. The English argued for Executive Directors who were only part-time, unsalaried, and only occasional overseers of the operations being carried out by the World Bank President, who was to be a full time 'international' official free from loyalties to any government. Again the British lost."[8]

As matters worked out in practice, members of the Bank's board of directors from the United States and other creditor nations "considered that their countries owned the Bank; if they were representatives of borrowing countries, they felt the Bank existed for the purpose of lending money to their countries."[9] But of course it was the U.S. Government that held veto power.

The executive directors, led by that of the United States, were to overshadow its president, who was supposed to be internationalist in outlook although an American appointee. His anticipated lack of authority within the Bank complicated the search for someone to fill the position. It was first offered to Assistant Secretary of Commerce William L. Clayton, who also was the Alternate U.S. Governor of the IMF, but Commerce Secretary Byrnes urged him to remain with the Commerce Department. Edward E. Brown, the only banker in the U.S. delegation to Bretton Woods, declined the job for reasons of health. Lewis Douglas was next offered the job – he who elicited Morgenthau's anguished comments cited above – and turned it down. Finally Eugene Meyer, publisher of the *Washington Post*, accepted the position in June 1946. But six months later, just as the Bank was to begin its loan operations, he resigned, "saying that he had agreed to stay only for a while and that, since the Bank was now ready to begin its loan operations, a permanent head should take over. To those who looked for deeper reasons, the Bank president's anomalous position seemed the most plausible. The World Bank was being run not by its president, but by directors expressing national policies. Though many would blame the president for the Bank's difficulties or failures, he had little real power to prevent them."[10]

The problem evidently was that Meyer "as president had less power than the American executive director, Emilio G. Collado," who was responsible under the Bretton Woods Agreements Act of July, 1945, to the National Advisory Council on International Monetary and Financial Problems (NAC), whose "task was to coordinate government lending policy and operations and particularly to keep our activities in the Fund and the Bank in line with national lending activities. . . . By statute, the American representatives on the Bank were subject to control by the NAC. That body' s approval was required whenever American agreement was essential for the Bank to act. The president, on the other hand, had to give his entire allegiance to the Bank, member countries being forbidden by the Articles of Agreement to influence him. He could not be the instrument of American policy, yet he could not run the Bank unless American policy supported him."[11] With these caveats now spelled out, "the search for a president began again, under less favorable circumstances than before."

The New York financial community meanwhile had acquired a virtual veto power over the choice of the new head. Unless they approved the man chosen, the Bank would have a hard time raising money from its largest potential investors. Clayton again was offered the post and again turned it down, followed by Herbert Lehman and Averill Harriman. Graham Towers, Governor of the Bank of Canada, was the first (and last) non-American to be offered the post, but turned it down upon advice from his government, no doubt on the ground that a non-American president of the Bank could only be a figurehead in the face of U.S. control of its stock. Alan Sproul, head of the Federal Reserve Board of New York, declined the position, as did John J. McCloy (former Assistant Secretary of War) and Daniel W. Bell (former Under-Secretary of the Treasury but by this time a Washington bank president).[12] All these rejections occurred within the space of just one month.

Finally, negotiations were reopened with McCloy, who accepted the post under certain definite conditions. "One became apparent when Collado resigned and was replaced by Eugene Black, a New York banker [associated with the Chase National Bank, for whom McCloy's law firm was Council]. As vice president of the Bank, McCloy picked Robert L. Garner, financial vice president of General Foods. By choosing his own team, the new president clearly expected to overcome the difficulties of the Bank's structure," as well as exacting a commitment from U.S. Government officials that the Bank's operating philosophy would favor "safer" loans than were originally anticipated for it, *i.e.*, loans on harder credit terms.[13]

McCloy also achieved an important change in the Bank's articles of agreement. The executive directors were to concern themselves with underlying long-term issues, not with day-to-day operations. The result of these changes, taken together, was to increase the voice of the Bank's president, a tendency which would become increasingly marked over future decades, culminating in Robert McNamara's tenure. *The New York Times* reported that "The election of John J. McCloy as president . . . is considered here a victory for Wall Street, and for British theories as to how the bank should have been organized in the first place." McCloy himself confirmed this view when he stated in May 1947 that "The necessity of going to private investors for funds, in addition to keeping the bank's management in touch with financial markets, also insures that its operations will be free of political influence."[14] For the time being, private finance capital seemed to have gained the ascendant hand over government.

The Bank's transition from reconstruction to development lending

It was not political self-interest so much as the shortcomings of orthodox economic thought that warped World Bank project lending after 1952, when it began to shift its focus from reconstruction loans to Europe to infrastructure loans to the less developed countries. In fact, perhaps the greatest shortcoming of the Bretton Woods agreements was their almost single-minded emphasis on helping Europe reconstruct from the war, to the exclusion of aid for the less developed countries that had not been belligerents in World War II. The Latin American delegates to Bretton Woods, to be sure, had succeeded in lengthening the World Bank's originally proposed title to the "International Bank for Reconstruction *and Development.*" They had also asked that its resources be divided equally between reconstruction and development aims, but were overruled by joint U.S. and European opposition.

From the outset, the World Bank's lending strategy in its application to the less developed countries did not extend beyond those areas in which industrialization of these countries served immediate U.S. interests. Morgenthau had believed that some liberal "harmony of economic interests between the more and less developed countries" existed, on the ground that "the process of industrialization, without which improvement of living standards is unattainable, can be most efficiently accomplished by an increasing volume of imports of machinery and equipment. And what could be more natural than for India and China to import such goods from England and the United States with their vastly expanded capacity for producing such goods?"[15] In keeping with this view, World Bank and IMF lending activities were designed to finance large-scale exports of capital goods and engineering services from the United States, and later from other developed nations, without actually financing the development of those sectors in the emerging countries, above all agriculture, which might have displaced U.S. exports.

The congressional hearings on the Bretton Woods agreements reveal a fear of Latin American and other countries underselling U.S. farmers or displacing U.S. agricultural exports, instead of the hope that these countries might indeed evolve toward agricultural self-sufficiency. The limited discussion of agricultural problems that did transpire in the U.S. hearings dealt entirely with the benefits to U.S. farm exports from World Bank and IMF lending activities.[16] Assistant Secretary of State Clayton observed that the World Bank lending program "would certainly be a very good one for agricultural exports, because as you help develop these countries, help develop their resources, and help develop·them industrially, you will shift their economy somewhat from an agricultural economy to an industrial economy, so that I think in the end you would create more markets for your agricultural products rather than otherwise."[17] In other words, industrialization of these countries was to be accompanied by growing food deficits and hence higher import dependency.

This self-centered U.S. agricultural preoccupation fostered a destructive theory of economic growth that has characterized the World Bank since its inception: the view that industrialization of impoverished food-deficit countries can be undertaken, within the context of some semblance of economic and social stability, without fundamentally modernizing their agricultural sectors. Rather than promoting increased agricultural productivity in those countries, Clayton merely observed that "if you have a country that today is devoting all of its labor and nearly all of its economic activity to the production of agricultural products for export, if you help develop them industrially, and use their labor and other things for industrial development, I think it will take something from their agricultural activities, and to some extent reduce the competition which we have in this country."[18]

Because of this narrow U.S. self-interest in formulating the World Bank's lending and development philosophy, the Bank was precluded from the outset from playing a positive role in the Third World's impending economic and social revolution. Of all the interests left unrequited at Bretton Woods, those of the agriculturally backward countries were the most serious. U.S. delegates simply anticipated that these countries would increase their purchases of American farm products, which they could have produced for themselves if only they had set out to restructure their agricultural sectors.

Without this structural economic dimension, macroeconomic policies were doomed to miss the important needs of countries in need of development aid. Alvan Hansen, for instance, rationalized that the United States could make its major contribution to world prosperity by promoting "domestic full employment. Under conditions of full employment the United States will be a heavy importer of raw materials and unprocessed foodstuffs, of tourist travel services abroad, of luxury products of all kinds, and of many specialized articles that can to advantage be imported from other countries,"[19] as if their interests really lay in becoming service economies for America.

What was to be developed was their export enclaves to produce raw materials needed by North American and European industry, at prices satisfactory to the user countries. The suppliers of these commodities must be willing to participate in the international division of labor as it then existed. This meant accepting their continued dependence on non-food, raw materials exports. Should they elect not to participate in this proposed trade-off of their long-term balanced growth and economic independence for immediate short-term U.S. resources, they would become exiles in the Western economic community, as became the case with Cuba following its 1959 revolution. They were asked to open their home markets in exchange for international commodity agreements designed to stabilize their terms of trade mainly in the interests of the industrialized raw materials-consuming nations.

U.S. foreign aid would compensate them for the presumably transitory economic difficulties that their acceptance of the existing world division of labor entailed, but the full scope and permanence of these difficulties was not faced either by the developed nations or by the governments then in power in the backward countries. The bylaws of the new U.S.-dominated economic institutions were designed to maximize U.S. diplomatic leverage over foreign governments so as to impose the existing international division of labor as a permanent pattern on the postwar world.

From the U.S. point of view the postwar laissez-faire institutions were protectionist in one key respect: they protected U.S. industrial and agricultural exporters and investors against foreign commercial nationalism. This was free trade imperialism in its classic form. Progress of the less developed countries toward agricultural and industrial self-sufficiency, which had begun to gain momentum during their years of war-enforced isolation, was halted and reversed. Their gold reserves were drained to the United States and Europe.

The result has been that the division of the world into developed and impoverished countries has increased since World War II. Not only have the underdeveloped countries failed to embark upon self-sustaining growth, they have failed even to increase food output in keeping with their population growth. During the 1960s their per capita food output even declined 2 per cent; in the non-Communist industrial countries it increased 11 per cent. The industrial nations thus have increased their productivity advantage over the poorer countries in agriculture as well as in manufactures. As a result, the overall U.S. trade surplus in agricultural products increased during the 1960s even as its trade balance in industrial manufactures was deteriorating.

Meanwhile, most agriculturally backward countries have seen their food deficits increase. Yet as recently as fifty years ago the doctrine of comparative advantage indicated that they would continue to export food surpluses to obtain industrial manufactures. What this glib doctrine failed to anticipate was that international productivity differentials continually evolve in agriculture as well as in industry, generally at the expense of the agriculturally backward countries. This is why the former grain-exporting regions of Latin America and Southeast Asia have deteriorated to food-deficit status. The international reserves with which they emerged from World War II were exhausted – one is tempted to say squandered – to finance their outmoded institutions of land tenure and the related technology that represents their burdensome agricultural heritage: in Latin America a quasi-feudal legacy descended from the Spanish land grants; in most of Africa collectivist forms of land tenure in the absence of modern farm technology; and in the Asian countries a heritage of microfundia interspersed with plantation export agriculture. The result has been that instead of developing, most of these countries are retrogressing.

It would be to the World Bank's credit that it attempted to move these countries toward industrialization were it not for the fact that its strategy of economic development has fostered their industrial growth without renovating the agricultural base requisite to this growth. Only 8 per cent of World Bank lending through 1962 was for agricultural purposes. Because no other international organization has existed to finance agricultural modernization, the effect of World Bank lending on balance has been to retard the evolution of agriculture in its client countries. By over-emphasizing the creation of an urban industrial infrastructure and export-oriented extractive and transport industries, its loan programs have stimulated an unmanageable rural exodus of untrained migrants into the cities, aggravating these countries' food deficits. Given the failure of agricultural output to increase sufficiently to make up for this attrition of farm labor, food shortages have developed and these led to an inflation of living costs and wage rates, and the exhaustion of international reserves to pay for increased food imports. Instead of spurring economic growth within a stable institutional framework, World Bank loans have worked to destabilize the economies of its loan applicants.

The Bank does not appear to have recognized this. It continues to be limited by a crudely technological view of growth that fails to take into account the dimension of social efficiency. It confuses the problem of economic advance within an established growth pattern with the problem of backwardness, which concerns the transformation of practices, institutions and fiscal policies that render labor and land uneconomic under existing methods of production and tenure. The Bank's diagnosis of the problems of backwardness shares the defect of most free enterprise academic economics today in limiting its scope to merely technical problems of resource allocation within existing institutional structures, not institutional and resource transformation.

This strategy has been reflected in the stabilization programs that the Bank and IMF have recommended to borrowing countries, and indeed, imposed on them for the past fifty years. These programs often have aggravated the borrowers' instability. Applying merely monetary solutions to structural defects attacks the symptoms instead of the underlying causes of the problems. By freezing the existing institutional structures of these countries with all their irrationalities and archaisms, and by conceiving of their needs merely in terms of financial stability within existing trade and investment patterns, the World Bank and IMF "development" and "stabi- lization" programs have resulted in the downfall of governments that have attempted to impose these artificial programs on their countries. Argentina and Turkey in 1958 are early cases in point.[20] Russia since 1991 is merely the most recent example in a long train of such misadventures.

The World Bank and IMF were designed to solve certain problems. Bringing about a revolution in agricultural productivity in the less developed countries was not among them. Nor was social restructuring of any kind. As a result, the problems of backwardness were left essentially untouched, by writing a narrow-minded operational vision into the Bank's articles of agreement.

For one thing, the Bank was permitted to lend only to governments and official agencies. But many governments, particularly those dominated by landed oligarchies, were not at all eager to implement agricultural modernization and its associated land reform. The original reason given for this constraint was that a major factor dictating relatively high interest rates to borrowers in the less developed countries was their historically high rate of default. This led to a correspondingly low creditworthiness of private sector borrowers in these countries. By restricting loans to public entities, the Bank obtained official guarantees against default.

But as so often happens to economic planners (especially to laissez-faire planners), the attempt to resolve one problem created another. Inasmuch as many governments were (and are) dominated or strongly influenced by the very classes whose power must be reduced by the process of economic modernization, particularly in agriculture, this provision limited the Bank's ability to transform social institutions in the backward countries. As J. J. Spengler observed in 1954, "it being the purpose of a mission to induce action on the part of the government of a visited country, its recommendations must be limited to those which it feels that the government can, as a practical matter, carry out. Accordingly, missions must necessarily refrain from suggesting institutional or other changes which are completely beyond the scope of practical politics."[21] The interests of many governments in the food-deficit countries thus coincided with that of the United States in not pressing the Bank to emphasize the distinction between growth within an existing institutional framework and the need to modernize this framework.

In addition to overt U.S. self-interest in promoting these constraints on Bank operations, there were historical and doctrinal reasons why its articles of agreement were designed along these lines. Historically, the authors of the articles of agreement looked back toward the problems of the 1930s, not forward toward the problems of the 1950s and 1960s.

One of the problems of interwar lending that the Bank had sought to overcome, for instance, was that bilateral aid often was accompanied by political pressures, being given as part of an economic, political or military trade-off. To ensure that the Bank would not be involved in such coercion, the framers of its articles of agreement (Art. IV, s. 10) prohibited it from using economic pressure, *e.g.*, the withholding of loans, as a political lever with which to effect economic change. But here again, by solving one problem, the Bank created another, for it was just such pressure and just such change that were needed to bring about a revision of fiscal policies and modernize land ownership patterns in most of the countries borrowing from the Bank.

The effect of this prohibition against social pressure was to curtail positive political pressures that the Bank might have exerted toward institutional change, while not preventing it from indirectly exerting social pressures of a contrary nature. Borrowing countries found themselves tied to the comparatively conservative financial policies and philosophy of economic growth implicit in the Bank's lending operations. As a condition for receiving loans they were required to undertake stabilization programs that increasingly resulted in widespread strikes, unemployment and political upheavals, and that froze existing inequities rather than dissolving them. Beyond a point financial stability spells social rigidity.

Another problem working against lending to modernize agriculture to a degree that would have helped the Bank's customers maintain or achieve self-sufficiency in basic food production was that the Bank was permitted only to lend foreign currencies. This constraint was imposed mainly because the Bank was designed primarily to promote U.S. exports, not foreign development and resources. Agricultural modernization requires expenditure in local currencies for educational and extension services, transport and marketing services, and associated rural programs. The Bank was precluded from lending local currencies for these purposes. To make things worse, it could lend only for profit-making projects, whereas agricultural modernization requires subsidized infrastructure expenditures. That is the lesson of 150 years of U.S. experience, certainly the most successful modernization program in modern history.

A rationale for opposing local currency loans was that some degree of self-help was necessary to prevent the squandering of funds on unproductive projects – something which had indeed characterized many of the interwar aid loans to governments. While this foreign currency provision did have the positive effect of requiring recipients of loans to commit a substantial amount of their own funds to finance the domestic expenditure portion of their development plans, it unfortunately precluded the Bank lending in such areas as financing the purchase of lands by tenants and serfs, for restructuring the agriculture of backward countries, financing rural credit facilities and cooperatives, development of a crop distribution infrastructure, and other projects calling mainly for domestic currency expenditures. Thus, to the extent that the Bank has been able to make loans for agricultural purposes, it has been limited to the financing of only that aspect of agricultural technology which can be imported from the more advanced nations. As early as 1951, a group of UN experts observed: "What is important is to build up the capacity of underdeveloped countries to produce goods and services. The Bank should start from this point rather than from the measurement of foreign currency needs. And if development succeeds, the transfer problem of meeting the debt charges should take care of itself. At present the Bank puts the cart of foreign exchange difficulties before the horse of economic development."[22]

In addressing itself mainly to the problems of the past, the Bank created new ones which in fact were implicit in its operating philosophy, above all the laissez-faire doctrine of comparative advantage, bolstered by a generalized productivity-maximization theory of economic growth dominated more by macroeconomic income theory than by the concept of improving physical output. Existing free trade patterns were locked in or imposed by fiat by Bank planners and the government strategists who shaped their policies.

The Bank was constrained to make loans for productive purposes only, with "productive" being defined as capable of generating a financial surplus to amortize the loan and pay interest upon it in a definable time span. The concentration of Bank loans for such self-liquidating projects as electric power was taken in many quarters to imply an identification of growth with monetary accumulation, and not with social change. A 1958 report by the RAND Corporation, for example, concluded that in view of the fact that most of the Bank's loans were for electric power utilities and transportation, "it is clear . . . that the Bank regards these kinds of investment as the key to economic development."[23]

Yet the published country reports of most of the World Bank's survey missions have placed major emphasis on agricultural development, as did the Bank's soft loan affiliate, the International Development Agency (IDA). It probably is more appropriate to say that while the Bank realized that profitable loans could finance only a small part of the agriculturally backward countries' total development needs, it is prohibited by its articles of agreement from making loans for any purposes other than those that generate a revenue sufficient to amortize its loan with interest. The Bank makes loans by borrowing in the open market at going commercial rates, supplying these funds to borrowing countries with a 1 per cent to 1½ per cent premium as compensation for risk. It has itself decried the lack of suitable projects to qualify for its loan funds.

The result of these institutional limitations, however, has been to bias Bank lending against agriculture. Its loans have been mainly for electric power and transportation facilities to accommodate commodities produced by the export sector. The Bank's constraints also have increased its proneness to the notion that technological and financial inputs by themselves can suffice to accelerate and ensure economic evolution on the pattern experienced by today's developed nations.

This failure to recognize the social and political dimension of the problems inherent in development lending was reinforced by the World Bank's initial success in extending reconstruction loans to the European nations, which did not require fundamental social restructuring. The Bank believed it could repeat this early salutary aid experience in Latin America, Africa and other less developed regions. On the assumption that their growth simply was a matter of providing adequate technological and financial inputs, it followed that money and technology could finance a take-off into non-Communist (even if non-participatory) democracy. Economies were deemed capable of taking care of themselves once these technical inputs were provided, thereby completing the postwar peaceful revolution into prosperity.

It was as if highly sophisticated capital can be applied by quasi-serfs such as Chile's *inquilinos* on rented land as readily as by trained farmers on large, American, owner-operated farms. But in many countries World Bank lending went hand in hand with right-wing death squads descending on the landscape to block attempts at land redistribution. In other countries, World Bank programs became associated with the privatization of land and natural resources which went hand in hand with the modern equivalent of the sixteenth–eighteenth-century enclosure movement in England, all in the name of promoting raw materials exports without increasing self-sufficiency in food.

As long as this technocratic and politically narrow-minded philosophy persists on the part of the World Bank and its administrators, its lending policies will be unable to address (much less to solve) the structural problems of backwardness. Sophisticated technology barely is relevant in agriculturally backward countries, as long as present forms of land tenure prevail. Perhaps new seed varieties and fertilizers might increase output on an Indian allotment one foot wide and fifty feet long, but to what avail? A Chilean *inquilino* could, technically speaking, apply fertilizer to his plot of land and increase crop yields. But without land reform he will be thwarted by the country's archaic system of land tenure, under which increased yields are appropriated by the landlord.

Technology is not something merely technical, but is social in nature. Can any other premise explain why food-deficit Chile is a net exporter of guano and other nitrates, while its own lands are under-fertilized? Or why most citizens of India, with 20 per cent of the world's cattle population, should subsist on milk-deficit and meat-deficit diets? The promise of modern technology may indeed hold out a bright potential for future food output, but this promise cannot be realized under today's social constraints that maintain the institutional backwardness of the food-deficit countries.

Because the Bank's agricultural lending is limited to the importation of a farm technology that is inapplicable by the vast majority of the tillers of the food-deficit countries' soils, it can only aggravate the dual-economy structure of these countries. Because the Bank is permitted to lend only to governments, with no option to lay down social conditions for its loans (except, since 1990, to demand privatization and trickle-down fiscal policies), its lending activities must work to entrench these governments and vested interests, despite their failure to lead their societies to the point of sustained development. Transforming the institutions of land tenure has been deemed to lie outside the Bank's development activities, as have most of the social, political and other not obviously commercial aspects of economic development.

Some Bank economists and survey missions in fact have taken pains to assert that the Bank's aim is not to achieve an agricultural revolution upon which to base industrial development, but merely to increase productivity in whatever sector offers the greatest opportunity. Typical of this attitude is the report of the Bank's first survey mission, to Colombia: "Increased productivity," it asserted, "permits the release of resources that can be devoted to the production of more essential or useful objects. Hence, it is not a question of stressing productivity per capita, or efficiency, in all fields . . ."[24] Emphasis was placed on nonagricultural industry, on the ground that it offered the greatest scope for specialization of labor under the prevailing conditions in most food-deficit countries. No attempt was made to alter prevailing conditions or modernize Colombia's social and political institutions.

In fact, the Bank's implied productivity focus stands in contradiction to the experience of the United States. The productivity gains of American farmers in the postwar period have outstripped the gains of any industry in any country of the world, including the United States itself. The foreseen gains from industrial growth in food-deficit countries were portrayed as consisting of import substitution through growth in industrial manufactures. What was not emphasized were the losses suffered in the form of diseconomies associated with a dual economy – the rural exodus into the cities and decline in agricultural output.

These problems often have been catalyzed, as in India, by pricing policies aimed at reducing crop prices instead of supporting them at a level sufficient to induce broad application of capital to land. On balance, these "external" diseconomies often exceed those that would have been associated with a policy of institutional reform and an initial emphasis on agriculture as the basis for balanced growth.

Voicing his own and other World Bank economists' convictions, however, John H. Adler, director of the Bank's Nigerian survey mission, asserted that "while it may be true that emphasis on agricultural improvements may yield positive and welcome results in the form of larger availabilities of foodstuffs and agricultural raw materials, and therefore of a higher real per capita income, these improvements will not set into motion a cumulative process of development which has characterized the economic history of the countries which enjoy the highest per capita income."[25] The reason, he declared, is mainly the absence in agriculture of the external economies which occur in industry.

In one sense this is true. The development of a large plantation, export-oriented agriculture will have no more salubrious impact in creating a home market or in nurturing a trained class of rural entrepreneurs in today's backward countries than it did in the Southern States of America prior to the Civil War. But without a primary focus on agricultural reform – including land reform and tax reform – as the mainspring of economic development and self-dependency, the food-deficit countries will be deprived of the basic institutional prerequisites to growth that the Bank's neoclassical (and neoconservative) growth models dismiss as "external" economies, that is, economies extraneous to the scope of their development philosophy.

Despite such examples of the Bank's anti-agricultural prejudice, most of its survey missions themselves have placed primary emphasis on the need to develop the agricultural sectors of client countries. The missions generally are in agreement that agriculture provides the greatest number of forward and backward linkages, affects the largest sector of the population and generates the major portion of national income in less developed countries.[26] Indeed, the missions have been among the leaders in enumerating the disadvantages of land tenure systems characterized by insecurity of title or proprietorship, and of tenant-farmer and *inquilino* institutions that stifle incentive on the part of those who work the soil. These Bank missions are generally in accord with the observations of the United Nations important studies of *Land Reform* and *Progress in Land Reform*, published in 1951 and 1952 respectively.

The 1951 land reform study points out that, "In the first place, the tenant has little incentive to increase his output, since a large share of any such increase will accrue to the landowner, who has incurred no part of its cost. In the second place, the high share of the produce taken by the landowner may leave the peasant with a bare subsistence minimum with no margin for investment . . . Thirdly, it means that wealth is held in the form of land, and that the accumulation of capital does not lead to productive investment."[27]

Other disadvantages of existing patterns of land tenure have been enumerated by various World Bank missions. The mission to Ceylon observed that land without title cannot be used as security for loans, and that "insecurity of title also means that he [the peasant] will find it impossible to borrow, even for improvements to his land."[28] Of course, where land has been able to be pledged, the creditor is able to foreclose and turn the holder into a financial serf. No programs have been developed to provide rural credit in the context of security of widespread land tenure.

The Bank's survey mission to Jamaica reported that the "size of farms . . . is more important than questions of ownership and tenancy. Many farms are too small to support a family."[29] Often the two extremes of excessive fragmentation of land and excessive holdings are to be found side by side. In Colombia, for example, "Large numbers of farm families . . . trying to eke out an existence on too little land, often on slopes of 50 or even 100 per cent (45 degrees) or more. As a result, they exploit the land very severely, adding to erosion and other problems, and even so are not able to make a decent living."[30] In the face of such methods, although "the good, level, arable land situated near populous centers is strictly limited," it is for the most part "devoted to the grazing of cattle, and is customarily owned by absentee landlords."[31]

Although the Bank's Colombia mission gave first priority to the solution of what the United Nations' *Progress in Land Reform* termed the "uneconomic and paradoxical use of land,"[32] such survey missions do not find their opinions echoed in the day-to-day workings of the Bank. Farm size, for instance, is inextricably linked with the problem of land tenure, as are the problems of introducing improved technological practices, providing rural credit and marketing facilities, and modernizing the tax systems in the food-deficit countries. But as long as the Bank's articles of agreement preclude it from fostering development in these directions, it cannot claim to make the needed beginning in renovating the agricultural sectors of its client countries and enabling their domestic farms to feed their growing populations.

Modern agricultural technology gives no country any excuse for being in a food-deficit position, save for very small, densely populated, industrial nations such as England and Japan. Certainly no country whose human resources are primarily devoted to agriculture – as are those of Latin America and Asia – may be complimented for slipping back from food-surplus to food-deficit status since World War II. This is not to say that all these countries need is an importation of sophisticated agricultural technology. The point is rather that this technology is irrelevant to countries whose institutions of land tenure, food pricing and distribution remain such as to prohibit application of technology. The inadequacy of today's international lending agencies lies in their failure to have helped bring about this needed transformation.

How World Bank operations are biased to aid the United States

During 1946–52, the World Bank's prime objective was to help finance the reconstruction of Europe, not to aid the United States directly. It was understood that many of the capital goods and services purchased under Bank programs would be supplied by U.S. exporters, but funding for these activities also was raised largely in the United States. The Bank provided Europe with some $700 million of loans, about one-half of overall World Bank lending during these seven years.

From 1952 onward, the Bank's lending activities expanded and were concentrated in the less developed countries, financing some $9.8 billion of exports from the industrial nations to these countries. About one-third of these exports were from the United States, the balance from non-U.S. sources of supply. During 1960–69, Bank operations contributed an average $240 million per year to the United States' balance of payments on current account, for a total of $2.6 billion net inflow since the Bank had been founded. This sum included net payments to the United States by the World Bank, exclusive of special transfer payments from Europe to the United States through the sale of dollar-denominated bond issues that absorbed surplus dollars held by Europeans. Half of this $2.6 billion consisted of long-term World Bank investments in the United States. Goods purchased in the United States by Bank-financed programs totaled $3.3 billion from the Bank's inception; interest payments to the United States and its citizens, about $860 million.

From the U.S. point of view, its total public and private investments in the Bank, approximating $2,443 million at the close of 1969, was an excellent investment. The aggregate return to this country, on its total net investment position in the Bank, had exceeded 100 per cent from the Bank's inception of through 1969 (see Table 7.1). On public and private account the United States still held a $2.4 billion investment in the Bank at 1969 year-end. On balance-of-payments account, U.S. receipts from Bank operations approximated 2.1 times its investments in the institution. The Bank thus was not exactly an instrument of altruistic American generosity.

In fact, U.S. officials began to acknowledge the degree to which the Bank's operations had served to benefit the United States. It was this advantage to which Robert McNamara pointed when he resigned his post as U.S. Secretary of Defense to become the World Bank's president. In his maiden speech as president he stated that a new function of its operations would be to transfer funds from payment-surplus to payments-deficit countries, *i.e.*, from Europe to the United States.

McNamara's appointment may be viewed as an extension of his authority as strategist of Pax Americana from national to global scope. Having enlarged the Pentagon's role in American society to one of dominance, he was elevated to the position as head of the world's major development-lending institution, able to lay down explicit social policy conditions to be adopted by applicants for World Bank loans.

To assert that he personally transformed the Bank's operating philosophy into a vehicle for U.S. Cold War aims is not to put forth an argument *ad hominem*. In view of the linking of World Bank operations to Pax Americana strategy after he took office, and in light of the convergence of views of the reports of the Peterson and Pearson Commissions and

Table 7.1 **Estimated IBRD Effects on U.S. Balance of Payments, from Inception of IBRD Through Calendar Year 1969**
(in millions of U.S. dollars)

	Inception to 12/31/59	Calendar Year									Inception to 1969	Inception to 12/31/69
		1960	1961	1962	1963	1964	1965	1966	1967	1968	1969	12/31/69
U.S. Payment of 1 per cent subscription	64	—	—	—	—	—	—	—	—	—	—	64
U.S. Payment of 9 per cent subscription	571	—	—	—	—	—	—	—	—	—	—	571
IBRD bonds sold in United States, net of redemptions	957	32	41	68	-19	-40	141	6	187	213	64	1,650
Net IBRD loan sales in United States	146	44	2	79	76	22	-35	-50	-55	-27	-44	158
Investment income earned by IBRD in United States	137	42	42	54	54	51	54	54	56	59	92	695
	1,875	118	85	201	111	33	160	10	188	245	112	3,138
IBRD-financed goods bought in United States[1]	1,783	148	136	176	209	146	136	148	147	140	110	3,279
Interest paid by IBRD to U.S. bondholders	187	38	40	42	42	43	45	50	58	72	87	704
Interest paid by IBRD borrowers to U.S. loan holders	28	7	12	12	14	17	17	16	13	11	9	156
IBRD administrative expenses in United States (including bond issuance cost)	84	10	11	13	15	17	22	27	29	36	40	304
Total paid by IBRD to United States	2,082	203	199	243	280	223	220	241	247	259	246	4,443
Net paid by IBRD to United States	207	85	144	42	169	190	60	231	59	14	134	1,305
IBRD-Long-Term Investments in United States[2]	—	—	—	—	—	—	240	341	179	161	382	1,303
Net paid by IBRD to United States	207	85	114	42	169	190	300	572	238	175	516	2,608

1 Includes procurement specifically identifiable as originating in the United States and the same proportion of procurement not identifiable by country of origin.
2 Maturities over one year.

Source: World Bank, Controller's Department: Accounting Division, February 6, 1970.

198

McNamara's maiden speech, the question must be raised as to whether his appointment epitomized the final subversion of World Bank operations to U.S. Cold War policies for the 1970s. For in the same way that U.S. foreign aid became increasingly military and paramilitary in character under his regime as Secretary of Defense, more and more employed to prop up politically friendly and anti-democratic governments, so the resources of the World Bank were mobilized as a vehicle for militant U.S. policy abroad.

This is not to deny that McNamara faced very real institutional problems upon joining the Bank. It was obvious that he was taking over an institution unable to expand indefinitely its lending under the constraints imposed by its 1944 articles of agreement. Whereas the Bank had been able to borrow long-term funds at less than 3 per cent in the early years of its lending, it found itself obliged to pay nearly 7 per cent by 1968. This burdened the aid-borrowing countries with interest charges nearly three times as high as those of the 1940s. As loans were recycled upon maturity, their interest rates increased.

But as noted above, the Bank was permitted to lend only for self-amortizing projects, that is, for projects that would generate a direct, hard-currency earnings flow, either by increasing exports or displacing imports in amounts sufficient to amortize the Bank's loan and meet its interest charges. Fewer such projects became available as the creditworthiness of aid-borrowing countries declined in the face of more and more of their balance-of-payments inflows being earmarked to repay past borrowings. And at the same time that these countries found their debt-servicing costs increasing, they found their net balance-of-payments positions deteriorating. The more they borrowed to industrialize, the greater became their adverse trade balances – especially on food account – and the smaller their ability to attract further foreign credit.

As early as 1963, the year in which McNamara's predecessor George Woods became the Bank's president, it was recognized that there was a scarcity of projects qualifying for investment on the Bank's hard-loan terms. This led Woods to press for supplementary financing for the Bank's soft loan affiliate, the International Development Association (IDA), but the Bank member governments elected not to provide IDA with the funds it required. This was largely the result of growing disillusion at the deteriorating economic position of the aid-borrowing countries. In recognition of this governmental inertia, McNamara observed in his speech to the Bank's September 1968 annual meeting that "blatant mismanagement of economies; diversion of scarce resources to wars of nationalism; perpetuation of discriminatory systems of social behavior and income distribution have been all too common in these countries. . . . But it is equally clear that the political will to foster development has weakened, is weakening further and needs desperately to be strengthened."

Faced with these problems, McNamara effected a fundamental policy change in Bank operations. Without explicitly calling attention to the fact, he renounced Article IV, s. 10 of the Bank's charter, which prohibited it from exerting political pressure upon member nations to alter their social institutions. He also, in effect, rescinded the article obligating it to make loans for productive, *i.e.*, self-amortizing purposes only.

Article IV had been intended to limit the kind of conflict of interest between borrower and lender that often characterizes bilateral intergovernmental lending. Such loans often are granted in exchange for political or military favors that may not be in the best interests of the borrowing country. But McNamara perceived that the Bank's inability to lay down social-political preconditions for its loans had been a major factor in the disappointing results of its lending. It had been obliged to work within the existing contexts of politically repressive, polarized economies.

The hard loan provision had been designed to avoid squandering funds on showcase projects, by requiring each project to amortize its own cost. But the effect of this project-by-project approach was to force the Bank into a narrow view of economic development that weighed only the immediate internal economies of projects under consideration, to the neglect of the external economies inherent in development lending. The Bank's move under McNamara toward viewing the overall financial effects of projects, and toward program lending in general, thus represented a tendency toward a more dynamic evaluation of the effects of its loan projects – in economic jargon, a transition from partial equilibrium to general equilibrium analysis.

These policy changes were potentially salutary. Dropping the constraints of self-amortization of loans and non-interference in the social structures of aid clients broadened the scope of World Bank operations as it entered the 1970s. But unfortunately, McNamara chose as the principal vehicle through which to introduce these changes a Malthusian policy of population control. The Bank's first course, he announced, would be "to let the developing nations know the extent to which rapid population growth slows down their potential development, and that, in consequence, the optimum employment of the world's scarce development funds requires attention to this problem." In this statement he declared his intention that the use of Bank funds would be conditional upon population control in borrowing countries, even where such a policy was repugnant to their governments and often to their dominant religious beliefs as well as pressures for social reform.

Although McNamara observed that outmoded social institutions represented a check to the expansion of food output needed to sustain population growth at then current rates, he did not go so far as to demand that these institutions be transformed, particularly land tenure. Just the opposite. He advocated that population growth be curtailed to match the modest rate of gain in food output which existing institutional and political constraints would permit.

McNamara's speech was widely popularized in the Anglo-Saxon nations, but was generally received with misgivings in Roman Catholic countries and in the more race-conscious of the nonwhite nations. An illustration of the anti-American attitudes already emerging prior to his speech appeared in the editorial comment of the November 1968 issue of *Communication Social*, a monthly periodical published by the Latin American Bishops' Conference (CELAM). Summing up world press reactions to Pope Paul's August 1968 encyclical *Human Life* opposing birth control, delivered just one month before McNamara's initial World Bank presidential speech, the report asked: "Where did the greatest opposition [to the encyclical] come from? From the rich; from the powerful nations defending lucrative interests in underdeveloped countries."[33]

The resulting clash of views ushered in a long-needed debate as to the assumptions and values inherent in proposed economic development. McNamara seized the initiative in August 1968 by appointing Canada's recent Prime Minister, Lester Pearson, to head a commission whose conclusions, McNamara correctly anticipated, would endorse his Malthusianism. The commission's report, *Partners in Development*, was published one year later. It proposed a ten-point program:

1. *To create a framework for free and equitable international trade.* But free trade is essentially a doctrine of the status quo. Its workings tend to perpetuate existing patterns of comparative advantage – and disadvantage – among nations. Thus, in advocating free trade the Pearson Report, like the Peterson Report, would prevent less developed countries – and food-deficit countries in particular – from shaping their own development. They must not insulate their low-productivity economies from existing international competition that must necessarily swamp their domestic producers in the absence of tariffs or other barriers to imports. They must not follow the path of development that enabled the United States to industrialize in the face of European competition in the nineteenth century. They must be

passive rather than active with regard to their trade patterns and the economic institutions largely responsible for determining them.

2. *To promote mutually beneficial flows of foreign private investment.* Aid-recipient countries must provide a "general climate for private activity. Disincentives to such activity should be identified and removed wherever consistent with legitimate national goals." In other words, the main growth sectors of these countries must be permitted to fall into foreign hands. This means that the consequent outflow of profits, interest, depreciation and amortization funds, insurance and reinsurance must be permitted to contribute to the now-chronic payments deficits that have stifled their attempts at development over the past two generations.

Reviewing the Pearson Report, Charles Elliot observed that it "rightly urges that the auction that has developed for foreign private funds is not in the best interests of the developing countries themselves (though it misses the important analytical point that such incentives distort the choice of technologies in the direction of capital intensity), but does not see that this auction has developed precisely because some developing countries find that they need a constantly increasing inflow of foreign funds to offset the outflow resulting from the repatriation of profits generated by already existing foreign capital."[34] This foreign exchange outflow also is imposed by the aid recipients' debt service charges on past borrowings. Given today's rules of international finance, aid lending leads to a loss of commercial autonomy for less developed countries, and to their resources being turned over to foreign ownership.

3. *To establish a better partnership, a clearer purpose, and a greater coherence in development aid.* But partnership in what? In progress or backwardness? And on whose terms? On these sensitive points the report is discreetly silent. "There is very little suggestion in the report that aid can in fact be obstructive to development and even growth," notes Elliot. "Even in the discussion of food aid it is hard to perceive that the Commission has considered seriously the mounting volume of evidence that food aid has acted as a real constraint on the development of agriculture in the food deficit countries. While the report seeks to explode the myth that aid has been wasteful in the sense of misappropriated or misapplied, it comes nowhere near to discussing the way it has been used as a political tool to keep in power obstructive and regressive regimes, particularly in Latin America."[35]

4. *To increase the volume of aid.* The world is now rich enough to afford the economic bondage of entire nations whose vested interests are supported by donations from the wealthier countries. It is as if the issue

was one of income distribution among nations, not productive capacity. The report recommends that 1 per cent of the wealthier nations' GNP be "given," by which they mean lent abroad at interest. The Pearson Commission apparently felt no twinge of embarrassment at using the term "aid" throughout the report with no qualifying quotation marks around it. Interest-bearing debt, military assistance, U.S. export promotion and administrative overhead are all lumped together as aid.

5. *To meet the problem of mounting debts.* These debts are caused in large part by the failure of past aid-lending and the misshapen profiles of development it has helped foster. The report did not advocate a moratorium on aid debts. It was no more ready to see these debts wiped off the books than the United States would agree in 1931 to excise the Inter-Ally World War I debts. Instead, the Pearson Report proposed to constrain future economic evolution in the debtor, food-deficit countries by their existing debt burden and food dependency, and indeed to make this burden heavier: "If future debt crises are to be forestalled, sound financial policies must be pursued and the terms of aid must be lenient." By "sound financial policies" the commission meant that deflationary austerity programs must be imposed on countries suffering heavy debt burdens, even though such policies block the use of expansionary monetary policies to promote their growth.

The stabilization plans recommended by the IMF and World Bank missions to Argentina and Turkey in 1958 contributed to the fall of governments in both countries. Such programs have become causes of national discontent wherever applied. They place international payments balance above the goal of domestic equilibrium in developing countries. There is a striking contrast between the Pearson Commission's call for balance-of-payments equilibrium in debtor countries and the full-employment policies pursued by the United States and other industrial creditor nations without regard to the massive deficits that even the advanced nations suffer under such policies.

A recent study conducted by the U.S. Government Accounting Office (GAO) concluded that during 1966–70 the World Bank took in more funds from twenty of its less developed member countries than it disbursed. In other words, its collection of interest and principal from these countries exceeded the new loans extended to them. For the seventy-two less developed countries taken as a whole, "the bank disbursed an average $535 million a year . . . But repayments of principal and interest averaged $427 million, leaving an average net transfer of only $108 million annually." In view of this, the GAO concluded, the World Bank "has not been a significant factor in the net transfer of resources to developing countries."[36]

In part this was because of a bureaucratic lag in loan disbursements. As of June 30, 1972, the World Bank had accumulated nearly $4.1 billion in undisbursed project funds. Most of this was on deposit in U.S. banks, thereby benefiting the U.S. balance of payments rather than that of the aid-borrowing countries. This $4.1 billion represented nearly a fourfold growth in undisbursed funds in only four years, representing what the GAO termed "the slow growth of project implementation."

6. *To make aid administration more effective.* Although the commission's recommendation that aid be freed of tied-aid requirements was laudable, it found no ready response in the United States. If the United States did indeed proceed to untie its aid, the result would be a still sharper deterioration of its balance of payments, which the economy hardly could sustain.

The degree to which the United States has proceeded to tie its aid even to ostensibly multinational organizations such as the Asian Development Bank is not broadly recognized. The amended Asian Development Bank Act provided that all of the $100 million U.S. contribution to that Bank's Special Fund – its soft loan window – be tied. "The United States Special Resources may be expended by the Bank only for procurement in the United States of goods produced in, or services supplied from, the United States, except that the United States Government, in consultation with the National Advisory Council on International Monetary and Financial Policies, may allow eligibility for procurement in other member countries from the United States Special Resources if he determines that such procurement eligibility would materially improve the ability of the bank to carry out the objectives of its special funds resources and would be compatible with the international financial position of the United States."[37]

Loan terms seem to be hardening for U.S. subscriptions to international lending organizations. As Representative Reuss of Wisconsin observed: "Looking at the Inter-American Development Bank in the early 1960s, the first years of the Bank, for every $1 of Latin American money the United States contributed $11 to the soft loan resources of the Bank. In 1964 the ratio was $1 to $8, in 1965 $1 to $5, and in 1968 $1 to $3. Under the provisions of this bill, this ratio would be further reduced to $1 to $2."[38]

7. *To redirect technical assistance.* The report pays lip-service to the fact that "strong institutional support" is requisite for technical assistance to have a positive effect, "particularly in the fields of agriculture and education." But its attempt to portray agricultural productivity as evolving rapidly under the impulse of modern technology is misleading. Not only does it ignore the problem of the rural exodus, but as Elliot observed, "by being sufficiently vague, because aggregative, the report can sound more

optimistic than a disaggregated analysis of the facts would really justify. Another more alarming example is the way in which the 'green revolution' is described. All the figures quoted are from climatically good years and the comparisons are drawn with climatically bad years. Similarly, the report nowhere allows for inflation and can therefore make optimistic comparisons of *money* values in the future, ignoring *real* values." Elliot suspects the reasoning to be that "to have emphasized the pessimistic appreciation of the situation would merely have strengthened the disillusionment."[39]

8. *To slow the growth of population.* Nations must follow Malthusian policies in order to qualify for future Bank loans. "Aid-givers cannot be indifferent to whether population problems receive the attention they require, and both bilateral and international agencies should press for adequate analysis of these problems and their bearing on development programs . . . In particular, social policies which reduce the dependence on the family as the sole source of security would lessen the need and desire for large families."

It seems that aid recipients must abolish their welfare systems so as to stop subsidizing child-bearing! The less capable their institutions are at sustaining their economic growth, the more they must cut back their population growth so as to live within the constraints imposed by their political institutions. Their prescribed retardation of population growth thus becomes a direct function of their institutional obsolescence. They must break down their traditional family structures, in contrast to the social justice programs pursued in the United States and other creditor nations.

9. *To revitalize aid to education and research.* This is a valid element of the report's advocated strategy, but it is not attainable within the confines of an open global economy. The problem is that education and research must be financed by either the private sector or the government sector. If the labor force and its employers are to finance education, they must do so out of higher wages. This requires protected industries. On the other hand, to finance a rapid increase in public education requires government spending, which must be inflationary unless it is matched by tax increases. But higher taxes would add to the cost structure of these countries, and perhaps require some degree of tariff protection against imports, unless taxes were levied on the land and monopolies held by the vested interests in these countries – interests supported by U.S. policies. So this element of the Pearson Report may be paraphrased as "If we had some ham, we could have some ham and eggs, if we had some eggs." It does not explain why neither ham nor eggs are available.

10. *To strengthen the multilateral aid system*, by moving from bilateral to multilateral aid. The report does not acknowledge the degree to which allegedly multilateral institutions – the World Bank, IDA, IFC and IMF – are dominated by U.S. and British government appointees who steer their course to meet the dictates of U.S. world strategy. At first sight one is tempted to laud the proposal that balance-of-payments surplus countries transfer a given portion of their surplus to the debtor countries to ease their debt problems, up to, say, $5 billion per year in the form of Special Drawing Rights transfers, as has been proposed by monetary authorities. However, under the U.S. plan the main beneficiary of this income transfer would be the United States itself. SDRs are created by countries' payments deficits, mainly by those of the United States and Britain. Thus, the foreign exchange resources of certain creditor nations – mainly Continental Europe and Japan – would be transferred to Latin America and other debtor regions, largely to enable them to repay dollar borrowings and to purchase dollar goods and services. A triangular flow would be set in motion from Europe and Japan to the debtor countries on SDR aid account, and then to the United States in the form of earnings and amortization remitted on U.S. investments and past aid lending. This would help finance the U.S. payments deficit, caused at the time of the Pearson Report by the government's military and agency spending.

On February 20, 1973, the World Bank borrowed nearly $0.5 billion (135 billion yen) from Japan, at 6.74 per cent interest, its largest single borrowing to date. Of this sum, about one-fifth was a rollover of an earlier 28 billion yen borrowing from the Bank of Japan. Repayment would have obliged the World Bank to transfer funds out of dollars into yen. Its new borrowing, by contrast, was for conversion from yen to dollars. Instead of U.S. investors having to finance dollar exports to World Bank borrows, the Central Bank of Japan supplied the credits.[40]

In effect the Pearson Report proposed that loan activities be conditional on their proving to be of measurable assistance to the United States. This was nothing new. It was a condition that had characterized the World Bank virtually from its inception. The amounts loaned to aid-borrowing countries were massive, yet many aspects of these loans worked against their development rather than promoting it. Bank loans were concentrated on the export sectors of borrowers with little practical concern for their domestic sectors. Such aid lending served to promote expansion in minerals and other raw materials exports to the industrial nations, creating dual economies in which modernized export sectors existed as enclaves alongside backward agricultural sectors. The result was that food deficits consumed the foreign exchange provided by minerals and plantation exports.

The World Bank's theory was that expansion of export capabilities would have a double effect upon domestic economies. Growing export receipts would permit the importation of agricultural and industrial consumer items, and by generating incomes within the borrower countries, it presumably would help build up markets for local agriculture and consumer goods industries. This would stabilize domestic consumption in the Bank's client nations and simultaneously enrich them industrially by expanding their export potentials.

The theory would have been impeccable if only the facts had been different from what they were. Loans, as inputs, might indeed have produced the effects thought likely. But what were the effects of repaying these loans? This question was not recognized as being important. It was as if loans were a species of gift, hence the term "aid loans" without any sense that the term was an oxymoron. Their repayment, with interest, was assumed to be smaller in hard-currency terms than the export incomes they would generate. This view involved treating countries as though they were corporations, whose cash returns on the use of borrowed funds could be depended to be in excess of the stipulated outflows for debt retirement and interest charges.

But it was precisely the absence of this characteristic that distinguished the debtor countries. Large capital inputs into their non-consumption sectors did not induce a corresponding increase in output by their consumption goods sectors. Instead, imports were stimulated, while World Bank loans contributed to an overproduction of raw materials exports which held down their prices. These effects significantly reduced the effective capacity of these countries to meet their debt service obligations out of increased export receipts.

Another effect of sudden industrialization was to draw population from the countryside to the cities in search of employment. But the growth of industrial hiring was insufficient to absorb this rural exodus. However miserable their previous standard of living was, whether as farmers or laborers, they at least had been self-sustaining. Drawn from the land by the magnet of industry that could not absorb them at their rate of flight, they ceased to be self-sufficient, and therefore became drains on national resources. Meanwhile, the foodstuffs they once had produced ceased to be grown or garnered. This caused a secondary demand for more imports, now of food products, which accelerated with the passage of time and the continued flight of people from the land.

Food prices soared in country after country as the flight to the towns reduced agricultural output while increasing market demand for staples. The effect of sudden industrialization thus was to destabilize the economies of developing nations by reducing their capacity for self-sufficiency and, by their resulting inflations, increasing the prices as well as the volume of imports.

These dynamics help explain why annual debt service costs of the developing countries had grown by 1968 to $4.7 billion, equal to about 20 per cent of their aggregate exports as compared to only about 10 per cent at the start of the 1960s.[41] The aid-borrowing countries had reached the limit of their creditworthiness in terms of hard currencies. Debt service charges for interest and principal payments on past aid borrowings had to be met out of deteriorating net balances on their commercial trade and services accounts. To refinance their outstanding debts so as to remain at least nominally solvent, these countries were compelled to change direction in their economic growth, limiting expansion of their agriculture and consumer-goods industries in order to concentrate still further on their export sectors.

This constituted a form of forced savings, focusing their economies on foreign debt service requirements rather than on the domestic needs and aspirations of their peoples. The result was a series of warped patterns of growth in country after country. Economic expansion was encouraged only in areas that generated the means of foreign debt service, so as to be in a position to borrow enough to finance more growth in areas that might generate yet further means of foreign debt service, and so on *ad infinitum*. On an international scale, Joe Hill's "We go to work to get the cash to buy the food to get the strength to go to work to get the cash to buy the food to get the strength to go to work to get the cash to buy the food . . ." became reality. The World Bank was pauperizing the countries that it had been designed, in theory, to assist. Its functioning and its avowed purposes contradicted each other.

This self-defeating character of World Bank and U.S. State Department foreign aid policy was not merely the result of faulty post-Keynesian or other superficial views of economic development. Less innocently, it was the product in large part of specific U.S. Cold War aims, above all that of preserving the U.S.-centered international status quo. Economic reasoning that challenged the viability of the status quo was rejected out of hand by the U.S. Government and its aid-lending instrumentalities.

The difficulty in replacing outmoded aid and development doctrines with more appropriate strategies lies precisely in the fact that sounder strategies would run counter to U.S. Cold War aims. Development of a thriving Third World Bloc is manifestly at odds with every element of strategy of the militant American nation-state. Thus, even though a more effective development philosophy can be formulated – as its outlines have been – it is merely wishful thinking to assume that it could gain sponsorship by the World Bank or the U.S. State Department. Freeing debtor, food-deficit countries from their yoke of obsolete political and social systems therefore must entail not only a re-education of U.S. strategists, but at some point direct political action by the developing countries to thwart their strategies.

The ultimate action would be for these countries to withdraw from the World Bank, GATT and the IMF altogether and to form a new set of development institutions run by themselves in their own self-interest. Until such a set of institutions is developed they can benefit only incidentally, never directly, from U.S. and European economic growth. They will be "aided" only to the extent that their growth patterns conform to increasingly rigid concepts as to what constitutes U.S. or European self-interest. For the developing countries, capitulation to foreign dictation guised in neoclassical growth doctrines offers no promise of economic or social evolution.

Despite the fact that the World Bank is dominated mainly by U.S. self-interest, it still might be argued that borrowing countries may benefit from membership in the Bank, on the logic that the net borrowing of resources, even on suboptimal terms, is better than obtaining no resources at all. The judgment call depends upon the facts of the situation, and specifically on whether the economic development of borrowers on balance is fostered or impaired by World Bank loan programs.

According to most economic models, any capital input tends to increase economic growth. The neoclassical model computes a capital-to-output ratio, according to which the dollar value of existing aggregate capital is balanced against dollar GNP. Each average or marginal dollar of new capital inputs is associated or correlated with X dollars of added output. This approach hypothesizes that incremental foreign direct investments and aid dollars contribute to the GNP of foreign countries by a multiplier based on the national capital-to-output ratio. If a nation's output is four times its measured capital resources, then each additional $1 of capital is expected to contribute $4 to its GNP. Yet in 1970 two authors published a study that indicates that "the opposite hypothesis is closer to the truth: in general, foreign assistance is not associated with progress and, indeed, may deter it. If the growth which a nation achieves, or fails to achieve, is related to the assistance it receives, one finds that there is no support for the view that aid encourages growth . . . Taking the average rate of growth of GNP over the years 1957–64 for the twelve [Latin American] countries for which figures are available, we find that it is inversely related to the ratio of foreign aid to GNP."[42] "If anything," the authors conclude, "aid may have retarded development by leading to lower domestic savings, by distorting the composition of investment and thereby raising the capital-output ratio, by frustrating the emergence of an indigenous entrepreneurial class, and by inhibiting institutional reforms."[43]

Why has this inverse correlation between economic growth and foreign aid loans occurred? One reason, the authors suggest, is that foreign resources may displace domestic investment rather than supplement it. Foreign private capital tends to preempt the economy's growth areas, and aid resources may reduce the urgency for governments to foster an investment climate to mobilize domestic resources. "Moreover, governments, finding abundant resources abroad, expand their consumption, too, and refrain from raising taxes. In other words, aid frequently becomes a substitute for tax reforms."[44]

But the major adverse effect of foreign aid is less direct. A typical diplomatic precondition for U.S. or World Bank aid is that no move be taken to protect the client economy or challenge vested interests, especially those of land owners or foreign investors. "Perhaps the most important reason why foreign assistance frequently hinders growth is that it prevents . . . institutional changes. In part because the lending country may not accept the wisdom of such changes, in part because aid enables the borrowing country to postpone them, such reforms as changes in land tenure patterns are not instituted. Foreign aid tends to strengthen the status quo; it enables those in power to evade and avoid fundamental reforms; it does little more than patch plaster on the deteriorating social edifice."[45] Questions of the effectiveness of U.S. State Department and World Bank strategies of economic development abroad thus resolve themselves ultimately into political questions, above all on the retarding effect of loan programs on positive institutional reforms in debtor food-deficit countries.

Although many of these countries were net food exporters immediately following World War II thanks to the unique wartime factors, their food surpluses have diminished steadily since then. In many cases they have turned to deficits. Shrinking per capita food production has elicited two responses: one radical, the other Malthusian. The World Bank and the United States have chosen Malthusianism as an alternative to radicalism.

To many development planners, the solution to declining agricultural self-sufficiency does not lie in further emphasis on mining, petroleum or industrial manufactures with which to earn the funds to purchase more food imports. The indicated path lies rather in a structural transformation of agriculture, through methods similar to those employed successfully in the United States over the past seventy years, namely, educational extension services to promote an evolving agricultural technology; rural credit banks and price-support programs to finance it; subsidized or at least regulated transport and crop distribution services; and a general sponsorship of owner-operated farms. In most of the impoverished countries such patterns are not possible under the existing exploitative patterns of land tenure and related fiscal institutions. The required path toward economic transformation of the countryside is thus political and social. In many cases it is a problem of social and political evolution, for only by breaking down institutional impediments to modernized agriculture can these countries hope to attain self-sufficiency in food.

To U.S. State Department strategists, to the World Bank, Ford Foundation planners and a rising proportion of the U.S. academic community, failure of the impoverished countries to extend their agriculture to meet the needs of growing populations foretells a rising revolutionary pressure for social transformation, with all of its attendant dangers of economic isolation. This school of thought does not look directly at the cause of declining self-sufficiency in food production. It accepts it as somehow a fact in being, effectively as a result of natural law. It thus seems that nature or technology is at fault, not man's political institutions. The response is a political repression of the left and of land reform advocates generally, not a shift to help modernize backward agricultural sectors and dysfunctional fiscal and related economic policies.

Assuming that existing trends in farm productivity in developing countries persist, the political effect must indeed be revolution at some point. "As Secretary of Defense," McNamara reminisced in his September 1968 speech, "I have observed, and spoken publicly about, the connection between world poverty and unstable relations among nations." However, instead of advocating a transformation of the institutions responsible for this poverty, he advised that population growth in agriculturally retarded countries be curtailed to sustain the very institutions whose shortcomings he had just decried.

For a man in the position of heading the world's major development-lending agency, McNamara has been strangely quiet about all aspects of socio-economic transformation save those of birth control and the technological revolution. He has made no major remarks concerning archaic systems of land tenure in backward countries, farm credits, crop distribution patterns, the structural inadequacy of existing educational and tax systems or other socioeconomic impediments to agricultural evolution. By stressing population control as the unique area in which the Bank is to exert pressure for social change in impoverished debtor countries, McNamara has preempted the World Bank from involving itself in the agricultural modernization of these economies. The food problem, which is essentially one of social-institutional backwardness, has become construed as a population problem, with birth control and labor-displacing agribusiness technology proposed as palliatives rather than as complementary parts of a broader strategy to transform the economic and social systems of agriculturally backward countries.

The effect of this Malthusianism has been to debar the World Bank and the U.S. foreign aid program from playing any role in pursuing new policies to correct economic backwardness. The shortcoming of the Bank's applied theories lies in the assumption that technological and financial inputs of themselves suffice to foster growth even in the absence of an institutional environment within which these inputs may be utilized productively. For over thirty years the Bank has been entrapped in the view that the effect of poverty – a high rate of population growth that exacerbates poverty – can be attacked without attacking its causes in the form of social backwardness and institutional limitations on the capacity to develop the soil. Aid proposals are put forth as alternatives to social and economic modernization, not as means to this end.

The ex-Secretary of Defense might have suggested, for instance, that social reforms should be nurtured by a new lending authority established for that specific purpose, perhaps by a radically transformed World Bank itself. He might have theorized that the tendency of the rate of population growth to decline steadily with rising per capita incomes in developed countries would repeat itself in developing countries if institutional changes within them permitted the self-same increase in per capita incomes among their peoples.

This he did not do. He chose instead the Malthusian course of advocating that population be fitted to existing food resources, not that food resources be expanded to meet the needs of existing or growing populations. One need not involve oneself in the dispute over whether family planning, birth control by mechanical or chemical means, or other aspects of the birth control issue represent a form of genocide. There are moral questions here, however, which the World Bank has swept aside. What is significant is that there is an essential difference between birth control employed as a matter of personal conscience or choice, and birth control as a national and international policy of governments imposed upon peoples for political-strategic ends. Whatever the merits of birth control as a matter of personal choice, they become degraded as soon as birth control becomes a political device to prevent needed social changes of a basic character. Advocacy of birth control, by the World Bank in its demands upon its client nations, is principally for the antisocial purpose of deterring political change.

For instance, the World Bank is essentially an American instrument, and the United States is a food-surplus nation threatened with loss of foreign markets for farm products as modernization of European agriculture proceeds. For the World Bank to finance such institutional reforms in developing nations as would lead them toward self-sufficiency on food account would run counter to American interests. U.S. farm surpluses would become unmanageable as the overseas market for U.S. farm products dwindled. Hence, the World Bank prefers perpetuation of world poverty to the development of adequate overseas capacity to feed the peoples of developing countries.

There is a yet more subtle point to be considered. Mineral resources represent diminishing assets. It is in the interest of developing peoples to conserve such assets for their own ultimate use in manufacturing industries, as these develop within the borders of nations rich in raw materials but backward in general development. In the short run such domestic use of mineral resources is not possible because of inadequate industrial capital and consumer markets. The specter is thus raised that in the long run these countries will find themselves depleted of resources as World Bank programs accelerate the exploitation of their mineral deposits for use by other nations.

The long-term prospect is thus for these countries to be unable to earn foreign exchange on export account sufficient to finance their required food imports. The World Bank has foreseen this. Its proposals for population limitation in these countries is a cold-blooded attempt to extort from them their mineral resources, without assuming responsibility for the sustenance of these peoples once the industrialized West has stripped them of their fuel and mineral deposits.

Consider the alternative, that World Bank loans and technical assistance foster agricultural self-sufficiency among these peoples. Assume substantial success in this endeavor in, say, a decade. Thereafter, exportation of fuels and minerals would become a matter of choice by these peoples, not a necessity. Such export might continue at current levels; it might increase, or it might diminish. The decision to conserve or to dissipate exhaustible resources would be autonomous, a matter of choice by these peoples and their governments, not something imposed upon them from outside. The decision about desirable levels of population also would be a local matter, not something demanded among the terms on which capital resources are obtained from foreign suppliers. The peoples now dependent would escape that trap. This is not intended or desired by the World Bank or by the U.S. Government and its client regimes.

It is only a seeming paradox that the World Bank simultaneously fosters the development of resources in impoverished countries while demanding reduction of their population's rate of increase. What seems to be planned by the West is a reduction in the rate of population growth in these countries sufficient to permit the continued dissipation of their irreplaceable resources while postponing indefinitely their total immiserization. In the estimation of the World Bank, the ideal eventual population for these countries is the number of people that can be sustained from their domestic agriculture above the basic poverty level, once the West has taken away the last of their recoverable minerals. The ideal short-run population is the number needed to operate the enterprises whose intent is precisely to exhaust the resources of these countries and, meanwhile, can be sustained by imported foodstuffs paid for by the minerals irretrievably lost by exportation.

The issue, therefore, is not between a higher rate of growth in population than in resources. It is that populations in impoverished and politically backward countries today, whatever the rate of development of their mineral resources, exceed the number of people that eventually can be fed once these minerals have been exhausted. The logic of the situation, dictated by the callousness of the West, is that populations in these countries must decline in symmetry with the approaching – no matter how gradual – exhaustion of their minerals.

Whether the United States and the World Bank have been led to this objective by their intention to preserve the obsolete and oppressive militaristic class institutions in developing nations, or whether they have been led to the preservation of these institutions in order that the mineral resources of these countries can continue to be stripped from them, may be a matter for conjecture. But the facts remain, whatever the dominant motives at work. Excessive industrialization in the United States, coupled with increasingly wasteful uses of resources on armaments and on personal luxuries that are essentially trivial in terms of human well-being, makes essential the U.S. exploitation of the developing countries, their resources and peoples. The United States is in deficit on raw materials account, but is unwilling to limit its industrial expansion correspondingly. It is in surplus on farm products account, but is unwilling to limit its agriculture accordingly. The peoples of developing countries therefore are to be turned into the instrument through which the otherwise untenable U.S. economic process is perpetuated.

The customary pro-and-con arguments regarding birth control in these countries are blind to the realities of the situation. Reduction of population growth might well prove desirable, but not for the reasons advanced to the impoverished countries by the World Bank and the United States. Balanced economic development, with ample sustenance from thriving agriculture, is the prerequisite not only for the healthy evolution of these countries but also for postulation of what size of population is desirable for them. It bears repeating that beyond some point above the poverty level, population growth rates tend to diminish as per capita real incomes rise. To assume that this is something peculiar to Western peoples is absurd. The anti-Malthusian argument – that beyond a point resources tend to increase more rapidly than population – is the universal experience of every developed country. The Malthus doctrine holds true only in conditions where per capita food resources are so low as to leave no surplus of human energy to devote to pursuits above the mere gathering and cultivation of crops. Malthusian advocacy by the World Bank is thus a pronouncement that the Bank intends to leave the economies of impoverished countries in the eventual condition of zero surplus of human energy.

Espousal of Malthusian doctrines, at first in U.S. foreign aid programs and soon afterward by the World Bank, is not surprising. It is in keeping with the evolving purpose of U.S.-centered aid programs. The motive for urging and even demanding population control as the remedy for malnutrition of average citizens in politically backward countries rests on the same grounds as those of Malthus during England's Poor Law debates: deliberate social retardation of the many to serve the vested interests of the few. In today's case the few tend to be foreigners and foreign commercial and financial interests, including the U.S. economy's own minerals-import and food-export requirements. Foreign populations are to supply raw materials and exchange them for U.S. food exports, not grow their own food and consume their fuels and minerals themselves or work them into manufactured goods to compete with U.S. producers.

Beyond this narrow economic interest is the more ancient specter that a large increase in world population may bring into question the balance of international military and political power. Centuries ago, mercantilist theorizing had viewed population growth largely as a military input. A similar view remains today. "Nothing is more menacing to world security," testified Secretary of the Treasury Henry Morgenthau to the Senate in its 1945 hearings on the World Bank, "than to have the less developed countries, comprising more than half the population of the world, ranged in economic battle against the less populous but industrially more advanced nations of the west."[46] It thus was historically logical that Secretary of Defense Robert McNamara should become president of the World Bank upon leaving his position as architect of America's war in Southeast Asia.

Jose de Castro, a Brazilian sociologist, demographer and former president of the United Nations Food and Agriculture Organization (FAO), published remarks in SLASC, the monthly organ of the Latin American Christian Workers Confederation, praising the encyclical *Human Life* as the most progressive the Church had yet published: "The United States imposes birth control, not to help the poor countries – no one believes any more in its 'disinterested' aid programs – but because that is its strategic defense policy. We must realize that the pill is North America's best guarantee of continuing a dominant minority . . . If ever the Third World achieves normal development, Washington's 'Roman Empire' will disappear."[47]

This interpretation poses the problem of political morality for liberals in the developed nations. Genuinely concerned over poverty in their own and other lands, they have seized upon regulation of population size as an immediate and automatic solution to the prevalence of malnutrition. They fail to perceive that among the many exploitations in this imperfect world is the exploitation of their very morality, that which in their fiber compels them on the course of liberalism. The easy kind of liberalism, with its hope for ready-to-hand technocratic solutions to social problems, has led them to support the major way in which liberal institutions among backward peoples can be prevented from evolving. Their support for higher living standards for all has been exploited into *de facto* support of the oppressive and militarist regimes in backward countries. That indeed has become the purpose of the Malthusianism promoted by the World Bank and the government of the United States. American liberals have been its unwitting allies, and thereby the allies of the world's most reactionary regimes.

8 The Imperialism of U.S. Foreign Aid

Let their lives be saved, lest the wrath of the Lord be stirred up against us . . . But so let them live as to serve the whole multitude in hewing wood and drawing water.

Joshua 9:20–1

Most Americans still believe that their nation's foreign aid programs supply poorer countries with needed resources as outright gifts, or on easy credit terms at very low prices. Even those who are aware of the link between food aid and U.S. farm surpluses do not widely recognize the ways in which the United States has used food aid as a lever to dissuade foreign governments from achieving self-sufficiency in food to feed their populations. Yet what started out as a system of benevolent grants and loans to underdeveloped economies, at a real but moderate cost to the ample resources of America, has evolved into a strategy of international client patronage and dependency based on U.S. political and military control over aid recipients. Not only the incidental effect of U.S. aid but its stated purpose has been to restrict rather than enlarge the capacity for evolution of aid-dependent countries toward greater self-reliance.

Since the 1960s a major aim of foreign aid has been to help the U.S. balance of payments, not that of aid recipients. In a travesty of economic terminology, any loan extended by the U.S. or foreign governments is classified as "aid," *ipso facto*, even when the balance-of-payments effect is from aid recipients to donors. Reflecting the self-interest that characterizes U.S. aid in general, payments made by the government to farmers to produce crops that cannot be consumed at home or sold abroad on commercial terms take on the guise of foreign aid. Thus, in the curious system of U.S. accounts, the domestic costs of crop purchase by the government – outlays intended since the Agricultural Adjustment Act of 1933 to support prices above their free market levels – are transformed into components of the cost of foreign aid.

"It is easy," wrote one agricultural economist, "to rationalize our farm surpluses into international assets. But in so doing, we deceive no one but ourselves. We can go on making a virtue of them, but thoughtful people and informed leaders abroad are not deceived by what we say; they see clearly that we have been making our foreign economic policy fit our internal convenience."[1] To be sure, Congressmen and aid diplomats are much more aware than is the public of the many ways in which U.S. and World Bank loans are extended to low-income countries on terms whose aggregate effects often prove more onerous than commercial loans.

Over the years, these loans grow into principal-and-interest-payments requirements so large as to prohibit accumulation by the aid recipients of the foreign exchange they need to finance autonomous development of their economies. Additionally, the terms on which aid is advanced often involve recipient nations in expensive military programs that cannot be met out of domestic resources without the imposition of repressive military regimes. Impoverished but peaceful peoples have been transformed into even more impoverished but warlike peoples whose military expenditures filch the resources required for their economic growth and for the democratic evolution of their political forms.

The U.S. approach to foreign aid was appraised in terms of *realpolitik* as early as 1957, in the Senate's report on the concept, objectives, and evaluation of foreign assistance:

> The subcommittee has conducted its study on the premise that the sole test of technical assistance is the national interest of the United States. Technical assistance is not something to be done, as a Government enterprise, for its own sake or for the sake of others. The United States Government is not a charitable institution, nor is it an appropriate outlet for the charitable spirit of the American people. That spirit finds its proper instrumentality in the numerous private philanthropic and religious institutions which have done so much good work abroad.
>
> Technical assistance is only one of a number of instruments available to the United States to carry out its foreign policy and to promote its national interests abroad. Besides technical assistance, these tools of foreign policy include economic aid, military assistance, security treaties, tax and commercial treaties, overseas information programs; participation in the United Nations and other international organizations, the exchange of persons program, tariff and trade policies, surplus agricultural commodity disposal policies, and the traditional processes of diplomatic representation.
>
> None of these tools has any particular inherent merit; any of them may be useful in a given situation . . . The proper measure of a program's cost . . . is the relationship of cost to benefits. International affairs are made up of too many intangibles for a mathematical cost-benefit ratio to be worked out as in the case of a multipurpose dam in the United

States. But the same general concept is applicable: the cost of any foreign activity of the United States becomes significant only when it is related to the benefits which the United States receives from that activity.[2]

Not originally intended, and no doubt repugnant to those men who originally saw the role of the United States vis-à-vis agriculturally retarded nations as munificent (although founded upon eventual mutual benefits), the system of foreign aid now is implemented callously, coldly and with deliberate intent to enlarge U.S. military and political influence. Benevolence has degenerated into hostility toward the legitimate desires of poorer peoples to develop economically, socially, independently and according to their own norms, a hostility which all the world is now asked to share. To make matters worse, other developed nations are now asked to bear part of the cost of this U.S. drive toward hegemony.

Any loan to a foreign country is nominally recorded as "aid" if it is made within the context of a government program or is approved by some government agency. This produces the seemingly odd result that if a commercial bank or other private lender finances U.S. exports to Europe or Latin America, the loan is recorded as private investment, but if the U.S. Government provides the financing, or a credit guarantee to a private loan through the Export-Import Bank (Eximbank) or the Agency for International Development (AID), or if the government simply provides its offices in the transaction, it is recorded as foreign aid. Loans and grants associated with the war in Southeast Asia also were treated as foreign aid.

The United States is not alone in such euphemistic distortion. The statistical reports of Germany, France and almost all the developed nations treat as "aid" virtually all of their commercial loans and financing of exports to developing countries as long as these loans and export credits can somehow be fitted into the context of some government program. The criterion for what constitutes aid, it seems, is whether it is sponsored by the governments of developed countries, without regard for who actually pays the bills or the terms on which they are paid.

One therefore is tempted to question just what the term "aid" has come to mean. Etymologically, aid in its modem sense means to help, assist, afford support or relief. But in feudal law it meant a customary payment made by a vassal or tenant to his lord. There is a certain irony here, because what has principally been helped by U.S. aid programs is the U.S. balance of payments, U.S. industry and commerce, and long-range U.S. strategic goals. Over time the net flow of foreign exchange is not from the United States to aid-borrowing countries as implied in the modern connotation of the term "aid," but from the borrowers to the United States as in the feudal connotation. So-called foreign aid is, indeed, feudatory. Aid has imposed vassalage on developing countries in the form of contractual debt services which represent mortgages on their future balance-of-payments earning power, as well as heavy opportunity costs of foregoing actions designed to guide their economies towards self-sustaining growth according to their independent desires.

In 1970 the Peterson Report acknowledged that Eximbank operations "are designed to promote U.S. exports and only incidentally contribute to international development . . ."[3] Incorporated in 1934 to provide government financing for U.S. exports to countries that did not qualify for private credit, the Eximbank has provided U.S. exporters with a substantial competitive advantage in the terms on which their goods are financed relative to those of other countries. Available data indicate that export credit, not relative prices, has been the major factor underlying U.S. commercial supremacy in many commodity lines, for price differentials alone cannot explain the evolution of U.S. exports over time. Yet export promotion by the developed nations to the underdeveloped at prices often higher than those prevailing in world markets hardly can be considered aid. Britain's Radcliffe Report cited the Eximbank's explicit strategy that although its loans "usually are defined by the countries to which the financed exports go, the direct and immediate beneficiaries of these credits are United States labor and industry . . . United States exports, not the Bank's dollars go overseas."[4]

In the process, producers in the less developed countries may be thwarted. This is particularly true of the food aid which the agriculturally backward countries have received through Public Law 480, and which has often worked to stave off urgent agrarian reforms. Had these countries chosen not to accept these aid loans, it is not at all unlikely that their economic growth and self-sufficiency would have been greater. Their postwar evolution would have been more inward-looking and would necessarily have called forth a much more rapid socio-economic evolution than has taken place. But as events have turned out, technological aid has helped to displace rural peasants and throw them into urban slums. Food-deficit economies have become increasingly unstable, and in many cases increasingly militarist as well, particularly in the forward-defense countries bordering the Soviet Union and China.

U.S. aid strategy thus has been designed to further America's foreign policies, whether or not these coincided with the real needs of the borrowing countries. Viewed in its broad outlines, U.S. foreign aid has provided short-term resources to the recipients in exchange for long-term strategic, military and economic gains to the donor. An open international economy has been brought into being, founded upon a military and para-military alliance whose cost-effectiveness as weighed by U.S. strategists, has exceeded in value those goods and services the U.S. Government has lent, and to a much smaller extent donated, to other national governments.

US aid policy during the postwar period reveals a steady tightening of political, military and economic control over inter-governmental lending, subordinating the assistance aspects increasingly to U.S. military strategy. In the immediate postwar years, for example, the successful launching of the World Bank, IMF, GATT and other international organizations required Britain's membership and the adherence of Britain and its Sterling Area. In a series of bilateral negotiations, U.S. diplomats first gained British compliance in a world free trade strategy, and then moved successfully in a united Anglo-American Bloc to bargain with Continental Europe. Having gained European compliance through Marshall Plan aid and NATO military resources, the United States became the initiator of a broad exploitative move by the industrialized nations against the less developed countries, forcing them to orient their economies to the commercial, raw materials, and strategic needs of the developed nations.

This strategy minimized any possible organized opposition by developing countries against the trend of U.S. policies. Nation was set against nation, region against region. Today, individual countries may withdraw from this "world village" only at the cost of becoming exiles: Cuba under Castro, Indonesia under Sukarno, Egypt with its Aswan Dam and the short-lived revolutionary regimes of Brazil and Ghana.

The militarization of U.S. foreign aid

By 1969 military aid ("security assistance") made up 52 per cent of U.S. aid. This hardly can be said to have fostered the economic and social evolution of recipient countries, but has imposed socially destructive military overheads on them. As the Peterson Report observed: "Of the appropriations for economic programs under the Foreign Assistance Act, 26 percent was actually for security purposes," raising the military share of U.S. foreign aid to 63 per cent.[5] On January 5, 1971, *The New York Times* reported: "The General Accounting Office told a Congressional subcom-mittee today that the Food for Peace program has permitted foreign countries to purchase nearly $700 million in military equipment in the last five years. Senator William Proxmire, chairman . . . said that the use of

Food for Peace funds to purchase weapons smacked of an 'Orwellian operation,' an example in 'double-think' in which 'Food for Peace has been converted into Food for War.'"[6]

Two days later *The New York Times* reported that "U.S. Foreign Military Assistance for 1970 Is Put at 8 Times That Figure in Budget." It quoted Deputy Assistant Secretary of Defense for International Security Armistead I. Selden, Jr as testifying that the U.S. aid programs provided "a total of $4.896 billion for military assistance in the last fiscal year. Included in this total were $2.4 billion in grants, primarily for nations in Southeast Asia, $518 million in support assistance, $108 million through use of local currencies obtained through the food-for-peace program, $1.4 billion in military sales and $224 million in transfer of surplus military equipment." This figure did not include "the amounts of surplus equipment given to South Vietnam or the installations turned over to South Vietnam or Thailand . . . because of 'wartime conditions,' these figures were not available."

Recipients of this military aid were divided into two categories: the forward-defense countries bordering the Communist Bloc, and the less strategically placed countries within which or upon whose borders threat of Communist military presence was viewed as less dangerous by the United States. Of paramount importance in the forward-defense countries was preservation of the *status quo ante*, whatever its implications for their long-term economic growth. Any disturbance of this status, it was hypothesized, might work to Communist advantage simply by introducing a new element of risk.[7]

U.S. aid to this military ring was designed to minimize the risk of the unknown by supporting existing governments and social systems, directly through transfers of arms and military personnel, and indirectly through economic aid to mitigate discontent which, if unchecked, might impel these nations out of the U.S. orbit. This explains U.S. support of the Greek dictatorship, of half-starving India and Pakistan each with military ambitions, and of the Southeast Asian countries whose development potentials in the short run clearly were unable to justify the massive infusions of resources the United States injected.

Four forward-defense nations received 70 per cent of all U.S. military support assistance in 1968: Korea, Taiwan, Greece and Turkey. In view of the Greek colonels' treatment of their country's democracy, the official rationale underlying this military assistance to these countries appears somewhat tongue-in-cheek. "Each is exposed to and threatened by the substantial military power of a nearby Communist neighbor whose belligerence may increase that threat with little or no warning, as has been the case with North Korea. The more than 1.8 million men in armed forces of these four countries make a vital contribution to the military posture upon which U.S. forward strategy for free world defense in part depends."[8] Nor were South Korea under Park and Taiwan under Chiang Kai-shek models of modern democracy.

Taken on balance, all U.S. foreign assistance is ultimately military or paramilitary in purpose, even its ostensibly economic aid. It is designed primarily to enable foreign countries to support a military superstructure capable of saving the United States the necessity of deploying its own armed forces in these countries. In the words of the Korry Report of March 1970: "The magnitude of the U.S. aid effort was largely justified on national-interest grounds, with the annual level determined less by abstract development goals than by the level of additional resources thought necessary to support a military establishment adequate to assure national independence under the U.S. nuclear umbrella."[9] Also promoted are policing operations within underdeveloped countries, to contain incipient revolutionary movements that might threaten the status quo. The objective is for aid clients to grow or remain able to purchase U.S. exports on commercial terms in accordance with some growth factor over time, where purchase of imports still is possible after meeting the balance-of-payments costs of their military budgets. This desired commercial benefit is merely a hoped-for residuum, secondary to U.S. military strategic aims.

Foreign military strength has been encouraged to the extent that it is, or becomes, a component of U.S. military objectives and is subject to U.S. control. Discouraged, however, are tendencies toward developing independent military forces capable of initiating acts that might not serve U.S. policy ends. Yugoslavia was, for a time, denied U.S. economic assistance when it embarked upon a policy of building its own air-arm. The threat of withholding further military and related aid is a major U.S. tactic. It has become an especially persuasive bargaining tool in the hands of U.S. military planners as today's weapons systems have become dependent on the United States for replacements and spare parts as well as for more efficient weapons as American military technology evolves.

According to the Peterson Report, export promotion made up 42 per cent of U.S. aid in fiscal year 1969, 6 per cent alone being left for welfare and emergency relief. Here, again, U.S. strategists divided clients into two categories: developed and underdeveloped countries. The developed nations may, at some point, put forth national strategies of their own to rival U.S. commercial objectives. Such is the case with the Common

Market's protectionist agricultural policy and its Associate Membership status for selected African countries which, among other results, tends to channel Africa's mineral resources toward Europe. Aid-recipient countries are not able to seek new spheres of influence and, in general, can decide only by which industrial sphere they prefer to be entrapped. They may move into the U.S. policy sphere, into an open international economy revolving around the axis of U.S. military and commercial supremacy; they may align themselves with some other developed nation or group of nations, in the Sterling and Franc Areas or with the Common Market; or they may develop their own self-contained protectionist regions. Thus, the African nations recently freed from colonialism are now obliged to choose between applying for Associate Membership in the European Common Market, which disqualifies them from proposed U.S. special tariff concessions to less developed countries, or to pursue an Open Door trading policy which might qualify them for especially low U.S. tariffs, but would exclude them from the Common Market's preference system.

Economic growth abroad is encouraged by the United States, as is military preparedness, to the extent that it coincides with U.S. commercial and military objectives, but only to that extent. From the viewpoint of U.S. self-interest, optimum foreign growth is not easy to quantify; it tends to be ambiguous in its implications for U.S. commerce. For instance, rising income abroad is viewed as favorable to the United States if it generates demand for U.S. commercial exports, but unfavorable if it is generated or accompanied by a displacement of other U.S. exports. Determination of the probability of a net favorable result for the United States is obviously difficult. From the U.S. point of view, foreign economic growth would ideally express itself in a continuous net increase in demand for U.S. commercial exports, plus less direct but real contributions to the U.S. balance of payments and military position. The roundaboutness of world trade makes even approximate calculation of these net effects of foreign economic growth upon the United States extremely complex and subject to error.

The role of aid recipients in America's balance of trade and payments

Most certainly, a visible adverse balance of trade between this country and any one given nation is not necessarily a threat to the overall balance of payments of the United States. If the U.S. trade deficit with the given nation is spent largely on the products of less developed countries, it might in fact have the effect of alleviating the need for U.S. foreign aid expenditures. Also, if the country with a trading surplus with the United States also holds its central banking assets principally in non-negotiable U.S. Treasury issues or in U.S. Treasury bills, the apparent adverse trade balance of the United States is negated by the capital inflow to purchase Treasury issues, which absorbs the trading deficit. This follows the long-recognized rule that, whatever appearances may be, a nation enjoying a trade surplus must, ultimately, finance that surplus itself by supplying credit or by capital exports.

The case of Japan is crucial in this respect. Japanese world trade, although in surplus with the United States, has benefited the U.S. balance of payments in a number of direct and indirect ways. It has been Japanese practice, since the two-tier price of gold was established in the monetary crisis of 1968, to hold Japan's central banking assets in dollars or dollar equivalents, and not to add to its minuscule gold reserves. Consequently, the favorable balance of trade of Japan with the United States, approximately $3.7 billion during 1968–70, represented no threat whatever to U.S. gold reserves. The bilateral U.S. trade deficit with Japan was financed in exactly the same way that domestic budget deficits of the United States have been financed: by the printing of dollars and dollar equivalents. It was not financed by diminution of U.S. monetary reserve assets.

Moreover, Japan's favorable trading balance with the United States has principally been spent on Japanese purchases of ores, lumber, metals, petroleum and other raw materials, and of foodstuffs in which it is deficient. Many of these imports are the products of American-owned companies in third countries. A case in point is the Japanese financing of mine development of new ore discoveries made by Granby Mining Company of Canada. In return for the required advance of capital, Granby allocated the output of copper from the new ore bodies entirely to Japan, at London Metal Exchange prices minus some interest factor on the funds advanced.

The shipment of these ores and concentrates to Japan removed an equivalent volume of market demand for copper from the London market, tending to minimize the upward movement of copper prices. The United States is a net importer of copper and is critically interested in minimizing U.S. import costs of this essential raw material. Thus, Japanese investment in – or more properly, advance payment for – Canadian copper has been of direct assistance toward reducing U.S. import expenditures.

Moreover, Granby Mining Company is controlled through a majority stock interest by Zapata Norness, Inc., an American corporation. The apparent expenditure of some part of Japan's trading surplus with countries other than the United States is thus illusory. The purchases from Granby have been from a U.S. affiliate. There is no way of knowing how many such instances exist. What is known is that to the extent that Japan's trading surplus is used to buy the products of American corporations operating in third countries, it induces a flow of profits, dividends, interest payments and capital consumption allowances to the United States.

The story does not end here. Japan's international trade is finely balanced. In 1968, for example, its global exports were reported at $12,972 million, global imports at $12,987 million. No economic statistics can be as exact as these numbers suggest, but there is no doubt that Japanese imports–exports approximated a perfect balance, allowance being made for statistical error, returns and allowances, and time-lag effects. In that year Japan had a trading surplus of $1.1 billion with the United States, the whole of which was employed in financing needed imports into Japan. That country's payments for this trade provided third countries with the revenue to increase their demand for U.S. exports.

However, the loss in U.S. export potential caused by the increased domestic demand induced by the U.S. war in Southeast Asia meant that not all of this demand could be met by the United States. Triangularity of trade broke down, to U.S. disadvantage, not because of excessive U.S. imports from Japan but because of diversion of U.S. industrial output from commodity production to arms production, and because of inordinate domestic demand resulting from the generation of spendable civilian incomes brought about by the war.

At that point, and only at that point, did Japan's trading surplus with the United States become a burden to the U.S. balance of payments. Previously, triangularity had brought about a fair balance between Japan's surplus with this country and America's surplus with some other countries. With the triangular process interrupted by America's war, the Japanese surplus was transferred, via Japanese imports from third countries, into increased dollar holdings by her supplier nations. These countries in general were not constrained by firm agreements not to draw down monetary reserve assets or bank deposits from the United States as they repatriated their dollar receipts. U.S.–Japanese economic tensions thus only became problematic at the point where the U.S. economy itself became distorted and undermined by the war in Southeast Asia.

How America's military spending deranged its international payments and aid programs

Faulty economic theory and basic – but politically motivated and thus willful – lack of foresight deterred the United States from limiting domestic demand for goods when the nation escalated its Vietnam invasion in 1965. The exportable surplus therefore dwindled – and foreign suppliers expanded to take up the slack. During 1965–70 world trade patterns shifted in ways that were adverse to the U.S. economic position. This shift was of America's own making, but was not foreseen by the U.S. Government, although the long history of international trade should have indicated clearly enough that it is inescapable for a major nation to embark upon a major war without imposing economic controls on home demand and consumption. The United States itself had done this in World War II. But by refusing to face up to this reality during the Vietnam years with its attempts to create a "guns and butter economy," its government planners from Robert McNamara to chairman of the Council of Economic Advisors Gardner Ackley played a major role in destroying America's competitive advantage in world trade.

Under these conditions the problem of estimating the net favorable effects upon the United States of stimulating foreign economies, whether in advanced or retarded nations, not only cannot be solved but ceases to exist. Foreign economies, even those of developing countries, cannot expand in ways advantageous to the United States. The American official ideal of a continuous increase in foreign demand for U.S. commercial exports meets head on the reality of U.S. inability to be both extravagant at home and have a surplus production to export abroad. The quintessence of U.S. strategy thus turns out to be essentially self-contradictory.

As a result, the United States in 1971 resorted to demanding from the rest of the world a slowdown in its economic production, an increase in its income payments and the granting of special economic assistance to the United States by all trading nations. Foreign aid had come full circle. It was now the United States that was to be the universal recipient of aid, and on terms that it would dictate unilaterally. The implied alternative: repudiation of the U.S. overseas debt that would wreck the monetary and credit systems of every nation. The world outside of the United States was to be treated as a defeated enemy or an indicated ally.

This upshot has been implicit in American economic strategy since 1948. It has featured in the spurious theory that the backward countries should foster their growth by transferring resources from domestic consumption to the export sector and pursue free trade import policies instead of fostering self-sufficiency. Such recommendations are made not only through U.S. aid missions directly, but also indirectly, via the World Bank and other international lending organizations influenced by U.S. political-economic decisions.

Where export-oriented growth occurs, U.S. negotiators find it preferable that these exports be made by foreign affiliates of U.S. companies, so that the U.S. balance of payments may benefit from the remitted earnings on these sales or from the build-up of U.S. capital assets abroad via reinvested earnings. Economic growth of the import-displacing type, growth in the direction of commercial self-sufficiency, does not satisfy U.S. self-interest, except where the import-displacing firms are owned by U.S. investors. Whether greater dependence on U.S. exports and capital investment is the conscious motive of today's development planners or whether, as is more likely, it is an incidental result of promoting capital-intensive industries in the extractive and manufacturing sectors of developing countries, its effect is to bias economic growth in foreign lands toward dependence on the international and U.S. economies instead of on their domestic production and home markets.

Accelerated growth abroad may be deemed antagonistic to specific U.S. interests even where it works, on balance, to increase the overall net demand for U.S. goods and services. For instance, the Common Market's agricultural program has generated demand for U.S. farm equipment and fertilizer inputs and feed grains, but has at the same time restricted other classes of U.S. agricultural exports. U.S. trade negotiators have responded by demanding the best of both worlds. Europe should continue to increase its imports of U.S. farm products, but simultaneously guarantee that importation of other U.S. products not be limited by the effect of Europe's imports of U.S. foods on Europe's trade balance, already in deficit with the United States. To industrial and raw materials exporters alike, U.S. negotiators have offered short-term aid, conditional upon long-term political and economic adherence to U.S. policies.

This policy was formalized as early as 1946, when Assistant Secretary of State Clayton withdrew U.S. support from the United Nations Relief and Reconstruction Administration (UNRRA), although contractual U.S. contributions to UNRRA and its successor agencies continued at a high level through 1948.[10] To the United States, the problem of the UNRRA was precisely its multilateralism. It was obliged to distribute aid according to economic need, which included Eastern Europe and other areas outside the U.S. sphere. The four largest recipients' of UNRRA aid were China, Poland, Italy and Yugoslavia. With the exception of Italy, this distribution was deemed not to be conducive to U.S. strategic aims in 1946.

After 1948 virtually all U.S. aid was bilateral, save for that extended through the World Bank and IMF, whose functioning stimulated demand for U.S. exports and opened up the international economy in accordance with U.S. designs.[11] Apart from the British Loan, major U.S. lending was channeled through the Eximbank, which provided U.S. companies with about $0.5 billion annually to lend to foreign purchasers of U.S. exports. Until Public Law (P.L.) 480 was passed in 1954, the remaining U.S. official nonmilitary lending comprised mainly program loans under the Mutual Security and related Acts. For the period 1948–60 taken as a whole, mutual security grants amounted to nearly $1 billion annually, accounting for about 80 per cent of total U.S. grants, the rest being mainly P.L. 480 aid.

Until about 1952, over 95 per cent of U.S. aid was extended to Europe to help reconstruct its economy, enabling Europe to become once again a growing market for U.S. exports while strengthening it as an anti-Communist ally. By 1953, European reconstruction was well underway, and the United States turned to the less industrialized countries, which had become the new battleground for social, political, and economic transformation.

How food aid promotes agricultural dependency

The incoming Eisenhower Administration secured enactment of the Mutual Security Act and radically revised the foreign assistance program in the following year. The major innovation was P.L. 480, formally known as the Agricultural Trade Development Assistance Act. Its purpose was to develop U.S. agricultural exports, not the farm sectors of the client countries. Its subtitle described it as "An act to increase the consumption of United States agricultural commodities in foreign countries, to improve the foreign relations of the United States, and for other purposes." According to section 2 of the Act, "The Congress hereby declares it to be the policy of the United States to expand international trade; to develop and expand export markets for United States agricultural commodities; to use the abundant agricultural productivity of the United States to combat hunger and malnutrition and to encourage economic development in the developing countries, with particular emphasis on assistance to those countries that are determined to improve their own agricultural production; and to promote in other ways the foreign policy of the United States." Above all, it was designed to reduce the massive farm surpluses accumulating in the silos and warehouses of the Commodity Credit Corporation (CCC) without burning them or dumping them in the ocean.

The Act enabled the U.S. Government to assist the overseas marketing of U.S. farm surpluses by acting as its own foreign exchange broker. It was to purchase surplus commodities from the CCC and sell them to foreign governments in exchange for the local currencies of these governments, instead of for dollars or other hard currencies. These local currencies would then be resold to other U.S. Government agencies and, when the currencies on hand exceeded the government's operating needs, to private U.S. investors and travelers as well.

P.L. 480 rapidly became a major channel for U.S. foreign aid. The foreign currencies received in exchange for its food sales were used by eight different U.S. Government agencies for some twenty-one different purposes. About one-half of U.S. Government expenditures of these currencies was used directly by the Pentagon, the remainder by other government agencies and in "Cooley loan" sales to U.S. businessmen.[12] "Public Law 480-generated foreign currencies," the 1965 Annual Report on P.L. 480 observed, "continued to be used to pay embassy operating costs and other overseas expenses of the Government, conserving dollars and strengthening the U.S. balance of payments position. In the last two years, over $2.7 billion in such foreign currencies have been disbursed in place of dollar payments that would, in almost all cases, otherwise have been made."[13]

Nor do P.L. 480 sales work directly to displace U.S. commercial farm exports, or to increase the agricultural exports from the client countries, thanks to special safeguards written into the act. "Public Law 480 requires that shipments of commodities made under its authority are not trans-shipped or diverted, that they are used within the recipient country, that normal U.S. commercial marketings and world patterns of trade are not upset, that suitable deposits of local currency are made to the credit of the United States when called for in the agreement, and that proceeds of the sale of food and fiber are applied as specified in the agreements."[14] U.S. Government agencies are thus saved from having to throw dollars into foreign exchange markets to purchase the client countries' currencies. The net effect is equivalent to a hard-dollar sale.

A further balance-of-payments contribution of the program is its stimulus to bona fide commercial farm exports. "Expansion of dollar sales," the 1969 report on P.L. 480 notes, "owes much to aggressive worldwide development efforts initiated under P.L. 480."[15] As a precondition for granting P.L. 480 aid, the U.S. Department of Agriculture "develops a program which provides for suitable quantities, establishes levels of required commercial imports from the United States and friendly countries (usual marketing requirements), and includes self-help measures suitable to the needs of the requesting country."[16] As an example of such marketing efforts, the report cites the country's agreement with Iran to provide 18,000 metric tons of U.S. vegetable oils through P.L. 480 on the condition that

Iran buy 55,000 additional tons on world commercial markets. This helped reverse the downtrend in U.S. vegetable oil exports to Iran, and therefore tended to displace third-country suppliers to that country.

Sometimes the commercial returns are less direct. For instance, "proceeds from the sale of Public Law 480 oils used to finance private sector agricultural and livestock development projects are expected to result in sales of other U.S. agricultural commodities such as feed grains and livestock breeding stock as well as suppliers and equipment needed in constructing additional facilities for livestock and meat production, processing and distribution."

This requirement that foreign purchases of U.S. farm commodities on commercial terms reach prescribed levels is based on the principle of fixed market share: the larger the foreign food market grows, the more it must import from the United States. "Usual marketing requirements," the report specifies, "are generally incorporated in agreements, and are based on historical import levels. Commercial imports may be required from global Free World sources, from the United States, or from a combination of both, and must be accomplished within the supply period of the agreement. Provisions are also included in agreements to prevent resale, diversion, or transshipment of Public Law 480 commodities." Hence, the aid borrower must increase its aggregate farm imports from the United States in accordance with its domestic market growth, while its farm exports must not so increase that they might potentially displace U.S. commercial exports. Meanwhile, it must pay increasing debt service to the United States for the past P.L. 480 food aid it has received.

This does not constitute constructive long-term assistance to the aid-borrowing countries. Neither their farm sectors nor their balance-of-payments position are helped. They are contractually obliged not to implement policies of domestic agricultural self-sufficiency and must enter into agreements assuring the United States a guaranteed future share in their domestic markets. Self-help therefore must be narrowly constrained within existing income and distribution patterns, that is, in the context of a continued deterioration in the agricultural trade accounts of the aid recipients. "On the surface, food aid appeared to offer a convenient combination: it promoted economic development in the recipient countries and at the same time allowed the United States to defer a politically risky reform of its domestic agricultural price support policy, which was fostering surpluses. Soon, however, certain economists voiced fears that the proponents of PL 480 were ignoring a potential danger. By relieving the recipient countries of the necessity of supplying their ever increasing demands for food on their own, food aid may discourage them from attempting increased internal production."[17]

Of the ten nominal categories of self-help, Number 10, the final provision, calls for "carrying out voluntary programs to control population," although how such a provision could be voluntary is hard to define.[18] Not less than 5 per cent of the sales proceeds are to be made available on request to the foreign country for family planning programs.[19] It is necessary to control population precisely because of the program's requirements that population growth and widening markets entail a mounting food deficit, through the "historical market-share" provision concerning purchases from the United States and its allies.

Nor is domestic banking in these countries to be aided. P.L. 480 recipients must carry out all transactions through foreign branches of U.S. banks.[20] Receipt of U.S. aid commodities tends to depress domestic food prices, discouraging agricultural production and retarding capital formation in agriculture. Such complex dependency patterns associated with U.S. aid lending have prompted one observer to comment that "the recommended self-help policies tend to be those which contribute to the U.S. trade and investment position, as is the case particularly in the fostering of technology-intensive farm investment. The planting of new hybrid varieties of wheat and other crops, for instance, entails the importation of new seeds and farm machinery from the United States."

When a suggestion is put forth to increase agricultural self-sufficiency abroad, some special interest group is usually quick to lobby against it. For instance, when President Nixon proposed to drop the tied aid policy in 1970, the president of the Fertilizer Institute protested that this would "undermine American opportunities to develop long-range trade relationships with these nations. Experience shows that as emerging nations grow into a viable economy, they tend to do business with the commercial ties developed under AID programs," which have included fertilizer exports.[21]

How food aid has helped the U.S. balance of payments

During 1955–69, P.L. 480 accounted for some 23 per cent of total U.S. farm exports. Mutual Security food sales extended through the State Department's Agency for International Development (AID) accounted for 4 per cent, and raw materials barter programs arranged through the Defense Department approximated 2 per cent. (See Table 8.1.) Thus, all government export programs taken together accounted for some 29 per cent of total U.S. farm exports. This ratio had been even higher during the

Table 8.1 Value of U.S. farm products shipped under Public Law 480 compared with total exports of U.S. farm products, July 1, 1954 through December 31, 1969[1] (in millions of dollars)

	Public Law 480							Total agricultural exports			
Calendar year	Sales for foreign currency	Long-term dollar and convertible foreign currency credit sales	Government-to-government donations for disaster relief and economic development	Donations through voluntary relief agencies	Barter[2]	Total Public Law 480	Mutual Security (AID)[3]	Total Government programs	Commercial sales[4]	Total agricultural exports	Public Law 480 as per cent of total
1954 July–December	—	—	28	20	22	70	211	281	1,304	1,585	4%
1955	263	—	56	186	262	767	351	1,118	2,081	3,199	24
1956	638	—	65	187	372	1,262	449	1,711	2,459	4,170	30
1957	760	—	39	175	244	1,218	318	1,536	2,970	4,506	27
1958	752	—	43	159	65	1,019	214	1,233	2,622	3,855	26
1959	732	—	32	111	175	1,050	158	1,208	2,747	3,955	27
1960	1,014	—	49	124	117	1,304	157	1,461	3,371	4,832	27
1961	878	1	93	151	181	1,304	579	1,483	3,541	5,024	26
1962	1,006	42	81	178	137	1,444	35	1,479	3,555	5,034	29
1963	1,161	52	99	160	37	1,509	11	1,520	4,064	5,584	27
1964	1,233	97	62	186	43	1,621	23	1,644	4,704	6,348	26
1965	899	152	73	180	19	1,323	26	1,349	4,880	6,229	21
1966	815	239	79	132	41	1,306	47	1,353	5,528	6,881	19
1967	736	193	108	179	13	1,229	33	1,262	5,118	6,380	19
1968	540	384	101	150	3	1,178	11	1,189	5,039	6,228	19
1969	335	427	103	153	—	1,018	NA[5]	1,018	4,918	5,936	17
July 1, 1954 through December 31, 1969	$11,762	$1,587	$1,111	$2,431	$1,731	$18,622	$2,223	$20,845	$58,901	$79,746	23%

Source: P.L. 480 Annual Report, 1969.
1 Export market value.
2 Annual exports have been adjusted for 1963 and subsequent years by deducting exports under barter contracts which improve the balance of payments and rely primarily on authority other than Public Law 480. These exports are included in the column headed "Commercial Sales."
3 Sales for foreign currency, economic aid, and expenditures under development loans.
4 Commercial sales for dollars include, in addition to unassisted commercial transactions, shipments of some commodities with governmental assistance in the form of short- and medium-term credit, export payments, sales of Government-owned commodities at less than domestic market prices, and, for 1963 and subsequent years, exports under barter contracts which benefit the balance of payment and rely primarily on authority other than Public Law 480.
5 Not available.

1950s, when it averaged some 36 per cent. In 1969 four countries accounted for 69 per cent of P.L. 480 aid, led by India (29 per cent), Indonesia (15 per cent) and Korea (11 per cent). Wheat made up 40 per cent of the crop shipments.

The P.L. 480 crop disposal program has been achieved at no economic cost to the United States. The country's farm surpluses would have been purchased by the CCC as part of its farm price support program, regardless of whether they could be marketed abroad. In fact, "operations under Public Law 480 have assisted in reducing costs to the American taxpayer of storing and servicing food surpluses."[22] According to the Peterson Report, the true economic cost of making these export sales was only 50 per cent of their nominal aid transfer price, as "more than half the budgetary cost would be required in any event to support farm incomes in the United States."[23] Thus, the effective cost to the United States of its $16.2 billion in the P.L. 480 program through 1969 was cut by some $8.1 billion.

Furthermore, the government disbursed some $3 billion of its foreign currencies obtained through the program to its various agencies, sold $0.5 billion to private enterprise, and expended some $1.3 billion for "common defense" through the Pentagon, mainly in Korea and Vietnam. The Defense Department used $1.7 billion in barter for strategic raw materials. Long-term dollar and other convertible currency sales made up another $1.6 billion, so that the total balance-of-payments credits amounted to $8.1 billion, just matching the domestic $8.1 billion in what the CCC would have had to expend to store or otherwise dispose of these crops.

A policy change was enacted in 1966, calling for the State Department to shift completely to hard currency sales by 1971.[24] Thus, by 1969, "Among Title I sales agreements made with 22 countries only six provided for any local currency financing (Ghana, India, Korea, Pakistan, Tunisia and Vietnam), and only one exclusively (Vietnam)."[25]

Among the domestic currency expenditures under the P.L. 480 program, "Market development projects include sponsoring trade mission tours of the United States by foreign buyers, participation in trade fairs overseas, and publicity and advertising campaigns. Promotional activities reach 70 countries. Some 40 private U.S. agricultural trade and producer groups were working on continuing project agreements with the Department of Agriculture's Foreign Agricultural Service."[26] Section 104(b) (1) of P.L. 480 "provides that not less than 5% of these currencies may be used to maintain, expand, or develop foreign markets for U.S. agricultural commodities,"[27] with some $116 million having been spent for such purposes since the program's inception. Four tobacco export associations are cooperators in this P.L. 480-sponsored market development program. Among the commodities financed through P.L. 480 sales have been $24.5 million in tobacco, half of it going to Vietnam.

Additional self-interest of a political-economic nature was written into the Act through the Hickenlooper Amendment which, until Peru successfully challenged it in 1968, called for food and other forms of aid to be used as a threat to autonomous decisions by client countries. Any foreign country that nationalized U.S. investments without satisfactory and prompt compensation to U.S. investors would have its food aid withheld. The idea was to reduce the riskiness of U.S. foreign investments in aid-recipient countries.

Secretary of Agriculture Orville Freeman openly acknowledged the use of food trade and aid as a political lever in an important policy-setting article entitled "Malthus, Marx and the North American Breadbasket."[28] "Our unmatched food-producing capability," he asserted, "has strengthened our foreign policy immeasurably."[29] Its first effect was upon "the balance of power between East and West." North America became a vital supplier of Communist nations' food needs, with the result that their food deficits "are causing them to become politically and militarily vulnerable." The United States has supplanted China as Japan's main source of food imports. China, in fact, is dependent today on Western Hemisphere grain supplies. "Without our ability to generate huge farm exports, these strong economic ties could not have developed. In geographic terms Japan is off the coast of California. This is but one of the more dramatic illustrations of the value of a productive farm sector in supporting our foreign policy."

In 1961 the Kennedy Administration brought about, as part of its enlargement of presidential powers, a fundamental restructuring of aid programs, centralizing all activities in the State Department under the newly created Agency for International Development. The most important feature of the new program was the enlistment of aid activities to help reduce the rising deficit in the U.S. balance of payments. Unless the payments deficit were overcome, U.S. strategists argued, a transfer of economic and diplomatic power to Continental Europe would take place, proportionate to the outflow of U.S. gold. To assist low-income countries without further strengthening Europe as an economic rival, all aid became tied to the purchase of U.S. goods and services, except in the case of specifically military or paramilitary assistance to Asia where security aims outweighed economics. A Gold Budget was established as an accounting control device to maximize the aid program's balance-of-payments contribution. Recipients of U.S. "aid," in short, were required to subsidize the U.S. balance of payments.

New export credits under all aid programs were to be compensated in counterpart funds. In addition, all aid-financed commodities had to be shipped in U.S. flagships at freight rates above world tramp rates. Commerce Department figures show that some 39 per cent of total U.S. flagships' receipts from foreigners on ocean freight in 1961 derived from the transport of U.S. aid commodities.[30] The Peterson Report estimated that the cost of U.S. aid to its recipients approximates 15 per cent more than going world prices.[31] This combination of high commodity prices and extremely high shipping costs has led some countries to withdraw from the U.S. aid program, on the grounds that they simply cannot afford further U.S. assistance.

In order to make certain that no displacement of commercial exports took place, foreign aid was subjected to what was termed an additionality provision: "Additionality measures were an attempt to prevent AID financing of goods that might otherwise have been exported through regular commercial transactions. The principal device used was limiting the selection of U.S. products permissible for AID financing to those in which the U.S. share of the local commercial market was small, so that AID-financed imports of these products would very likely be additional to normal commercial purchases from the United States."[32] The report adds that "Difficulties arose because local businessmen – not host governments – do most of the importing of AID-financed commodities. These private importers act according to commercial motives. Their governments often had to use unpopular restrictive exchange, import, or credit arrangements to induce private importers to buy the less competitive U.S. products permissible for AID financing."

The official AID estimate that this measure worked to benefit the U.S. balance of payments by only some $35 million per year seems low. By 1968, U.S. aid was contributing massively to the balance of payments, accounting for a $904 million surplus for the United States, the amount by which $1.5 billion, received by U.S. aid, exceeded the direct cost of new aid extended.[33] (See Table 8.2.) Some 95 per cent of this new aid was tied directly to purchases of U.S. goods and services. This may understate the full contribution to the U.S. balance of payments. According to the AID annual report for 1969, "The AID program contributed a net surplus estimated at $242 million to the U.S. balance of payments in fiscal 1969. The 1968 surplus was $81 million."[34] According to the Eximbank's 1968 report, "Repayments and interest on loans made by Eximbank and on

Table 8.2 "Foreign Aid" in the U.S. balance of payments: 1960–1970* (millions of dollars)

	Reference to O.B.E. Table 1	1960	1961	1962	1963	1964	1965	1966	1967	1968	1969	1970
Nonmilitary grants and loans, and their associated payments-flows		$(300)	(329)	(186)	13	40	70	319	537	903	1,145	1,329
1. New grants and other capital outflows: net funds spent abroad		(1,125)	(1,144)	(1,042)	(813)	(691)	(753)	(734)	(726)	(641)	(734)	(687)
A. Total new grants and capital outflows	29*, 42*, 43*	(3,617)	(4,298)	(4,555)	(4,794)	(4,614)	(4,527)	(4,655)	(5,238)	(5,093)	(4,838)	(4,935)
1. Nonmilitary grants	29	(1,664)	(1,853)	(1,919)	(1,917)	(1,888)	(1,808)	(1,910)	(1,802)	(1,706)	(1,644)	(1,647)
2. Loans and other long-term assets	42	(1,213)	(1,939)	(1,129)	(2,201)	(2,375)	(2,454)	(2,501)	(3,634)	(3,713)	(3,477)	(3,284)
3. Net foreign currencies and other assets (increase)	43	(528)	(261)	(245)	(447)	(19)	(16)	(265)	209	72	89	(23)
4. Less credits to finance military sales contracts	42*	26	33	13	36	16	90	291	390	554	528	361
Memo: Foreign currencies used by U.S. Government other than for grants or credits	43*	238	278	275	265	349	340	270	401	300	334	342
B. Spent in the United States	3*	2,492	3,185	3,512	3,981	3,922	3,774	3,921	4,511	4,452	4,104	4,248
1. On merchandise exports.	6*	2,046	2,396	2,503	2,882	3,032	2,952	3,152	3,523	3,331	3,097	3,026
2. On services		368	497	670	785	690	748	798	767	855	791	844
a. Transport	9*	162	218	230	252	244	209	192	185	200	225	230
b. Private services		75	75	75	75	75	75	75	75	75	75	75
c. Interest on prior U.S. Government credits	13*	69	74	114	147	168	183	181	171	196	200	196
d. U.S. Government services	10*	102	109	121	154	126	91	133	112	149	40	102
e. All other services, n.i.e.	60*	40	21	130	157	177	190	217	224	235	251	241
3. U.S. Government credits to repay prior U.S. private credits (mainly bank credits)	38*	—	111	93	34	—	5	14	104	116	88	234
4. U.S. Government credits to repay prior U.S. Government credits	44*	37	71	100	186	151	154	162	201	148	144	174
5. Increase in U.S. Government liabilities associated with specific grants and capital outflows	56*	41	80	147	94	49	(86)	(205)	(84)	2	(16)	(30)
2. Income received on U.S. Government loans and other assets, net		279	307	357	351	288	326	412	467	569	732	715
A. Total	13	348	381	471	498	456	509	593	638	765	932	911
B. Financed by U.S. Government credit	44*	(69)	(74)	(114)	(147)	(168)	(183)	(181)	(171)	(196)	(200)	(196)
3. Net receipt of principal repayment on past credit (scheduled only)		546	508	499	475	443	497	641	796	975	1,147	1,301
A. Total	44	583	579	599	661	594	651	803	997	1,123	1,291	1,475
B. Financed by new U.S. Government credit		(37)	(71)	(100)	(186)	(151)	(154)	(162)	(201)	(148)	(144)	(174)

* Source: U.S. Dept. of Commerce, Office of Business Economics, Table 5 and unpublished O.B.E. estimates.

export loans guaranteed or insured by it are estimated to have contributed over $1.7 billion to the United States balance of payments during the year."[35] It seems probable that repayments of military loans brought the foreign aid program's net contribution to the U.S. balance of payments to over $2 billion in 1968. Thus did the aid-borrowing countries finance their own submission, and thus has the U.S. foreign aid program been one of the major sources of strength in the nation's balance of payments, a remunerative investment of government finance capital and not the net economic cost which the term "aid" supposedly connotes.

Foreign aid and Cold War geopolitics

To integrate export promotion with diplomatic aims, P.L. 480 aid was transferred out of the Department of Agriculture into the State Department. This centralization of all foreign assistance within AID reinforced the State Department's capacity to secure leases on military bases, signatures on diplomatic agreements, and the general military and political loyalty of foreign governments. The biennial aid packages offered to Spain in exchange for airbase rights are cases in point. It was in recognition of this political service of aid that the Korry Report accused U.S. foreign aid of holding too tightly to the position "that development assistance provided by the U.S. should secure political support for the U.S. on important current issues."[36]

Meanwhile, the Peace Corps replaced the more belligerent instruments of prewar diplomacy and yielded a political gain at home by attracting the support of many groups that would have opposed an outright increase in military involvement abroad. Aid strategy was shifted to emphasize economic development as a social alternative to Communism rather than a military offset to revolutionary movements abroad. The threat to the status quo among America's aid clients, it was recognized, was becoming more internal than external in nature, more political than overtly military.

This broadened the scope of Cold War strategy, and was defended with disarming simplicity on the grounds that it would inhibit revolutionary sentiments abroad by relieving poverty. Secretary of Defense Robert McNamara asserted in his congressional testimony on the Foreign Assistance Act of 1964:

In my considered judgment, this program, and the foreign aid program generally, has now become the most critical element of our overall national security effort . . . If we are to meet the avowed Communist threat across the entire spectrum of conflict, then we must also be ready to take whatever measures are necessary to counter their efforts to promote guerrilla wars and insurrections. And much of this task can be accomplished only by the assistance, both military and economic, we give our less prosperous allies . . . As President Johnson recently stated, the foreign-aid program is the best weapon we have to insure that our own men in uniform need not go into combat.[37]

The Peterson Report virtually rephrased Mr McNamara's strategy: "In the past, the line of demarcation between security and development interests was blurred. The United States faced a divided world, in which foreign assistance was justified in terms of the conflict between East and West. Today all countries have a common interest in building and maintaining a global environment in which each can prosper."[38]

After the May 1965 build-up in Vietnam the days of bilateral aid were numbered, curtailing the United States' ability directly to manage its foreign assistance program. In 1966 President Johnson asked Edward Korry, then U.S. ambassador to Ethiopia, to draft a new aid strategy to multilateralize it. Korry's 1966 report was followed by that of Sir Robert Jackson for the United Nations in 1968, and by another prepared by a committee headed by James A. Perkins, president of Cornell University and a director of the Chase Manhattan Bank. By this time antiwar sentiment had come to threaten the entire aid program, inducing the Perkins Committee to conclude: "Fundamentally the committee believes that development cooperation provides the U.S. with an alternative to military involvement for playing a continuing role in the less developed world. Doves or Hawks on our military commitment in Vietnam can equally support assistance for development."

When the new Republican Administration took office in 1969 a further recasting of the U.S. aid program seemed required. Congressional opposition to the President's military commitment of the nation's resources was increasing rapidly. If the overall aims of U.S. strategy were to be pursued into the 1970s, then its aid aspects would have to be submerged in the anonymity of multilateral programs. Not only might this mobilize foreign official resources to supplement those of the United States in pursuing its world designs, it also would be less subject to domestic opposition to U.S. involvement abroad.

The Peterson Report was the result of this perception. Released in April 1970, its theme was that bilateralism must give way to a new policy, one that would be more multilateral in appearance. "A predominantly bilateral

United States program," it asserted, "is no longer politically tenable in our relations with many developing countries, nor is it advisable in view of what other countries are doing in international development."[39] As Representative Reuss of Wisconsin expressed this idea: "The principal advantages of multilateral financial institutions . . . are burden-sharing and economic expertise. Through these institutions other developed countries share with the United States the cost of providing development assistance, as other nations have grown in economic strength, our share of the financial cost has declined."[40] Regarding the Asian Development Bank, for instance, "while it is true that Japan plays a big role in the Asian Bank, that is good, not bad. I think it is fine that we are getting others to bear what should properly be their share of the burden, and if we can get the Japanese in Asia assuming a large scale development role, I think that is one of the more hopeful signs . . . in terms of the Asian Bank, I submit that our diplomatists have done an excellent job in compelling burden-sharing on the part of Japan."[41]

This tactic already had been recommended by Congress in its 1957 report on Technical Assistance, noting: "1. The multilateral character of the U.S. program affords a means of utilizing the resources of other nations. 2. A multilateral approach through the U.N. program is particularly appropriate in fields where bilateral efforts are likely to encounter national sensitivities and resistance on the grounds of outside interference. Public administration is one such field. Another, in some countries, is in areas where there is substantial private American investment."[42]

As an alternative it drafted a militant strategy on four fronts:

1. to transfer the disposition of foreign aid from the Legislative to the Executive arm of the government, bypassing congressional opposition to the President's use of aid strategy as a means for expanding paramilitary involvement abroad;
2. to adopt a low-profile military posture by inducing foreign governments to recruit their own people in place of United States troops in existing and future military involvements, *e.g.*, the Vietnamization of the Southeast Asian conflict;
3. to use bilateral and multilateral aid as an economic lever against the European Common Market;
4. to implement a more realistic strategy against social revolution abroad and its associated threats of nationalism and regional blocism.

To prevent congressional budget cuts in the foreign aid program and to reduce its net burden on the federal budget, the Peterson Commission urged establishment of a new lending agency, the International Development Bank, empowered to issue its own public bonds and hence to be independent of congressional funding or approval. This meant that if Congress were to reduce aid appropriations or vote against strategic use of foreign assistance, as it did in October 1971, the proposed new bank could obtain funds from private lenders in the United States or abroad. The military and paramilitary purposes of the U.S. aid program thus could be secured even over the opposition of the Congress. The Cold War machine would become self-financing and self-perpetuating.

The Eximbank was already doing this on a substantial scale. In 1962 it "initiated the sale of guaranteed certificates of participation in pools of its loans. . . . The Bank has sold in all, some $3.5 billion of participation certificates with maturities varying from three to fifteen years."[43] Participations in Eximbank's financing of exports are now also being sold to foreigners and foreign branches of U.S. commercial banks, enlisting overseas funds for the promotion of U.S. exports.

The Peterson Commission believed that the United States could phase out its military grant program, as the nation's allies had become so enmeshed in U.S. weapons systems that they had no choice but to continue to depend on U.S. arms. Easy credit policies employed by the Defense Department to finance military sales had succeeded in Americanizing the armament systems of most non-Communist countries. The path thus had been paved from military aid to armaments trade. "In the past, these countries needed the close involvement of U.S. military advisers to ensure the effective integration of United States arms and equipment into their forces. By now, however, military officials in most of these countries have achieved adequate levels of professional competence and facility with modem arms."[44] Military grants in the future "should be determined on a cost-benefit basis. The risks involved for the United States and the need for United States forces that would arise if funds were not provided should be specified."

The proposed new strategy required foreign countries to finance and operate their own military systems. The United States would sell them the hardware, foreign countries would provide the manpower. Security assistance in the 1970s, the report concluded, should be aimed at improving the "military defenses of our allies and move them toward greater military self-reliance, to serve as a substitute for the deployment of U.S. forces abroad, to pay for U.S. base Fights, and to deal with crisis situations."[45]

A major reason for the Peterson Report's emphasis on multilateralism was its desire to shift the burden of financing U.S. world strategy onto

Europe's shoulders specifically. Thus, whereas the Kennedy Administration's tied-aid policies were designed to prevent the U.S. expenditures on foreign aid from spilling over to Europe's advantage, the Peterson strategy was more aggressively designed to involve Europe's treasuries in U.S. loan programs.

The Peterson Report was not unmindful that the burdens of interest and principal repayments weigh heavily upon the aid-borrowing countries. "The debt burden," it observed, "was foreseen, but not faced, a decade ago. It stems from a combination of causes: excessive export credits on terms that the developing countries cannot meet; insufficient attention to exports; and in some cases, excessive military purchases or financial mismanagement . . . Whatever the causes, future export earnings of some countries are so heavily mortgaged as to endanger continuing imports, investment and development. All countries will have to address this problem together."[46]

The Third World's dollar-debt problems

Most of the aid debt burden was owed to the United States, or at least was denominated in U.S. dollars as, for example, World Bank loans financed by dollar borrowings abroad. According to the World Bank's 1970 *Annual Report*, as of 1969 the external governmental debt of eighty less developed countries stood at $59.3 billion, exceeding by more than $40 billion the $18.8 billion in private U.S. direct investment in these countries. Official debt service of these countries amounted to $5 billion, compared with $2.9 billion remitted on U.S. direct investments. Latin America alone owed $17.7 billion on governmental capital account and paid $2.2 billion in official interest and amortization charges on these debts, compared with $13.8 billion of U.S. direct investments in Latin America and an associated $1.2 billion flow of income remittances to U.S. private investors in 1969. Statistics for other regions are comparable.[47] Government borrowings had come to exceed liabilities on direct investment account throughout the whole of the world's less developed areas. This was true in even greater degree of U.S. official obligations to the developed nations.

These statistics point up the shift of inter-governmental capital loans since World War II, from productive reconstruction lending to Europe toward less productive consumption loans to less developing countries, and from credits by the United States to credits from the United States. A growing portion of intergovernmental claims since World War II has represented the debt owed by aid-borrowing countries for such foreign assistance as P.L. 480 food aid and arms support. Many of these loans are not for directly productive purposes as is generally connoted in the business sense of the term. Toward the underdeveloped countries, lending policies of the United States, and of the IMF and World Bank which the United States created, have assumed a character not dissimilar from that of the United States after World War I toward its wartime allies.

It is impossible for the developing countries indefinitely to continue servicing their accumulating debts to the United States and to the international lending institutions. They do not possess even nominal reparations payments on which to rely for part of their debt-service needs. And their borrowings have not been essentially autonomous decisions. Much of their borrowing has been for debt service recycling, increasing their capital obligations and magnifying the interest cost burdens as their debts have grown and interest rates have risen.

The proposal that all countries help amortize this dollar debt to the United States was a request for a net foreign exchange transfer from other developed nations, specifically from Europe and Japan, to America. Foreign governments were asked to realign their aid policies in such a manner as to help the United States recoup the costs of its investment in past programs of bilateral aid, including the cost of U.S. armaments. The entire world was to pay the economic cost of the American drive toward world domination.

The Peterson Report rightly observed that "keeping these countries on a short leash by emergency debt rescheduling operations does not show the necessary foresight. Countries with serious debt problems, in trying to avoid default, are likely to impose more internal and exchange restrictions and thereby intensify their future difficulties."[48] Yet the Report effectively insisted that these countries be kept on a leash, and that any given country's debt be rescheduled only if it demonstrates "by its plans and policies that it is pursuing a coherent development program of appropriate fiscal and financial policies," *i.e.*, deflation and a dismantling of whatever protectionist trade and monetary policies these countries might have enacted. They must open their economies to foreign trade and investment and must "show determination to develop" by reducing growth in their populations.

The Peterson Commission sought to prevent the African countries from accepting Associate Membership in the Common Market, urging the United States to retaliate by offering special tariff preferences to Latin America, foreclosing U.S. markets to Africa in commercial competition with Latin America. "If the United States cannot reach agreement with other industrial countries on this nondiscriminatory approach, it should unilaterally extend such tariff preferences to all developing countries except those that choose to remain in existing preferential trade agreements with industrial countries."[49] The Report specifically recommended that quotas be dropped on sugar, textiles and meat. It recognized that it would be too much to expect Europe, in the absence of advantage to it, to subscribe to the Inter-American Development Bank (IDB) or to participate in concessional lending to the more backward Latin American countries. The IDB, it concluded, would have to continue being funded by the United States, although it might borrow in Canada, Europe and Japan.

The U.S. aid program had thus taken on two new forms. First, it was directed against the Associate Members of the European Economic Community (EEC), and thus against Common Market Europe itself. Second, it had begun to move away from U.S. congressional funding toward borrowing in international capital markets, thus toward an existence independent of public will in the United States, *i.e.*, toward self-perpetuation as Cold War policy by the United States, whatever the changing attitude of the citizens and the Congress of the United States toward the Cold War. U.S. Government international finance capital had prepared to sever itself from domestic constraints. It was emerging as an autonomous institution capable of effectuating policy decisions without the need to secure the support of the American people.

U.S. strategists also moved to mobilize the non-Communist world's multinational aid organizations to serve U.S. ends rather than those of the aid-borrowing countries. The intent of this multilateralization of U.S. aid strategy was to transfer European, Japanese and Canadian resources to the United States. American representatives to the World Bank, for instance, asked that purchases of capital and services financed by its loans be made on the basis of each member nation's subscription to World Bank stock, not according to competitive bidding as in the past, that is, at a time when most of the competitive bids had come from U.S. suppliers.

As early as 1962 Frank Coffin, a State Department aid administrator, testified before a congressional subcommittee that the "aid efforts of other donor countries have an important indirect beneficial effect on the U.S. balance of payments that is probably roughly proportional to the amount of their aid."[50] This benefit to the U.S. balance of payments by foreign countries' multilateral aid, extended via the World Bank and other institutions, was now to be made more direct. In February 1971, U.S. officials asked that a World Bank loan to finance a Brazilian steel mill be tied to the purchase of 25 per cent U.S. goods and services, *i.e.*, in proportion to the U.S. Government's 25 per cent stock ownership in the Bank.[51]

The U.S. Government sought to use the World Bank much in the manner it had wielded bilateral aid, as a lever against foreign moves against U.S. investments. McNamara argued against the non-U.S. bank directors on loans to Bolivia and Guyana, on the ground that

> In both countries there are actual or impending cases of seizure of United States companies with unsettled questions of compensation. At issue, essentially, was the United States interpretation of the World Bank's own policy on the nationalization question. The long-standing bank policy is not to lend to any country that is in dispute with another member country over expropriation, where no "reasonable and speedy" attempt to negotiate a settlement is under way. Egypt was barred from loans for a long period after seizure of the Suez Canal under this policy, for example. In the debate in the bank's board of directors on the two recent cases, it is understood, the United States was largely isolated. It was the other directors, not the president of the bank, Robert S. McNamara, who disputed the arguments of Robert E. Wieczorowski, the United States director.[52]

The U.S. Government was claiming, in effect, that it could determine the price at which Anaconda's and Kennecott's Chilean copper mines could sell their copper to their U.S. parent companies – at so-called "producer's" prices, about one-third of the going world market price – but that foreign countries could not move to prevent this action by regulating, purchasing or otherwise "interfering" with foreign affiliates of U.S. firms.

Failure of the World Bank to acquiesce in serving as an arm of the U.S. State Department was instrumental in the nationalist opposition developing within the United States against aid in general. Representative of this attitude is that of John Connally, U.S. Secretary of the Treasury, who was reported to be

> taking a "get tough" stance with developing countries which expropriate U.S. investments without reimbursing the companies promptly and adequately. The crackdown showed up last week in this country's abstention on two votes for loans to Bolivia, one a $23 million loan from the World Bank and the other a $19 million loan from the Inter-American Development Bank . . . the U.S. was serving notice of its anger over Bolivia's nationalization of a $2 million operation of the Texas

based International Metals Corporation . . . Implicit in the vote abstention is the possibility of further U.S. retaliation against governments that take a cavalier attitude toward U.S. property rights. . . . The latest abstentions follow up two earlier abstentions on small loans, one of $6 million to Bolivia for cattle development from the World Bank, another a $5.4 million World Bank loan to Guyana to build dikes against the sea. Mr. Connally apparently hopes these abstentions will deter Guyana from its rumored intention to nationalize some bauxite mines owned by Reynolds Metals Corporation . . . Key congressmen are urging the administration not only to cast its own votes against loans to countries which take over U.S. investments, but to lobby actively within the international banks against such loans.[53]

Most of all, however, opposition to the U.S. foreign aid program developed within the American liberal community as the naked self-interest of American aid came to be perceived, and as its implicit conflict with the interests of aid-recipient countries – as distinct from the existing governing regimes of these countries – became apparent. By 1970 a Twentieth Century Fund study remarked that underlying the Rockefeller Report on Latin America "was the assumption on which U.S. policy in this hemisphere has traditionally been based: that the United States must continue to dominate Latin America and that any basic change in the established structure of Latin American society would be detrimental to the security interests of the United States."[54]

Professor Joseph Page, in reviewing this work, commented that the

rhetoric that promised Latin America a peaceful revolution implied the need for basic structural change that would inevitably create a certain amount of instability. Yet United States corporate officials, who were supposed to participate in the Alliance by exporting capital and technology to Latin America, held that unstable conditions amounted to an unfavorable business climate and threatened existing business interests. And the Pentagon, C.I.A. *et al.*, believed that instability jeopardized United States security. The history of the 1960s teaches that the political and social goals of the Alliance were quickly sacrificed whenever confronted with competing United States security or economic interests. As Levinson and de Onis forthrightly state: "If the Alliance is defined as a policy based on this proposition (that economic growth, social reform, and political democracy are mutually reinforcing aspects of an effective development program), the pertinent question becomes not whether it has failed but to what extent it has been attempted."[55]

The foreign aid program had come to play a perverse role in the development of foreign countries.

The U.S. aid program thus had come full circle. In its early postwar phase, 1945–52, it had been primarily multilateral, through UNRRA, the World Bank and, less visibly, through the IMF. This was a period when U.S. balance-of-payments outflows were desired to help alleviate the world's dollar shortage. U.S. aid was comprised largely of grants to Europe and of loans that were not tied. But between the late 1950s and 1970 U.S. foreign aid became increasingly bilateral in nature, increasingly tied to U.S. balance-of-payments aims. Its function no longer was to put U.S. dollars into the treasuries of foreign governments, but to dispose of surplus food and other exports produced in the United States and to obtain for the U.S. Government and its agencies cash payment in return.

In 1970 the U.S. Government earned $1.3 billion on its foreign aid programs, the amount by which its hard currency interest and principal repayments of $2 billion exceeded the $0.7 billion balance-of-payments cost of its new aid extensions. Toward the end of further aiding the U.S. balance of payments, the U.S. Government, in keeping with the Peterson Report's suggestion, moved once again toward multilateral forms of aid. But this time the organization of world aid was to be much different from that which had followed World War II. It was to become a program of compulsory burden-sharing by Europe, Japan and Canada in America's aid domination and militarization of the Third World. This time there was to be no balance-of-payments cost to the U.S. Government of its aid, which was to be tied to the greatest extent possible. In effect, multilateralization of U.S. foreign aid in the 1970s was to mean foreign governments paying the cost of American aid. Specifically, the flow of multilateral aid payments was to flow from the developed nations outside of the United States, to Latin America and other less developed countries, and from them to the United States.

9   GATT and the Double Standard

. . . we have at present the Means in our Power of treating with the Northern Potentates of *Europe* on very advantageous Terms: That is, we may signify to each of them (as we did formerly to *Portugal*) that in what Proportion soever, they will favour the Introduction of the *English* Manufactures into their Territories by the Repeal or Diminution of Taxes; in the same Proportion will we admit their Bar Iron, Hemp, Pitch, Tar, Turpentine, &c. into *Great-Britain.*

> Josiah Tucker, *A Series of Answers to Certain Popular*
> *Objections against Separating From the Rebellious Colonies,*
> *and Discarding them Entirely* . . . (Gloucester: 1776), p. 49

Unanimity as to the rules of conduct governing world trade hardly can be achieved in a system of nation-states in which each economy is at a different stage of development, and therefore has different needs and ideas as to what constitutes its self-interest. The most that can be accomplished is a pragmatic grouping of nations at a given point in time. Often the closest trade relations are found among complementary economies, for the more similar the specialization of production is among countries, the more rivalry tends to develop. Even among complementary economies, of course, a jockeying for gain develops as to the terms of trade, most notably between industrial economies, food and raw materials exporters.

Trading rules, tariff and quota systems, subsidies, public transport and other infrastructure spending, pricing and tax systems in such circumstances tend to reflect the uneven development of nations within the shifting world economic system. At the time any such set of rules are drawn up and generally accepted, it is almost impossible to anticipate the subsequent uneven rates and directions of development, or the new opportunities or changes that may occur in the economic environment. *Ad hoc* initiatives and responses therefore play an important role in shaping the world trade system.

The U.S. Congress has recognized this intuitively, and has persistently refused to abdicate its authority over the trading rules governing U.S. imports and exports. Each member of the House of Representatives and Senate is in almost constant touch with the management and labor representatives of local industries, which are as sensitive to changes in world trade as barometers are to changes in atmospheric pressure. In fact, political pressure on Congress by these local industries is the most sensitive measure the United States possesses regarding the real or anticipated effects of changes in the rules of international trade on domestic interests. It is the quintessence of commercial politics to translate these domestic pressures into positive or negative legislation.

To some extent this also is true of other nations, and becomes increasingly true as their industries expand and diversify. It is especially true of non-democratic countries, where the link between legislation and vested interests is undisguised and trade interests are openly subordinated to those of industry and the state. On purely abstract grounds, one therefore cannot expect any economy with any claim to national independence to accept dictation from without, even from an international body of which it is a member, regarding the terms on which it will trade with the rest of the world.

Permanent agreement among nations as to the terms of international trade is ruled out by the very fact of nationhood. Only if one trading nation is dominant over all others in all significant respects can such agreement be imposed. The terms on which it would do this deny the autonomy of other nations, and thus of nationhood as a concept. Such terms therefore are inherently transitory, unless the world system rigidifies and shrinks.

The position of one nation being dominant over all others did exist when World War II ended, to be sure. The United States which was unquestioned as to dominance and planners of the postwar world order factored this into their world designs as though it would remain a constant.

Congress was more dubious, more realistic perhaps. It listened more intently to the arguments of local industries in the electoral areas than to the administrators and planners in Washington. After all, it was in these electoral districts that votes were gathered, not in Moravia, Tanganyika, France or Britain. It also was in these electoral districts that the effects of proposed rules for world trade on U.S. domestic industry could best be anticipated. Even if these local and special-interest anticipations were incorrect, they still needed to be voiced if the harvest of votes were to be reaped.

For the United States this ruled out absolutely free trade from the start, even though it seemed an essential policy to maintain U.S. dominance in the world. Such dominance was desired by local interests as much as by national politicians. But its economic cost could not be equalized over every American industry or local factory. Unanimous industrial support envisaged gains for every interest, not gains by some and losses by others. But free trade in the absolute sense would have involved losses for some, especially in the farming areas but also for steel, autos and other "old" industries. Unanimity of economic support for free trade thus could not be obtained politically. Congress was split on the issue, and the Truman Administration had to bow before this fact.

What U.S. planners originally had intended for the postwar world, with the hearty support of Britain, was a system of regulated free trade binding upon all signatory countries, including the United States itself. In November 1945 the government's trade strategists, in conjunction with the first massive postwar U.S. loan to Britain, published a report entitled *Proposals for Expansion of World Trade and Employment* calling for establishment of an International Trade Organization (ITO). This statements of intent was elaborated in September 1946 in the *Suggested Charter for an International Trade Organization of the United Nations*. The first official ITO negotiations took place in London the following month, and in March 1948 the *Draft Charter for an International Trade Organization* was signed in Havana. President Truman presented it to Congress for approval early in 1949.

Support for the ITO was widespread in the United States, but was by no means unanimous. Organized labor viewed it with suspicion, industries traditionally protected by tariffs and import quotas with open hostility. The most protectionist sectors were chemicals, dairy products, livestock, nut growers, glassware, woolens, independent petroleum producers, rayon, and pulp and paper. Organized labor joined with management in some industries to oppose the ITO through the National Labor-Management Council on Foreign Trade and the A. F. of L.'s Wage Earners' Protective Conference. Their views were echoed by the American Tariff League.[1]

In addition to this special-interest pleading, ideological resistance was based on political concepts as to America's place in a changing world. Senator Millikin urged the United States to obtain voting power in ITO equivalent to its share of world trade.[2] Others depicted the ITO as "a superstate capable of directing American trade policy."[3] The fears of free trade, even if regulated, thus were based on many separate interests, each of whose arguments had a certain logic.

The first steps toward what eventually would become the General Agreement on Tariffs and Trade (GATT), the world body to regulate international commerce, were taken under circumstances that bode ill for its future. After 1948, U.S. participation in international agreements to regulate world trade, or even in negotiations along these lines, was constrained by considerations reflecting powerful special interests, as well as by rising economic nationalism that quickly overcame the free trade idealism of 1945.

The Trade Agreement Act of 1945 had been drawn up in the knowledge that recovery by the devastated nations and restoration of world trade were in American interests as well as those of the world. This was the basic idea that underlay that year's *Proposals for Expansion of World Trade and Employment*. The Trade Agreement Act, however, was susceptible to amendment. Such amendment has been recurrent as the Act has been renewed by Congress periodically. Each renewal had afforded wider opportunities for domestic industries and corporations to claim injury from the importation of specific products under existing tariff and trade arrangements.

One example occurred in 1963, when the United States raised its tariffs on imported sheet glass, principally Belgian glass, although importation from Communist countries was also involved. The new duties followed Tariff Commission hearings held in response to complaints by the domestic glass industry. The European Common Market retaliated by raising its own tariffs on poultry imports from the United States, poultry being selected because the value of EEC imports from the United States in this category approximated the loss by Belgium of exports of sheet glass to the United States. The episode became known in America as the Chicken War of 1963.

Events at the genesis of what was to become GATT therefore were not propitious. In fact, although GATT is a device of American creation, the United States never even became a full treaty member. Its participation was by presidential order only, as Congress refused to relinquish its authority to rule upon foreign trade agreements. Consequently, U.S. domestic law predominates over international agreements on trade relations. This is of course the antithesis of international treaty law, which takes precedence over municipal law in all instances. Tentative agreements reached between U.S. trade representatives and the general GATT membership could be repudiated by Congress and often were, most notoriously in the case of the promised removal of the American Selling Price (ASP) system of tariff valuation which concluded the Kennedy Round of negotiated tariff reductions in 1967.

From the outset, therefore, the U.S. position on liberalizing world trade has involved a double standard. America has insisted that other countries adhere to fixed principles of free trade, modified only by international agreements on tariffs and import quotas, while it alone is permitted to abrogate those principles and agreements unilaterally, whenever Congress shall so determine. This double standard understandably was unwelcome to other countries.

Negotiations for the establishment of the ITO proceeded with much less smoothness and unanimity than had the Bretton Woods financial and aid agreements. An immediate sticking point was the refusal by other nations to permit voting power in the ITO to be allocated in proportion to each nation's share of world trade. They insisted that each member nation be given one vote only, making it impossible for the United States unilaterally to dictate or block ITO policies. This distinguished the proposed world trade agreements from U.S. dominance and veto power in the IMF and the World Bank. As late as 1971 the United States still was trying to demand non-equality even in GATT, a far less sweeping institution than the ITO was planned to be.

Had one been fully alert in 1948 to the implications of the double standard that U.S. officials tried to build into international agreements, and especially to the control functions of the United States in the IMF and World Bank as compared to their absence over the proposed ITO, the latter's failure could have been predicted with fair accuracy. But the necessity for such prediction seemed absent at a time when almost every international action by the United States not only seemed benevolent but was indeed tinged with benevolence. And yet even though most nations were recipients of massive U.S. assistance, they were well aware of the power function that eventually emerges to dominate critical actions by nations. This power function is the essence of economic diplomacy. Recognizing that American benevolence was genuine and American concern over the future of the world no less than their own, other countries nonetheless revealed their disbelief in the persistence of such national generosity by refusing to yield their equality in voting power in the proposed ITO.

This refusal has been of critical importance. In hindsight one can interpret it as evidence that the position of power reached by the United States in 1945–51 was the maximum it could attain in the world. America appeared all-powerful in the military, political and economic spheres, but the magnitude of this power obscured the fact that it nonetheless was limited. In fact, it had reached the limit. Future U.S. world power could be equal to or less than its relative power status of 1945–51, but could not exceed it. Even to maintain its unique position of relative strength, the U.S. economy would have to evolve in such a manner and degree as coincided with the evolution of all other nations in a position of dependency.

It probably was this perception that other nations in time would recover, and by doing so would be in a position to challenge America economically, that motivated Senator Millikin to demand U.S. voting power in the ITO equivalent to a veto privilege. Other nations would have to be so constrained as to leave U.S. economic supremacy unaffected, whatever their own needs and whatever the benevolence or otherwise of U.S. intentions. If the future offered zero probability of an increase in America's relative strength, the corollary was that relative U.S. power in the world had become diminishable, not able to be increased by U.S. will, and indeed with little likelihood that it could remain unchanged.

At the time, it seemed that this was not the case with regard to control of the world monetary system, given the pace of development of the less developed countries. The United States has remained in a position to dictate the functioning of the International Monetary Fund, by virtue of its veto power in that institution, the magnitude of its gold reserves, its once highly favorable balance of payments that gave it freedom of action within the international financial system, and most of all by the fact that other countries built dollar dependency into their own central bank systems and international reserve policies. This role was implicit in the dollar's role as key currency. The United States likewise created and dominated the World Bank because of its then unique capacity to lend and export investment and development capital in hard currency. In the IMF and the World Bank the United States could and did obtain effective veto power and the power to initiate the functioning of these critically important world bodies. No meaningful complaint was heard from Europe, Asia or the developing nations over the U.S. power to veto and initiate in these institutions because such power rested on the realities of the situation at the time. Actions initiated in these international bodies by the United States were largely synonymous with the needs and wishes of other member countries.

In the financial and development-lending spheres, American economic initiative in the years following World War II reflected the power relations existing at the end of that war. It has been and remains the object of American policy to preserve that power relationship, even though circumstances have evolved, at first gradually but with perceptible acceleration over the years, in ways that have eroded American supremacy. The facts have changed, and the realities of economic relationships and international diplomacy have changed with them.

U.S. policy has changed correspondingly, but in the reverse direction. Its purpose has been to preserve, and if necessary to attempt to restore, the degree of U.S. supremacy that once corresponded with reality, but which has grown dissonant with the changing realities of the world economy as time has passed.

Whether consciously or not, the double standard proposed for the ITO – the obligation by other nations to adhere to its rules, in the face of freedom by the United States to violate them – proved essential toward maintenance of American dominance. But the substantive economic relationships among nations were shifting. No U.S. strategists spelled out an analysis of the global future in terms of maintaining or relinquishing the 1948 equations of strength, for this would have reflected a prescience nowhere else displayed by them. They simply wanted always to be in a position of control so that they could respond to shifting circumstances in an *ad hoc* way that reflected U.S. national interests, whatever surprises or more underlying developments might occur.

Understanding the proposed structure of the ITO is essential to understanding the way in which the United States has conducted its ongoing campaign not so much to attain power but to maintain it. The inability of U.S. diplomats to obtain majority voting power in the ITO alarmed some Americans, who argued that it appeared "certain that the United States would consistently be on the losing end of arguments, with debtor countries, or control-minded governments, or underdeveloped countries, or countries in balance-of-payments difficulties, combining to defeat it on major issues."[4]

These fears were not without foundation. In agriculture, for example, other countries shared the United States' insistence upon maintaining autonomy in national farm policies, including tariff protection. The Latin American countries insisted at the 1945 Chapultepec Conference that their infant industries remain protected after the return to peace. They were just as adamant at the 1948 Havana Conference, as indicated by the assertion of Ramon Beteta Quintana, head of Mexico's delegation, that "we recognize the convenience of international economic cooperation, but we still must reject any plan to suppress all protective tariffs, because that would mean the economic destruction of the weak nations while entrenching the commercial supremacy of the stronger countries."[5]

Of more immediate concern to some nations was the fact that the U.S. economy was absorbing their gold reserves at an alarming rate. As early as 1942 foreign countries had succeeded in obtaining League of Nations endorsement of "the absolute necessity of adapting commercial policies to the circumstances influencing national balances of payments." In the ITO negotiations Britain spearheaded pressures to draw up a balance-of-payments escape clause that would enable countries to limit imports if these threatened to bring about a balance-of-payments crisis. This was inserted in the Draft Charter of the ITO over the opposition of U.S. negotiators.

Other nations wanted to emulate the U.S. policy of fostering domestic employment. The result was Article 21, para. 4(b) of the ITO Draft Charter, "which appeared to mean that no country could be required to alter policies directed toward the maintenance of full employment or the promotion of economic development even if these created balance-of-payments difficulties. This looked like a perfect loophole for the indefinite retention of controls, especially since most of the [U.S.] businessmen believed that government-sponsored full employment policies were bound, if they worked, to be inflationary and so to exercise pressure on foreign exchange reserves."[6]

Largely as a result of both U.S. and foreign desires to insert provisions circumventing the Draft Charter's free trade principles, plans to create the trade organization faltered. To start with, its rules would have required too many changes in U.S. statutes to be acceptable to the Congress. "Of course," summarized Diebold, "the United States was never prepared to accept the pure principles of the ITO in all its own commercial behavior. Loopholes of American design were built into the Charter to permit the use of import quotas in connection with domestic farm programs and the withdrawal of tariff concessions if imports damaged domestic producers. Shipping was excluded from the Charter largely because the United States was not prepared to alter its subsidy policy."[7]

Certainly the Export-Import Bank Act of 1945 violated ITO ideals. "Three conditions of Export-Import Bank loans seem to run contrary to the general American policy of liberalizing world trade and finance on a non-discriminatory basis," observed the Council on Foreign Relations.

First, the loans were tied; borrowers had to spend them in the United States and for specified purposes . . . Tying was not required by law, but the Bank's officials apparently felt that it carried out the intent of Congress, which established the Bank to make loans "for the purpose of aiding the financing and facilitating of exports" from the United States . . . Second, Public Resolution 17 of the 73rd Congress requires that goods bought with the proceeds of U.S. Government loans be transported on American ships unless such vessels are not available in sufficient numbers or in sufficient tonnage capacity or on necessary sailing schedules or at reasonable rates. In addition to discriminating against foreign shipping, full application of the resolution would increase foreign dollar requirements at a time when they were already very high and when one of the main purposes of our lending was to help overcome that difficulty.[8]

But only Norway complained and this provision was passed, although pressure to oblige Eximbank borrowers to insure their cargoes exclusively through U.S. companies was defeated.

To obtain compliance by foreign countries in the proposed new trade rules despite the extent to which they favored U.S. producers, American trade negotiators warned that it would be to the world's advantage to sign the agreements before an impatient Congress enacted protectionist legislation that might close off many sectors of the U.S. market to foreign producers. And indeed, the 1949 recession in the United States provided a momentum that prompted congressional opposition to free trade. Outbreak of the Korean War in 1950 and associated government controls over most areas of the economy, especially over imports and exports, ended U.S. interest in bringing the ITO into being. Mobilization of the U.S. economy, with all its controls, was at odds with almost every principle avowed in the ITO Charter. In 1950, at the Torquay conference on trade and trading rules, U.S. negotiators put it quite plainly that the State Department and President Truman had agreed that "the proposed Charter for an International Trade Organization shall not be resubmitted to Congress."[9] ITO was stillborn. In the words of William Diebold, Jr:

Rearmament not only disrupts trade and checks efforts to remove barriers. It substitutes a whole set of different criteria for the principles embodied in multilateral trade agreements such as GATT. The flow of strategic materials must be controlled, not set free. Prices may have to be manipulated, not left to the market. Cost must sometimes be disregarded. In a time of cold war, non-discrimination becomes strategically unwise and insistence on it would be stultifying. When last renewing the Trade Agreements Act, Congress excluded the countries of the Soviet orbit from its benefits by directing that American tariff concessions to them be withdrawn and that they be denied most-favored nation treatment. In trade terms the consequences were not great or the resulting sanctions very strong. The gesture was largely emotional. But the denial of the principle of non-discrimination goes much further, especially in the matter of export controls. ". . . For if there is anything that strategic considerations demand," says Professor Viner, "it is discrimination in the treatment of different countries, according as they are friends, or foes, or would-be neutrals."[10]

Not all observers believed that war situations were necessarily detrimental to opening U.S. foreign trade. Raymond Vernon viewed it as "illogical that nations should raise trade barriers instead of lowering them at a time when a more effective international division of labor would enable them to carry the burden of rearmament more easily."[11] But war is a political exercise, not an economic one, and there seemed to be logic in the Fortress America attitude that saw the birth of a defense-oriented energy policy and government stockpiling in response to the Paley Report on America's raw materials needs and shortages in time of war.

The first attempt to establish international rules of trade and its corresponding enforcement agencies had failed. Yet the negotiations and arguments among nations and the wrangling among the U.S. Congress, the administration and the special interest groups made clear to the world, in ways it came to accept, that a double standard must exist in any formal world body charged with regulating economic affairs. Rules binding all other nations must not necessarily bind the United States. Other nations must adhere, by the equivalent of treaty law, to the regulations imposed by such a body. The United States could be bound by them only to the extent that Congress permitted, and this could vary if Congress so willed. Effectively, therefore, further moves toward establishment of such a world organization must accept this double standard as a precondition. In mathematical terms, the conduct of other nations was to be a constant, that of the United States a variable. Only on these conditions could the United States join a world body to govern international trading practices, and without the United States such a body could neither be brought into being nor function if it were created. This amounted to a repudiation by the United States of the principles it itself had proposed for ITO in 1945, 1946 and 1948. Something much more limited, less principled and more truly reflective of the realities of the postwar world would have to take the place of the ITO. Otherwise, nothing.

Perhaps by coincidence, possibly by design, such an agency was ready to hand. An Interim Commission for the ITO had been set up in 1947 as a subjunct of ITO, intended to be purely technical and temporary. Pending ratification of the 1948 Draft Charter for an International Trade Organization, coordination of interim trade negotiations was effected through a working agency called the General Agreement on Tariffs and Trade (GATT) founded in Geneva in 1947. It occupied the ITO offices, used the Interim Commission for ITO as its secretariat, and acted generally as an advance installment on the ITO charter. It sponsored tariff negotiation meetings in Geneva in 1947 (with twenty-three countries attending), in Annecy in 1949 (with forty countries) and in Torquay in 1950–51. It was left to this forum to pick up the pieces of what remained of the ITO. After the United States rejected the Havana Charter, GATT was established formally as a governing world body in 1951.

At the outset it was understood that the GATT would deal only with mutual tariff concessions, not with such problematic issues as quotas and other non-tariff barriers to international trade. Because the highest U.S. trade barriers were mainly of the non-tariff type, U.S. import policy was less affected by GATT tariff bargaining than was the trade of most other countries, which generally employed straightforward *ad valorem* tariffs. Thus, by the end of the Kennedy Round, world *ad valorem* tariffs had been reduced from their 1947 levels in accordance with early U.S. strategy, leaving America's own non-tariff barriers legally intact! Most other countries had not put such barriers in place. Those enacted since 1947 presumably were in violation of GATT's "grandfather" clause, which permitted pre-existing non-tariff trade barriers to be maintained but forbade new ones to be enacted. Here again the United States in 1971 would challenge the legality of such actions by other countries, specifically by the Common Market.

Nor were GATT's narrow tariff negotiations related to the broader problems of economic development, employment policy and the related social norms to which they were linked in the ITO Draft Charter. This effectively tabled some of the most important escape clauses that the less developed countries had written into the ITO charter. Indeed, when Norway proposed that the GATT agreements should be amended to include the ITO charter, or at least its statement of principles, U.S. delegates promptly squelched the suggestion.[12] The result was to confine the GATT negotiations substantially to mutual tariff reductions among the industrialized nations, leaving less developed countries to play only a passive role. They had little to offer and too much to ask.

GATT's articles of agreement comprise thirty-five rules and escape clauses. The first article forms the foundation of GATT itself by calling for universal Most Favored Nation (MFN) treatment of all trading parties. This is the Open Door principle of nondiscrimination, or what has been termed the Law of Commercial Supremacy. Some existing tariff preferences were permitted to be retained, however, typified by the Empire Preference policies that characterized the Sterling and Franc Areas.

Because of the double standard, the United States has not been required to adhere strictly to the MFN rule. Tied-aid clauses in almost all U.S. foreign aid agreements since the mid-1960s, as well as special restrictions on shipping and proposed U.S. tariff preferences for the products of developing countries, have been permissible for the United States but illegal for other GATT members. It may be argued, however, that the European Common Market also violated GATT principles in extending Associate Membership to Mediterranean and African countries with which its member nations had centuries-long trading ties based upon their colonial past, and in offering Associate Member status to still other countries. In practice, therefore, the double standard may be somewhat less double than appears. It certainly is less influential than the United States initially intended.

Article VII of the GATT provides that valuation of imports for customs purposes shall be based on their actual invoice value, not on the value of similar goods of domestic origin or on other arbitrary valuations. This article makes the United States, with its ASP system of tariff valuation, a major violator of the rules that others must obey. The European Common Market, by contrast, follows the rules of the Brussels Convention which prohibits practices that artificially increase customs duties. Abandonment of the ASP system was to have represented the first major removal of a non-tariff barrier to international trade negotiated within GATT, as part of the chemicals agreement which concluded the Kennedy Round. Popularized at the time as having special symbolic value, it came instead to symbolize American intransigence on the issue of non-tariff barriers to imports.

Article XI calls for the elimination of quantitative trade restrictions such as quotas, although it leaves some exceptions concerning agricultural trade. These escape clauses were inserted at U.S. insistence, but have not saved it from being in violation of the article. Paragraph XI(2) permits price-support programs and their attendant import quotas to be applied only "to restrict domestic production and marketing," not to increase sales. This obviously has not been the case with U.S. farm support programs, which have enormously increased U.S. farm output. In March 1955 the United States obtained a general GATT waiver allowing it to impose whatever import quotas or tariffs it might desire to implement its agricultural programs, but this hardly was an equitable transfiguration of GATT rules. As one specialist commented: "The broad, general terms of this waiver have . . . created a situation in which other countries feel that the United States has, more or less, been freed of the obligations under Art. XI, whereas they are being requested, and, in particular, requested by the

United States, to live up to these obligations . . . harm[ing] our case for obtaining liberalization of trade-restricting practices of other countries."[13] In fact, section 22 of the Agricultural Adjustment Act was amended in 1951 to make the imposition of import quotas mandatory whenever imports might interfere with America's agricultural price supports, regardless of any "trade agreement or any other international agreement heretofore or hereafter entered into by the United States." A rider to that year's Defense Production Act (s. 104) broadened the imposition of quotas to cover dairy products and other farm commodities.

Article XII is the balance-of-payments escape clause that foreign countries managed to retain from the ITO Draft Charter in exchange for their promise that any special trade restrictions they might impose to alleviate payments difficulties would be relaxed the moment their international solvency permitted. This shifted the problem of defining adequate balance-of-payments status from the GATT to the IMF, where U.S. influence was greater because of the weighted voting system. The early U.S. desire to maximize its voting weight within GATT was expressed by Vernon in his observation that "the United States carried a weighted vote in the Fund, representing about a third of the total vote in that body, whereas it voted as only one among a score of nations in the GATT. It was felt, therefore, that the scope of GATT's balance-of-payments discussions ought to be confined to such narrowly circumscribed issues as whether a nation was relaxing its restrictions as far as its reserves permitted, whether it was taking adequate measures to minimize commercial damage, and like questions."[14]

Countries with balance-of-payments deficits, of unspecified size, were permitted under Article XII of the GATT to use some import quotas to conserve foreign exchange needed to purchase vital imports. This article was carried into the GATT regulations partly as a result of the German balance-of-payments crisis of 1950. Although the United States viewed this article with disfavor, it was itself moving in 1950 to violate GATT regulations by imposing new quotas on cheese imports. In fact, many countries used Article XII, especially its section 3(b), as a back door device "to encourage expansion of internal agricultural production and restrict agricultural imports to the quantities, if any, by which their internal production fell short of internal demand. By doing this, they largely disregarded cost differentials . . . much of Western Europe's and Japan's postwar systems of agricultural support and protection was built up behind, or even by means of, trade controls originally imposed on balance-of-payments grounds."[15] These trade controls were discriminatory against

U.S. exports, but they were only an emulation of America's own agricultural practices.

Article XIII prescribes that when quantitative restrictions are employed, they must be nondiscriminatory in nature so as to facilitate attainment of an import mix that approaches as closely as possible the shares that supplier nations might be expected to obtain in the absence of such trade restrictions. However, U.S. representatives have demanded of Europe that American farmers be guaranteed a constant share of the British and Common Market grain markets. This would result in a product mix of imports quite different from that which open market forces might bring about in an evolving world economy. The United States would be made a guaranteed supplier of grains to Europe, leaving Canada, Australia, Argentina and other countries with unconsumable surpluses, except for purchases by Russia, China and other Communist countries. U.S. fruits and other products would be similarly affected.

Continental Europe refused to concede this perpetual share of its food market. Britain accepted the American proposal for its own market, but this became a major problem blocking its entry into the European Community. Meanwhile, U.S. initiatives in 1971–72 to normalize relations with China and the Soviet Union reflected in large part the need to find new markets for U.S. farm products.

Article XIV deals with exceptions to the preceding rule of nondiscrimination in levying quotas. It permits a nation accumulating inconvertible foreign currency, *i.e.*, one that can be used only to pay for imports from an aid donor, to give preferences to imports from that country. This was one of the articles designed to maintain the Franc and Sterling Areas. It could have caused problems in the 1970s when the United States granted import preference to Latin American goods. Most Latin American countries run a payments deficit with the United States, and many of their currencies are inconvertible, in particular the counterpart funds held by the U.S. Government for its P.L. 480 sales. Use of these currencies to promote Latin American preference under this clause represents a return to the blocked-currency practices of the 1930s and the early years after World War II.

Article XVII calls for nondiscriminatory treatment on the part of government enterprises. This article recalls the original U.S. proposal for the ITO, which urged that nations engaged in state trading should base their purchases from abroad solely on commercial considerations of price, quality and marketability. The United States at that time requested that the centrally planned economies, with their state monopolies over foreign trade, agree to buy a stipulated amount of foreign goods each year. This was in striking contrast to the Buy American policies employed by the United States at the federal, state and local levels. California, for instance, has long engaged in practices that have drawn vigorous complaints from Canada. And at the height of the protectionist flurry centering on the Mills bill in November 1970, the Washington D.C. transit authority announced that it would give a 15 per cent preference to U.S. suppliers in the competitive bids it was inviting for the projected expansion of its transport system. Other countries also employ domestic favoritism, of course, but have not loudly demanded that it be relinquished by their trading partners.

Article XVIII is the GATT's infant industry clause, and recognizes the need for less developed countries to develop industries that otherwise might be restricted by the free trade policies called for in the other articles of agreement. However, prior approval of the other contracting parties to the GATT is required for such tariffs and other trade restrictions to be imposed.

Article XIX is an import injury clause permitting countries to take emergency action on imports of particular products if injury to home producers results from unforeseen developments attributed to negotiated tariff concessions. Here again there must be consultation with the affected parties. This clause has considerably reduced the value of the tariff concessions the United States has offered its trading partners, especially under the broader interpretations given in the language of repeated congressional amendments of the U.S. Foreign Trade Act. Despite the fact that these escape clauses taken together have favored the United States in most areas, they have paved the way for such tariff reduction negotiations as the Dillon Round of 1960–62 and the Kennedy Round of 1964–67.

All this ground was lost in 1971 when the U.S. Government demanded of the world at large a guaranteed annual $13 billion improvement in the U.S. balance of payments. There was to be no more nonsense about free trade. The world was to accept, as though by natural law, that the United States be in a permanent state of balance-of-payments surplus, and that *ipso facto* the rest of the world must hold itself in perpetual dependency upon the United States.

The first step was to embargo gold payments by the United States. The dollar was made unconvertible, which meant that more than $50 billion of short-term liabilities to foreigners owed by the United States on public and private account could not be used as claims on America's gold stock. They could be used to buy U.S. exports, to pay current obligations to U.S. public and private creditors, to invest in government and corporate securities or even to buy control of American businesses in sectors where this was not proscribed by law. The cloudy legal status of America's huge foreign indebtedness had obvious Buy American implications. Excluding outright repudiation of its foreign debt, but including its possible amalgamation into a new world monetary base, there is an automatic creation of effective demand for U.S. goods abroad, circuitously or not. The alternative was to swap one dollar obligation for another *ad infinitum*, an economically meaningless exercise. Taking the long view, the gold embargo created an export potential for the United States capable of overriding tariff barriers anywhere. The alternative was for foreigners to accept a total loss on their holdings of U.S. obligations, including their bank deposits held in the United States.

The GATT's articles of agreement constrained it from ruling on such non-tariff hindrances to free trade and indeed on trade matters of broad conceptual importance. But America's actions were illegal under the IMF's rules. Even if they were not, they created effective trading preferences in favor of the United States as opposed to the commercial interests of other nations, at variance with the spirit and intent of the GATT and of the concepts inherent in the originally U.S.-proposed ITO.

Even this was not the full extent of moves in 1971 to protect U.S. foreign trade. The United States insisted that foreign currencies be revalued upward, by 10 per cent for the Deutschmark, 12 to 15 per cent for Japan's yen, and varying rates for all other currencies significant in world trade and finance. Properly interpreted, this amounted to a 10 per cent tariff on German imports to the United States, a 12 to 15 per cent tariff on Japanese imports, and so on, while simultaneously granting an equivalent subsidy for U.S. exports.

It had the additional effect, if not the outright intent, of bringing the trade of other nations into great confusion. Contracted sales prices among them, unless accompanied by fixed-parity agreements, became largely incalculable as foreign exchange rates moved in unpredictable amounts and directions. Barter deals accordingly began to proliferate, such as initially had been developed for trade between the West and the Soviet Union and its satellites.

In addition a temporary 10 per cent tariff surcharge was levied on all dutiable imports not already subject to agreed import quotas. Special tariff agreements, such as the pact between the United States and Canada over the importation of Canadian-built automobiles in exchange for Canada's permission for U.S. auto companies to expand their investments in Canada, were simply disregarded. The surcharge was applied to imports from Canada in spite of the agreements that had been reached by such intensive negotiation between the two governments. GATT did not die; it was smashed.

The U.S. Government extended wage and price controls over most of the economy, violating agreements between management and labor over wages, pensions, working conditions, cost-of-living clauses and other matters affecting employee compensation and product pricing. The purpose was to foster the export potential of the United States by keeping the rate of cost and price increases, already below those of most industrialized nations, still further below them.

The United States declared that this set of policies would be maintained until such time as other countries collectively guaranteed a $13 billion improvement in the annual U.S. balance of payments. This was 2.5 times the annual excess of U.S. exports and re-exports over general imports in 1946–50, excluding capital movements.[16] On trade account the United States in 1971 thus demanded not only that the surplus it had enjoyed in the early postwar years be restored, but that the rest of the world should give its exporters something approximating what this world trading power might have become by 1971 if other nations had not developed into powerful economies in their own right. Stated another way, the rest of the world was supposed to enable America to export enough of its food and manufactures to generate the foreign exchange needed by its industrialists and financiers to buy controlling shares in the major industries in Europe, Asia and elsewhere.

The clock was to be turned back. Other countries were once more to become, and to remain indefinitely, markets for U.S. products but not suppliers. They were to serve as hosts for U.S. private investors, but with no counterpart in the form of U.S. imports of the products of the foreign subsidiaries of American firms. To make matters worse, these foreign investments were to be given free of charge to America under its demand for a perpetually guaranteed balance-of-payments surplus.

Economic imperialism has produced some weird and almost incomprehensible results in its history, but never before has a bankrupt nation dared insist that its bankruptcy become the foundation of world economic policy. But U.S. officials now insisted that because of their nation's bankruptcy on international account, all other nations must warp their economies toward transferring its bankruptcy to themselves, stultifying their industries and paying tribute to the beggar. Like the ITO before it, the GATT no longer served the interests of the United States. As ITO was aborted, so the GATT was destroyed, whatever the legal pretense of its status. The world body whose functions had coincided with political and economic realities in 1951 became a contradiction with the American reality of 1971. The United States did not hesitate to reject it and to reassert its right to act unilaterally at all times.

10 Dollar Domination through the International Monetary Fund, 1945–46

What occurred after World War II was nothing less than an inversion of the law of nations as it had been evolving for centuries, at least on the part of Europe if not that of the United States. The most basic principle of international law is that nations are equals with regard to their rights and policy-making autonomy. In addition to this legal principle is a basic behavioral law of diplomacy: in a world of nation-states it is unnatural for any nation to abrogate its international position voluntarily. Treaties and agreements are arrived at by a process of negotiation and trade-offs among governments that are politically if not economically equal, and seek to maintain the right to manage their own economies. Liability therefore lies with Europe, and with Britain in particular, for acquiescing so passively to American designs for the postwar world. Europe demurred from pressing its self-interest at any point where this conflicted with that of the United States. Exhausted by war, it voluntarily abrogated what had been more than four centuries of imperial ambitions.

To American diplomats the United States simply was living up to its historic destiny as world leader when they formulated their plans for the postwar world at Bretton Woods. In their idealism they anticipated that the breakup of nationhood – at least on the part of foreign countries – would inaugurate a world economy of peaceful interdependence and perhaps even altruism. They did not ponder how alien this concept was to the basic principle of nationhood, that no nation can be expected to relinquish its independence with regard to economic policy-making. Nonetheless, America now asked, and received, European capitulation on every major point of postwar relations.

In an important sense Europe had began to relinquish its independence when it agreed to repay America's war loans after World War I. To be sure, a debt was a debt, or so it seemed necessary to claim in order to preserve the sanctity of Europe's property relations in general. Still, Europe had the option to renounce the world debtor–creditor system to the extent that it encroached on their options to manage their own economies. It could have bargained with the United States as follows: "It is in your own interest to retain us as a market for your exports and as a source of profits on your international investments. But we cannot remain so if you insist that we repay our debts while, at the same time, you deny us the opportunity to raise the requisite dollars by exporting goods to you. If you do not change either your tariff or your financial policy, we will be forced to withdraw from the system as it now stands." Europe did not draw this line, and it was left for the United States itself to do so in the 1930s, in an attempt to salvage at least the most creditorworthy of its loans (*e.g.*, that to Finland).

Britain, the nation most able to lead a non-American world at that time, instead led Europe's capitulation to American Inter-Ally debt demands. It was the first nation to reach an agreement to repay the debts, and this seemed to oblige its European allies to reach similar agreements, although most of them were able to obtain better terms.

Why did Britain do this? The main reason seems to be that it put its domestic class and property bias over international considerations, as did other European nations. Previously, foreign policy had tended to take the lead in shaping domestic policy. This was how Europe's central governments usurped the rights of parliamentary democracy during the period of colonial empire-building, 1870–1914. But now the reverse was true. Europe placed its notions of the sanctity of debt – in this case its own debts, behind which lay ultimately the idea of property itself – above the goal of maintaining its own national economic independence and viability. The result fragmented the European continent, forcing its nations to act selfishly, one by one, as a penalty for not having acted in concert vis-à-vis the United States.

The events that had followed World War I seemed to be repeating themselves after World War II. Britain once again led its sterling bloc into the dollar sphere instead of taking the lead in building an independent united Europe. It could have confronted the United States with the following dilemma: "If you insist in breaking up our empire as a condition for lending us the dollars necessary to keep us afloat under laissez-faire conditions, we must choose to withdraw from the Open Door commercial system you are proposing. We prefer to remain on terms of equality of power with you. We are sure you would prefer to make us a gift instead of a loan, in order to prevent our reverting to economic autarchy. We will not join an integrated world system on your terms, for these terms conflict with the most vital principles of our own economic independence. We will maintain our Commonwealth tariff preferences, and we will raise the funds necessary to balance our international payments by devaluing our currency."

Britain did not say this. Instead, it acquiesced to American pressure. Having used free trade policies for two centuries to break down foreign tariff barriers to its own manufactures, Britain now permitted this same rhetoric and strategy to be exercised on itself by U.S. diplomats. Run largely by academics, the British Labour Party ended up believing the free trade doctrines that the nation's economists had used to convince less industrialized economies not to go to the expense of protecting the economic potential of their own populations. Believing this mythology, British negotiators acted almost as if America's gain was a gain for own economy.

British thinking perhaps had become enslaved by its own slogans, etched into the minds of its college students over two centuries. Perhaps its leaders had, at this critical juncture in history, come to abhor the violent results of national drives and rivalries, *e.g.*, two world wars. Perhaps Britain felt that U.S. power was at one remove, or at least ensured the reestablishment of English-speaking domination over the world's surface. Whatever its reasons, Britain once again led Europe's march into the American economic orbit, leaving U.S. diplomats to set the terms of entry for better or worse.

It was only natural for American diplomats to start by putting forth a strategy for the world to be impelled mainly by U.S. economic drives. That is the nature of national diplomacy. But it also seemed to be the essence of nationhood for other countries to translate their own self-interest into national policy, perhaps making *quid pro quo* trade-offs with the United States to achieve some fair balance of benefits. This was not done. One hardly can find an American conspiracy to defraud Europe, any more than its earlier request for its Inter-Ally loans to be repaid at 100 cents on the dollar. Europe simply did not attempt to bargain, in a situation where hard bargaining was called for.

Perhaps it believed that a new world state was at hand, to be conceived under U.S. leadership and purging the particular national rivalries that had torn asunder earlier periods of world history. Perhaps this is why Britain opened its Sterling Area to U.S. exports and relinquished its historical trade position in Latin America. It even transformed its $14 billion in sterling balances from advance payments on postwar exports, which could have been restricted by blocking the balances, into a generalized debt which could be used to finance Sterling Area purchases of U.S. exports. The British Labour Party boycotted the cause of continental European integration in order to integrate its economy and diplomacy with that of the United States, all under no threat of physical duress.

Here was something unique in the experience of nations, a shift in the momentum of world relations undreamed of by prewar theorists of international diplomacy. It was left for the United States merely to pick up the pieces and arrange them in its preferred order.

The U.S. Government extended some $8.8 billion in new foreign loans during the eighteen months ending December 31, 1946. "Export-Import Bank loans and surplus property credits provided over $3.3 billion. Lend-lease credits came to approximately $1.4 billion and the British loan added $3.75 billion."[1] In addition, the United States subscribed $3 billion to the IMF and World Bank. To the American public these credits represented an investment in securing a final and permanent peace, by making possible an era of world economic cooperation upon which political and military peace could be firmly based. However, in the diplomatic meeting rooms the American negotiators made it clear that cooperation among the world's central banks would start from the financial status quo as it existed upon the return to peace. This status quo found the U.S. Treasury holding 60 per cent of the world's monetary gold, making the dollar the world currency most in demand.

Congress exploited this opportunity to its utmost, urging that "the advantages afforded by United States loans and other settlements are our best bargaining asset in securing political and economic concessions in the interest of world stability."[2] What was desired in particular was the breakup of the Sterling Area. More and more, multilateralism for the United States had come to connote the end of the British Empire and the forging of a concentric Dollar Area revolving around American gold, American economic power and American full-employment levels.

The U.S. concept of multilateratism as expressed in Lend-Lease, the British Loan of 1946 and the Bretton Woods agreements called for the dollar to supplant sterling as the world's reserve currency. In effect the Sterling Area was to be absorbed into the Dollar Area, which would be extended throughout the world. Britain was to remain in the weakened position in which it found itself at the end of World War II, with barely any free monetary reserves and dependent on dollar borrowings to meet its current obligations. The United States would gain access to Britain's prewar markets in Latin America, Africa, the Middle East and Far East.

How Britain was ruined

The first loan on the postwar agenda was the British Loan which, as President Truman announced in forwarding it to Congress, would set the course of American and British economic relations for many years to come."[3] He was right, for the Anglo-American Loan Agreement spelled the end of Britain as a Great Power.

American politicians took the hardest line toward Britain, not private businessmen. Leon Fraser of First National City Bank, Winthrop Aldrich of the Chase National Bank, John H. Williams of the New York Federal Reserve Bank, and Joseph Kennedy, former U.S. ambassador to Britain, urged that an outright gift be made to Britain on the ground that Britain was in no position to service a loan. The intention of Congress and the President, however, was similar to that which had underlain Lend-Lease: to keep Britain dependent upon the U.S. Treasury so that it would be obliged to follow policies desired by the U.S. Government.

The Bretton Woods institutions had not yet been established, and Britain was virtually devoid of liquid international reserves. It was into this virtual economic vacuum that the United States moved to secure subjugation of sterling by the dollar.

The loan negotiations were difficult, lasting three months. During this time Britain found itself floundering as its foreign exchange position deteriorated steadily. During 1945–46 it sold half the foreign investments it had sequestered during the war.[4] Finally, the U.S. Government agreed to extend it a line of credit amounting to $3.75 billion, drawable to the end of 1951. Repayment was to be in fifty equal annual installments beginning December 31, 1951, with interest at 2 per cent and special considerations that would waive interest payments in the early years of the loan if Britain's balance of payments continued to falter. The $650 million that the United States had levied on Britain for Lend-Lease was lent on the same terms. Simultaneously, Canada lent Britain $1.25 billion, bringing the total postwar North American loans to support sterling to $5 billion.

What proved so troublesome to the British loan negotiators were the conditions the U.S. Government attached to the loan. Historically speaking, these represent the genesis of the infamous IMF "conditionalities" that have been imposed on debtor countries ever since. It was these negotiations that cast the die. British negotiators gave way on every point critical to its postwar self-interest, each time in exchange for additional U.S. financial assistance. "Not many people in this country," The Economist concluded in 1947 when the totality of British capitulation had become clear, "believe the Communist thesis that it is the deliberate and conscious aim of American policy to ruin Britain and everything that Britain stands for in the world. But the evidence can certainly be read that way. And if every time that aid is extended, conditions are attached which make it impossible for Britain ever to escape the necessity of going back for still more aid, to be obtained with still more self-abasement and on still more crippling terms, then the result will certainly be what the Communists predict."[5]

To the Americans, Britain's Sterling Area represented a potential threat. Indeed, it was the Sterling Area much more than Russia that triggered America's fear of state-controlled economies following World War II, for it was Britain, not Russia, that represented the most immediate threat to postwar U.S. penetration of markets in Latin America and Asia. "For example," describes Feis, "in the agreements negotiated between the United Kingdom and Argentina since 1933, there are specifications as to the uses to which the sterling proceeds acquired by the sale of Argentine goods in the British market are to be put. It is specified that after a reasonable deduction required by the Argentine Government to meet the service of its foreign debt outside of the United Kingdom, the rest of the sterling should be set aside to pay for Argentine purchases of British goods, or for the shipping services of British vessels, or for the payment of interest and dividends on Argentine securities in British possession."[6]

The $14 billion in sterling balances represented an opportunity for Britain to create domestic prosperity on the wave of a postwar export boom. Transforming these balances into blocked exchange would forced its foreign trade into bilateral balance in cases where it would otherwise be in deficit, *e.g.* as occurred in fact when Sterling Area countries converted their sterling balances into dollars to spend in the United States. If the sterling debts to countries that had exported raw materials during the war to fuel Allied war effort had not been made convertible to become general claims on Britain's international reserves, they would have represented a store of value that could be used only to purchase British exports.

This would have given Britain a strong head start in appropriating postwar world markets. "Britain's share of the world market for manufactured exports, amounting to 19 percent in 1937, far exceeded America's and certainly would not diminish if the sterling bloc remained intact after the war," reflected Joyce and Gabriel Kolko on this period. "Even the dollar earnings of bloc members were not convertible to other currencies, leaving India, Argentina, and other large creditors fully integrated in the British trade system. England's indebtedness, therefore, in its wartime form represented a very great threat to America's postwar plans and to the Bretton Woods Agreement, which England had yet to ratify."[7]

Paramount among these policies was opening Britain's domestic and imperial markets to U.S. economic penetration. "If we fail to make this loan," asserted Secretary of State James Byrnes, "Britain will be forced to do business by barter with a bloc of nations. These nations will be forced to do business with Britain in preference to other nations, which means dividing the world into economic blocs, thereby endangering the peace of the world."[8] Without the loan, Britain would join neither the Bretton Woods institutions nor the proposed International Trade Organization. Devaluation of sterling would have been necessary, reducing the market price of English exports and displacing many U.S. exports in the process. A devalued sterling might well have continued to be the world's major trading currency.

Even maintenance of blocked sterling represented a threat to dollar supremacy, because the sterling balances could be sold at a discount, achieving the equivalent of devaluation. This explains U.S. insistence that Britain make all sterling freely convertible into any currency starting one year from the date of the loan.[9] Yet the U.S. Government was tying Eximbank lending to purchases in the United States at the same time that it objected strongly to the prospect of "Britain put[ting] Argentina in possession of pounds by purchase of goods and stipulat[ing] that these pounds shall be spent in Britain."[10]

Britain also gave up "its rather important right . . . to impose exchange controls without the consent of the International Monetary Fund during the postwar transition period." The safety valve of devaluation to cure payments disequilibrium thus was closed to Britain. As Representative Frederick Smith summarized the loan conditions to his fellow congressmen: "This loan was negotiated by our old friend Fred Vinson. He never sold the United States down the river. You can be sure that he drove as good a bargain as could be had. If we're going to help our foreign trade we're going to have to break that [sterling] bloc. And that's what Fred Vinson did."[11]

Still, the loan took seven months to clear Congress, and instead of being granted to Britain in March was held back until July, although Britain's position was deteriorating rapidly. It took only two weeks of debate for Parliament to authorize the borrowing, along with British adherence to the IMF. At Churchill's direction many Conservatives abstained from the voting, and the Labour Left also opposed the loan conditions. There was widespread comparison between the loan and the debt that had followed World War I. Robert Boothby, MP, declared that "Lord Baldwin has been much criticized for the 1923 debt settlement; but the terms he obtained then were princely by comparison with these terms." H. Norman Smith stated that Britain was now being treated "like a defeated nation, in the way Germany was treated under the Dawes and Young loans." "It is aggravating," wrote *The Economist*, "to find that our reward for losing a quarter of our national wealth in the common cause is to pay tribute for half a century to those who have been enriched by the war."[12]

The United States reverted to its interwar policy of aiding the defeated powers more than its wartime allies. The costs of occupying Germany continued to drain Britain's balance of payments, while Germany's internal debt was canceled and its economy was free to start anew, unburdened by indebtedness – the basis for the German miracle of the next quarter-century. Britain was permitted no such miracle. Its foreign exchange cost of occupying Germany totaled £363 million in 1946 and £230 million in 1947, pushing its balance of payments into deficit on current account to £344 million and £545 million in those two years. The whole of Britain's 1946 deficit resulted from its military expenditures in Germany. Britain asked that the United States bear some portion of these costs in view of their war-related nature and the "equality of sacrifice" principle. However, Byrnes reminisced later, "I thought it unwise for Britain to be in the position of a poor relative or a junior partner by contributing less than 50 per cent. They are a proud people. It would be apt to cause irritation. It seemed much better to aid Britain in some other way."[13]

Equality for Britain on the spending side of the ledger sheet, second-rate status on the income side – this was to become the U.S. strategy toward Britain, which now owed more than all the rest of Western Europe combined. British exports to Latin America fell from 40 per cent of that region's imports in 1938 to only 8 per cent in 1948.[14] Similar declines occurred in Britain's trade with other countries. Throughout the Near East it had to yield some of its exclusive oil rights. America's strategy was threefold. First, Britain would bear the cost of paying Sterling Area countries for the material support they had given during the war. Second, these funds would be made generally available to buy U.S. exports. And third, Britain's currency, the pound sterling, would remain overvalued rather than set at the level to which it was allowed to decline only in 1949.

This strategy succeeded only as a result of British war-weariness and the special love of its political leaders for the United States, even at the cost of sacrificing Britain's own world position. In exchange, the United States provided loans, not gifts or a clean slate. In retrospect, one can see that the loans did not serve to put Britain back on its feet. Rather, they subsidized Britain in a condition where its economic viability – that is, its ability to compete with the United States – was not restored.

The first condition was that Britain would be obliged to join the International Monetary Fund, but to relinquish the right, given to all other

IMF members, to avail itself of the five-year transition period during which currencies could remain inconvertible. Within one year of the loan agreement's ratification, by July 1947, the pound sterling was to be made convertible, so that no sterling funds could trade below the $4.20 parity that Britain still retained from the prewar period.

This condition meant that despite Britain's exhausted economic conditions, it could not devalue sterling to rebuild its reserves. Nor could it resort to special Sterling Area trade agreements, but was obliged to endorse the free trade principles of the International Trade Organization. It was not to discriminate against Dollar Area imports in any way, and would have to abandon Imperial Preference – the very condition that Roosevelt had assured Churchill was not the purpose of the Lend-Lease agreement signed by Britain on February 23, 1942.

This was the economic setting for introducing the IMF and its program for stabilizing world currency parities. At the Bretton Woods meetings there had been general agreement on two points: competitive devaluations of national currencies must not occur in the postwar world, and all major trading currencies must be tied to gold. In a sense these two principles were almost identical: to prevent competitive devaluations, the value of each leading currency must be defined by international agreement as to the quantity of gold it represented. This meant that it must be freely convertible into gold in international settlements at a fixed rate, or convertible into some other currency universally accepted "as good or better than gold," to use President Johnson's famous phrase of 1968.

Because the United States was already principal holder of the world's monetary gold, and because the national currencies of Germany, Italy, Japan and their allies would be of doubtful and in some cases zero value in the postwar world, the IMF as a world system could not be brought into universal and automatic operation with the ending of the war. Time must elapse before definition could be reached on feasible exchange rates for the new currencies of the defeated nations.

Stabilizing currencies to protect against competitive devaluations

The ostensible reasoning that underlay the IMF's design was as follows. Currency stability required international reserves sufficient to sustain the needs of the system. A build-up of such reserves, apart from gold itself, required a high degree of currency stability and minimization of central bank risk. This could be assured only by international cooperation and consultation through the Fund so that countries would not suffer major foreign exchange losses or be left holding such inconvertible currencies as the blocked reichsmarks of the 1930s. However, devaluation could not be absolutely prohibited, as excessive rigidity of parities was as undesirable as floating exchanges. "It is extremely difficult," the League of Nations had observed, "to ascertain and establish the correct equilibrium rates of exchange when economic relations are resumed after a global war."

But as long as foreign central banks could minimize their foreign exchange risk and reject the currency dumping that had characterized the 1930s, they would find their interest to lie in the mutual support of each other's currencies. "So long as exchange adjustments are confined to the correction of a fundamental and persistent disequilibrium of this kind," the League of Nations study continued,

> they cannot be any more objectionable to other countries than wage-reductions or unemployment in the country suffering from an overvalued currency. On the contrary, exchange adjustment in such circumstances is likely to prove beneficial all round, since the country in question is enabled to restore not only its exports but also its imports along with its domestic income, production and employment, so that a balance is achieved at a higher level of trade. . . . What actually happened during the twenties was that one country after another established its gold parity by its own independent choice without much regard to the resulting interrelationship of currency values. Had the stabilization problem been attacked by concerted international action, there might have been a better chance of securing a set of workable exchange ratios from the start and less need for subsequent readjustments . . . The important case of exchange dumping which arose from the undervaluation of the French franc in the years leading up to the depression came about by mistake rather than by deliberate design.[15]

This logic became the basis for permitting exchange rate adjustments under IMF rules. Devaluations even were encouraged to the extent that they reestablished long-term equilibrium, but they were discouraged as means of securing short-term balance. Above the 10 per cent devaluation permitted by Article IV, parity changes could be multilaterally negotiated. A margin of 1 per cent on each side of parity was permitted as leeway for day-to-day fluctuations.

It was critical that the IMF members agreed to stabilize their currencies "in terms of gold as the common denominator or in terms of the United States dollar of the weight and fineness in effect on July 1, 1944," that is, at $35 an ounce. However arbitrarily this price had been fixed in 1934, it now became the essence of the IMF's stable parity system. Had foreign currencies been priced higher relative to gold and to the U.S. dollar, they would have experienced a gold outflow to the United States. This was universally undesirable, as the United States already held nearly three-fourths of the world's monetary gold. Further additions to its gold stock could only have threatened the continued use of gold as the world's monetary metal.

On the other hand, had Britain and other countries been permitted to lower the value of their currencies relative to gold, there would have been a gold outflow from the United States. Devaluation of sterling and other currencies against gold at the outset of IMF operations in 1946 would have reduced foreign export prices on world markets, and raised gold prices as expressed in their domestic currencies. It would also have attracted international capital flows to the devaluing countries and prevented much of the gold loss of Europe and Latin America in the early postwar years.

The argument made to Britain and other countries against such a policy was that it would thwart the spirit of international cooperation that was the bulwark of the IMF. What went under the name of international cooperation thus connoted, in practical terms, foreign submission to the United States on this critical issue. The $35 an ounce price of gold protected the U.S. gold stock from being drained to Britain or to any other country that might have devalued its currency against gold. In practice this meant that the United States would keep the more than $10 billion in gold that had fled Europe and Asia in the years leading up to World War II. This gold stock had not been earned through normal economic activities but represented flight capital. After the Axis Powers declared war on the United States in December 1941, it had been added to the nation's monetary base, enabling America to finance much of its war effort with other countries' gold instead of by increasing domestic taxes in the degree required. The long-term result was to blind the United States to the realities of the gold stock. What was technically a U.S. asset was practically the property of anyone who accumulated dollars abroad and, under the IMF rules, cashed these in for gold.

As early as 1943 the Department of Commerce expressed the U.S. logic (or at least the cover story) regarding postwar exchange rates: "Exchange rates, price levels, labor standards, and other basic conditions influencing exports of foreign countries may be subject to flux for some time after the war and may afford temporary advantages to foreign producers that could not be maintained in the long run. To expose domestic producers to sharp disturbances emanating from short-run situations of this character would be undesirable."[16] In practice, this meant that exchange rates would be pegged so as to prevent any sudden increase in exports by foreign countries, but not to prevent expansion of U.S. exports toward the $10 billion annual rate aimed at by U.S. trade strategists as necessary to full employment in the United States. U.S. imports could rise only as long as U.S. exports rose even more – that was the U.S. concept of expanding world trade under the aegis of the IMF.

This only aggravated the problem, already apparent at Bretton Woods, that there were not enough gold and dollars to go round. International reserves of most countries were depleted to minimum working levels. The U.S. Government did not wish to give up its gold or to supply dollars generally beyond its $2.75 billion IMF subscription. Under the world realities of 1944–45, an increased dollar supply would have involved essentially a giveaway. It therefore was desirable to establish the pound sterling, the French franc and the Canadian, New Zealand and Australian currencies as recognized central bank assets. This required their legal and practical convertibility into gold or U.S. dollars.

This obviously required time, as recognized in the IMF's Article XIV which dealt with the Fund's proposed transition period of at least five years. But Britain had signed away its rights to make use of this period when it agreed to the loan conditions imposed by the United States in 1946. The question thus arises as to the much claimed necessity for the IMF to insist on relatively fixed parities during the transition period.

The IMF was to operate universally and in no respect as a punitive weapon against recent aggressors. It was in fact to be the principal instrument to secure a peaceful and stable world economic order embracing victor and vanquished alike. But it was to do so on terms that would promote U.S. exports above all. At least this was a tacit calculation made by America's negotiators at Bretton Woods over every detail of the negotiations.

To begin with, establishing a fixed gold value for currencies benefited the United States as the world's major gold holder. The objective was to prevent postwar trade patterns from being disrupted by the competitive devaluations and currency wars of the 1930s. A basis for limiting such destructive national acts already was at hand in the form of the Tripartite Agreement of 1936, in which the United States, Britain and France agreed to economize on the world's supply of monetary gold and avoid sudden, unmanageable runs on national currencies. Unlike the International Monetary Fund, this agreement was not based on fixed gold parities for currencies, but accepted flexible parities as a fact of life. It was a means whereby the Exchange Funds of countries with fixed and flexible gold prices could have access to each other's markets and could cooperate in the management of gold shipments in both directions. The prices governing official transactions in the countries with flexible gold prices were held stable for a period of time (twenty-four hours) long enough to enable the authorities of countries with fixed gold prices to complete the conversion operation without risk. The importance of this agreement was in the antecedent understandings concerning the exchange rates on which the gold prices were based, and its effect was to allow the various Exchange Funds, Central Banks and Treasuries to operate an international gold settlement system that was an amalgam of conflicting techniques and principles.[17]

A not dissimilar proposal had been rejected by the United States at the 1933 World Economic Conference in London. The U.S. motive at that time was to permit the dollar to be devalued relative to all other currencies. The result was a massive inflow of gold into the United States, enlarged by the flight of refugee capital to America as World War II loomed. But U.S. motivation at Bretton Woods was quite different. America already held most of the world's gold, and intended to hold on to it, or at least to enough of it to make the dollar the *de facto* world currency, whatever the *de jure* position of sterling or other currencies. The United States insisted that the IMF establish fixed gold parities for all convertible currencies so as to prevent others, above all sterling, from being devalued so as to promote foreign export trade in competition with that of the United States. The corollary was that Britain's export trade would have to be sacrificed. This was the unstated theme of the 1945–46 negotiations between America and Britain.

In most other respects the IMF embraced the Tripartite Agreement's thinking as to a system of international settlements through gold or gold equivalents. To assure that central banks and the IMF itself would not be left holding depreciating foreign exchange assets, a three-day warning period was chosen (Article IV, s. 5) to enable the world's central banks to move out of currencies about to be devalued. This was three times the period called for in the 1936 agreements. The IMF rule explains why devaluations almost always are announced over the weekend.

An alternative would have been simply to give a gold guarantee on official currency holdings, such as was provided to the IMF itself by Article IV, s. 8. Rather than endorsing IMF policy, the key-currency approach endorsed by Williams, Aldrich and Fraser took this line, based on the

Tripartite Agreement. The postwar system was seen as an extension of the 1936 agreements that had left room for flexible limits within which currencies could vary marginally as normalcy was restored. Williams in particular warned of the imminent weakness of sterling under the IMF rules, for Article IV of the IMF charter forbidding member nations from devaluing their currencies by more than 10 per cent, without express permission by the IMF. Britain signed the IMF agreement without insisting upon special exemption from this article for a period of two years or so.

How fixed currency parities led to sterling's overvaluation

It was obvious to many economists that the postwar dollar price of sterling was an overvaluation. Britain was almost hopelessly indebted on sterling account at the going rate for the pound, despite the fact that it was in dire need of reviving the export industries that had languished during the war. Devaluation no later than the end of 1946 was the obvious answer to this problem, a solution long noted by international trade theory. Instead, the pound was supported artificially by U.S. dollar loans until 1949. What should have been the 1945 year-end dollar price for sterling was not initiated until four years later, by which time it occurred under crisis conditions.

America's multi-billion dollar loan was persuasive. Maintenance of sterling's 1945 parity, subsidized by the massive British Loan, ended up providing the United States with a net equivalent value in the form of a large share of what otherwise might have been an expansion of British export trade. Stated another way, Britain itself might have obtained a trade benefit equal in magnitude to its dollar borrowings from the United States, if it had set sterling's exchange rate at its 1949 level. The ability of the Commonwealth countries' sterling balances to buy U.S. exports would have been halved, for instance, favoring British suppliers accordingly. But Britain was convinced to keep its high prewar and wartime value of sterling, on the logic that a high parity would hold down the price of imports, minimizing food and raw materials costs and stemming whatever postwar inflation Britain might suffer.

The arguments against this logic were more persuasive in principle, and indeed have been borne out by subsequent events, but they were brushed aside. Devaluation of sterling in 1945 would have provoked an inflow of gold, partly out of the refugee dollar hoard in the United States. Also, reduced British export prices would have drawn enough gold to Britain, from the United States gold hoard and from newly mined gold, to lay a firm foundation for sterling as a truly convertible currency. The argument that import prices would have risen can be given no great weight because, even without devaluation, Britain continued a system of rationing for years following the war, *i.e.*, there was no effectively free market price for staples even with an artificially high parity for sterling.

In the negotiations with Washington over the British Loan that paved the way for Britain's acquiescence in the IMF system, Britain's Board of Trade recognized that its sterling obligations might be treated as blocked balances to induce foreign countries to use for the purchase of British exports. To be sure, this would have reduced domestic living standards, as goods produced by British labor were shipped and consumed abroad rather than retained within Britain. But as matters turned out, rationing was worse after the war than during the war. In 1947 bread was rationed for the first time. The meat ration was reduced and many Britons learned to eat whale. And despite the enormous effort made during the war to raise the self-sufficiency in food above the prewar 30 per cent, British agriculture still fell short of what was needed. The nation's diet and cuisine had become adapted to North American hard wheat and Virginia tobacco, as well as Argentine beef and linseed oil.

Britain could have retained the right to devalue through more skillful negotiation. Indeed, notes Skidelsky, "expectation of a British devaluation was one reason Harry White gave to the Senate Banking Committee in the summer of 1945 for denying that Britain would need extensive transitional assistance."[18] But Keynes opposed devaluation, on the ground that devaluation would reduce the price of British exports to a greater degree than it would have increased their volume, given Britain's productivity and supply constraints. But its fatal promise to maintain the value of sterling prevented it from devaluing until 1949, by which time holders of sterling had spent their money at a high creditor-oriented rate. Cultural attitudes played a role. It was as if Britain continued to think of herself as a creditor, not as a debtor.

Fixing sterling's parity at its overstated wartime value set it at a level that made exports denominated in that currency uncompetitive with the exports of Germany, Italy and Japan, although membership by these countries in the IMF lay some years in the future. Italy was admitted to the IMF in 1947, and Germany and Japan in 1952. As with Britain, these three countries were committed under Article IV to maintain fixed parities for their currencies in relation to the dollar. However, these parities represented the realities of events at the time, two years and seven years after World War II respectively. In this sense the IMF favored the defeated countries at the expense of Britain as the United States returned to its interwar stance of veiled aggression against Britain and open support of the erstwhile aggressors. Sterling, with its parity fixed at the wartime rate, was disadvantaged when the defeated powers were admitted to the IMF with their parities reflecting the new realities.

Britain's loss proved to be America's gain as world trade expanded rapidly, especially of U.S. merchandise exports, helped by a monetary system that counted world reserves as consisting mainly of the U.S. gold stock plus dollar equivalents located abroad based on this gold stock. Use of the dollar as the preferred means of settlement followed from its status as a proxy for gold. The IMF's rules encouraged an accelerated velocity of the dollar in the world economy, but no corresponding acceleration in the velocity of sterling. The latter's overvaluation, written into the IMF articles of agreement and confirmed by America's British Loan, had the effect of dislodging sterling and enthroning the dollar.

No other result could have ensued from establishing the IMF on the basis of fixed parities. Exchange rates were set beyond the point of tolerability for individual currencies. Sterling, devalued in 1949, four years too late for Britain to catch up in the race for expansion into world markets, had to be devalued again in 1967, once more too late to undo the damage that the IMF, reflecting its domination by the United States, had inflicted upon Britain. America's main objective was attained by reducing Britain to the status of a second-rate industrial power and the penetration by the United States into markets once specifically British.

How the United States set the quotas

American dominance over the IMF lay directly in its veto power over IMF decision-making, based on the subscribed quotas that each member nation was required to contribute to the Fund. Of the $7.3 billion in subscribed quotas as of year-end 1945, the five largest IMF member nations controlled $5.5 billion. The $2.75 billion United States quota was more than twice that of Britain ($1.3 billion), followed by China ($550 million), France ($450 million) and India ($400 million). One reason for India's rather large quota was the intention to provide the British Empire as a unit with voting power approximating that of the United States. Britain's $1,300 million quota and India's $400 million quota were to be supplemented by quotas for Canada, New Zealand and Australia of $300 million, $275 million and $200 million, respectively, for an Empire total of $2,475 million. This would have been enough to provide the British Empire collectively with veto power, that is, with more than 20 per cent of IMF voting rights. However, Australia and New Zealand did not join the Fund until 1947 and 1961, respectively, while Canada was more a member of the Dollar Area than the Sterling Area. As a result, Britain could not mobilize veto power in the IMF without raising the most serious of political questions between the Commonwealth countries and the United States. Bilateral exercise of veto power by Britain and, say, India, with joint voting power of over 23 per cent in the Fund, would have been interpreted as political aggression against the United States, unless it should occur at hidden U.S. initiative. The United States already had veto power – and of course, gold.

The original IMF quotas were based on a composite index representing national income as of 1940, foreign trade volume during 1934–38, gold and foreign exchange reserves as of 1943, and some factor for political weighting. Professor Mosse of the French delegation to Bretton Woods reflected that "in the end, quotas were established more or less arbitrarily by the United States in a series of deals."[19] Skidelsky notes that "India wanted equality with China. France would accept a smaller quota than China 'for political reasons,' but insisted on a larger quota than India. The Americans, with an eye on voting strength in the Fund, took up the demand for larger quotas for the Latin Americans."[20] Countries wanted as large quotas as possible so as to maximize their borrowing power in the Fund, as well as to reflect national prestige. France's request for a larger quota was granted in 1947.

Other countries, and particularly Britain, acquiesced to U.S. wishes, although the United States could not have revalued in retaliation against foreign devaluations, as this would have prompted recurrence of the beggar-my-neighbor devaluations of the 1930s. The United States' only alternative to seeing some of its gold return to Europe would have been to embargo official gold sales, which would have undercut the IMF's currency convertibility provision and broken the world then and there into national currency and trading blocs. This in turn would have thwarted the recovery and expansion of U.S. exports.

As matters worked out, it was other countries' gold that flowed into the United States. Latin America lost more than one-third, more than $1 billion, of its gold during 1945–46, most of it from Argentina and Mexico, the two most developed Latin American economies. Europe also found its international reserves draining to the United States, forcing France to devalue by 44 per cent in 1948 and Britain by 30 per cent in 1949. Thus, by failing to devalue against the dollar at the end of the war, which would have conserved their international reserves, Europe and Latin America saw the remnants of their gold resources drained to the United States during the transition period which was supposedly to have strengthened their financial position.

Let us pause a moment to contrast Britain's response to its insolvent but potentially strong position in 1945 with U.S. actions as it moved into a similar position a quarter-century later.

Britain, although having fallen to the status of world debtor, continued to abide by a strategy much more suited to its prewar creditor status. It acquiesced in a system of international laissez-faire that favored U.S. exporters, and it relinquished its blocked sterling accounts which could have guaranteed it a $14 billion market within its Commonwealth. Twenty-five years later the United States was to make a virtue out of just such a status, by discovering the inherent advantage of being a world debtor. Foreign holders of any nation's promissory notes are obliged to become a market for its exports as the means of obtaining satisfaction of their debts. This fact is what enabled the United States to ask Europe to let it amortize its $75 billion in official intergovernmental debt by improving its balance of payments by an annual $13 billion, to be achieved largely by growth in exports.

Britain could have taken a similar position in 1945. It could have said that the degree to which foreign holders of sterling balances accepted British exports represented the degree to which they wished to be repaid. It could have refused to free these balances for conversion into dollars, could have turned down the Anglo-American loan, could have devalued its currency, and thereby would have moved to regain its position in Latin American and other world markets, much as the United States did in the 1970s.

Instead, Britain adhered to an overvalued sterling and dissipated the leverage inherent in its debtor status. At a meeting on February 12, 1946 at the U.S. Treasury, reports Skidelsky, "Keynes claimed that with their overvalued exchange rates India, Egypt and some colonies would be a 'sink for imports and would be able to export little or nothing,' thus causing a drain of their balances from London. He wanted to bring these countries 'brutally up against the need for them either to devalue or to restrict imports by simply blocking a large part of their balances . . .' These were tough words, but in the end even Keynes's resolve failed before the complexity of the problem."[21] It was of course not the "complexity" that was the problem, but U.S. intransigence wearing down Keynes and his fellow negotiators.

Britain also dissipated its scarce international reserves by financing the cost of an obsolete world empire. "It was rearmament," reviews Kolko, "that caused the most serious structural shift in the British economy, dealing the final blow from which it never fully recovered. The industries that the English most relied on for export were those that were diverted to arms. England made a greater effort at rearmament than any other Western European nation and paid a cost not only in terms of current economic austerity but also in the loss of markets, permanently affecting its future trade."[22] It had hoped that rearmament might stabilize its economy; instead, it diverted resources from Britain's export sector.

Yet Britain was obliged by force of circumstances to put balance-of-payments objectives above that of promoting domestic economic growth. This was the beginning of the so-called stop–go policy that would lead its government to stifle every business upswing, as recovery generally is accompanied by a worsening international payments position. Currency stability thus ended up being enshrined above the goal of national prosperity.

Britain's problems were not made easier by the fact that the United States demanded that 25 per cent of its quota be paid in dollars and/or gold, a sum amounting to about $300 million. That Britain could not afford this was evidenced by her withdrawal of this sum – her maximum drawing privilege for any one year – in 1947. Because quotas had to be paid in gold or dollars, and because permission to withdraw funds was limited under the IMF rules, the Fund was not able to help countries during the 1947 world currency crisis.

The marginal character of early IMF loan operations

The International Monetary Fund had been created merely as a pool of national currencies and gold, not as a bank that could create generalized credits. It permitted the conversion of some portion of its currency deposits into other currencies, but only to the extent of its holdings on a currency-by-currency basis. It was a financial intermediary that could lend out only what was put into it. Its stated purpose was not to provide a solution to the major long-term problems as they existed in 1945, not to provide the liquidity required to finance the growth of world trade, and not to act as an aid-lending institution, but only marginally to supplement the exchange stabilization funds of its member countries and, specifically, to stabilize foreign currencies vis-à-vis the dollar at existing parities. This was reflected in the relatively modest size of its quotas, which were sufficient only to meet the less vexatious problems which were expected to remain once the transition to a peacetime economy had been completed.

By the deadline date of December 31, 1945, thirty-five countries had subscribed to the IMF charter, to the extent of $7.3 billion in quotas. This was $1.5 billion less than the originally scheduled $8.8 billion, the difference mainly representing Russia's scheduled $1.2 billion quota. In proportion to total world trade and payments, the IMF's hard currency holdings did not represent a large sum. To quote the IMF's official historian, J. Keith Horsefield: "The original plan for the Fund was more heavily influenced by the caution proper to the United States, whose resources would be chiefly in demand, than by the expansionist hopes of the United Kingdom and some other powers. It therefore took the form of a fixed subscription, rather than of an open-ended commitment to permit overdrafts, for which Keynes had hoped. And the total of quotas, $8.8 billion, while appreciably larger than the $5 billion originally mentioned by White, was only about one third the size of the resources which Keynes wished to make available."[23]

Keynes' plan for a $33 billion clearing union had been for generalized credit to be made available, not limited on any currency-by-currency basis to the original national currency subscriptions, but only by the borrowing members' quotas. Under the U.S. plan ultimately adopted, the maximum amount of dollars that could be drawn from the IMF was little more than $2 billion. It was apparent that the IMF was not to be primarily a provider of world liquidity but mainly a system for facilitating settlements at the margin.

"The British wanted an automatic source of credit, the Americans a financial policeman," reports Skidelsky. "Keynes's main purpose was to protect the Fund from preponderant U.S. political control." Toward that end, he believed: "The main function of the executive directors was not to manage the Fund, but to be the link between the Fund and the national treasuries and central banks from which they were seconded . . . By contrast, American conception of the Fund was hegemonic. Clayton insisted that it needed a strong, full-time executive board and a large specialist bureaucracy to police the policies of its members."[24]

The Fund's Article V established rules for member countries' borrowings from the Fund and the extent of any country's liability under the rules. Countries were permitted to borrow 25 per cent of their quota annually, up to the point at which IMF holdings equaled 200 per cent of their quota. This was not a particularly generous allotment. Furthermore, to ensure that countries made only short-term use of IMF resources they were permitted to be debtors for only five years. This was the ground on which Cuba was expelled from the Fund in 1964. As shown by the case of Czechoslovakia, failure to supply monetary and balance-of-payments data was also grounds for expulsion. For this reason the Fund was permitted to make loans for brief periods only, to ensure that its resources would not be used to finance Europe's reconstruction needs. Nor could its resources be drawn upon to finance capital transfers of any other kind. Its purpose was initially to foster balance-of-payments stability on current account, leaving its members to maintain capital controls until such time as their overall balance-of-payments positions could sustain their removal.

Toward this end Article VI, dealing with capital transfers, specified that members borrowing from the Fund at the same time that they ran substantial capital outflows might be declared ineligible to use IMF resources. But the technical difficulty of segregating capital transactions from other payments transactions led to this article never being enforced. It was relaxed fully in 1961 when a legal ruling of the IMF permitted its resources to be used to finance overall payments deficits, not merely deficits on current account. This ruling was on the ground that most of the major nations had abolished their capital controls and their currencies had become fully convertible. As the next chapter will describe, this article hardly could stem America's practice of running deficits while its investors were buying up Europe's leading companies from 1964 onward.

The first borrowings from the IMF were made by France and the Netherlands in May 1947, for a total of only $25 million and $12 million, respectively. Borrowings remained at low levels throughout the early years of Fund operations, and the Fund's official history adjudges that "the reconstitution of the economic viability of Europe proceeded without the Fund's participation."[25] For it indeed was not a bank, and was not intended to function as such. Despite the troubled condition of world finance in the early postwar years, not a dollar was drawn from the IMF in 1950, and only moderate drawings were made in 1951. In part this was because the Korean War was transferring U.S. dollars abroad, initiating the U.S. move into a position of almost chronic payments deficit. A contributing reason for the very small use of Fund resources was formation of the European Payments Union which largely supplanted IMF activities among the European countries, emphasizing that the Fund indeed was designed to operate at the margin and not in the body of the international economy.

The Netherlands and Australia protested the impracticality of the Fund operating as a merely marginal lender in a world of major economic distortions. By 1951, the year in which capital controls by major member nations were scheduled to have been removed and full external convertibility established, capital controls remained in effect, including blocked sterling. Multiple currency practices were still widespread, and currency floating by the less developed countries was on the increase. The avowed purposes of the IMF had not been fulfilled.

Yet there was one net gainer: the United States. By international law the U.S. dollar and gold were made virtual identities. What then did the world have to fear from U.S. deficits on international account? The build-up of dollar assets abroad, declared by the IMF to be the equivalent of gold, allowed the United States to finance its deficits with the printing press. And, because of the IMF, the world's central banks were led to accept this dollar paper. That is what the IMF was for, and that is all it has accomplished.

Looking back fifty years to evaluate Keynes's contribution to British diplomacy in 1945–46, his biographer Skidelsky notes his basic failure. Most tangible of his economic bequests "was the American loan of $3.75 billion he had negotiated in 1945 to see Britain through the immediate post-war years. This proved the least durable of his legacies, quickly dissipated – though, without its false promise, the British welfare state might never have taken root." However, Skidelsky adds: "The convertibility of the pound into dollars, started on 15 July 1947, had to be suspended six weeks later, as Britain's and the world's hunger for dollars caused a flight of sterling from London. The IMF was put in cold storage, its co-founder Harry White dying in 1948 under suspicion of being a Russian spy. The Cold War had started."[26]

The IMF's effect was felt not so much as a maker of loans but as a setter of policy. It was in this sphere that the IMF exerted its control functions over the international financial system. This control reflected U.S. policy at one remove, for the IMF's adopted a deflationary monetarist philosophy of operations with regard to all countries except for the United States.

Thus, however idealistic some aspects of the IMF's philosophy initially appeared, their international effects in the 1950s strongly served exclusive U.S. national interests on every major point. Only the United States then possessed sufficient gold reserves to persist for any length of time in deficit status, so that it alone could place the goal of rising incomes, full employment and growth of productive powers above the goal of international payments stability. Moreover, the dollar meant gold in IMF law. Other countries at that time could accelerate their growth only to the extent permitted by their modest – and shrinking – stock of foreign exchange reserves, IMF drawings, World Bank borrowings and bilateral loans from the U.S. Government. Both Europe's growth and the growth of the less developed countries were thus constrained by the need for payments equilibrium, second by World Bank lending policies which reinforced the IMF's emphasis on investment in export-oriented sectors, and finally by U.S. Government aid strategy toward this same end. The turning point, however, was at hand.

Events began to move away from U.S. dominance and toward new power relations antithetical to the monolith which the United States had created. But in response to these events the United States was to pursue just the opposite policy after 1964 to that which Britain pursued after World War II. It gave priority to domestic expansion, treating its balance-of-payments problem and the dollar's value with a policy of benign neglect, refusing to act "responsibly" on international account, and benefited from the ensuing devaluation of its currency and its spur to domestic exports. In short, the United States showed what debtor economies could achieve when they applied a flexible policy to their world position, pursuing a creditor-oriented policy only toward countries with which they enjoyed a payments surplus, while pursuing debtor-oriented policies in all cases suggested by their payments deficit position.

Part III

Monetary Imperialism and the U.S. Treasury Bill Standard

11 Financing America's Wars with Other Nations' Resources, 1964–68

As the case stands, as it would ruin England to lose her Empire in India, it is stretching our own finances with ruin, to be obliged to keep it.

J. Dickinson, *The Government of India under a Bureaucracy*
(London: 1853), p. 50

Since 1914 the world has been no stranger to the financing of one nation's war with other nations' funds. War debts among the Allies of World War I were of this character. There is therefore nothing basically surprising in U.S. military actions in Korea, South Vietnam, Cambodia and Laos having been financed by borrowings from other foreign countries. Nonetheless, there are novel aspects to this transfer of the costs of U.S. aggression to other peoples. The fundamental difference between the American method of financing its wars out of other nations' treasuries and the ways in which other countries financed their wars in earlier years lay in the structure of the world monetary system. The United States did not run into debt in the conventional sense of the term. It did not borrow abroad under the kind of contractual conditions it had imposed upon the Allied Powers in World War I, except in very limited instances. What it did primarily was to inject paper dollars into the world economy, creating debts that it did everything it could to avoid repaying.

As early as 1963, what Robert McNamara termed "the Columbia University Group" cautioned that U.S. overseas military spending, even in the absence of overt aggressive action, had become so massive as to threaten the gold cover of the U.S. dollar.[1] This group perceived that overseas military spending by the United States and maintenance of the gold cover were incompatible. The gold stock itself was threatened as the legal limits upon money creation under the gold cover clause of U.S. domestic law raised fears abroad that America might sooner or later embargo gold payments. This apprehension caused draw-downs by foreign central banks on the U.S. gold stock. The possibility of an embargo almost universally was denied in the United States, but lurked among the fears of Europeans.

Foreign governments, particularly those of Common Market members, began to reemphasize the role of gold as the soundest of international monetary assets. They urged the United States to take steps to curtail its overseas spending, especially since the major factors in the U.S. payments deficits were overseas military operations and U.S. private capital investments in Europe. Although no serious trouble had yet developed, it began to appear that the United States must slow its rate of monetary expansion in order to curb its payments deficits.

American planners themselves were beginning to grow concerned about the deficits, and when IMF quotas were increased by 50 per cent in 1959, the U.S. Treasury was not above arranging a window-dressing stratagem that called for the IMF to redeposit some $300 million of its gold in the United States. This IMF gold became double-counted, appearing as an IMF asset even while it continued to be included in U.S. gold reserves. The rationale was that because all IMF quota increases had to be paid 25 per cent in gold, the less developed debtor countries probably would elect to obtain this gold by cashing in some of their dollar holdings with the U.S. Treasury. The IMF agreed to close this triangular payments circle by redepositing the entire $300 million gold receipt from less developed countries back in the U.S. Treasury. A similar practice was employed when IMF quotas were increased again in 1966 and 1970.

It may provide some perspective on the subsequent evolution of the U.S. payments deficit, *i.e.*, the transfer of U.S. military costs to other nations, to observe that even the modest deficits that the nation was running toward the end of the 1950s were enough to excite speculation that the $35 per ounce price of gold could not long hold. European observers speculated that inflationary policies in the United States would accelerate under a Democratic Party Administration. After John Kennedy won the 1960 presidential election the price of gold was bid up to nearly $41 an ounce in the London gold market. This induced U.S. monetary authorities to take the lead in forming the Gold Pool to drive down the price of gold to the U.S. parity.

One of President Kennedy's first official acts was to deliver a speech on the balance of payments, pledging to restore it to equilibrium, despite the expanded pace of military and welfare spending under his inflationary administration. His appointees moved rapidly to apply palliatives to the U.S. deficits. Robert Roosa, international economist for the New York Federal Reserve Bank, negotiated a series of currency swap agreements with foreign central banks. These agreements established lines of reciprocal credit between the United States and other countries. Although the United

States was a net lender of $116 million in 1961, it soon became a net borrower from the Common Market nations.

Europe tried to help the United States resolve its payments problems. Led by France, which was just entering a period of payments surplus, it began to prepay its World War II reconstruction debts to the United States. Germany agreed to buy increasing amounts of U.S. military goods to help offset U.S. military spending within its borders. U.S. military exports negotiated by the Pentagon jumped some $700 million in 1962, to $1.1 billion, and contributed about $1 billion annually to U.S. exports for many years.

U.S. authorities made broad attempts to reduce the payments deficit while maintaining existing programs, but their efforts were more in the nature of economizing on foreign exchange payments than of reorienting national policy. The foreign aid program, for instance, introduced a balance-of-payments control device known as the Gold Budget accounting format to track and minimize the foreign exchange costs of military and aid activities. Foreign aid was tied to purchases of U.S. goods and services, as were the Pentagon's military support programs.

Window-dressing policies were devised to create the impression that the government was reducing the nation's payments deficit. Among these devices was issuance of ostensibly nonmarketable, nonconvertible, medium-term U.S. Treasury securities to foreign central banks in lieu of gold. Because the nominal maturity date of these securities was over one year, their purchase by foreign banks was recorded in the U.S. payments statistics as a long-term capital inflow rather than as a means of financing the deficit. In reality these nonmarketable and nonconvertible Treasury securities were potentially liquid debt instruments, their nominal illiquidity being a mere disguise. They required only from two to nine days to be exchanged for fully marketable liquid securities that could, in turn, be converted into gold upon demand. A three-day advance warning period was required for them to be converted into a convertible security, another three-day period for them to be converted into a marketable security, and finally another three days for them to be marketed or exchanged for gold or short-term capital assets. Thus, foreign central banks were offered an interest-bearing instrument in place of gold, while the Treasury reduced the apparent, publicly reported size of the U.S. payments deficit by the euphemism of calling these instruments a capital inflow.

It was widely recognized that such accounting techniques were mere deceptions, but American officials balked at taking more meaningful steps. In fact, they showed disdain at the thought that European governments might seek to impose their will upon the United States. It was soon recognized that in order for net military spending abroad to continue running at about $3 billion annually, the private sector would have to bear the brunt of financing it. Either the trade surplus or the investment-and-income balance would have to grow sufficiently to cover the payments deficit on military account, but military expenditures must not be reduced. At the 1962 hearings of the Joint Economic Committee of Congress, held some three years before the Vietnam build-up of May 1965, Professor Seymour Harris announced in his introductory speech that, "Given the need of large expenditures abroad for military purposes and for aid and also large capital exports, the United States must have a large volume of exports vis-à-vis imports . . . Insofar as the excess of exports is not adequate to finance those items in the balance of payments, a deficit emerges."[2]

This was no tautology but a doctrine that the government sector was to remain outside balance-of-payments constraints. It implied that the balance of trade must and should be manipulated to finance the deficit on overseas military account, and also compensate for the foreign exchange costs of the takeover of European industry by U.S. companies. The burden of America's deteriorating balance of payments was to be borne by foreign central banks and, domestically, by the private commercial sector accumulating surplus dollars so as to finance military operations abroad.

Restrictions were imposed on the private sector to reduce its investment outflows, particularly those which did not result in direct ownership of foreign firms and thus did not result in the possibility of transmitting the entire net cash flow back to the United States. In 1962 the Kennedy Administration levied an Interest Equalization Tax on foreign bonds, offsetting higher interest rates abroad by imposing a 15 per cent tax on net interest receipts by U.S. residents. In February 1965, "voluntary" guidelines were announced to limit private overseas direct investment and commercial bank lending to foreigners, made retroactive to December 1964. These restrictions became compulsory in 1968. In addition new quotas were announced on imports of oil, steel, textiles and other commodities.

The result was that while U.S. diplomats preached laissez-faire to the rest of the world, U.S. Government foreign operations obliged the United States to practice increasingly restrictive policies at home. Yet the private sector's balance on basic long-term transactions – foreign trade, services and direct investment – continued to deteriorate. This required that the burden of U.S. deficits be shifted increasingly to foreign central banks.

Valéry Giscard d'Estaing of France expressed the unease of his Common Market compatriots in observing, at the IMF's 1963 meetings:

The present situation, whereby central banks accumulate holdings of the currencies of other countries, does not include any automatic machinery for a prompt return to equilibrium. The creditor country which accumulates foreign exchange congratulates itself on the increase in its holdings, while overlooking some of the unsound aspects of these gains. The deficit country tends to attach insufficient importance to the increase in foreign holdings of its currency, all the more so since, at the outset, losses of gold represent only a small part of its deficit.[3]

Furthermore, he noted, the persistent U.S. deficit was causing monetary imbalance by exporting America's inflation to Europe. This damaged Europe's internal financial stability and, in the process, enabled the United States to avoid paying the price of its economic and military policies. "The inflationary effect resulting in the creditor country from a lasting surplus in the balance of payments is matched in the debtor country by that which comes from the use that foreign central banks make of their holdings in its currency . . . Without overrating the size of this phenomenon in relation to the evolution of the money supply, one must admit that it tends to offset one of the automatic corrective mechanisms."[4]

European central bankers warned that expanding IMF quotas for the purpose of helping the United States sustain its payments deficits would violate Article XIII of the IMF charter, which prohibited IMF credits from being used for more than temporary stabilization purposes. Germany's representative to the 1963 IMF meetings stated:

I should like to warn against the illusion that, as if by some purely technical reform, one could solve in an automatic or painless way the adjustment problems which are due either to structural distortions or to policy discrepancies between the member countries of our international system . . .

I want to stress that any improvements that might be thought out for our international monetary system . . . should not be concentrated only on the question how best *to finance* balance of payments deficits, but also on the even more important question of how to provide sufficient incentives for *curing* them.[5]

Article VI of the IMF agreement forbade IMF resources to be used to finance deficits on capital account, something which the United States seemed to be using them for. Common Market economists complained of America's growing investment in European industry, and correlated this investment outflow with the size of the overall U.S. payments deficit to demonstrate that the United States was, in effect, obtaining a cost-free takeover of Europe's economy. Private U.S. investors spent dollars to buy private European enterprises. The European recipients of these funds exchanged their dollar proceeds with their central banks to obtain local currency or other, non-dollar currencies. These central banks in turn were pressured by the U.S. Treasury to refrain from cashing in their dollars for U.S. gold, on the ground that this might disrupt world financial conditions. There seemed to be no effective limit on how far this process might go as long as the United States was not compelled to part with its monetary gold in payment for the increase in its private sector's net investment in Europe. U.S. Treasury bonds were being exchanged for higher-paying direct ownership of European assets.

In an attempt to stop this nationalist U.S. monetary policy, the Common Market nations insisted that the IMF's 1963 annual report conclude that there was no overall shortage of world liquidity. They got the United States to agree that in the event an increase in world liquidity were to be enacted through an increase in IMF quotas, the United States would not be freed of its obligation to reestablish balance in its external accounts.

But in 1964, foreign dollar holdings grew to exceed the U.S. gold stock. This threatened an embargo on U.S. gold sales – the very point the Columbia University Group had made. This was hardly an auspicious time for the Vietnam War to be accelerated. It imposed a new and immense strain on the dollar. The shift of U.S. military focus from Europe to Southeast Asia distressed Europe all the more as the United States began to shift troops from Germany to Vietnam. Some Europeans felt themselves left open to the threat of military aggression from the East. France announced her intention to withdraw from NATO, and pressed for an independent European nuclear deterrent. Britain opted to link her defense system with that of the United States, only to see the Pentagon abruptly cancel the Skybolt program, leaving Britain effectively disarmed as far as its missile delivery system was concerned.

Because the military aspects of the U.S. payments deficit grew increasingly U.S.-Asian in character and less and less European, the 1964 IMF meetings were dominated by discussions by the European representatives over whether any need existed for increasing IMF quotas. "Very rightly," stated Germany's representative, Karl Blessing, "the Fund so far has held that balance of payments deficits, which are the self-inflicted consequences of inflationary policies, should not be financed indefinitely by means of the Fund, but that the inflationary causes must be removed. This policy should be carried on without compromise." Blessing went on to emphasize that he

> would have preferred to see the [annual] Report place greater emphasis on the need for stricter monetary discipline on the part of the deficit countries [i.e., the United States and Britain]. I am entirely in agreement with those who think that supplies of gold and reserve currencies are fully adequate for the present, and are likely to be for the near future.
>
> I am glad that the review of the existing international monetary system has not led to any basic change. In my opinion, there is not so much need for an improvement of the system as for an improvement of national policies of adjustment. No system, however ingeniously conceived, can function satisfactorily without monetary discipline. Under the system of fixed exchange rates, even countries with sound monetary policies have to import inflation if other countries do not maintain sufficient monetary discipline. If we want to avoid further creeping inflation, deficit countries, too, must take corrective measures, however painful they may be.[6]

Under an overly abundant provision of international liquidity, "corrective internal policies may be delayed too long and the inflationary tendencies will tend to prevail," the Dutch representative Mr Holtrop asserted.[7] "There is agreement," he concluded, "that it is both unlikely and undesirable that in the future the supply of international liquidity, originating from the balance of payments deficit of the United States, should continue to flow at the present rate." Italy endorsed the "proposed 'multilateral surveillance' of the means of financing balance of payments disequilibria,"[8] while France added its voice to warn that "excessive facilities may be granted which may lead to the spreading of international inflation. It may even lead to the strange paradox that, since the system in practice permits the deficits of the reserve currency countries to be financed without limit, the creditor countries are somehow invited to 'create a deficit' in order to compensate for the outflow of reserve currencies, which is a phenomenon for which they have no responsibility however."[9] France spoke for all six Common Market countries in urging that "reference will have to be made in gold" in financing future balance-of-payments deficits, as "the only monetary element outside the scope of government action."

Politically, Germany would do nothing to oppose the U.S. war in Asia regardless of its cost, a stance assumed also by Britain. France not only opposed the war, on grounds of historical stupidity as much as on the moral issues involved, but actively showed its opposition to it by drawing down the U.S. monetary gold stock. This was a positive act to counter America's striving for world hegemony. It was in fact the only act of opposition by any Western power. Its results, however, were to multiply the difficulties America experienced in financing the war without loss of U.S. domination over Europe. In fact, it is hardly too much to say that France effectively destroyed that hegemony, and contributed to the transformation of the United States from a dictator of the direction of Europe's evolution to a beggar at the doors of Europe's central banks.

Such a change in the world position of the United States may have been implicit in the cost of its Asian war. It was made explicit, and was precipitated as active antagonism between Europe's and America's monetary and trading interests, by a shrewd and calculated move by France.

At the 1964 meetings the Anglo-American axis proposed something akin to what subsequently would become Special Drawing Rights or "paper gold." The suggestion was that IMF quotas be increased and paid for entirely out of paper as a book-keeping entry, not in gold. Europe squelched this plan, the Dutch representative insisting that "in accordance with the precedent of the increase of the Fund's resources in 1959, the obligation to pay 25% of the increase in quota in gold should be maintained." If the United States would not itself impose corrective measures, they would be imposed by the payments-surplus economies.

The problem was that the traditional balance-of-payments adjustment process was not sufficient to counteract the military disequilibrium in America's international payments. The normal deflationary policies applied in stabilization programs serve only to cure payments deficits resulting from adverse price movements and monetary inflation in private sectors with excess income and liquidity and excessively low interest rates. The appropriate response to a situation where the payments deficit results mainly from spending on government account for policy reasons that are not price-responsive is to stop the spending at its source, by altering public policies. However, these policies generally are not responsive to price and liquidity movements in the marketplace. They are the results of strategy in which economic considerations tend to be subordinated to political objectives. Neither excessive wage payments nor excessive investment spending were in themselves the cause of the U.S. payments difficulties. The problem was excessive military spending, especially overseas.

Because the costs of the Vietnam War were superimposed on an economy not far from effectively full employment, the U.S. domestic sector was severely destabilized. Instead of taxing the nation to pay for the war, the government engaged in the more politically acceptable practice of deficit financing. The balance of payments thus deteriorated not only from the Pentagon's direct foreign exchange expenditures associated with its war in Asia, but from that portion of the private sector's surplus liquidity that expressed itself via the foreign investment and import accounts as a demand for European assets and industrial goods. So great was the net infusion of funds into the economy that what did not result in pushing up price levels through demand-inflation expressed itself as a demand for imports, worsening the trade balance.

Part of the problem was simply that the United States did not want to pay for its war in Vietnam. The Korean War had been financed essentially by the Federal Reserve's monetizing the federal deficit, an effort that transferred the war's cost onto some future generation, or more accurately from future taxpayers to future bondholders. But in 1964, as the United States once again committed itself to military involvement, the likelihood of its settling its payments deficit in the foreseeable future declined. Foreign central banks would have to bear at least the foreign exchange costs of the war. Toward this end U.S. financial strategists sought to restructure the International Monetary Fund, regardless of Europe's wishes. If the U.S. payments deficit were to persist indefinitely, the IMF would have to be be transformed to accommodate it. This posed with utmost clarity the question of the degree to which Europe could be induced to absorb the costs of an aggressive American war over which Europe had no control and in whose outcome it had no real interest.

Since 1914, war had been the major factor in European–U.S. balance-of-payments relations. World War I and its aftermath had transferred the world's financial power from Europe to the United States, and World War II pushed this balance even further to U.S. advantage. Now the war in Southeast Asia threatened to reverse the flow of financial power, despite the build-up of long-term assets abroad by U.S. private investors. This danger to U.S. hegemony prompted U.S. monetary officials to take the lead in restructuring the world monetary system.

That the direction of change would be away from gold was apparent. With the world's gold threatening to return to Europe, the United States saw its financial power dwindling. Gold, American strategists recognized, was indeed power. If U.S. gold were flowing out, the basis of world financial power must be changed in order that U.S. diplomatic and financial hegemony be maintained. U.S. monetary strategists therefore attempted to shift the basis of financial power away from gold toward debt, and more specifically away from the creditor-oriented rules of international finance that the United States had voiced at Bretton Woods to the debtor-oriented proposals it had repudiated when they had been put forth by Keynes in 1943.

The pretext for reforming the IMF was of course not America's need to finance the war in Southeast Asia and its purchase of European industry with Europe's funds, but the politically less touchy thesis that, for world trade to continue to grow at historic rates, a proportional increase in world liquidity was necessary. Because of private hoarding, this increase was not being supplied by newly mined gold. The balance therefore would have to come either through increased use of the dollar as the key currency or through Special Drawing Rights. Under the new U.S. plan the Fund would cease to be a mere pool of national currencies, but would develop overdraft facilities for use by deficit countries, headed by the United States.

To this suggestion Europeans replied that the function of international liquidity was not so much to finance trade as such, but imbalances in world trade and payments. Exports and imports could perhaps multiply tenfold, but if they remained in balance there would be no increase in deficits needing financing. The solution to the U.S. balance-of-payments problem was thus a U.S. economic policy aimed at financing its own international payments, not really to finance the deficits of other countries. Still, Europe permitted the IMF to increase its quotas by 25 per cent in 1966, and allowed it once more to redeposit most of its increased gold holdings in the U.S. Treasury.

The limiting factor on how long this global inflationary policy could persist was the ability of the world's gold markets to withstand its growing pressures. In the background was the fact that the domestic U.S. currency – that is, its Federal Reserve notes in circulation – was legally backed 25 per cent by gold. As the U.S. domestic money supply increased and as U.S. gold flowed out, the intercept of these trends visibly approached. The 25 per cent legal gold backing in effect froze a corresponding volume of gold from being used by the United States to settle its payments deficits. Less and less would be available for this purpose as more and more money was created, even if U.S. gold holdings were to remain stable.

As noted above, one step to help conserve its gold was taken by the Treasury in organizing the Gold Pool early in 1961, following the sharp increase in gold prices during the Kennedy–Nixon presidential campaign. To alleviate future gold speculation, U.S. monetary authorities took the lead in getting Britain, the six Common Market nations and Switzerland to pledge their gold reserves to support the price of gold. These eight

European countries accepted the burden of meeting 50 per cent of the Pool's net sales or, alternatively, of purchasing half the gold offered to the Pool so as to maintain a stable price by supplying or buying the metal at $35 an ounce.

The magnitude of America's defeat when the Gold Pool was disbanded on Sunday, March 17, 1968 may be indicated by the intensity with which the United States had fought to preserve it intact. Through the Gold Pool the U.S. Government had given visible evidence to the world that the dollar was "as good as gold" by being worth $\frac{1}{35}$ of a troy ounce of the metal. By supporting the value of the dollar at this price, the Pool encouraged individuals and governments to hold on to their dollars, which they could invest in income-earning assets that at any time, they were led to believe, they could convert into gold.

Despite the Pool's activities, gold speculation accelerated in 1964 when foreign official short-term dollar claims grew to exceed the stated value of the U.S. gold stock. Nor were fears mitigated as the United States exerted conspicuous pressure on Europe's governments not to cash in their dollars for gold. It became clear that some political solution to the disparity between the value of foreign dollar holdings and the U.S. gold stock would have to be found. This solution ultimately would have to entail a revaluation of gold.

Despite this long-term inevitability, the Gold Pool succeeded for nearly seven years in holding the price of gold at $35 an ounce on London markets, although prices in other markets frequently jumped above this level. Gradually, as the position of the dollar deteriorated under the burden of America's continued balance-of-payments deficits, it became impossible to maintain the orderly market that the Pool was formed to ensure.

The Pool's collapse came at the end of a series of crises dating from June 1967, when France withdrew from the pooling agreement, although at U.S. request it remained a nominal member for public relations purposes. By withdrawing, France took the lead among its European neighbors in refusing to suffer any further gold losses as the penalty that it, not the United States, was obliged to suffer as a result of America's overseas military involvement and expanding U.S. foreign investment. To preserve the Pool intact the U.S. Treasury picked up France's 9 per cent share, increasing its gold subscription to 59 per cent of net Pool sales.

Gold losses by the Pool's active members proceeded for years at a moderate rate, but havoc ensued after the pound sterling was forced to devalue on November 18, 1967. Gold Pool sales amounted to nearly $800 million during the rest of November alone, with the United States putting up some $475 million of this sum. Nor was the furor mitigated when France, in order to prevent a run on the franc, felt itself obliged to reveal publicly that in June it had terminated active membership in the Gold Pool. Only by so doing could France assure foreign exchange dealers that the reserves of the Bank of France itself were not being drained by the massive gold speculation. The announcement, however, was construed with somewhat more sinister overtones in some quarters, which speculated that France had joined Russia and South Africa in pressing for a higher gold price out of motives unrelated to the realities of the world monetary situation.

In an attempt to stem the movement out of paper into gold, the remaining Gold Pool nations met in Frankfurt on November 27, 1967. At the conclusion of this conference they announced their joint determination to continue meeting any and all demands for gold at $35 at ounce. This statement temporarily squelched speculative activity.

News soon leaked out that U.S. officials had set forth a number of proposals at this meeting. First, pressure was brought to bear upon Canada and Australia, among other nations, to join the Pool to demonstrate international solidarity vis-à-vis the world's gold speculators. This met with a cold response in view of the clear likelihood of further gold losses during 1968 by gold-holding countries. Canada nevertheless agreed to sell or lend the United States some $100 million of its gold stock.

Another American proposal, adopted without publicity, was for Gold Pool members to be billed only at the end of each month for their sales commitments, instead of being required to meet these commitments on a current basis. The balance apparently was to be met out of Bank of England reserves. This proved a boon to the United States, for even though the Gold Pool lost approximately $1 billion in the month of December, following upon November's $1 billion loss, the 59 per cent U.S. contribution was not reflected until January 1968. By that time some reflux probably had occurred in speculative activity and, of greater importance, after the Federal Reserve's currency in circulation had been seasonally reduced following the Christmas holidays. Thanks to this postponement, and also because of the roughly $1.2 billion double-counting of IMF gold as part of U.S. gold holdings, the gold cover was maintained at over 28 per cent of Federal Reserve notes outstanding. More timely and meaningful accounting would have reduced the American gold cover by over $1.7 billion, moving it below the legal 25 per cent backing for the nation's currency. That would have set off a panic, as the United States would have been left with no gold with which to settle foreign claims.

American representatives at the November 1967 meeting also suggested a three-tiered price of gold. The idea was to divide the London gold market into three distinct markets, each with its own price of gold set by its own set of buyers and sellers. One market would be for official sales among governments at $35 an ounce. A second was to be restricted to *bona fide* industrial users at a floating price, comparable to the system that governed prices for copper, zinc and other metals traded on the London Metal Exchange. Prices in this market would reflect demand forces within the gold-consuming countries, and might exceed $35 an ounce. Admission to this market, which was limited to preexisting gold, would require specific authorization from the central bank of the nation of which the prospective purchaser was a citizen or legal resident. The third market would be for newly mined gold. All speculative demand among non-industrial gold users would be limited to this market. It would have been here, therefore, that prices presumably would have been highest, effectively revaluing the price of gold so far as the mining industry was concerned.

This multi-tiered system was designed to enable the United States to maintain its commitment to buy and sell gold at $35 an ounce to settle official intergovernmental transactions, but for no other purpose. It was summarily rejected by the other Gold Pool members, largely because of its inherent uncertainties. For instance, with gold hoarders being able to sell their accumulated gold only to industrial users, presumably at relatively low prices compared with newly mined gold, some illegal market was bound to develop elsewhere to bridge the widening price gap.

The most radical of U.S. proposals, which also was rejected, called for creation of "gold deposit certificates," a kind of fractional reserve double-counting of gold that would help phase out the metal as the major international reserve asset. Bankbooks would be created for the Gold Pool members. Each member would be credited with an amount equal to its sale of gold, despite the fact that this gold had been sold through the Pool and therefore had ceased to be available either to the Pool or to its member nations. Thus, if the Gold Pool were to sell $1 billion of gold in any given month, the United States, with its 59 per cent share, would turn over $590 million in gold at the end of the month and would receive a bankbook credit for this amount. According to this U.S. plan, the $590 million would be treated not merely as a simple receipt for the gold sold, but as a *bona fide* asset of the United States, continuing to be counted among its international reserves. Consequently, despite speculation against the dollar that could take the form of a flight out of paper into gold, reported U.S. international financial reserves would not be diminished, nor would those of other nations adhering to this plan.

However, America's arguments for this proposal were ill timed. Its representatives cited as a precedent for such double-counting the fact that the Federal Reserve already was counting over $1 billion of the IMF's gold kept in the United States as belonging to U.S. gold holdings. This sum even served as part of the legal gold backing for the dollar. It was treated not only as part of the IMF's total $3.8 billion net gold subscriptions, but at the time of removal of the 25 per cent gold cover for Federal Reserve currency in circulation, on March 18, 1968, was contributing some 2.7 percentage points to the currency's legal gold backing.

The U.S. plan would have transformed the Gold Pool into an international gold bank operating on the fractional reserve principle with credits for member nations' sales continuing to be counted as officially held reserves. France's monetary representatives responded to this suggestion by requesting that a prorated portion of the IMF's imminent $1.4 billion stabilization loan to Britain following its sterling devaluation be taken out of the proposed special IMF gold deposit. This French proposal was rejected by the Gold Pool members, but so was the American gold certificate device.

The U.S. proposals were leaked by Paul Fabra, financial editor of Le Monde, in that newspaper's issue of December 8, 1967. It was revealed that the United States proposed to establish bankbooks for the Gold Pool members, each member to be credited with an amount equal to its sales of gold. Gold Pool members would thereby treat "their contributions as they count gold now," summarized the Wall Street Journal, noting that this "certificate plan . . . would keep contributions from statistically shrinking their reserves."[10] On the day following the Le Monde story The New York Times reported that "officials ridiculed the suggestion as 'silly' and 'stupid.' . . . I've never heard of such a silly thing,' said one well-informed central banking source. 'I would hope that Mr. Hayes and Mr. Coombs would have more brains than to propose such a stupid thing.'"[11] Another source commented: "This is a ridiculous proposition. Nobody would ever accept it." U.S. Government spokesmen flatly denied that any such proposals had ever been made.

It must have been with some twinge of embarrassment, therefore, that two days later the U.S. Government made public the fact that it had indeed made these proposals. As could be expected, the awkward and belated handling of the situation by the United States served only to accelerate speculation that changes were underway in the gold markets. Renewed gold buying, this time feverish, struck London, Paris and Zurich.

This was met by near-panic in Congress. On December 12, Senators Jacob Javits of New York and Vance Hartke of Indiana proposed that the United States amend its Gold Reserve Act of 1934 so as to suspend all further sale of gold to France until that nation had redeemed in full its World War I debt.[12] These two senators also anticipated the events of August 1971 by suggesting that the United States simply embargo gold so as to oblige Europe to float its currencies upward relative to the dollar.

The Gold Pool was maintained in its previous form, although continuing pressures on the dollar undermined its activities. The United States was unwilling to take corrective measures to reduce its payments deficit, whether by increasing taxes, reducing the budget deficit or slowing its rate of monetary inflation. Increasing talk of a further build-up of forces in Vietnam implied an even more rapid deterioration in the U.S. balance of payments. The Tet offensive of February 1968, followed by North Korea's seizure of the U.S. naval vessel *Pueblo*, strengthened this speculation.

U.S. military strategy in Asia had not envisaged an upper limit on how much foreign exchange could be spent on war without weakening the U.S. position in all other areas of the world. So strong had the U.S. economy seemed in the early postwar years that U.S. diplomats did not foresee that U.S. military overheads might become so costly at some point as to negate the general aims of U.S. diplomacy. By 1968, however, the direct foreign exchange cost of U.S. military activity abroad was running at about $4.5 billion annually, of which about $2.5 billion was the direct result of the war in Vietnam. The indirect overseas costs of the Vietnam War amounted to another $2 billion, including the adverse effect of intensified war production and high defense spending on the balance of trade. The Vietnam War resulted in a shortage of domestic capital and skilled labor, an increased rate of domestic inflation, special and enlarged import needs, and diversion of facilities from production of export items. "To put it bluntly," asserted Senator Hartke, "Vietnam has ruined any chance we might have had for attaining equilibrium in our balance of payments. . . . Until recently there was curiously little official acknowledgment that after all Vietnam is the real culprit."[13]

Such recognition was by no means universal, especially among Johnson appointees. Under-Secretary of State Nicholas Katzenbach gave it little acknowledgment as late as January 1968. Even if Vietnam did not exist, he asserted, the U.S. payments deficit would be about equal to what it then was. Regardless of official blindness on the part of U.S. spokesmen, however, Europeans insisted on relating the question of further extension of credits to the United States to that of the Vietnam War. The Italian

Foreign Minister's reply to Mr Katzenbach, for example, was that "a prompt end to the Vietnam War would help solve the U.S. balance-of-payments problem."[14]

Italy in fact took the lead among Europe's central banks in balking at further financing of the U.S. deficit. In January 1968 the Bank of Italy proposed that all future swap transactions between the U.S. and European central banks be channeled through the IMF, obliging the United States to assure Europe of serious policies being taken to end U.S. payments deficit. In other words, the United States would have to subject its domestic policies to the scrutiny of foreign creditors as the price for maintaining its financial solvency. IMF surveillance mechanisms, it was proposed, would be brought to bear.

However, the United States had it in its power to provoke a world monetary breakdown by repudiating its overseas obligations. Recognizing this fact, Europe capitulated. On March 18, 1968, the day the Gold Pool was officially disbanded, the swap agreements were increased by $9 billion, raising the total U.S. swap network to $20 billion. Of this sum, foreign central banks agreed to accept $10.5 billion of U.S. currency without cashing it in for gold.[15]

By early March 1968 the death of the Gold Pool seemed imminent. In effect its members were quietly withdrawing. The Bank of Italy, for example, was using the currencies it received for the gold it provided to the Pool to go out and buy more gold elsewhere so as to replenish its gold stock. Belgium, seeing Italy's gold holdings rise rather than decline, was balking at future contributions. The Bank of England's ability to meet further gold sales out of its own reserves was virtually exhausted.

On March 12, 1968, a bare two days before all the U.S. gold not tied up in the 25 per cent legal backing for Federal Reserve currency was depleted, the connection between war and the gold drain was clearly made in Congress. Senate doves joined to oppose a waiver of the 25 per cent gold cover on the dollar, recognizing that if they could effectively prevent the release of any more gold to settle the U.S. payments deficits, the Johnson Administration would be forced to ask Congress for an official Declaration of War in order to continue financing military activity in Southeast Asia. The Senate narrowly voted, by 39 to 37, to remove the gold cover, with Senators Aiken, Church, Gruening, Hatfield, McGovern and Young in dissent, joined by numerous hawks who had their own reasons for wanting to exert congressional restraint over President Johnson.

Nonetheless, the Gold Pool, the fixed link between the dollar and gold, was not to survive the coming weekend. By the close of trading on

Thursday, March 14, 1968, the United States, because of the necessity to maintain a 25 per cent legal gold cover for its Federal Reserve notes, was unable to supply the Pool with enough gold to meet another day's sales. The Hartke–Javits proposal to suspend future gold sales to France until such time as it began to repay its World War I debt was reintroduced into the Senate. It was supported by antiwar Senators Hatfield, Church, McGovern and Scott. This was at best a desperation move as well as political failure by these opponents of the Vietnam War to perceive that France was their sole *de facto* ally in the West in that opposition. In response to the growing panic, the London gold market closed down. Three days later the seven remaining active Gold Pool nations, meeting in Washington, announced that the Gold Pool had been dissolved.

Collapse of the Gold Pool gave way to a two-tiered pricing system for gold based on the U.S. proposals made the preceding November. The only modification was that *bona fide* industrial users were lumped together with all other gold consumers and hoarders, as there was no practical way to determine the extent to which jewelry represented a form of hoarding. The price of gold immediately moved against the dollar, to approximately $38 an ounce.

One response to this *de facto* devaluation of the dollar vis-à-vis gold was that the oil-producing countries demanded, through their cartel OPEC, an immediate increase in royalties and taxes from U.S. and British petroleum companies in proportion to the declines of the dollar and sterling relative to gold. If the price of gold were to remain at, say, $38 an ounce, the existing contractual dollar or sterling royalty and tax payments would have to be increased by $3/35$ to maintain a constant gold value of these payments as measured on the open market. Through this policy the OPEC nations tried to conserve the purchasing power of their income flows in terms of gold. They later backed down, pressing their attack in more direct areas by simply demanding higher royalty payments outright.

On March 31, 1968, millions of Americans heard Lyndon Johnson announce on television that he would not run again for the presidency, and that he would not substantially escalate the Vietnam War despite the Tet offensive. Unperceived by the public at large, the point finally had been reached at which depletion of U.S. gold holdings abruptly altered the country's military policy. As one expert noted: "The European financiers are forcing peace on us. For the first time in American history, our European creditors have forced the resignation of an American president."[16]

The tide, it seemed, had turned against the United States. Its position of preeminence in the world had required total success in the functioning of the world monetary system it had created. That system was now basically jeopardized. Oddly, this was not because gold had drained from the system, but because it had become translocated within the system. The international monetary order had not really been an international order, but a national system that managed to extend itself over the entire globe. As it grew more international in character with the redistribution of gold reserves, it grew more fragile, for the U.S. dollar and gold had become synonymous, in law as well as in fact. When factually they ceased to be synonymous, when the gold cover of other currencies began to exceed that of the dollar, the legal equivalence between gold and the dollar became dubious.

Yet it remained a legal fiction. In 1971 the United States formally repudiated gold claims on its monetary reserves. But the world was not yet ready to repudiate in turn the IMF and the rest of the American creations that had grown to represent the world order. Yet all constraints were removed on U.S. economic profligacy. The U.S. budget deficit for the fiscal year ending June 30, 1972 was calmly forecast by the Treasury at close to $39 billion. By September 1971, U.S. liquid liabilities to foreign official institutions had grown to about $43 billion, an increase of about $25 billion in less than a year. Liquid liabilities to all foreigners, public and private, had risen to almost $61 billion, an increase of $33 billion or so since the Vietnam War build-up had begun in early 1965.

Effectively speaking, not only had the United States compelled the other nations of the West to pay for the overseas costs of the U.S. war in Asia, it had accomplished something of far greater significance. Those overseas military costs were now the central banking assets of the non-U.S. members of the IMF. Whatever they might desire, the central banks of Europe had no choice but to continue to accept the paper dollar equivalents annually created as the domestic and overseas deficits of the United States increased. Otherwise the whole shaky structure of the world monetary system would collapse into rubble. America had succeeded in forcing other countries to pay for its wars regardless of their choice in the matter. This was something never before accomplished by any nation in history.

12 Power through Bankruptcy, 1968–70

Considering the present state of *Europe, France* and *Spain* being Masters of the Mines. The other Nations seem to be under a necessity of setting up another Money. The only Reason can be given why it has not yet been done, is, that the nature of Money has not been rightly understood . . .

John Law, *Money and Trade Considered, with a Proposal for Supplying the Nation with Money* (Edinburgh: 1705), p. 77

Three courses were open to the U.S. Government upon the collapse of the Gold Pool in 1968: immediately to pull out of the war in Southeast Asia and cut back overseas and domestic military expenditures to allow the dollar to firm again on world markets; to continue the war, paying for its foreign exchange costs with further losses of gold; or to induce Europe and other payments-surplus areas to continue to accumulate dollars and dollar equivalents exchangeable only for other dollar equivalents not convertible into gold.

The first option would have involved acceptance of defeat of the world's superpower by a handful of half-armed peasants, and hence an impertinent destruction of the American myth of world military supremacy. 1968 was an election year, and the Democratic Party dared not approach the electorate with military defeat as the outcome of its policies. Political fear thus foreclosed the first option.

The second option open to the administration in 1968 was highly limited, for the gold cover had shrunk while the nation's money supply was expanding rapidly in the Johnson Administration's "guns and butter" economy. The U.S. gold stock had fallen to $10 billion by year end 1968, a decline of $6.9 billion since 1960 and $2.9 billion since 1965. Meanwhile, the narrowly defined money supply in December 1968 had grown to $195 billion, about eighteen times the gold reserve. This ratio compared to $166.7 billion in 1965, twelve times that year's gold stock. The narrowly defined money supply – currency in circulation outside banks, plus demand deposits – had grown in excess of $28 billion in three years, while the more broadly defined money supply – currency in circulation outside banks, plus demand deposits, plus time deposits – grew by $86.3 billion from 1965 to 1968.

During these three years the federal government debt had risen by $31.3 billion, to $344.4 billion. Rolling over of this public debt became increasingly difficult as the amount due within one year rose from $88 billion in 1965 to $106 billion in 1968. Obviously the second option – paying for the war by a continued drain on gold – could be sustained only briefly.

This left the United States with only one practical option: to induce the central banks and Treasuries of foreign countries to refrain from cashing in any more dollars for gold, but to accumulate dollar assets in growing amounts, whatever their fears regarding the stability of the dollar. By its nature, this option could not be a wholly autonomous decision of the United States. In the last analysis the decision had to be made by the IMF, the Group of Ten and political leaders in the payments surplus nations of Europe and Asia. It had to be secured by at least a token reflux of gold to America, *i.e.*, a halt to the hemorrhage of gold, at least temporarily.

It was to achieve this objective that U.S. monetary officials developed plans for international financial reform immediately following dissolution of the Gold Pool. The Pool had been designed to tap other nations' gold reserves to support the U.S. balance of payments. Now, the U.S. Government wished to move away from gold altogether and supplant it with some new monetary instrument based mainly on the U.S. payments deficit. If possible, the United States should receive credits from Europe, Japan and other payments surplus nations automatically. This idea was to become the plan for Special Drawing Rights (SDRs) within the IMF, or "paper gold" as it was widely called.

To transform central bank arrangements along these lines it was first necessary to terminate Europe's gold purchases from the U.S. Treasury. In the aftermath of the collapse of the Gold Pool, the major industrial nations, with the notable exception of France, agreed not to cash in their gold holdings of U.S. Treasury instruments for gold. France, the danger point in this system because of its insistence on accumulating gold, was taken out of the picture in May 1968 by its student riots and the attendant flight of gold from France, which continued to deplete that nation's monetary reserves until early 1971.

Various arrangements were made by U.S. Treasury officials to ensure that foreign countries would relend their dollar accumulations to the U.S. Treasury. Not only would this not drain away the nation's remaining gold supply, it would help finance the federal debt, which by 1968 was exerting major pressures on the New York capital market. Also, foreign private hoarders of gold found it increasingly difficult to secure U.S. gold via their national central banks. American political pressures along these lines produced an increase in U.S. gold reserves of $967 million in 1969.

One country that was accumulating surplus dollars was Canada, in part because of the average $1 billion annual borrowings by her municipalities and corporations in U.S. markets during the late 1960s. The Interest Equalization Tax had closed off this market, producing financial stringency in Canada. The U.S. Treasury agreed to exempt Canadian borrowers from this tax only if its Treasury took steps to offset the adverse balance-of-payments effect of this borrowing on the United States. Since July 21, 1963, Canada had been investing its foreign exchange reserves, over and above the usual operating levels, in special U.S. Treasury securities instead of cashing them in for U.S. gold or holding them in negotiable or marketable claims on the United Statess. "In particular," wrote Canada's Minister of Finance E. J. Benson to U.S. Secretary of the Treasury Henry Fowler on December 16, 1968,

> we have taken steps to prevent Canada from becoming a "pass-through" channel for the flow of funds from the United States. We have also found various appropriate means of supporting the payments position of the United States. Thus the Canadian Government has invested its United States dollar reserves (in excess of working balances) in Special non-marketable issues of the United States Treasury. It also turned to the expanding capital markets of Europe to find funds with which to rebuild Canada's foreign exchange reserves. In the course of this year substantial sums have been added to our reserves as a result of borrowings of the Government of Canada and other Canadians outside the United States, and the investment of these sums has provided support to the payments position of the United States. . . . In the light of all these considerations I can reiterate to you that it is not an objective of Canadian policy to achieve permanent increases in our exchange reserves through unnecessary borrowing in the United States.

The U.S.–Canadian agreement was a model for subsequent agreements, both formal and informal. Much as Britain had asked the United States in 1945 to reinvest the proceeds of its foreign investments abroad so as to help stabilize the economies of dollar-deficit countries, the United States now asked Europe, Japan, and Canada to reinvest their central bank dollar holdings in the U.S. economy, specifically in U.S. Treasury securities, in order to recycle the funds thrown off by the U.S. deficit. America thus joined the ranks of the world's dollar-deficit economies!

In one respect Europe and Japan had little choice. Europe's official dollar balances were in effect frozen, as sterling balances had been in 1945. These balances could not be cashed in for American gold because of their very size, $12.5 billion by the end of 1968, a sum that exceeded total U.S. gold holdings. Most of these dollars therefore were invested in illiquid U.S. Treasury securities. A Dollar Bloc financed by blocked dollar deposits had been created.

The central banks of major powers that did wish to add to their gold holdings did so from sources other than the U.S. Treasury. Japan's $366 million in gold holdings in 1966, for instance, rose only to $737 million in 1971, a modest increase achieved by way of the International Monetary Fund. Most nations that ended up with the dollars being thrown off by America's payments deficits continued to recycle their funds back to the United States. Thus, the more the U.S. deficit persisted, the larger became the volume of intergovernmental claims on the U.S. Government. The interwar position of the United States as the world's great intergovernmental creditor was reversed. The United States was now the single largest intergovernmental debtor.

This fact meant that the constraints implicit in the gold exchange standard were nullified. It became possible for a single nation, the United States, to export its inflation by settling its payments deficit with paper instead of with gold. There was no limit to ability of the United States to print paper or create new credit, despite the fact that there was a visible limit to its gold stock.

To be sure, in accepting U.S. paper instead of gold, foreign central banks were accepting paper that was still the world's reserve currency. Consequently, each new injection of U.S. paper into the monetary reserves of foreign countries inflated their monetary base. Whatever the realities, the dollar was still, at least in legal fiction, a gold equivalent for the world's central banks. America's payments deficits therefore worked to inflate the currencies of other nations, becoming the engine of global inflation in the late 1960s.

A rising world price level thus became, in effect, a derivative function of U.S. monetary policy. The United States gave notice that it henceforth would act vis-à-vis the world without economic constraints, and the world would have to accommodate itself to this fact.

It was in this setting that U.S. monetary officials proposed creation of Special Drawing Rights, a variant of the Common Reserve Units (CRUs) that had been discussed but not created in 1964. They were an intellectual counterpart to Keynes's original proposals for paper gold. At Bretton Woods he had proposed that the IMF should create an international unit-of-account, which would be distributed to deficit countries to settle their payments deficits with the United States and with other payments-surplus nations in the postwar period. This paper credit, he proposed, was to be accepted by the United States and all surplus nations as equivalent to gold. At the end of the reconstruction process, according to Keynes's plan, the United States would be left with international reserves comprising paper credits and gold. Europe and Asia for their part would suffer no loss in net reserves, but instead would have a massive accumulation of real capital. This stratagem would have enabled Europe to retain what meager gold stocks it still possessed. The continent would have been able to finance its reconstruction with imported capital goods from the United States, and to pay in time out of the real net proceeds of future production rather than in gold, which was needed to back the growth in credit that would fuel the required new direct investment.

U.S. representatives to Bretton Woods dismissed this proposal. One reason was that if this paper credit were to count among U.S. international reserves, it would be equivalent in inflationary potential to a vast inflow of gold itself. The United States would wind up importing Europe's inflation. On the other hand, not to count this paper gold as *bona fide* monetary reserves would mean that America would have to make outright gifts of its output. U.S. diplomats did not foresee that some day it would be the United States that would beg for such credit. They therefore demanded that the IMF be created as a literal fund of gold and foreign currencies. Their ideas ultimately became the Fund's Articles of Agreement. IMF resources would be lent to deficit countries to help them tide over temporary balance-of-payments deficits, but would neither create international credit nor finance payments deficits.

By 1968 all this had changed. Acting in concert, the United States and Britain urged a new debt instrument to be accepted by payments-surplus nations, to be given free of charge to payments-deficit countries in proportion to their IMF quotas. Instead of accumulating more gold, dollars or pounds, which would represent potential claims on U.S. and British gold stocks, payments-surplus nations would be offered Special Drawing Rights on the IMF. These credits eventually would be repaid by the deficit countries, but they would be permitted automatically to draw on the resources of payments-surplus nations without drawing down their existing international reserves.

These Special Drawing Rights would be created and distributed by the IMF in keeping with its members' gold tranches, that is, in proportion to their original subscriptions to the IMF, which also determined their voting power in the Fund. This meant that the United States would receive more than one-fifth of the $5 billion in SDRs proposed to be created over a five-year period, starting in 1970. Britain and the United States would be given a painless means by which to incur more deficits, avoiding the adjustment process and loss of gold they otherwise would suffer.

Creation of Special Drawing Rights was a fundamental departure from the Fund's creditor-oriented philosophy. The use of SDRs to sustain long-term payments imbalance made it necessary to drop Article I, s. 6 of the IMF charter, which stated the Fund's purpose as being "to shorten the duration and lessen the degree of disequilibrium in the international balances of payments of members." The idea indeed was to permit the United States, Britain and other payments-deficit countries to afford a higher and longer degree of disequilibrium without having to submit to the classical financial adjustment process.

The SDR proposal also was in violation of Article XIII, which stated that IMF credit must not be used to "serve to compensate large or protracted outflows of capital on the part of member states." Europeans were quick to point out that acceleration of American capital investment in Europe was a major factor in the U.S. payments deficit, and that SDRs would accelerate this outflow.

The SDR proposal also contradicted Europe's insistence that there was no need to supplement existing international reserve assets, and that what was required was rather some means of imposing constraints on the payments deficits and inflationary policies of the United States and Britain. The Common Market nations were emphatic about this, but they controlled only 17 per cent of the IMF's voting power, 3 per cent less than the votes required to veto IMF proposals. The United States, with its 22 per cent of the voting power, was alone in its unilateral ability to veto any proposal that it found to run counter to its national interests. To the EEC's objections U.S. negotiators retorted that the Common Market could increase its proportional voting power in the IMF by raising its gold tranche subscription to the IMF, *i.e.*, by surrendering gold to the IMF. This would have swelled the Fund's loanable resources further, aggravating the liquidity plethora to which the central banks of Common Market countries were objecting.

Ultimately, the Common Market won the concession that although a 20 per cent vote would remain necessary to veto the establishment of

SDRS, a 15 per cent veto would suffice to block the SDRs from being activated. This meant that the Common Market nations could use their 17 per cent vote to postpone activation of SDRs until such time as they deemed them necessary and desirable.

The remaining problem to be settled was when – and indeed, even whether – the SDRs would have to be repaid. U.S. representatives were obliged to relinquish their early stance for non-repayment of the SDRs with foreign exchange or gold, and for the IMF simply to liquidate them at some point, as Keynes had wished to do with his "bancor" credits in his 1943 draft for the IMF. A five-year repayment period was settled upon, so that the SDR credits would represent medium-term rather than short- or long-term financing.

But just what was to happen at the end of the five years if the SDR credits were not repaid was not spelled out. There was a provision specifying that "a member's average use of SDRs over a basic period is not to exceed 70 per cent of its average allocation . . . However, the reconstitution provision does not prevent a country from using all its SDRs when its balance-of-payments difficulties are temporary in nature."[1] IMF members subscribing to the SDR plan were obliged to accept SDRs up to an amount equal to twice their own original allocation, in addition to this initial allocation itself.

Although the New York Federal Reserve Bank claimed that "this new facility to some extent represents a logical extension of the Fund's current operations," its economists proceeded to demonstrate how the SDR proposal in fact reversed the IMF's operating philosophy. "First, SDRs will be more readily available than the credit that the IMF now provides through drawings in the credit tranches." At the time, a country was able to draw on its credit tranche, that is, sums in excess of its gold subscription, "only after it has agreed to take measures to correct its balance of payments." But there were no such constraints on a country's use of automatic SDR credits. That was the essence of their being automatic. "Its exercise of this right will not be subject to consultation or prior challenge nor contingent on the adoption of prescribed policies designed to restore balance-of-payments equilibrium," the New York Fed continued. "Second, the SDRs are intended to provide a permanent addition to international reserves, whereas most current IMF transactions give rise to only a temporary increase. Third, the SDRs will be distributed to all participants in proportion to their IMF quotas. On the other hand, reserves that arise as a by-product of the Fund's credit operations normally add, in the first instance, to the total reserves of the borrowing country alone and only indirectly to the reserves of other countries. Finally, the use of SDRs does not entail repayment according to a fixed schedule, as does the use of the Fund's ordinary resources, although SDR balances must be partially reconstituted following large and prolonged use."

Automatic paper credit without the famous IMF "conditionalities" thus was to replace gold and hard money as the new basis of world liquidity. If the United States were to lose its gold to other nations, no such nation could use that gold as the basis for autonomous economic power. The United States would draw on other nations' funds to continue financing its payments deficit, institutionalizing not only this deficit itself but also the disequilibrating government spending policies, particularly in the military sector, which were the major cause of this deficit.

The spirit of the U.S. proposals for Special Drawing Rights had been anticipated as long ago as 1682 by an anonymous British advocate of paper money who perceived that

whatsoever quantity of credit shall be raised in this office, will be as good, and of as much use, as if there were so much money in specie added to the present stock of the nation . . . 'tis more prudent and advantageous to a nation, to have the common standard or medium of their trade within their power, and to arise from their native product, than to be at the mercy of a foreign prince for his gold and silver, which he may at pleasure behold. . . . Credit can neither be hoarded up, nor transported to the nation's disadvantage; which consequently frees us from the care and necessity of making laws to prevent exportation of bullion or coin, being always able to command a credit of our own, . . . as useful, and as much as shall be necessary.[2]

Under such conditions in the modern world the proposed structural reform of the IMF was akin to a tax levied upon payments-surplus nations by the United States to pay the foreign exchange costs of the American departure from classical economic drives to a drive toward classical military imperialism. It was a tax because it represented a transfer of goods and resources from the civilian and government sectors of payments-surplus nations to payments-deficit countries, a transfer for which no tangible *quid pro quo* was to be received by the nations who had refrained from embarking upon the extravagance of war.

In September 1969 the IMF nations voted to activate $825 million of SDRs on January 1, 1970, to be followed by equivalent distribution every three months for the next three years. Only seven members elected not to subscribe to the SDR plan: the Arab oil-producing states of Kuwait, Saudi

Arabia and Libya, plus Lebanon, Ethiopia, Singapore and Portugal. These nations therefore did not have to accept SDRs in lieu of gold, dollars or other more tangible assets.

The new arrangements enabled the U.S. payments deficit to widen still further. In the first quarter of 1970 it amounted to $3.1 billion as measured on the official transactions basis, followed by $2 billion in the second quarter, another $2 billion in the third, and $3.5 billion in the final quarter. This prompted Europeans publicly to express regret that the SDRs had ever been issued in the first place. According to the *Journal of Commerce*, they proposed to undo some of what had been done by suggesting a formula for creating SDRs after 1972 that would link their creation to "some index that will slow the increase in world reserves from other sources, such as dollar outflow and purchases of gold by IMF and South Africa."[3] The IMF also suggested,

> although it did not actually state it, that the new special drawing rights (SDR) might not have been activated if it had known that the U.S. would continue to run a very large deficit in its balance of payments. The continued outpouring of dollars plus the creation of $3.4 billion of SDR on Jan. 1 increased world liquidity by about double the amount that the fund earlier had estimated. "The SDR allocation proposal made an allowance for a possible rise in official holdings of U.S. dollars over the ensuing three to five years of some $0.5 billion to $1 billion on average," IMF noted . . . the fund stated that "it regards the need to rectify the U.S. payments position as the most urgent task remaining in the field of international payments."

Pierre-Paul Schweitzer, the Fund's managing director, went so far as to suggest that foreign central banks cash in all new dollar accumulations for U.S. gold so as to begin laying down the law to U.S. authorities. "Until the payments position of the United States is brought into balance," he stated, "it is important that the deficit should be financed by the use of United States reserve assets to the extent necessary to avoid an excessive expansion of official holdings of dollars by other countries. A policy of this kind is indeed necessary if control over the issuance of Special Drawing Rights is also to provide the means of regulating the aggregate volume of world reserves."[4]

This statement gave the lie to the New York Federal Reserve Bank's assertion, popularly accepted in the United States, that France's position within the Common Market toward the U.S. payments deficit was unique.

"The position of the French government," Barrett and Greene wrote, "as stated by Michel Debre, Minister of Economy and Finance, is 'that the mechanism cannot come into play until the balance-of-payments deficits affecting the countries whose currencies are designated as "reserve currency" have disappeared.' This is an extreme view which has not been taken by other countries."[5] Not only was this view not extreme – and by no means unique to France – but it had become the majority view of the non-U.S. IMF leadership. Indeed, Mr Schweitzer's statement of September 21, 1970 had been anticipated two weeks earlier when the IMF released its report for the year at its annual joint meeting with the World Bank. "If the United States' payments deficit on the official settlements basis continues," *The New York Times* summarized the IMF's position, "it might be better to finance 'a substantial portion' of it by running down United States monetary reserves and thus avoid 'an excessive expansion of official holdings of dollars of other countries and of international reserves in general.'"[6]

The IMF itself set the pace by cashing in some $400 million of its dollar-denominated Treasury securities for U.S. gold, withdrawing part of the deposit that had been double-counted in world liquidity as belonging separately to the IMF and to the U.S. Treasury. The Fund and its member countries also turned SDRs over to the U.S. Government. It thus turned out to be the United States that was receiving paper gold, although most of it was coming from the less developed countries that could not have paid in gold anyway. Foreign central banks were holding their gold purchases in abeyance, pending the outcome of the protectionist Mills tariff bill and a political assessment of just how their governments might best respond politically and economically.

U.S. monetary officials and economists embarked on a campaign to rationalize the U.S. payments deficit, hoping to deter Europe from calling the U.S. Government to account and to persuade foreign central banks to acquiesce in further expanding world liquidity through continued U.S. deficits. Two main lines of apologetics were put forth: a Structuralist Rationale, which sought to justify the deficit on the grounds of inherent world forces that could not be manipulated to restore payments equilibrium for the United States, and a theory called the International Financial Intermediary Hypothesis, which sought to explain away the deficit as merely a statistical anomaly.

The Structuralist Rationale held that the United States occupied a unique position in the world economy because, as Robert Roosa said, the United States had "undertaken external commitments, both military and economic." Given America's assertion of its position as Cold War leader, and the consequent requirements for payments outflows on military account and for related government transactions, "how can the balance of payments of such a country be expected to conform to the same pattern, and correct its aberrations by resort to the same means, as those indicated by the traditional norms?"[7] In other words, deflationary monetary policies at home would not affect the government's foreign policy, which was acknowledged to lie at the root of the deficit. The price non-Communist countries had to pay in exchange for the U.S. protective umbrella was to absorb this deficit.

America's foreign programs, Mr. Roosa continued, "by their nature and because of their critical importance for other prime objectives . . . cannot be left to vary purely as balancing residuals of trade accounts of leading countries." It followed that the U.S. Government and its military agencies could not be expected or required to spend funds only in accordance with what the private sector might generate through its foreign transactions. The government deficit must be accepted as an unchallengeable category of expenditures, whose magnitude must not be constrained by balance-of-payments considerations. Foreign nations must either provide the U.S. Treasury with the requisite funds directly, by holding their international reserves in U.S. Treasury securities or "Roosa Loans" negotiated with the Federal Reserve System or, by expanding their imports from the United States and limiting their exports, must permit the U.S. private sector to run a surplus of whatever magnitude was needed to balance the government outflow. In either case the traditional adjustment process would not be appropriate for the United States. It was up to foreign countries to adjust their economies to the payments needs of the United States. "Perhaps," Mr Roosa speculated, "by conventional standards, the United States would have to become a habitual renegade, barely able to keep its trade accounts in balance, with a modest surplus on current account, with an entrepot role for vast flows of capital both in and out, with a more or less regular increase in the short-term dollar liabilities used for transactions purposes around the world . . ."

This Structuralist Rationale went a step further by recognizing that the payments outflow on government account could not be compensated by surpluses on private transactions, contrary to what had been believed possible in the early 1960s. A study made by Hendrik Houthakker of the Council of Economic Advisers and Stephen Magee indicated that U.S. economic growth tended to be accompanied by imports rising more rapidly than exports, so that continued economic growth implied a dwindling trade balance. Data covering the years 1953–66 "suggested that as long as incomes rose, the United States economy, in its present form, would continue to draw in a more-than-proportional rise of imports – that the relevant elasticity determining purchases of goods abroad was income change in the United States, and that even if relative price stability could be attained, imports would go on rising at about the same pace." There seemed to be little America could do to alter these built-in structural relationships, The Houthakker–Magee study concluded. Indeed, "prospective deterioration in the United States trade balance will probably be especially marked vis-à-vis Japan and Canada, unless these countries maintain much higher rates of growth and inflation than the United States."[8]

This study may have been partially responsible for the hard-line U.S. position toward Japan regarding its widening trade surplus with the United States. At any rate, Mr. Roosa concluded from this study: "Since no economic policy for the United States could contemplate static incomes over time, the chances of regaining a trade surplus sufficient to carry most of the other United States overseas disbursements on capital and Government account were beginning to seem remote indeed." The alternative would be for the U.S. economy to stop growing.

On the other hand, an increase in domestic income, particularly one stemming from inflationary pressures, would tend to increase the U.S. payments surplus on capital account. Although inflation might slightly impair the U.S. trade balance, it was likely to spill over into the U.S. stock market, pushing up stock prices and attracting foreign speculative capital, while its upward impact on interest rates might attract foreign funds. This was after all what had happened during 1928–29. The resulting capital inflow might not have been desirable then, but it was desired now.

Allied to this structuralist argument was the assertion that if the United States actually were to begin putting its house in order, Europe would protest just as vigorously as it did about the U.S. deficits. "Our deficits have been continually criticized," argued Mr Roosa, "our efforts to correct them, particularly when the traditional formulae of deflation were being applied, have brought anguished complaints." U.S. deficits, it was implied, were the byproduct of America remaining a thriving market for foreign output, and hence were necessary for continued smooth functioning of the world economy and its credit system. The deficits seemed to be enriching all nations in their effects. However bad world inflation might be, it was more desirable than world deflation.

Such reasoning led to what was termed the International Financial Intermediary (IFI) hypothesis, which asserted that the U.S. payments deficit was just a statistical illusion.[9] The U.S. economy, it was argued, functioned much like a savings bank or a savings and loan association, which are called financial intermediaries because they borrow short-term savings and reinvest them in long-term assets, mainly mortgages. Much like a savings bank, the United States borrowed, *i.e.*, received short-term deposits from foreign dollar holders, and reinvested these funds long, *e.g.* in buying out European companies. Foreign investors elected to lend their dollar balances to foreign branches of U.S. banks instead of exchanging them for local currencies, partly in search for security against foreign currency devaluations, partly because Europe's credit markets were not as sophisticated as those in the United States and European stock markets likewise were not as open and active. Also, foreign central banks chose to invest their dollar surpluses in interest-bearing U.S. Treasury securities instead of in gold, as the latter earned no interest. U.S. international banks turned around and lent their Eurodollars to U.S. international corporations wishing to finance their foreign investment activities, including the buy-out of foreign companies. The U.S. Treasury used its inflow of foreign funds to finance U.S. Government operations abroad. Everything was a matter of choice, which is how economists tended to define every kind of transaction. The implication was that foreign holders of liquid funds, including central banks, just happened to have an exactly matching reciprocity of investment preferences with U.S. long-term investors and spenders, including the U.S. Government.

In such a situation one could not measure U.S. international financial imbalance simply by the liquidity deficit, defined as gold sales to foreign countries plus net U.S. short-term borrowings from foreigners. Just as a savings bank was not really in deficit when it invested its deposits in long-term mortgages, neither was the U.S. economy in deficit in borrowing short and lending long. Its short-term borrowing simply indicated "that foreigners had (and have) a positive demand for liquid dollar assets."[10] By definition, the theory stated, "assets and liabilities must be willingly held. Willingness to purchase and sell the existing flow of goods and services and to hold the existing stock of assets at existing prices is the definition of equilibrium in other parts of economic theory; it should be in explanations of the balance of payments, too. The existence of a positive foreign net demand for liquid dollar assets and gold combined implies, in the absence of an increase in world monetary gold stocks, that a U.S. deficit on the liquidity definition is not only consistent with equilibrium in the foreign exchange market but is a necessary condition of it . . ."

This purported to explain the dollar's strength in foreign exchange markets at times when its payment deficits were widening. In such cases, the theory claimed, there was no real movement out of the dollar, no dissatisfaction abroad with the U.S. payments deficit, no monetary disequilibrium stemming from this deficit, but merely a preference by foreign residents and central banks to hold their balance-of-payments surpluses in short-term dollar assets. This preference found its complement in the equal but opposite preference of Americans to make the much higher returns available from buying out the commanding heights of foreign economies, seeking Cold War military supremacy, and going into debt to sustain rising living standards in excess of more prudent and less debt-happy foreign consumers.

This theory was promulgated by semi-governmental economic research organizations in the United States such as Mr Salant's Brookings Institution, which sponsored a Universities Conference meeting of the National Bureau of Economic Research to discuss the new doctrine. But its depiction of the lines of causality at work was wholly imaginary. Throughout the 1960s it had been U.S. entities, both private and governmental, that had initiated the build-up of international liquid assets, or hot money as it was termed by the popular press. U.S. companies bought up foreign firms while the U.S. Government spent funds abroad to finance military and related operations. These activities put dollars into the hands of foreigners in excess of their demand for U.S. goods and services. It was then up to foreigners to respond, headed by the central banks in which the surplus dollars built up. At this point, what the Americans represented as a matter of economic choice became a product of political and diplomatic coercion.

Foreign dollar holders either could turn these dollars over to their central banks in exchange for local currencies, or they could deposit or otherwise relend them directly to other U.S. borrowers via the Eurodollar market. As long as interest rates in the United States were higher than in foreign countries (partly as a result of the U.S. inflation), or as long as U.S. banks were prevented by the Federal Reserve's Regulation Q from borrowing via Certificates of Deposit from U.S. residents, these banks would find it in their interest to borrow back the dollars thrown off by the U.S. payments deficit by offering attractive interest rates to foreign dollar-holders, including foreign affiliates of U.S. firms. The circle could continue unbroken. However, when interest rates began to fall in the United States, and when Regulation Q was relaxed following the Penn-Central bankruptcy in May 1970, U.S. commercial banks stopped borrowing funds abroad and focused their attention on attracting deposits at a lower cost from U.S. residents. Between June 1970 and June 1971 foreign Eurodollar deposits with U.S. banks, held mainly by foreign private sector residents, fell by more than $10 billion. These dollars, the accumulated proceeds of years of U.S. payment deficits during the late 1960s, ended up in foreign central banks. These central banks had little choice but to hold on to them, short of asking for U.S. gold. They were compelled to hold U.S. Treasury promissory notes, *faute de mieux*.

This certainly was not *quid pro quo* lending, and in fact was the reverse of how financial intermediaries operate. A savings institution first receives funds from depositors, and then relends them long in the form of real estate mortgages. Matters would be different if it were to begin financing mortgages by printing its own bank notes and afterwards obliging the person to whom it lent this mortgage money – or to whom that borrower in turn paid the money – to redeposit the private savings bank's notes in the same institution that had issued them.

Professor Triffin was one leading economist who criticized the analogy between savings bank operations and U.S. behavior during the 1960s, on the ground that "the initiative certainly lies far more with the American investor than with the autonomous desire of Europeans to raise long-term funds in the United States, as assumed by our three anthors."[11] Mr Salant replied that "it makes no difference to the validity of the analysis whether buyers or sellers take the initiative."[12] But it certainly does! Private dollar-holders abroad, the foreign companies that are bought out, did indeed wish to divest themselves of these funds by turning them over to their central banks, and these banks wished to obtain something better than U.S. Treasury promissory notes, which was precisely why they complained about U.S. financial policy and did what they could to exchange their surplus dollars for U.S. gold! But the Washington economists pretended not to understand any of this.

In a sense the IFI hypothesis was an extension into the realm of international finance capital of Say's Law of Markets. All surplus funds thrown off by U.S. direct investment abroad and war-related spending created their own demand, which expressed itself in the form of increased foreign holdings of U.S. Treasury securities. This, however, was a forced demand, not exactly a voluntary one. It was irrelevant to assert that Europe "wanted" or "chose" to hold short-term claims on the U.S. Treasury, simply on the ground that it did in fact hold such claims. A more realistic interpretation would have been that Europe and Japan accepted this option reluctantly, partly out of sympathy with U.S. war aims to be sure, and partly to avert a world political showdown and monetary collapse. The important point was that foreign central banks held their liquid claims on the U.S. Treasury not because that was their first preference, but simply because they feared to do otherwise, because they feared bringing about a breakdown in international finance and trade.

As Arthur Laffer summarized the issue: "In their now classic article, Despres, Kindleberger and Salant set forth an altogether novel framework for analyzing the U.S. balance of payments. If correct, their analysis points out (i) that U.S. deficits, within some limits, do not represent a disequilibrium position, but, in fact, are necessary for a healthy world economy; (ii) any lack of confidence in the dollar is brought about by a failure to understand the role of the dollar; and (iii) unless there are a myriad of controls the normal macro-economic tools are likely to fail in controlling the deficit."[13] The three authors are quoted to the effect that "banks and other financial intermediaries, unlike traders, are paid to give up liquidity. The United States is no more in deficit when it lends long and borrows short than is a bank when it makes a loan and enters a deposit on its books."[14] Thus, Laffer concluded, "the unique role of the United States is as the major supplier of liquidity to the rest of the world."[15] Translated into political terms, this meant that (i) the Vietnam War and its associated payments deficits were necessary to provide international reserves to insure a healthy world economy; (ii) people who do not understand this fail to understand both the ineffable benefits of slaughter and the financial mechanisms at work, and (iii) there is nothing to be done about the U.S. deficit short of transforming the nature of American and foreign political society, which is precisely what the American strategy was designed to prevent.

Logically speaking, the IFI hypothesis applied only to the private sector's investment and payments transactions. It maintained the fictions that government finance capital played no role in the world economy, and that some investment alternative was always available to foreign dollar holders. However, because the parameters of international transactions in real life are manipulated by political policy and not by free market forces, any general equilibrium theory is inapplicable to modern balance-of-payments analysis. The hypothesized voluntariness of most private transactions therefore must be replaced by an analysis of economic behavior taking government diplomacy into account.

The International Financial Intermediary Hypothesis would have merit only if there were no official transactions deficit, that is, no build-up of U.S. official liabilities to foreign governments, but merely an offsetting exchange of private liabilities of differing maturities. Such an approach might, for example, help explain the U.S. payments surplus on capital account during the 1950s, when the dollar was much more secure than it later became in relation to European currencies. But the approach was inapplicable to the international financial transactions of the 1960s and 1970s, for in light of the substantial role played by government transactions – and hence, of diplomatic arm-twisting – the critical assumption of mutuality became unrealistic. In the final analysis the United States remained liquid only by imposing a *de facto* embargo on its gold sales, and in August 1971 an outright embargo. Foreign desires to purchase U.S. gold with their surplus dollars were denied, pending some resolution of the U.S. monetary dilemma.

The most serious defect of the IFI hypothesis was its attempt to divert attention from analysis of how the world inflation actually was being transmitted and where its origins lay. It interpreted the politically inspired U.S. payments deficit, which stemmed from government actions and transactions designed to maintain U.S. hegemony, as an interest-rate responsive exercise in liquidity preference between long- and short-term investments. It did not ask what was responsible for creating the capital funds that comprised the reserve assets of the world's central banks.

It was almost inevitable that the attempts by Salant and his colleagues to explain away the U.S. payment deficits would inspire self-serving official statistical attempts to minimize these deficits. During the 1960s the payments deficit was redefined from a measure of net economic imbalance in U.S. international transactions to a more nebulous category, which the Department of Commerce termed "transactions in U.S. monetary assets." One effect of this was to treat foreign, mainly British, drawings on U.S. swap agreements as adding to U.S. reserves rather than as part of the deficit. Britain borrowed dollars, and gave the New York Federal Reserve Bank an equivalent amount of sterling. This swap was treated synthetically as reducing the statistical deficit by as much as $1 billion for a number of years.[16] Similarly, SDR creations were recorded "below the line," as offsets to the sale of gold and the growth of official U.S. indebtedness abroad. (Surplus nations such as France recorded their SDR allotment differently, as was discussed in various meetings of the IMF's Working Party III.)

According to Robert Solomon of the Federal Reserve Board, the choice of how to treat SDR disbursements

> lies in the behavior of governments and their monetary authorities. Some governments have as an explicit objective an increasing level of reserves [and] are apt to take defensive actions when their reserves decrease substantially. These defensive actions can take the form of restrictions on

trade, tourism and capital movements or of fiscal and monetary policies that are more restrictive than needed for domestic reasons . . . Unless there is room in the system for these aims to be satisfied, countries will take actions – such as restricting their trade and payments or deflating excessively – that are detrimental to themselves and to their trading partners. Thus an increasing volume of world reserves is a way to reconcile the conflicting balance of payments objectives of countries and of doing so in a way that facilitates economic welfare.[17]

By facilitating economic welfare Solomon meant pursuing expansionary income and monetary policies, which might not facilitate monetary stability. Reporting SDRs as a growth in reserves – as if they stemmed from a balance-of-payments surplus – would tempt them to avoid imposing monetary deflation, which would have tended to cut back their imports from other countries, including the United States.

It was officially suggested that the concept of economic equilibrium in the balance of payments be shifted away from actual commercial supply-demand conditions toward a measure of whether the deficit might in practice be continued over time, whatever its degree of involuntariness. Because SDRs would continue to be granted to the United States, so it was argued, they should be deemed part of the new world monetary equilibrium, not as part of the deficit!

The point is that economic forces would not necessarily be automatically set into motion *within the United States* to shift the economy out of its presumed 'disequilibrium' with the rest of the world; yet the operation of such forces is, as has been stated, part of the definition of "disequilibrium." To be sure, an official reserve transactions deficit may indicate a "political" deficit for the United States, in that foreign governments may be unhappy with the accumulation of dollar balances by their central banks; and "political" deficits can hardly be ignored by U.S. officials. However, this kind of disequilibrium is most appropriately evaluated by politicians schooled in making such normative appraisals, not by economists or statisticians.[18]

In other words, whatever situation might exist in the U.S. balance of payments, whether surplus or deficit, whether short-term or long-term, was to be defined as equilibrium *ipso facto*. To rational minds, economics itself was becoming incomprehensible and devoid of scientific analytic process.

To be sure, the proposed measure is asymmetrical in the sense that foreign central banks properly count increases in their dollar balances held in this country as surpluses (other things being the same), while under the proposed measure the United States would not consider these increases to show a deficit. This asymmetry appears to be appropriate, for it corresponds to an asymmetry in the real world. It is a shortcoming of the currently published official measures that they fail to take account of this asymmetry.

Henceforth, it was suggested, America's unique debtor position was to be recognized and institutionalized, not constrained or curtailed.

13   Perfecting Empire through Monetary Crisis, 1970–72

> . . . the state incurs [national] debts for politics, wars, and other higher causes and "progress" . . . The assumption is that the future will honor this relationship in perpetuity. The state has learned from the merchants and industrialists how to exploit credit; it defies the nation ever to let it go into bankruptcy.
>   Alongside all swindlers the state now stands there as swindler-in-chief.
>   Jacob Burckhardt, *Judgments on History and Historians*
>   (tr. Boston: 1958), p. 171

In May 1970, Secretary of the U.S. Treasury David Kennedy warned that if foreign countries did not make it feasible for the United States to increase its exports, Congress might restrict imports into the United States. "Is it not the surplus countries," he asked, "that have a special responsibility to take positive action towards their elimination?"

What Kennedy was asking was something wholly new in relations among peoples. In essence he was stating that as U.S. private capital continued to take over the industries and companies of Europe and Asia, establishing a U.S. deficit in its balance of payments on capital account, the nations that were forced into a surplus position by receiving these dollars should increase their imports from the United States in amounts equivalent to the U.S. cost of seizing control of their industries and enterprises. If, in addition, the United States should continue to unbalance its payments position by military acts in any part of the globe, the nations forced into a surplus position must expose their domestic industries to artificially sponsored competition from the export sector of the U.S. economy.

Stated succinctly, the monetary, investment and trading policies of the rest of the world were to be determined by whatever was happening in the domestic and international economic and political affairs of the United States. Shifting responsibility for the U.S. payments deficit from U.S. domestic and overseas policies onto Europe and Japan, Kennedy asserted that it was "inconsistent for foreign countries to urge the United States to run a balance-of-payments surplus and then adopt policies that tend to thwart achievement of that very objective."[1]

Just how this was to be brought about was not spelled out. Nor, for that matter, was it made absolutely plain to the peoples of the world at that time that the United States was in earnest. Kennedy's statement was not so much a plea for international cooperation as a direct threat that America would take whatever measures it thought necessary to compel Europe and Asia to accept the instructions that he imperiously had given to them.

America's illegal textile quotas spur foreign retaliation

At the time this hardly was sensed abroad, much less at home. Affairs in fact seemed to be going in the opposite direction. Nations had begun to resist U.S. economic aggression, or so it appeared. Japan was a case in point. In winter 1970 the State Department had requested it to impose voluntary quotas on its textile exports to the United States. Japan rejected this as flatly as the United States would have rejected a suggestion that it impose export quotas on its farm products. Wilbur Mills of Arkansas, Chairman of the House Ways and Means Committee, thereupon prepared a bill calling for mandatory quotas on textile and footwear imports, along with other protectionist measures.

Japanese trade officials threatened to enact trade legislation retaliating in kind against any U.S. impediments to its textile sales in the United States. By June, a half-hearted attempt at agreement was abandoned. On June 8, President Nixon met with textile industry leaders and indicated that he would not oppose congressional proposals for quotas to roll imports back some 40 per cent, to their 1967–68 level.

Harking back to Nixon's election pledge to the textile industry in 1968, this policy stance was the opening of a major U.S. trade aggression against other countries. On June 25, 1970, Secretary of Commerce Maurice Stans announced the administration's "reluctant" support of mandatory quotas on textiles as called for in the Mills bill, which had now come before the House Ways and Means Committee. Stans concluded that despite the special escape clauses enjoyed by the United States under GATT agreement, "in many respects we have been Uncle Sucker to the rest of the world." This set the stage for the posture of the abuse of the United States by its creditors that government spokesmen were henceforth to take. The *Wall Street Journal* found it ironic that on the same day that Stans was backing the Mills bill, "Federal Reserve Chairman Arthur F. Burns was in Seoul commending Korea for its 'amazing record' in expanding total exports. . . . In a text prepared before the Administration took its position, Mr. Burns said it is 'gratifying to see that the practical statesmen of the world' are rediscovering such classic economic concepts as freedom of trade, adding that 'we owe a great deal to countries like the Republic of Korea, Nationalist China, Hong Kong and Thailand that have most recently demonstrated how men operating in free markets can outperform totalitarianism."[2]

The Common Market was outraged by the U.S. quota threats. Its proposed multilateral talks on world textile trade, however, were turned down by U.S. negotiators. In a divide-and-conquer strategy they invited EEC spokesmen to Washington to discuss the problem bilaterally. On July 1, 1970 Edmund Wallenstein, the Common Market's Director of Foreign Trade, and Fernand Braun, Deputy Director of Industrial Affairs, arrived in Washington. They received assurances that the United States did not intend to protect its textile markets against European producers, but only against those of the Far East. No quotas would be imposed on woolen goods and man-made textiles or synthetic filament fibers, products more of European than of Japanese industries. Furthermore, the administration promised that it would press once again for removal of the American Selling Price tariff system to which Europe objected vigorously.

This offer failed to mollify the Common Market negotiators. If textile quotas were enacted, they argued, additional quotas probably would be imposed on shoes, steel, electronics goods and other commodities as textile interests in Congress sought legislative support from other protectionist-minded industries. Furthermore, the Asian textiles diverted from the U.S. market probably would be channeled toward Europe. U.S. import quotas thus would render the EEC a preferential trading area for exports from the Far East and the developing countries, unless the Common Market imposed import quotas of its own. Common Market economists estimated that America's proposed textile and shoe quotas would cost the EEC some $500 million in annual sales to the United States. British economists computed that the U.S. trade legislation would cut their nation's sales by an equal amount. They spoke of retaliation against U.S. soybean and soy oil exports, which would make American farmers secondary victims of the U.S. textile quotas. The stage thus was set for the opening scenes of the drama of confrontation between the United States and the rest of the world.

A Big Four GATT meeting of the United States, the Common Market, Japan and Britain was convened in Geneva on July 31 and August 1. The Common Market again threatened to retaliate against the Mills bill if it were enacted, and protested against any candidate for the U.S. presidency, or other office-seeker, ever again promising to violate GATT rules in order to win an election. U.S. protectionists, however, surmised that European retaliation on the trade front would be somewhat futile. From where would Europe obtain her soybeans, they asked, if not from the United States?

Europe's threats of financial and trade retaliation

The Common Market's spokesmen explained that EEC retaliation might not come in the area of foreign trade at all, but in international finance and investment. For instance, on the last day of 1969 Germany had done the favor of selling $500 million in gold to the U.S. Treasury. It had now accumulated more than enough dollars to repurchase this gold. And France quietly informed U.S. bankers that it was prepared to begin cashing in its dollar surpluses for gold on a monthly basis, as it had been doing regularly before May 1968. Germany and France refrained from such actions as long as the Mills bill did not pass, partly to maintain their liquid official dollar balances as bargaining power, partly in recognition of the rapid growth of nationalist protectionist sentiment in the U.S. Congress.

What had been uttered, however, was the one unforgivable threat. Europe, no matter how gently and indirectly, had in fact, for the first time since World War II, threatened to use its unquestioned financial strength against the United States. This could not be tolerated. Europe was still in America's official eyes a U.S. dependency. It could no more be permitted autonomous action than the American colonies were permitted such action by George III. The United States would not back down, and indeed its assertion of imperial power did not permit it to do so. The issue had expanded from pragmatic one of trade to the principled question of power and its exercise.

On August 13, 1970, after five weeks of hearings, the House Ways and Means Committee approved the Mills bill by a vote of 17 to 7. This was the first step toward its passage by the full House, but not a word of protest was heard from President Nixon or his cabinet. In addition to imposing quotas on textile and shoe imports, the bill proposed modification of the escape clause so as to facilitate additional import quotas, and also a special tax deferment for exporters in the form of DISCS (Domestic International Sales Corporations). Industries seeking special tariff protection no longer would have to establish that imports were a major factor in their economic difficulties, but need only show that certain conditions were fulfilled: imports must be rising rapidly; unit labor costs of the imported commodities must be below those in the United States; and imports either must represent 15 per cent or more of U.S. consumption or else the domestic industry must be suffering from declining employment, hours worked and earnings. Under these conditions, the President would be obliged to impose import quotas, unless he gave Congress a detailed report on why it was not in the national interest to do so. The new legislation would put U.S. tariff policy in the hands of the nation's protectionist Tariff Commission, and would permit quotas to be imposed on autos, radios and electronic products, bicycles and other sports goods, as well as on many other commodities. It was thus the equivalent of a declaration of trade war.

The United States had thrown down the gauntlet to Europe and Asia: either submit, or retaliate under conditions where the appropriate tactical maxim is "Don't hit the leader unless you can kill him." In effect, America was asking the rest of the world just what it was going to do in response.

On November 6 a French political leader, Michel Poniatowski, Secretary General of the Independent Republican Party and close associate of Finance Minister Valéry Giscard d'Estaing, suggested that Common Market retaliation be focused on European subsidiaries of American multinational firms. He believed that "a monetary and tariff war is foreseeable, even probable, between now and 1973. . . . First, the United States would impose quotas on textiles. Then the European Economic Community would retaliate by limiting American sales of soybeans in Europe. Next, Congress would be 'outraged by such insolence' from Europe and in turn would retaliate by restricting European sales in the United States of shoes and carpets. The EEC would respond by hitting American aircraft and electronics exports to Europe. Then the United States would attack European glass and steel. Finally, the Europeans would be provoked into imposing curbs on American industrial activities in Europe, which he suggested as the ultimate weapon in the economic arsenal. 'This war is foreseeable,' Mr. Poniatowski declared. 'We must therefore do everything to avoid it. But, if it breaks out, it will frankly not be the fault of Europe.'"[3]

On November 19, 1970 the House of Representatives passed the Mills bill by a vote of 215 to 165. President Nixon still said nothing, and his press secretary stated that he was keeping an open mind on matters. Even the usually docile British trade diplomats protested. Peter Tennant, Director General of the British National Export Council, announced: "We have been too damn polite for too damn long."[4] Spain talked of "cutting back purchases by state-controlled concerns. A large part of American exports to Spain is heavy machinery and the bulk of this – power stations, aircraft and such – is bought by state-run companies."[5] The bill would have threatened about $100 million of Spain's shoe exports to the United States, despite the fact that "the military bases agreement signed earlier this year contained assurances that the United States would do whatever was possible to improve [Spain's] trade balance." Spain threatened to cut back its purchases of oil from U.S. affiliates abroad unless President Nixon provided special exemption for Spain from the quotas called for in the bill.

The Mills bill passed to the Senate Finance Committee headed by Senator Russell Long of Louisiana, who promised to attach it to the Social Security bill then pending. Supported by Senator Talmadge of Georgia, the trade bill received only one day of hearings, and these were called on only twenty-four hours' notice. As matters turned out, however, the Trade bill was not attached to the Social Security measure, but was superseded by subsequent U.S. trade and financial legislation.

In simplest terms the official position of the United States was that it alone was exempt from and immune to multilateral agreements. As in the typical posture of imperialists, veiled and open threats to the American ukase must be countered, and even the Mills bill was insufficient as a counter, for in economic terms far more was at issue than imports and exports. What lay at the root of matters was the persistence of American balance-of-payments deficits which, the United States demanded, must be financed by other countries. At stake was the very question of power in the world. If other countries could perpetually be bound by U.S. decisions, of whatever character and for whatever purpose, their autonomy would be negligible and their threats meaningless. What was needed therefore was a showdown between the United States and non-Communist Europe and Asia, a confrontation that would make clear the location of power once and for all.

The world was by no means certain where power actually lay. In terms of military capabilities vis-à-vis the United States, Europe counted for little and Japan for naught. Ultimate power therefore rested with the United States. It was not ultimate power that was at issue, however, but the more subtle and less definable relative strengths of national and regional economies.

The widening disparity between European and American economic strength only recently had begun to command general attention. Europe had kept quiet about the matter for understandable reasons. The United States had blinded itself by its assumption that national economic health and size of gross national product were identities, not measures of distinct and separate dimensions. Even the overseas deficits of the United States had alarmed few observers. That blindness was passing, however, along with the blind spot of economic theory that had produced it. Within the United States, slowly at first but with increasing acceleration, the most serious disquiet began to be felt. It expressed itself in what was to grow into a concerted private speculation by U.S. citizens and companies against the dollar. Funds fled the country, led by speculative ventures of U.S. corporate treasurers against maintenance of the dollar's *de facto* parity.

The summer 1971 dollar crisis forces up Europe's exchange rates

This currency and gold speculation reflected the growing doubts that the United States could continue to dictate fundamental economic decisions to the rest of the world. If it could not, its foreign debts might overwhelm it. These debts were euphemized throughout Europe and Asia by the expression "surplus dollars."

In March 1971 the Organization for Economic Cooperation and Development (OECD) published a study warning that surplus dollars would continue to plague Europe's monetary system at least throughout the year. A $6 billion U.S. payments deficit was projected for 1971, second only to 1970's all-time high of $11 billion. This quasi-official and inaccurately optimstic projection, issued with U.S. blessing, was a complement to President Nixon's simultaneous announcement that a tax reduction might be necessary to stimulate the economy if unemployment remained over 6 per cent by June of that year. Europeans adamantly opposed this plan, recognizing that a tax reduction would spill even more dollars into their markets. And as matters turned out, the U.S. payments deficit amounted to $6 billion in the first quarter alone, followed by another $6 billion in the second quarter. In April the U.S. trade balance moved into deficit for the first month since 1969, and remained in deficit thereafter. Movement out of the dollar accelerated into gold held abroad and into other currencies, with the Swiss franc and German mark being favored havens. Germany's international reserves rose to $16.7 billion, a gain of $3 billion from yearend 1970 and $9.6 billion from yearend 1969.

U.S. strategists did nothing to stem this flight out of the dollar. The central banks of the Netherlands, Belgium and France retaliated by cashing in $422 million of dollars for U.S. gold. Of this sum France accounted for $282 million, which it paid to the IMF to liquidate the balance of its borrowings made during the May 1968 crisis. Still, the Nixon administration did not tighten controls over U.S. capital movements.

On Tuesday, May 4, $1.2 billion in dollars flowed into Germany to be converted into marks, followed by another $1 billion in the first hour of trading on Wednesday, May 5. This brought German reserves to more than $19 billion, at which point the central bank closed its foreign exchange markets pending a decision on how to resolve its dilemma. Discussions were opened with the other Common Market countries and with the

United States on how the situation might be handled without bringing about a total breakdown of the international financial system.

On Friday, May 7, however, John Connally, newly appointed U.S. Secretary of the Treasury, indicated that the nation would emphatically not cooperate with Europeans by slowing the flow of dollars into foreign countries. He suggested, instead, that foreign countries step up their purchases of special U.S. Treasury securities and buy U.S. common stocks as a means of recycling their dollars to the United States.[6] *The New York Times* reported a few days later that "Washington concedes that its balance-of-payments priorities are pretty low. Europeans term the policy one of 'benign neglect' and in the corridors of the international meetings that have been taking place in Paris and Brussels they say that President Nixon is guided by only one thing – to get reelected in 1972. An editorial in the London *Financial Times* said that if the policy continues to be benign neglect, 'it will be up to the nations of Europe to take matters into their own hands.'"[7]

A group of prominent U.S. economists including Paul Samuelson, Milton Friedman and two former heads of the Council of Economic Advisers, Walter Heller and Arthur Okun, asked that Germany float the mark and that other countries follow suit. This was the exact opposite of the policy recommended by the Werner Commission, and would have impaired Common Market plans to align the currencies of the Inner Six more closely with each other. West Germany's Economic Minister Karl Schiller proposed a plan whereby "all Common Market central banks would stop acquiring dollars for an interim period. But while floating against the dollar, the currencies of the Six would maintain a fixed relationship" with one another.[8] He offered to provide German marks for a Common Market reserve fund to tide the weaker currencies of France and Italy over the transition period, and suggested that "such a fund could be the beginning of a 'Federal Reserve System' for Europe." France, however, did not wish to see Germany dominate the proposed monetary union. It announced that it would boycott the monetary union discussions as long as the mark floated. Italy also opposed a floating Common Market currency, fearing that a more expensive lira would force Italy to borrow increasingly from its Common Market partners, especially from Germany.

For the time being, proposals to establish an EEC Monetary Union, the equivalent of a central bank for Common Market Europe, had to be held in abeyance. This was at least a temporary victory for the United States, but it was no more than temporary. Moreover, a consistent U.S. objective since 1945 had been to open Europe's markets wide to U.S. farm exports.

The Common Market's agricultural policy had prohibited this. But to continue to succeed, this policy depended on fixed exchange rates among the currencies of the Inner Six. The outflow of funds from the United States, especially into the German mark, made maintenance of parities between the mark and the French franc impossible. Thus, the Common Market's agricultural policy, the indispensable foundation for harmonizing trading interests between France and Germany, hence the foundation of the Common Market itself, was brought into peril, threatened by the deluge of funds, largely American funds, that flooded into Germany.

Economic power in its reality was being demonstrated. The quiescence of U.S. officials at the flight out of the dollar was fully explained. Such flight was a necessary instrument of U.S. strategy, one of whose principal aims had been – and would remain – the rupture of the agricultural policy within the EEC.

So far, American strategy against Europe had succeeded without direct intervention by the U.S. Government. For the moment such open intervention was not necessary. So massive had been the flight from the dollar that Europe's currencies began to be floated even before the U.S. Government demanded that their parities be adjusted upward. On Sunday, May 9, 1971, Germany and the Netherlands floated their currencies, Switzerland revalued its franc by 7 per cent, and Austria increased the value of its schilling by 5 per cent. These moves were accompanied by plans for special capital controls to limit Eurodollar borrowings by Americans as well as by European firms. On June 1, the Bundesbank increased reserve requirements on foreign bank deposits to twice those required for domestic deposits. On July 2, German firms were obliged to make cash deposits with the Bundesbank to compensate for foreign currency borrowings made by them in the Eurodollar market. Thus it was not the United States that imposed capital controls to stop the flight from the dollar, but Germany, to stop the flight into the mark.

These European revaluations were the quintessence of U.S. strategy. Their effect was to increase the prices of German, Dutch, Swiss and Austrian goods in the U.S. and world markets, making U.S. exports correspondingly more competitive. "The President's economists have privately hailed the floating of the mark as a victory for United States policy, which they dislike calling 'benign neglect' because it upsets foreigners. If the mark finally settles at a higher exchange rate, this would help America's trade position by making our exports cheaper and imports dearer."[9] The fragmenting of parities was treated as Europe's problem, not that of the United States.

On May 10 an official U.S. Treasury statement observed that foreign exchange markets "appeared to be adjusting in orderly fashion," and reiterated that "no immediate action by the United States is called for."[10] Europe was compelled to choose between absorbing more and more U.S. dollars or stopping the purchase of dollars and letting European currencies appreciate still further, bestowing even more price advantage on U.S. exports. "Officials continued to maintain a polite silence about events that imposed difficult choices in Europe but no real problems, at least for the time being, for the United States. But there was no doubt that some officials were positively pleased by the weekend outcome."[11] Nobel Prizewinner Paul Samuelson typified the attitude of nationalistic U.S. economists, telling United Press International that "the outcome of the recent crisis was 'a very good thing . . . not a defeat for the dollar. This is a step in the right direction of equilibrium,' Mr. Samuelson said. 'It is good for the dollar because, in my judgment, the dollar is overvalued.' . . . He said he was 'especially pleased' that the Netherlands had joined West Germany in letting its currency float and added that he wished France had done the same thing. He laughingly expressed the hope for 'a healthy little crisis in Japan' leading to 'an upward floating of the yen.'"

Paul McCracken, chairman of President Nixon's Council of Economic Advisors, was quick to reject "a complaint by some European officials that United States policies were responsible for the dollar flows that have rocked the monetary system . . . this view, raised in the economic policy committee of the Organization for Economic Cooperation and Development, seemed 'lopsided.' 'If two people are out of step, it is not automatically clear who is out of step,' he said at a news conference later. . . . 'Let's not look for villains. Each nation has to look out for its own economy.'"[12] Senator Javitz teamed up with Wisconsin's Representative Reuss to introduce "a joint resolution asking President Nixon to consider calling for an international monetary conference. In a Senate speech, Mr. Javits proposed a formal end of convertibility of foreign-held dollars into gold and more flexibility of currency exchange rates."[13]

The United States began its official intervention in the power struggle over currency values by demanding, on May 17, 1971, that Japan revalue the yen.[14] "Pressure has been building up to revalue the yen. But as long as the yen stays pegged at 0.27777 United States cents, the Administration's economists cannot regard the recent crisis as having been truly 'constructive.' The United States Treasury has little liking for this policy of revaluation via crisis. Officials fear that it aggravates hostility between America and its trading partners and reveals the weakness of the dollar, thus exposing the dollar to attack."[15] U.S. officials went so far as to threaten Japan with a special unilateral tariff restricting certain categories of Japanese exports to the United States if Japan did not revalue the yen. It was reported that "one very high official made known his belief . . . that the yen is probably 'undervalued' by as much as 20 per cent . . . The imposition of a special duty on goods from only one country, through a unilateral determination by the United States – as distinct from the International Monetary Fund – that the country's currency is undervalued could have grave repercussions for both the world trading rules and the monetary rules."[16]

Japan at first refused to revalue the yen to a higher parity. Its officials pointed out that their country's trade surplus with the United States was not simply a problem of relative prices but of differing production structures that would be cured partially by a renewed upswing in the domestic Japanese economy.[17] In place of revaluation, it began to dismantle the capital controls that had been in effect since World War II, and undertook an eight-point program, including "import liberalization, preferential tariffs to the developing nations, tariff cuts, capital liberalization, removal of nontariff barriers, promotion of economic cooperation, normalization of exports and flexible manipulation of fiscal and monetary policies." Beginning July 1, 1971, Japanese citizens were permitted to buy foreign securities, and further capital liberalization moves were scheduled for August. In addition, Japan capitulated to U.S. interests by unilaterally restraining textile exports to the United States for a period of three years beginning July 1. Other Asian countries followed suit by reducing own textile sales, starting with Taiwan and South Korea announcing that "voluntary" export quotas were being imposed on their producers.

The result was that although the Kennedy Round seemed to be cutting tariff rates, "a new protectionist device has been invented . . . which gets around all international prohibitions and domestic inhibitions and which is compatible with an official posture of unalterable opposition to quotas," e.g. the so-called "voluntary" quota, ostensibly imposed by the exporting nation itself on its domestic producers. "Thus liberal consciences are assuaged while a particularly harmful form of restriction is spreading. That the exporter's restrictions are imposed under the threat that the exporter will otherwise use compulsion and that the 'voluntary' character is a myth does not seem to matter."[18]

To be sure, the new trade barrier was in violation of Article XI of GATT, which laid down that "No prohibitions and restrictions other than duties, taxes or other charges, whether made effective through quotas, import or export licenses *or other measures*, shall be instituted or maintained by any contracting party on the importation of any product of the territory of any other contracting party or on the exportation or sale for export of any product destined for the territory of any contracting party" (italics added). The formulators of the GATT agreements may well have had "voluntary quotas" in mind, inasmuch as they were first used by the Japanese in the late 1930s before being rediscovered and reimposed by the United States in the mid-1950s. As early as 1963 they covered about 27 per cent of Japan's exports to the United States.[19] An added feature was the fact that foreign governments could not claim ground for tariff retaliation against voluntary quotas, inasmuch as the reduction of exports to the United States was, after all, "voluntary."

These upheavals highlighted the link between financial and military power. It had come to light that "the United States threatened implicitly to withdraw its troops from West Germany three years ago if the German central bank did not renounce its rights to convert surplus dollars into American gold. The link between the troops and gold has always been assumed in international monetary circles. An interview published in *Der Spiegel*, the West German magazine, has now provided some of the details and the specific circumstances. The interview, with Dr Karl Blessing, president of the Bundesbank – he died April 25 – takes on particular significance because of the crisis over surplus dollars in Europe – most of them in West Germany – and the new moves in the Senate to pull the American forces out of that country."[20]

In the wake of the currency crisis Senator Mike Mansfield proposed, on May 11, 1971, that the United States cut its European troop commitments more than half, from 310,000 to 150,000 men in order to conserve the dollar outflow.[21] This suggestion was in direct opposition to the military strategy outlined by President Nixon in his State of the World Message delivered the preceding February. By May 13 the Nixon administration ruled out any compromise in its fight to defeat the Mansfield move. Senator Scott of Pennsylvania told reporters that the administration would "not accept any alternative that would have the effect of Congress determining the foreign policy of the United States toward NATO."[22]

The Nixon Administration was firm in its decision, for affairs were going exactly as it wished. Apparent weakness of the dollar, with corresponding firming of other currencies, was one of its objectives. The Mansfield amendment, designed to slow the outflow of dollars, was in contradiction of official policy to accelerate the outflow and force the central banks of other countries to pick up the short-term debt of the United States, by including this debt among their reserve banking assets. If this did not occur, the world could not be forced to adopt the U.S. dollar as its central banking currency without regard for the inadequacy of a gold cover. If they did accept the dollar in this role as the world's monetary reserve currency, the $61 billion in overseas debt of the United States would cease to exist for all practical purposes, at least as a debt that was expected to be paid.

The Nixon Administration was playing one of the most ambitious game in the economic history of mankind, but it was beyond the comprehension of the liberal senators of the United States, and it did not appear in the world's economic textbooks. The simple device of not hindering the outflow of dollar assets had the effect wiping out America's foreign debt even while seeming to increase it. At the same time, the simple utilization of the printing press – that is, new credit creation – widened the opportunities for penetrating foreign markets by taking over foreign companies.

August 15 and its aftermath

The policy was formalized on August 15, 1971. Upward adjustment of foreign exchange rates had not gone far enough to suit the administration. Foreign countries had submitted to the U.S. aegis, but their submission needed to be made more absolute. President Nixon therefore suspended all further sale of U.S. gold to foreign central banks. Henceforth the $61 billion of liquid debt owed to foreigners would be paid only in the form of other paper evidences of debt. Not only were gold payments suspended, the foreign overseas debt of the United States was, in effect, repudiated.

There was a devious legal aspect to this maneuver. The articles of the IMF that defined convertibility of currencies did not require their convertibility into gold, but into gold or U.S. dollars at their gold parity of 1944, *i.e.*, $35 an ounce. There was no requirement in the IMF articles that the United States in fact and forever must continue to buy and sell gold at $35 an ounce. Such was obviously understood when the IMF was founded, but it had not been spelled out. Therefore, the convertibility of other currencies could be construed as convertible into paper dollars, and this was how the Nixon Administration construed the rule. Inclusion of the U.S. short-term debt among the monetary reserves of foreign central banks thus satisfied all international legal requirements pertaining to gold reserves and the settlement of international payments imbalances.

One subtlety of this situation was that speculators could earn a profit by buying foreign currencies for dollars in the firm belief that the U.S. Government would force up the value of foreign currencies. This profit was guaranteed because the government of the United States required a massive outpouring of dollars into other currencies in order to further its foreign investment and export policies by forcing upward the exchange rates of other currencies vis-à-vis the dollar. To the U.S. Government this was a cost-free exercise, the only effort involved being that of creating dollars faster. Speculation against the dollar in fact had become the official international policy of the United States. It no longer involved an economic risk once gold payments were suspended.

Phase One of America's imperial monetary design was thus completed. Foreign currencies had been forced upward against the dollar, effectively supporting U.S. exports and minimizing U.S. imports to the extent that relative domestic and import prices were affected. Limitations were imposed on the export policies of certain nations and their official controls over capital movements weakened. Most important, the foreign debt of the United States was effectively repudiated.

Even this was not deemed sufficient, however. The revaluations of foreign currencies had not gone as far as the administration desired. That is to say, the competitive ability of foreign countries in U.S. and world markets, on the basis of product prices, still was too high for American comfort. To force these currencies up still further, President Nixon imposed a 10 per cent surcharge on imports to the United States not already limited by trade quotas. This unilateral surcharge, the government announced, would remain in effect until foreign countries, on a selective basis, revalued their currencies to the extent desired by the United States. Other limitations on their ability to export to the United States were spelled out as part of the price they would have to pay for removal of the surcharge. Export bounties in the form of tax rebates were granted to U.S. exporters, while wage and price controls were imposed on the domestic economy.

Faced with these aggressive economic policies the nations of the world capitulated, France again being the sole significant exception. The 10 per cent import surcharge negated all the tariff cuts reciprocally negotiated by the United States since the end of World War II. "The combination of the import surcharge and investment tax credit create a 22 per cent price barrier for other nations seeking to sell capital goods to American companies. . . . In addition, prices of foreign-made capital goods have been further increased in some cases by the upward revaluation of national currencies."[23] Administration spokesmen spoke of foreign revaluations of from 15 to 20 per cent, a set of quantum leaps that would have raised the total protection of the new program to the 37 to 42 per cent range.

GATT declared the United States in violation of its rules and announced that other member countries had the right to retaliate. But this did not save Japan, after two weeks of resistance, from finally having to float the yen on August 27, after the Bank of Japan was forced to absorb $4 billion in dollar inflows at existing dollar–yen parities. The yen immediately jumped by 5 per cent.

Revaluation of the yen was deemed urgent by U.S. strategists on the ground that "European countries will be more amenable to accepting some competitive disadvantage through higher rates for their own currencies now that they know Japan will accept a similar handicap."[24] A week later, on September 6, the Common Market indeed found itself obliged to follow suit by floating its currencies, although still intervening in an attempt to limit their appreciation against the dollar.

At a meeting of the Group of Ten on September 15, Treasury Secretary Connally "said blandly for the television cameras as he left the afternoon meeting . . . 'We had a problem and we are sharing it with the world just like we shared our prosperity . . . That's what friends are for.'"[25] He demanded that the rest of the world guarantee an annual $13 billion improvement in the U.S. balance of payments.

At this point the dollar had fallen by 2.9 per cent against the pound sterling, 6.4 per cent against the yen, 6 per cent against the Canadian dollar and 5.7 per cent against the Dutch guilder. This was not enough, U.S. monetary representatives insisted. If the United States were to relax its import controls, foreign countries would have to increase their currency values by some 10 to 20 per cent. To help encourage such shifts, U.S. officials leaked an IMF study estimating that, on the average, foreign currencies should appreciate by about 10 per cent relative to the dollar, with the yen rising 15 per cent and the German mark 12 per cent, the Canadian dollar 11 per cent and the pound sterling 7 per cent.[26] "The IMF study was based on the assumption that the exchange-rate changes would have to be large enough to restore equilibrium to the United States balance of payments at full employment."[27] In other words, foreign countries must accept increased unemployment at home resulting from loss of their export markets to U.S. producers, in order that full employment could be fostered in the United States. The double standard of international diplomacy pursued by the United States thus was laid bare for all to see.

What distressed European diplomats more than any other demand was American insistence that the Common Market weaken its agricultural program by opening its markets to U.S. producers at the expense of Europe's farmers. "We're interested in the whole package," asserted Mr

Connally, insisting that "currency changes, trade liberalization and sharing of American international aid and defense obligations should all be discussed in connection with lifting the surcharge."[28] American antipathy toward the EEC's agricultural policy had become all the more pressing as it now appeared certain that England would join the Common Market by January 1, 1973. This would mean a loss of $500 million in U.S. grain exports if England were to shift grain purchases from the United States to Europe as required under EEC rules. American officials also reiterated their long-standing antipathy toward extending Associate Membership status to non-Common Market countries.

On the eve of the Group of Ten meeting the U.S. Commission on Trade published its recommendations in a report entitled "Strategy for the Seventies," authored largely by Peter G. Peterson. The report singled out "the adverse effects on U.S. exports of European Community's common agricultural policy and preferential trade arrangements. We should seek a commitment to the elimination of illegal preferences, assurances that no further impairment of our agricultural trade interests will occur in the enlargement negotiations and a commitment on liberalization of the common agricultural policy as part of the negotiations on longer-term issues."[29]

Simultaneously, the Common Market issued a position paper at Brussels calling for a united front against the United States at the Group of Ten meetings to start the following day. "Realizing that if the present monetary difficulties continued too long, they would raise undoubted dangers for the good functioning of the Community, particularly the common agricultural policy, the Council asked the commission to draw up a special report on the consequences of the present situation on the functioning of the agricultural common market and confirmed the mandate given on August 19 to the monetary committee and the committee of central bank governors to seek as soon as possible methods enabling a stabilization of the Community's exchange relations."[30]

France as usual took the lead in opposing the U.S. demands. On August 18 it had announced that it would neither revalue nor float the French franc relative to the dollar. President Georges Pompidou, at his September 23 press conference, pointed out that "to arrive at an immediate solution would entail the risk, I am convinced, of leading the partners of the United States into exorbitant concessions and would finally render impossible a balanced solution."[31] The 10 per cent import surcharge, he said, was "just one element in the whole . . . a big stick that might possibly be transformed into a carrot if only one is disposed to play the role of the donkey, which is not our intention." He demanded an outright devaluation of the dollar in terms of gold.

It hardly was surprising when the Group of Ten meeting adjourned without any agreement, and U.S. officials turned to exert pressure on the Far East. First they asked Japan to emulate West Germany in agreeing to buy U.S. arms to offset the approximately $650 million annual U.S. military expenditures in Japan. "Japanese officials, and some American officials, argue that Japan is not getting a free ride at all. They note that the American military has rent-free use of thousands of acres of Japanese property. One estimate is that this saves the United States $450 million a year. These officials also argue that much of the American money is being spent more for the strategic defense of the United States than for the defense of Japan. And they point out that a large part of the $650 million – some say half – is spent not on defense, but on Japanese goods to stock American military post exchanges."[32] Furthermore, Japan already was spending $100 to $120 million annually in the United States to buy armaments.

U.S. policy was just as rough toward South Korea and other major Asian textile exporters. In mid-September the United States gave South Korea until October 15 to impose mandatory quotas slowing its export growth of woolens and manmade fiber products to 11 per cent in 1972, 10 per cent in 1973 and 9 per cent in 1974. "South Koreans had insisted on an annual increase of 23 per cent, maintaining that anything below that level would seriously hamper their third five year economic Plan, due to start next year."[33] By October 1, however, South Korea gave in to U.S. demands, effective retroactively to July 1971.[34]

Also on October 15, U.S. trade negotiators threatened Japan with even more restrictive textile curbs if it did not impose controls of its own.[35] The Sato Government was accused by the Japan Textile Foundation of suffering a humiliating agreement with the United States, threatening Japan's two million textile workers with unemployment.[36]

But Japan capitulated, agreeing to limit growth in textile sales to the United States to only 5 per cent annually, in exchange for the United States lifting its import surcharge on wool and synthetics.[37] Taiwan and Hong Kong signed similar agreements. "Industrial leaders predicted that the agreement would mean the loss of some 300,000 jobs in Japan. All four opposition parties issued statements . . . attacking the Government for initialing the agreement." In part-payment Japan regained control of Okinawa, whose return to Japan the U.S. Senate had held up pending satisfactory outcome of the textile negotiations. World trade thus was becoming more militarized than at any time since the 1930s.

Europe's autumn 1971 collapse

By the end of October 1971, Europe seemed to be heading into a recession, in part because of the U.S. tariff policy. Stock market prices on the French bourse had fallen by 15 per cent since August 15. British unemployment stood at a postwar high of 900,000 and was soon to exceed 1 million, while retail prices had risen more than 10 per cent from a year earlier. Industrial production was stagnant or declining throughout Europe, principally as a result of the uncertainties inflicted by the United States. The Nixon Administration did not help matters by announcing that it would keep the import surcharge as a bargaining lever until substantial improvement in the U.S. trade balance had been achieved. Denmark retaliated on October 19 by imposing a 10 per cent import surcharge of its own, and the threat of a world tariff war began to appear real.

Matters were not helped by the United States' "negotiating special exemptions from the surcharge for Canada and Mexico," along with proposals by Connally for "a selective lifting of the surcharge for West Germany because it has allowed its mark 'to float upwards to a realistic new parity with the dollar.'"[38] This was part of the emerging U.S. strategy to make a separate deal with West Germany and use it as a weapon against other Common Market countries. France's response was to insist that the franc would not be allowed to appreciate against the dollar, so that dollar devaluation would give it a competitive edge against Germany, whose mark had now soared about 9 per cent against the dollar.

Balance-of-payments deficits traditionally have been the setting for increased protectionism, and America's experience proved no exception. On November 4 the Senate Finance Committee voted to give the President authority, if the U.S. international position were found to be threatened, to increase the tariff surcharge to 15 per cent, and to extend it to cover all quota and non-tariff items that had been exempted from the August 15 surcharge. The President could also was empowered to impose import quotas.[39]

At this point the dollar had declined by only 4 per cent on a weighted average basis. At the GATT meetings in late November, U.S. negotiators used this fact to press for special trade favors quite apart from further devaluation. They were turned down by the Common Market countries, joined by Britain and Ireland. The United States also pressed once again for increased access to Europe's food markets, and the Common Market Executive Commission once again pointed out that the 10 per cent import surcharge had the effect of doubling effective U.S. tariff rates, to 19.3 per cent, affecting some $5.8 billion worth of Common Market exports.

U.S. delegates to a Group of Ten meeting in Rome on November 29 announced that the United States would rescind the import surcharge and its allied Buy-American tax credits if foreign countries appreciated their currencies by an average of 11 per cent. The U.S. monetary negotiator, Paul Volcker of the Treasury Department, brought agricultural and trade specialists to the meeting to press for what he called a big-package approach, but met solid European resistance. Finally, President Nixon and U.S. economic strategists met with a French mission headed by President Pompidou in the Azores on December 13–14, and reached a monetary agreement that was announced in Washington at the end of the week at a Group of Ten meeting. First of all, as of Monday, December 20, foreign currencies were appreciated by the 11 per cent figure demanded by the U.S. Treasury. The Japanese yen increased by 14.4 per cent, the German mark 11.9 per cent, the Belgian franc and Dutch guilder by 10.4 per cent each, the British pound and French franc 7.9 per cent each, and the Italian lira by 7 per cent. The Canadian dollar continued to float, and was up 8 per cent. In addition, the IMF rules were changed to permit wider parity banks of 2¼ per cent on either side of parity. This meant that the U.S. dollar could decline by an additional 2¼ per cent and other currencies could appreciate by a similar amount, so that a further 4½ per cent shift in exchange rates could take place without consultation with the IMF.

The U.S. representatives also agreed to ask Congress to authorize an increase in the official price of gold to $38 an ounce. Getting congressional approval for this agreement, the *Wall Street Journal* observed, might prove difficult inasmuch as "some Congressman is just bound to come up with a silly amendment, like for instance 'requiring everybody to pay off all their World War I debts first.' Every now and then Congress does take a keen interest in those World War I debts. At least enough interest, anyway, to keep the Treasury totting up the amount . . . Thanks to accrual of unpaid interest, as of mid-1970 the debts totaled a tempting $17,155,745,768.68."[40]

Senators Javits and Hatfield proposed to legalize gold ownership for U.S. citizens. In exchange for this agreement by Congress, President Nixon rescinded his import surcharge and extended his investment tax credit to cover capital goods of foreign manufacture. The Common Market responded by increasing its agricultural tariffs and price-support levels so as to prevent the United States from gaining any special farm export advantages from its devaluation.

Yet Europe's and Asia's capitulation had been total. The world henceforth would trade on terms dictated by the United States, whose massive foreign debt had become a bludgeon with which the world was beaten into submission. In so doing, however, the United States was impelling the world down a path that threatened to lead toward a Third Force, an enlarged Common Market embracing virtually the whole of Europe, with collective industrial capacity greater than that of the United States, with larger gold reserves and with some $43 billion of accumulated purchasing power for U.S. capital goods and industrial products which, if Europe so determined, could be employed for the acceleration of its own industrial growth at the expense of the United States. True, the United States would be paid for such exports, but such payment could constitute solely a reduction in U.S. liabilities to foreigners. If European central banks cashed in their Treasury bill holdings to cover their trade deficits with the United States, these securities would be thrown onto America's own financial markets, threatening to force up interest rates if the Federal Reserve did not simply monetize the bond sales or increase domestic taxes. The possibility thus was raised in principle that it would be the U.S. economy that might end up being squeezed.

The rate at which this transformation of U.S. paper liabilities into industrial exports might occur remained to be demonstrated. That it would come about seemed probable as countries set out during the 1970s to create a New International Economic Order. The world economy was fracturing, threatening the United States with the prospect that for the first time in its history it might have to pay the equivalent of economic tribute abroad for the military activities that had been responsible for its balance-of-payments deficits in the 1950s and 1960s.

In this alternative scenario, American success in forcing other nations to pay the costs of its overseas wars would prove an empty one. The United States would face a future of having to yield up the real products of its industry in exchange for the paper it has printed so assiduously and had forced upon other countries as central banking assets.

It was to discourage this prospect that the United States pressed its monetary imperialism to its new and present stage during 1972 and 1973.

14 The Monetary Offensive of Spring 1973

The monetary agreements reached at the Smithsonian Institution in December 1971 prompted U.S. officials to turn what they called "benign neglect" of the payments deficit into a willful policy. The idea was to oblige other governments either to finance the deficit by lending their surpluses to the U.S. Government – and, in the process, finance the domestic budget deficit – or let the dollar depreciate and thus favor U.S. exporters over European ones.

American strategists recognized that the excess dollars being thrown off by the U.S. payments deficit were being converted into marks and yen to force up the price of one currency after another. This financial instability threatened to render trade agreements unworkable, for the only way to defend against U.S. devaluation advantages would have been for foreign governments to compartmentalize their currency and trading systems, arranging barter deals to protect against shifting currency relations, and even to enact floating tariffs and export subsidies. U.S. strategists doubted that Europe and Asia would take these steps, and they were proved right. Foreign economies ended up supporting the dollar rather than risk the monetary anarchy threatened by U.S. actions.

The aim of U.S. policy was to continue running deficits for as long as possible. After all, who could tell how long the U.S. ability to bid up foreign goods and even companies on credit could continue, until other countries actually drew the line and stopped absorbing surplus dollars? The Americans saw that only a world monetary crisis could bring the free ride to an end. It was clear that the greater role played by foreign trade and investment in the economic life of foreign countries meant that such a crisis would hurt them more than the United States. The threat of triggering a world monetary breakdown accordingly became the U.S. bludgeon with which to threaten the world as the dollar glut intensified during 1972 and 1973.

The impotence of foreign governments to retaliate meaningfully, short of breaking totally with the United States and its dollar standard, was perceived as early as April 1967. Two bank economists, Rudolph Peterson of the Bank of America (subsequently head of the Peterson Commission on foreign aid) and John Deaver of the Chase Manhattan Bank (a protégé of the Chicago monetarist Milton Friedman) independently suggested that if Europe threatened to cash in its unwanted dollars for U.S. gold, the United States should simply suspend its gold sales, cut the dollar loose from gold and let it sink against the currencies of governments dumping their dollars. He wrote:

> If the Treasury began buying and selling only at its discretion, foreign central banks would be faced with a serious dilemma. With their dollars no longer freely convertible into gold, they would have to decide what to do with the dollars they own, and how to deal with the dollars that would be presented to then by their own commercial banks for conversion into local currencies. But this would be a most disagreeable choice. On the one hand, if they permitted the dollar to depreciate, prices of U.S. goods would drop relative to domestically produced goods. Furthermore, it would make U.S. exports more competitive in third markets. This solution would be vigorously opposed by most exporters and businessmen abroad. On the other hand, if foreign central banks continued to support the dollar at its present rate, this would place them more unequivocally than ever on a dollar standard . . . If it is made unmistakably clear that in the event of a crisis the U.S. would simply terminate the privilege now given to foreign central banks of buying gold freely, then the burden of decision regarding the defense of the dollar would be shifted even more than now from the U.S. to the shoulders of European and other central banks.[1]

American officials expressed some embarrassment at the naked offensiveness of these observations, and Deaver soon left Chase and disappeared from the economic scene. But his perceptions obviously were on target, for a year later, in April 1968, the first phase of this strategy was applied when the Treasury obtained "voluntary" agreement from the largest central banks not to cash in their dollars for U.S. gold.

In August 1971, President Nixon made the gold embargo an official pillar of his New Economic Policy. The suspension of gold convertibility did indeed force Europe to choose between holding dollars (mainly in the form of Treasury bills) or dumping them and thereby permitting the dollar to find its own level – a *de facto* U.S. devaluation. This made the U.S. payments deficit – that is, the world's dollar surplus – not a U.S. problem but one for Germany, Japan and other payments-surplus nations.

A year after Nixon took the dollar off gold, the well-known free trade economist Gottfried Haberler, a consultant to the U.S. Treasury, urged the government to continue pursuing its objectives without regard to the balance of payments. The first premise of U.S. economic policy, he emphasized, was that "U.S. macroeconomic policies (monetary, fiscal policies, 'demand management') should be guided by domestic policy objectives – employment, price stability, growth – and should not be used to influence the balance of payments." In keeping with his free market views, Haberler urged that the government "not try to improve the balance of payments by measures of control, such as import restrictions, export subsidies, capital export controls, 'buy American' policies, and the like." It should ignore the trade deficit and "pursue a passive balance of payments policy, a policy of 'benign neglect' . . . Actually, until August 1971, the Nixon Administration had been pursuing substantially a passive policy with respect to the balance of payments, although official statements vigorously denied that this was the case." In fact, Haberler observed, "the great sweep of monetary and fiscal policy" extending back into the Johnson Administration had been "independent of the balance of payments."[2]

Curiously, Haberler did not reflect that the absence of monetary self-control within the U.S. economy obliged other governments to impose controls over their own currency and capital markets in order to defend themselves against the dollar glut. His conclusion was simply that "The U.S. should not try to devalue the dollar, but leave it to other countries to change the par value of their currency, thereby changing the exchange value of the dollar." If the value of one currency after another could be forced up, the dollar would be left in a uniquely abandoned position at the end of the process, remaining low against the revaluing currencies. This would enable the U.S. Government to strike the moral pose that it was not devaluing; other economies were revaluing *their* currencies. But if the United States itself devalued the dollar, other governments probably would follow, so that the net effect would only be to revalue gold upwards.

Haberler echoed Peterson and Deaver in pointing out that the choices for the world's payments-surplus nations to cope with the U.S. payments deficit were "a) inflation, b) appreciation or floating of their currencies, and c) accumulation of dollar reserves." Any of these responses would be in the U.S. interest, as would be the policies of foreign countries importing more (especially from the United States) and being able to reduce their trade barriers.

This array of options would have an intriguing conclusion if countries experiencing dollar inflows let this money work in an inflationary way. In that case the U.S. payments deficit would inflate their economies until a new monetary equilibrium was reached. "It is not impossible that at some future date a foreign dollar holder may engage in excessive inflation," Haberler explained. "Then he would see his dollar reserves melt away. If this happened on a large scale in many countries it would bring back the days of the dollar shortage and imported inflation for the US."[3] World prices would increase as foreign countries bought U.S. exports and capital assets at inflated prices, thereby reducing the value of U.S. official foreign debt in terms of current world output. The United States would simply have inflated itself out of debt. If prices doubled after ten years, the outstanding real value of U.S. borrowings abroad would be halved.

This monetary adjustment process would enable the United States to repay its foreign debts in devalued dollars, that is, dollars that had been borrowed at a time when the dollar bought a maximum amount of foreign exchange to finance the U.S. investment takeover of foreign economies. By the time of repayment, the foreign exchange value of these dollars would have shrunk sharply. U.S. investors thus would pay back their debts with "cheap" dollars.

This was essentially the logic that prompted Nixon to escalate the policy of benign neglect. In late 1972 he removed the "Phase 2" wage and price controls and announced that by 1974 he intended to remove all controls limiting U.S. capital outflows. The Federal Reserve System proceeded to inflate the money supply to spur a boom, contributing to the most rapid inflation America had experienced since the Civil War.

The strategy was Machiavellian. Inflation in the United States would be conveyed abroad by the persistent and growing dollar glut, and the resulting rise in world prices would erode the value of the "dollar overhang." The $75 billion that the U.S. Treasury owed to the world's central banks at 1968–72 prices and exchange rates would be repaid with the equivalent of perhaps less than $40 billion in purchasing power as measured by the original debt. To the extent that gold was revalued and part of this $75 billion repaid in bullion, the gold tonnage price of this dollar borrowing would be written down to less than one-fifth of its original value as measured by the yearend 1974 price of almost $200 an ounce.

Gold prices subsequently soared to over $700 an ounce. U.S. monetary self-interest thus spurred a worldwide rise in commodity and gold prices. It was incidental to this strategy that it exerted a deflationary effect on Third World exporters of cereals, coffee, oil and other raw materials priced in dollars and thus worth less in exchange for European and Japanese products. But to the OPEC economies, the inflation became a major reason prompting them to quadruple oil prices.

Whereas foreign countries had been rendered satellites of the U.S. economy in the 1940s and 1950s by virtue of America's world creditor status, they now became satellitized by its debtor position. In fact, the words "satellitized" and "satellization" made their entry into the vocabulary of economic journalists as Europe seemed hopelessly fragmented in the face of America's new strategy. As Gordon Tether wrote in his "Lombard" column of the London *Financial Times*:

The Nixon Administration has already provided a working example of the way in which it intends to employ "divide and conquer" techniques to help it "discipline" the outside world through economic pressure in the same way as it kept it in its place through monetary manipulation for so long. It took the form of a refusal during the recent monetary conference to offer to collaborate in devising arrangements for joint support of the dollar in case of need . . . the absence of any firm U.S. commitment to support the dollar in a general way means that Washington retains full freedom to allow or even encourage market forces to bring about yet another American devaluation – should the rest of the world, for instance, not show a suitable readiness to indulge American wishes and ambitions in other directions.

Washington's refusal to discuss how [dollar support] would actually be apportioned between other currencies strikes . . . an even more sinister note. For what it means is that, to the extent that the U.S. plays a part in the work of preventing dollar weakness [from] revaluing other countries' it is free to decide which currencies it will help to keep down currencies, and which it will allow to go up.

Needless to say, this puts Washington in an excellent position not only to play one country off against another but also to bring pressure to bear on those that display less willingness to cooperate in making the economic satellisation plan work than the rest. For by inviting American discrimination against them in the exchange field, they will risk having unilateral revaluations that they do not want inflicted on them – with all that this entails. And this, of course, is only the start. The U.S. is equipping itself with the power to operate quota restrictions and tariff barriers on a discriminatory, country-by-country basis. And that will obviously put it in an even more favourable position to penalise any countries that resist.[4]

The problem, observed Tether, was Europe's inability to form a united front against the United States, especially as Germany had replaced Britain as America's cutting wedge against European unity. "The outcome of the recent crisis . . . revealed that the Germans are so vulnerable to the American threat to withdraw troops from Europe that they are apt to see things in very much the American way."

"It is no secret," Tether wrote in another column, "that an overriding purpose of the Administration's drive to cheapen the dollar to a sufficient extent to procure a massive excess of U.S. exports over imports is to provide scope for unlimited U.S. capital investment abroad." This might appeal to export-oriented businesses in the United States, he observed, but American consumers would suffer. "After all, the perpetual under-valuation of the dollar such a scenario requires will add unnecessarily to their cost-of-living it home . . ."[5] But American industry would be provided with the foreign exchange to buy up the most profitable and technologically critical sectors of European and Asian industry. This indeed has been the aim that has guided American policy for the past three decades, culminating in the purchase of public enterprises being privatized from Chile to Britain and Russia.

American strategies to deal with Europe's growing dollar holdings were grounded on the recognition that because of the many U.S. overseas transactions that were not functions of price (or, as economic jargon expresses it, were price-inelastic and had to be made regardless of price), the U.S. payments deficit in all likelihood would continue rather than responding positively to devaluation. In view of the major role played by price-insensitive raw materials such as oil, no protracted turnaround in the U.S. trade balance was likely. As the dollar fell in value, the dollar price of many imports from the industrial nations rose, but this did not induce a proportional decline in U.S. demand. Nor were exports helped much. More American goods were exported, but the foreign exchange equivalent of their sales proceeds was reduced by the dollar's devaluation.

In the spring of 1972 the International Economic Policy Association published a report on *The United States Balance of Payments: From Crisis to Controversy*. Its main author, Dr Danielian, acknowledged that foreigners had become "restive at giving real goods and services in exchange for 'paper,' which depreciated in value as American inflation grew; meanwhile, the money flows from the United States abroad increased foreign inflationary pressures."[6] But the system's strength lay in the fact that despite this foreign restiveness, there simply was little room to maneuver against the United States. Europeans were caught in an all-or-nothing dilemma.

The only way to protect themselves would be to make an outright break with the U.S. economy. It was precisely this threat that had led Britain to knuckle under to U.S. demands in the world War II Lend-Lease negotiations and the 1946 British Loan.

The 1971 dollar crisis all but precluded further rounds of world tariff cuts, so there was little likelihood of foreign economies lowering their tariffs against U.S. exports. "The average 11-percent devaluation of the dollar in return to major trading currencies effectively negated the average 10-percent tariff reductions granted by the United States in those negotiations . . . understandably, other industrial countries are determined to insist on reciprocal concessions in another round of trade negotiations to regain lost territory. They are also opposed to connecting monetary negotiations with discussions on trade matters."[7]

The major prospect for U.S. payments improvement seemed to lie on capital account. Foreign affiliates of U.S. firms might remit more of their earnings to their American head offices, and foreign investors might increase their stake in the United States. Former French Prime Minister Pierre Mendès France suggested that Europe use its surplus dollars to buy back U.S. affiliates in Europe, "presumably on a compulsory basis, and thus 'disenclave' the American investment presence. There are some precedents, as he points out, since both Britain and France were forced to requisition private assets abroad to pay [the United States] for their public external liabilities in connection with the two World Wars. An official of the United Auto Workers has advanced precisely this suggestion as a solution to the accumulated balance of payments deficit."[8]

But the United States did not intend to give any such *quid pro quo* for Europe's dollar holdings. More in mind was the Danielian Report's recommended solution that between $10 and $20 billion of foreign holdings should be converted into long-term (preferably non-marketable) Treasury obligations. This would prevent foreign central banks from converting their dollar holdings from liquid form, by turning them into a nearly sterilized asset.

The report found "both moral justification and economic logic" for other countries to reduce their trade barriers, especially in agriculture. "An additional billion dollars' worth of food products bought in the United States each year would neutralize the balance of payments cost of U.S. troops in Europe . . . A more felicitous concept of convertibility could hardly be conceived!"[9] Europe thus was to become dependent on the United States for feed grains, to complement and finance its military dependency.

American policy-makers knew that their European counterparts recognized as clearly as they themselves did that the U.S. payments deficit would continue at a rate of over $6 billion annually, even if the dollar was devalued or foreign currencies were forced up in value, and irrespective even of the likelihood of peace in Southeast Asia. "Only a drastic curtailment of military operations and closing of installations abroad, or a reimposition of the ban on dependants [accompanying soldiers overseas] can reduce the gross military outflow on the balance of payments account to manageable proportions. The latter would severely affect recruitment and re-enlistments, the former has major political and military consequences for the national interest."[10] It also would thwart President Nixon's hopes for an all-volunteer army, at least under circumstances in which a sizeable U.S. troop presence would remain in Europe. The report concluded that the government should accept, *a priori*, the fact that its annual $6 billion payments deficit would continue.

How small this appears from today's vantage point! Its hundredfold increase is a measure of the success America has achieved in getting foreigners to fund its payments deficit seemingly *ad infinitum*!

Given the fact that the U.S. payments deficit resulted mainly from military spending, not from a surplus of imports over exports, the Danielian proposals were, in effect, for American labor and capital to displace that of Europe and Japan in order to enable the government to pay for its Cold War programs and other international policies that it decided unilaterally. Foreign earnings remitted to U.S. buyers of overseas firms, and foreign markets promised to U.S. exporters regardless of price (especially for farm exports) would pay for U.S. government policies.

The Danielian Report's most novel proposal was to finance the dollar overhang by establishing a U.S. Public Development Corporation, which "would be established by law to borrow liquid dollar holdings on a long-term basis from foreign central banks, individuals, and institutions, and the IMF, at attractive interest rates, possible with a maintenance of value guarantee. The guarantee could be accomplished by denominating the Corporation notes in terms of SDRs, or in foreign currencies with the option of SDR conversion. The proceeds would be loaned to U.S. municipalities, states, and other agencies, for urban development, housing schools, transportation, sewage treatment plants, and other needed improvements. Interest rates would approximate those on tax-exempt bonds."[11]

The proposed financial intermediary would reduce America's need to fund such spending with tax money or domestic borrowing. This would permit taxes to be lowered, incidentally providing American exporters with a competitive advantage as foreign governments would tax their domestic residents to finance the dollar acquisitions that were lent to the U.S. Government corporation. In addition to lowering domestic tax needs, congressional restraints over government spending programs abroad and at home would be removed.

The proposal would establish a virtual perpetual motion vehicle for the U.S. federal spending. The government would run a domestic budgetary and balance-of-payments deficit to finance its military and related spending. These dollars would accrue to foreign central banks, which would re-lend them to finance America's development rather than that of their own economies.

The Danielian Report's suggestion that the U.S. Treasury offer a maintenance-of-value clause was to be made conditional on foreign countries agreeing "to carry their share of common defense costs and to supply a greater share of foreign aid in terms of absolute amounts." In other words, foreign governments would finance U.S. political, diplomatic and military aid via the World Bank, the Inter-American Development Bank and other institutions controlled by the U.S. Government, instead of through specifically European and Asian instruments serving their own national interests. Another condition was that Europe abandon its Common Agricultural Policy![12]

This report evidently formed the basis for official U.S. demands. In January 1973 the *Economic Report of the President* urged that the United States not participate in any international financial reform without obtaining substantial foreign trade and investment concessions, especially in agriculture. This stance was called the "single package approach." It aimed at unilaterally increasing U.S. tariffs against payments surplus economies such as Germany or Japan without violating the Most-Favored-Nation rule that underlies all international trade agreements. Injured economies are bound to retaliate under GATT rules, as had occurred in the 1962 Chicken War between the United States and Europe. Despite such trade sanctions, the government was backed by Congress and national labor unions in a plan to raise tariffs and impose special non-tariff barriers such as "voluntary" quotas. As Treasury Secretary Shultz had put matters at the 1972 annual meeting of the IMF and World Bank: "Such basic rules as 'no competitive devaluation' and 'most-favored-nation treatment' have served U.S. well, but they and others need to be reaffirmed, supplemented and made applicable to today's conditions." In other words, they no longer suited U.S. economic philosophy, and should be ignored.

A second U.S. objective spelled out in the 1973 *Economic Report* was to create a financial Procrustean bed by freezing the relative levels of world central bank reserves. Payments surplus nations whose reserves rose beyond a specified proportion of the world total would be obliged to revalue their currencies, presumably on the ground that this would hurt their balance of payments and restore equilibrium to the international economy. Conversely, when countries found their reserves falling below a specified limit, they could devalue, even if their deficit were caused by military spending rather than by private sector trade. Only their reserve levels would serve as "objective indicators for adjustment . . . not discriminat[ing] between one set of transactions and another."[13]

The onus of adjustment thus was to be placed on the payments surplus nations. If the value of Germany's mark or Japan's yen was pushed up by speculative capital inflows, U.S. troop spending or a U.S. investment takeover of their economies, they would be obliged to penalize their exporters by revaluing their currencies and realigning their economies to adjust to policies determined unilaterally in Washington.

Regarding the dollar overhang that had built up, the *Economic Report* suggested converting it from a U.S. liability into SDRs, *e.g.* into the liabilities of the IMF member nations generally rather than of the United States specifically. One problem standing in the way, of course, was the fact that countries were obliged at some point to repay their IMF borrowings. The economic advisors therefore advocated that the $75 billion in official U.S. Treasury debt to foreign central banks should be funded into world reserve assets without any corresponding liability! In line with the trial balloon sent up by the Danielian Report, they recommended that foreign central banks set up an "investment fund" to purchase U.S. common stocks and other securities. The scheme was aimed especially at the "oil producing countries with relatively large external assets."[14] Instead of using their export proceeds to modernize their own economies, payments-surplus countries were asked to finance U.S. spending and investment. (No such far-reaching proposal was made for Third World countries in deficit.)

Meeting with President Nixon in Honolulu in September 1972, Japan's Prime Minister Tanaka agreed to increase his nation's imports from the United States by over $1 billion. This sum included a $450 million increase in purchases of U.S. farm products, $320 million of civilian aircraft in an all-cash deal, and $320 million in uranium enrichment services. Japan also agreed to buy a $1 billion gaseous diffusion enrichment facility for peaceful atomic use. But despite these steps, its dollar holdings rose $1.4 billion in October, bringing its international reserves to $23.2 billion.[15]

On capital account the continuation of easy money conditions in the United States spurred some $8.5 billion in private investment outflows during 1972, and America's debt as a whole rose by a then massive $10.3 billion. This substantially exceeded the $6.9 billion trade deficit. The amount may seem small by today's standards, but at the time it was more than three times the 1971 trade deficit and would have cut the U.S. gold stock in half had gold convertibility been maintained. Military spending was held at $4.7 billion in 1972, but even though the United States was spending less in Southeast Asia, it was building up its military forces elsewhere in the world.

U.S. officials did nothing to stem the deficit. The Federal Reserve System continued to inflate the money supply and hold down interest rates so as to promote domestic expansion. Chairman Arthur Burns objected to Citibank's attempt to increase its prime lending rate, and convinced it to roll it back to 6 per cent. This level spurred capital to flow abroad, where higher interest rates could be obtained. In the first quarter of 1973 alone the U.S. payments deficit rose to $10.3 billion, an amount equal to the entire 1972 deficit. U.S. officials continued to act as if the U.S. deficit were a foreign problem, and made the usual suggestion that Europe dispose of its dollar surplus by buying more U.S. farm exports, letting American farmers displace European ones. To this demand President Pompidou of France made it clear that "There is not a chance that Europe can redress the American balance of payments through purchases. There is no chance at all." The deficit, he concluded, was "above all an American problem."[16]

Matters reached crises proportions in February and March 1973. By this time U.S. monetary strategy had taken on the contours that would remain through the 1980s. To begin with, U.S. officials complained that the Smithsonian agreements had not permitted the dollar to be adequately devalued. On February 7, Congressman Wilbur Mills announced that "the exchange relationship between the dollar and other major currencies will have to be realigned some more," above and beyond the 11 per cent December 1971 devaluation. Private dollar holders and speculators took their cue and began to sell dollar for marks and yen. During the week ending February 9, Germany's central bank found itself obliged to purchase some $6 billion of dollar inflows to save the mark from being forced up, including $2 billion on Friday alone in the wake of Mr Mills' statements.[17] Tokyo closed its foreign exchange market on Saturday, February 10, in response to rumors of a 25 per cent devaluation of the dollar against the yen and/or a special U.S. surcharge against Japanese exports.

Over the weekend the Common Market countries discussed how they might cope with their dollar inflows. Germany offered to take the lead in financing a joint float by the nine EEC countries, but was opposed by Italy, whose balance of payments was not as healthy as that of its Common Market partners. France also opposed a float that would increase the franc's value as much as that of the German mark, but it also opposed a unilateral Deutschmark revaluation on the ground that this would strain the Common Agricultural Policy. France and Italy therefore proposed a two-tier exchange structure. The rate for capital investment transactions would be free to rise to deter dollar investments in the French and other European economies, but the foreign trade rate would be held down so as not to impair French and Italian export opportunities.

Germany did not want to revalue the mark, which had risen by more than 25 per cent against the dollar during the preceding three years and over 15 per cent against other European currencies. The rising exchange rate had depressed German automotive, shipbuilding and steel industries. Volkswagen, for instance, sold one-third of its autos in the United States. The value of German exports to the United States was shrinking in D-mark terms, although it was still rising slightly in terms of the depreciating dollar.

Under-Secretary of the Treasury Paul Volcker met with central bankers from France and other European countries individually over the weekend, but avoided formal talks with of the Common Market in Brussels. His discussions with the central bankers sought to play off one country against another. "In Rome 15 months earlier," the *Wall Street Journal* observed, "Mr. Volcker and Mr. Connally had to deal with an institution, and they did not like it very much. The Common Market ministers caucused as a bloc and never agreed on anything except as a collective personality." The lesson was learned: "If you have to deal with the Common Market, don't." Go instead to Bonn, Paris and London. Anticipating that this policy might produce better results, the *Wall Street Journal* concluded, "The question being asked this week in several European capitals is whether this [divide-and-conquer strategy] will be the procedure in future crises and, if so, whether the Common Market is destined to have any real meaning."[18]

America had thrown down its geopolitical gauntlet. Europe refused to abort its agricultural policies, forcing the United States to settle its balance-of-payments problem on the monetary front alone. In this area Europe was frustrated. "It is true that there has been a revolt" against American monetary aggression, wrote the Federal Reserve Bank of Boston in its *New*

England Economic Review, "but it has been a bloodless revolt, limited in scope and unsure of its goals."[19]

The *Wall Street Journal* enumerated some of the benefits the United States was deriving from the monetary turmoil. "'In weakness there is strength,' one London-based American official says with a smile. The more the mark and the yen are buffeted upward, the more competitive dollar-priced goods become in world markets."[20] Even more important, the payments deficit was helping to finance the government's domestic budget deficit: "As foreign central banks acquire dollars through their market intervention, they ask the New York Federal Reserve Bank to purchase U.S. government securities for their accounts, thus gaining some yield on their reserve assets. Such purchases, amounting to $1.66 billion in the week ending last Wednesday [February 7], help finance the U.S. budget deficit and reduce borrowing costs in the U.S. market . . ."

During the year ending March 31, 1973, Japan invested $3.4 billion in U.S. Treasury securities, while Europe invested $13.6 billion and other areas some $0.5 billion more. This freed American residents from having to lend these funds to the Treasury, leaving them available for domestic capital expenditures and foreign investment.

The United States indicated that it preferred direct import controls to further devaluation and threatened to reimpose the illegal 15 per cent import surcharge of August 1971, supplemented by special tariffs and quotas against imports from Japan, Germany and other payments-surplus economies. "Is this the economic equivalent of the Christmas bombing in Vietnam?" asked one French businessman.[21]

Monday, February 12 was Lincoln's birthday and money markets were closed in the United States. They also remained closed in Europe and Japan because of the currency crisis. The next day foreign governments refused to revalue their currencies, obliging the United States to lose face by unilaterally devaluing the dollar by nearly 10 per cent, its second devaluation in fourteen months.

But what at first seemed to be a victory for the Europeans in making the United States act instead of themselves appeared to be what U.S. officials really had wanted all along. In addition to making foreign products more expensive than U.S. goods, the new devaluation resulted in a 10 per cent foreign exchange loss for central banks holding dollar reserves. The only concession (or "mini-concession" as it was termed) that U.S. negotiators gave Europe was to revalue gold by 10 per cent, to $44.20 per ounce. This enabled foreign central banks to offset their dollar exchange losses with nominal paper gains in the dollar value of their gold stocks (but of course at no increase in their own domestic currency values).

President Nixon warned that more U.S. turmoil was to come. Devaluation was "at best only a temporary solution . . . Only by getting trade legislation and changing or reducing the huge deficits can the pressure of the dollar be taken off." He made it clear that his ideas on trade reform hardly foreshadowed "another round of lowering trade barriers . . . We must go up [with barriers] as well as down." Making use of the Uncle Sucker myth, he reflected that the United States had entered into "too many negotiations abroad in which all we have done is negotiate down, whereas others have negotiated up." (He gave no examples.)

The protectionist pressures that had found expression in Wilbur Mills' Trade bill now were being exerted at the presidential level. The *Wall Street Journal* reported that "the President is likely to ask for authority to impose an import surcharge on a country-by-country basis . . . selectively applied against certain nations where large payments surpluses are accumulating."[22] But as the 1973 *Economic Report* noted, GATT rules forbade surcharges for balance-of-payments purposes.[23] A return to international tariff warfare was threatened as other nations were legally bound to retaliate under GATT rules under the Most Favored Nation clause that had governed trade liberalization since World War II. Nonetheless, Representative Mills took this opportunity to announce that he favored new import surcharges of between 10 and 15 per cent. President Nixon threatened to levy special import quotas on French steel for starters, and urged foreign governments to impose "voluntary" export quotas on all items whose sales to the United States were rising significantly.

With all semblance of free trade rhetoric abandoned, the American actions prompted a reaction in Japan, on which Europe had brought "unexpected pressure" to acquiesce in the American terms.[24] Opposition parties renewed their demands for Prime Minister Tanaka's resignation as the yen jumped 14 per cent against the dollar in hectic trading. Tanaka denied responsibility for the monetary developments, "placing the blame directly on the United States and pleading ignorance of the pre-devaluation conversations between his Finance Minister and the chief American negotiator."

European officials hastened to complete plans for full monetary union, which alone could enable them to become independent from U.S. balance-of-payments aggression. The free market price of gold, which had closed at $72.30 per troy ounce on Friday, February 9, jumped to $80 an ounce when markets finally were reopened on Wednesday, February 14, and to

$92 an ounce the next day. The U.S. stock market meanwhile fell by 5 points on Tuesday, 17 points on Wednesday and 6 more points on Thursday as capital funds moved out of the U.S. economy to seek more stable refuge abroad.

None of this induced the United States to do anything to stem the crisis. Treasury Secretary George Shultz made an effort to push down the dollar's value even further by announcing that the administration sought yet another devaluation, without specifying how much he wanted. "Announcement of a devaluation target," the *New York Times* explained, "could undermine Washington's position since – should the target be achieved – Washington might decide that it would like a little bit more." Shultz underscored the administration's aggressive trade stance by insisting on "selective authority to impose selective tariffs or quotas, or combinations of the two, to safeguard American industry."[25] Congress gave Nixon unprecedented personal authority to wage a tariff war against the rest of the world.

Europe was forced to choose between permitting the dollar to devalue further or acquiescing "voluntarily" in the U.S. tariff and quota offensive. U.S. officials were quite open in acknowledging how the crisis situation favored their maneuverability. "In an atmosphere of presumed crisis," Shultz explained, "one often finds that one can get something done if you know what it is you want to get done. The Administration has found a crisis it took an initiative, and it obtained results." His assistant Paul Volcker echoed these comments, observing that the monetary crisis and dollar devaluation had helped "to reinforce the thrust of a constructive reform of the international monetary system." This view was echoed throughout the Wall Street community. Sam Nakagama, chief economist for Kidder Peabody & Co., reflected that "The so-called crises of the past two months appear to have been almost deliberately induced by the Nixon Administration in order to achieve its monetary goals. Treasury Secretary Schultz appears to have almost everything he wanted in the way of creating a more flexible monetary system."[26]

The European response was angry, but was not backed up by any meaningful action. Jacques Serven-Schreiber, author of *The American Challenge,* attacked "the 'brutal act' of devaluation [which] would affect every family in Europe." The French socialist opposition leader François Mitterrand warned that "the devaluation marks the opening of commercial war."[27] Pierre-Paul Schweitzer, outgoing head of the IMF, sought to ward off further U.S. devaluation by emphasizing that the dollar already had become an undervalued currency. But Europe's fears of continued U.S.

dollar inflows for yet more investment takeovers were increased by President Nixon's announcement that he intended to remove all U.S. foreign investment restraints in 1974. The controls indeed were removed in January of that year.

Academic U.S. economists were as glib as administration officials in their proposed solutions to the dollar problem. Professor Richard Cooper of Yale, along with Charles Kindleberger of MIT and Lawrence Krause of the Brookings Institution suggested that the International Monetary Fund lend SDRs to the United States without limit – or, failing that, lend $6 billion which would be repaid over a forty-year period, by which time inflation no doubt would have wiped out most of its capital value).[28] This would require the IMF to eliminate its existing "holding limits" of SDRs for individual countries, which would find themselves stuck with SDRs as they earlier had been stuck with dollars.

The *New York Times* observed that,

From the end of 1969 to the fall of 1972, the United States covered the $45.5 billion increase in its dollar liabilities to other countries simply by requiring that the other nations add that amount of dollars to their monetary reserves [i.e., invest this amount in U.S. Treasury bills]. American officials think this dollar standard works tolerably well, and are in no hurry to change it. Some Europeans complain that the ability of the United States to create international monetary reserves by printing dollars gives it a free ride on foreign policy – and, in effect, has forced others to finance such American adventures as the Vietnam war. The Europeans see this ability of the United States to get credit without international constraints as an "exorbitant privilege," in the words of the late General de Gaulle. Some still regard an international credit system controlled by a single country as "a great obstacle in the way of perpetual peace," as Immanual Kant wrote in 1795. Prof. Robert Triffin of Yale notes that Kant also said: "The other States are justified in allying themselves against such a State and its pretensions."[29]

Raw materials exporters were hurt, as well as Europe and Japan. "The big Australian mining companies, whose contracts for ore have been written in American dollars [largely with Japan], estimate that the 10 per cent cut in the value of the United States currency this week will cost the industry up to $250 million a year in lost profits unless Australia also reduces the price of her money."[30] Dollar devaluation, which had already forced a number of Australian coal mines to shut down, threatened cotton growers in New South Wales with losses of more than $6.5 million, and wheat growers with losses of more than $20 million per annum. Oil-exporting countries suffered much more.

European economists stepped up their planning for the Common Market's Economic and Monetary Union (EMU) scheduled to begin in 1974. Their immediate desire was to replace the dollar with a more stable standard of value, one that did not oblige them to finance the U.S. Government's domestic budgetary deficit via the U.S. balance-of-payments deficits. Professor John Williamson of England and Senor Magnifico of Italy developed a plan that anticipated the euro which would be introduced 28 years later, in 2002. The plan "envisaged a European reserve bank issuing Europas to national central banks in return for their reserves and quotas of national currencies. It would act as central bank to commercial banks issuing bonds denominated in Europas. National central banks would manage their individual parities against the Europa, while the European reserve bank would manage the rate between the Europa and the dollar."[31] These Europas would supplant Eurodollars in European capital markets, restoring control of the money supply to Europe. Eurodollars would have nowhere to go except back to the United States, inflating the latter's economy instead of Europe's. For a change, good money might chase out bad.

Europe's choice lay between being divided and conquered, or proceeding full steam ahead toward economic and monetary integration. Most Europeans wanted the latter option, but the dollar outflow from America rose to such a pace that Germany and other payments surplus economies were unable to defend themselves. On March 5 the world's foreign exchange markets closed once again and remained closed for two weeks, an event unprecedented in modern history.

During this crisis U.S. negotiators refused to yield to Europe on any point. Treasury Secretary Shultz even rejected suggestions that the United States raise its interest rates to attract more dollars home, on the ground that "Domestic credit measures will be taken in the context of domestic economic development," not foreign concerns.[32] This inward-centeredness was reminiscent of the abortive London Conference of 1933.

As the price of gold pressed toward $100 an ounce, Jacques Rueff of France urged that the official price of gold at least be doubled, to about $80 an ounce. This would increase the value of U.S. monetary gold from $10 billion to $20 billion. Perhaps, he suggested, Europe could loan the gold revaluation profits back to the United States at low interest. But U.S. officials urged just the opposite policy, a reduction in the official price of gold leading to its demonetization, so that Europe and Asia could not use their gold reserves vis-à-vis the United States in the way that it had used its gold reserves itself against Europe in the 1920s, 1930s, 1940s and 1950s.

U.S. economic strategists discussed the prospect of the Treasury suddenly dumping its gold holdings on world markets, perhaps joined by Britain and a few other central banks in client countries. If America was to lose its gold, so its must allies, so the reasoning went. This would remove the last hope for an objective constraint on the ability of nations to run payments deficits at the expense of others.[33]

During February and early March 1973 the German central bank was obliged to purchase over $8 billion in dollars to support the latter's value against the Deutschmark. Finally, on March 14, Germany revalued the mark yet again. Two days later the finance ministers of thirteen countries, plus the United States, met in Paris and announced that all nine EEC members, except Italy, England and Ireland, would be joined by Sweden and Norway in maintaining their currencies within a 2¼ per cent margin. The three floating currency countries agreed to associate themselves with the new European fixed-rate system as soon as practicable. The United States agreed not to remove its controls on capital outflows in 1974 unless its balance of payments had improved, and also promised to "remove inhibitions on the inflow of capital into the United States." But as matters turned out, it broke its word and did just the opposite, removing its controls on capital outflows while making OPEC countries and other dollar holders promise not to buy any significant U.S. corporation.[34]

A number of European moves helped the dollar strengthen when world foreign exchange markets finally reopened on Monday, March 19. France announced that no interest payments would be permitted on foreign money deposited in French banks, and that 100 per cent reserve requirements would be imposed on these foreign deposits. To add bite, the new regulations were made retroactive to January 4. The Netherlands, Belgium and Luxembourg announced similar measures, and Germany already had imposed such restrictions. Belgium and Luxembourg imposed negative interest charges of 0.25 per cent per week to be paid by nonresidents on all growth in their bank accounts over a fixed base level.

These actions left little motive for Eurodollar holdings on the part either of foreign investors (who could earn no interest) or domestic banks (which found their foreign deposits sterilized). Even Spain moved to prevent its currency from becoming a speculative investment medium, forbidding foreigners and nonresidents to use their convertible peseta accounts for free currency transactions. They could convert their accounts back into their original currencies and remove them from Spain, but pesetas henceforth could be spent only within Spain. Payment of interest was forbidden on all foreign accounts, and 100 per cent reserve requirements were imposed.

American newspapers blamed the dollar's difficulties on multinational firms and Arab oil sheiks. On February 12, the Tariff Commission reported that U.S. multinational firms held some $268 billion in liquid assets. Much of this sum represented inventories, receivables and short-term credits to affiliates and other companies, and hence not available for currency speculation, but the impression was given that a mere 5 per cent shift in the currency form of these short-term assets could cause a world monetary crisis.

It remained true, of course, that financial resources in the hands of these companies were large, and could contribute to international currency instability simply by the practice of prepaying bills to nations that were revaluation candidates, and paying bills late to countries whose currencies seemed ripe for devaluation. International firms could shift deposits from one currency to another, but most did not want their corporate treasurers to act as currency speculators. A number of companies and banks had been badly burned doing this, and most large firms feared that controls might be imposed if they acted like bad monetary citizens.

Everyone seemed to have his own favorite villain. Persons with axes to grind against the Arab countries seized on rumors that the Sheik of Kuwait had turned most of his $2.5 billion dollar holdings into gold and hard currencies.[35] Franz Pick blamed Russia, accusing its foreign banks of profiting from a massive leveraged speculation against the dollar. This kind of movement out of dollars by corporations, Arab sheiks and perhaps Communist countries was depicted as being the primary cause of U.S. balance-of-payments troubles, as if the U.S. Government were just an innocent bystander.

Meanwhile, U.S. officials continued to make inflammatory statements about the need for further devaluations, monetary ease and removal of capital controls. Paul Volcker, addressing an American Bankers Association conference in Paris, stated that the United States was "skeptical of putting a very high degree of discretionary authority" in the IMF, as this would impair the fundamental principle of national sovereignty for the United States.[36]

Europeans replied that their virtual crucifixion on the cross of dollars threatened their economic sovereignty. French officials were rebuffed when they once again urged the United States to support the dollar. During the last two weeks of March the German Bundesbank absorbed $1.5 billion in U.S. currency transfers, largely from Belgium, the Netherlands and France. By the end of June, dollar inflows into Germany forced yet another revaluation of the mark on June 29, this time by 5.5 per cent. It was the fifth revaluation since 1969, bringing the D-mark's value to 41 cents, compared to 25 cents four years earlier.

A contributing factor to the German revaluation was the fact that no international gold sales were occurring at the "official" price of $44.22 per ounce. Demonetization of gold had removed it as a constraint on the ability of countries – or at least of the United States – to run balance-of-payments deficits. At the end of March the free price of gold had soared through the $100 an ounce level, and by June was pressing $125 per ounce. Italy was rumored to have sold 300 tons of gold on the free market to obtain dollars with which to settle its payments deficit with other Common Market central banks. But most countries running payments deficits sought to hold on to their gold, using their unwanted dollars to pay West Germany and other payments surplus nations.[37] The Soviet Union was said to be holding on to its gold until the price reached $200 per ounce.

Over the July 6 weekend U.S. diplomats apparently agreed to share equally with Europe in any exchange risks that might arise from borrowings of European currencies. The lack of such an agreement had been one of the principal obstacles to agreement on central bank intervention."[38] The idea was that if the United States borrowed marks or guilder to support the dollar, and the dollar was devalued before these borrowings were repaid, the United States would suffer only half of the devaluation burden. The other half would be borne by the central banks that had extended foreign currency loans to the United States. In the past, debtor countries such as Britain had been obliged to bear the full devaluation impact of their overseas borrowings, but the rules now were to be changed to accommodate the United States. In exchange for this quasi-concession the Federal Reserve increased its credit lines with foreign central banks from $12 to $18 billion, that is, by about 50 per cent, including $1 billion increases with the central banks of France, West Germany, Japan and Canada. This gave promise of official intervention to support the dollar's exchange rate, no such support having occurred from March through June.

But a greater ability of the U.S. Federal Reserve to intervene in support of the dollar did not mean that it would in fact do so. Writing in the New York Federal Reserve Bank's *Monthly Review*, Charles Coombs – head of U.S. official foreign exchange trading – attributed the dollar's weakness not to the payments deficit throwing increasing sums of dollars onto world markets, but to "sporadic bouts of nervous and, at times, heavy trading to levels unjustified and undesirable on any reasonable assessment of the U.S. payments position." He claimed that the problem concerned the price of American goods and services relative to those of foreign countries, not the volume of military spending and capital outflows to buy out foreign industry.

Coombs was putting forth what economists called the purchasing power parity theory of exchange rates, sometimes popularized as the "McDonald's principle" which defines a country's "natural" exchange rate as that at which a McDonald's hamburger will sell for a uniform world price. This would be the case were it not for international "distortions." Of course, the real world is driven by what academic economists belittle as "distortions," headed by government spending and private investment. The U.S. argument had been refuted already in the mid-nineteenth century by John Stuart Mill, and subjected to a more refined critique by Keynes in the 1920s, both of whom pointed to the impact of capital transfers or other non-trade spending on international pricing.

The German and French hyperinflations a half-century earlier had shown that exchange rates have more to do with structural factors, capital flows and relative interest rates than with relative product prices. This fact of life was clearly perceived in Europe. Labeling the U.S. devaluation a new form of protectionism, Mitterrand called for France to boycott the world trade liberalization negotiations scheduled for September. At the Bank for International Settlements in Basle, French officials threatened to press for "establishment of a Common Market gold bloc, which would in effect create a much higher official price for gold."[39] Europe and America prepared themselves for battle at the September IMF meetings.

Trade negotiations had become a dead issue. Freer trade was ruled out by the fact that the dollar's devaluation had wiped out most of the tariff concessions America had made during the 1960s. This was underscored on July 14 when Belgium's Sabena Airlines ordered ten Boeing 737 jets at about $6 million each, instead of the French twin-engine Mercure whose price had been increased in dollar terms to nearly $8 million each.[40] In 1969 the price for these two planes would have been roughly equivalent, throwing the advantage to the French plane inasmuch as its seating capacity was 140 passengers, compared to 115 for the Boeing jet. The result was a setback for Europe's hope to build an all-European aircraft industry as the foundation for military autonomy from the United States.

Another blow to free trade was struck when President Nixon obtained from Congress personal authority to impose import surcharges on a country-by-country basis if foreign economies did not acquiesce in U.S. trade plans and impose "voluntary" export quotas on their own producers. U.S. trade negotiators also asked for compensation for U.S. exports lost as a result of the Common Market's enlargement to include England, Ireland and Denmark. They estimated that the Common Agricultural Policy (CAP) would reduce U.S. grain exports to these three countries by some 10 million tons annually, and feared that within five years the Common Market might become a net grain exporter. The United States refused even to enter into global trade negotiations unless there was an advance commitment by other countries "to meaningful and realistic negotiations in the agricultural sectors," specifically a break-up of the CAP. This demand was still being made in the 1990s.

What the United States wanted from Europe and Japan was made evident by its proposed agreement with South Korea "to make it obligatory for South Korean exporters to the American market to import a certain amount of raw materials from the United States."[41] On another front the United States struck a blow at the Common Market's proposed associate membership status for its former African colonies by making it clear that it would not grant new U.S. tariff preferences for any Third World country that granted reverse preferences to other industrial nations.

What had appeared in 1945 as a liberating dissolution of European colonialism was taking the form of a U.S. attempt to lock the world's economies into a new dependency on the United States, above all American agricultural, aircraft and military-related technology. The American plan was for foreign countries to become dependent on the United States for basic food grains, arms and technology, and to sell their commanding heights to U.S. investors regardless of the fact that the U.S. economy was not generating the foreign exchange to pay for such control.

On May 9, Treasury Secretary Shultz told the House Ways and Means Committee that the forthcoming trade negotiations with other leading nations "probably should not be 'reciprocal,' adding that 'there may have to be more giving than taking as far as other people are concerned.'" The negotiations "won't be all tit for tat." The Nixon Administration threatened Europe that if its conditions were not met, Congress might pass the labor-backed Burke–Hartke bill, threatening to cut U.S. imports by $8 billion. France took the lead among its Common Market partners in seizing upon this statement to insist that failure to reform the monetary system would rule out further trade liberalization.[42]

What made the posturing so hypocritical was that the United States was enacting precisely the type of quota restrictions for which it was criticizing Europe. The Nixon Administration's omnibus Farm bill included a sleeper provision imposing permanent import quotas on dairy products, already limited under section 22 of the Agricultural Adjustment Act. The bill placed permanent limits on dairy imports, restricting them to only 2 per cent of the previous year's domestic U.S. consumption. "The President could increase this amount [of quota-free imports] only if he determines and proclaims that such increase is required by overriding economic or national-security interests of the United States. Such a finding would presumably be difficult to make in normal circumstances."[43]

Even more important was the fact that under pressure of a 15 per cent increase in wholesale prices and nearly a 50 per cent increase in food prices, the United States placed embargoes on its exports, abrogating existing sales commitments. So much for the free trade ideology America had sponsored after World War II. As early as March, U.S. officials had asked Japan to impose "voluntary" import quotas on U.S. timber in order to hold down the demand for U.S. exports. These quotas were to complement the equally coercive export controls on Japan's textile and steel exports to the United States. But if it were not to import U.S. forestry and farm products, how could it be expected to reduce its trade surplus with the United States?

Matters were aggravated on June 27, when America imposed export embargoes on soybeans, cottonseed and their products, save for sales actually in the process of being loaded on board ships. This broke the nation's export commitments, hurting Japan in particular. Further export controls were imposed a week later on scrap metal and on forty-one additional farm commodities, including livestock feed, edible oils and animal fats, peanuts, lard and tallow.

These unilateral actions made it clear that Europe and Japan no longer could depend on American supplies, but were expected to serve simply as residual markets for American agricultural and industrial surpluses on a commodity by commodity basis. And they would increase their consumption of U.S. products as U.S. output increased, but only to that extent. They would obligingly curtail their consumption when U.S. output diminished, so that domestic U.S. consumption and prices could remain stable.

American trade strategists urged nations accumulating large trade surpluses to purchase specific types of American exports, particularly those of a military character as the arms trade was one of the few areas in which the United States retained some competitive advantage. It sought to balance its oil imports from Iran by exporting jet fighters and other military equipment totaling nearly $4 billion, including laser bombs, heli-copters and other items which were to become part of the Shah's five-year modernization program.[44] In June, the Pentagon announced a $2 billion arms sale to Saudi Arabia and Kuwait, including some $14 million F-14 fighter planes so new they had not even been introduced into the U.S. armed forces. Rising U.S. oil exports from the Near East thus were financed by a rising stream of arms exports to the region.

It seemed that U.S. payments balance was to be achieved only by arming the rest of the world. The implicit end of this process was military hostility. An ideal scenario to U.S. eyes might have been one in which Iran, Saudi Arabia and other U.S. arms clients invaded OPEC countries that did not choose to recycle their oil-export proceeds to the Defense Department. Instead, the Arabs attacked Israel in October.

Even America's foreign aid programs were becoming militarized. On June 5, President Nixon reversed the official ban on aid-financed military exports, citing the fact that the United States was losing foreign arms markets to French and Russian producers. Even Communist Chile was included in the list of candidates for American arms aid in an attempt to induce it not to buy Russian MIG-21s. Secretary of State William Rogers rationalized the change of policy by testifying before the House Foreign Affairs Committee that "The United States should no longer attempt to determine for the Latin Americans what their reasonable military needs should be."[45] It should sell them whatever their regimes wanted on credit to be repaid by future generations.

U.S. aid strategists had pondered the question of export credit for some time. In February 1972, the National Advisory Council on International Monetary and Financial Policies argued that the U.S. payments deficit prevented the government from promoting exports on a no-cash, pay-later basis. The report urged nations to avoid a "credit race" in export financing by eliminating credit "as a factor of export sales competition."[46] In other words, to prevent other governments from using their balance-of-payments strength to offer more favorable terms, the Council urged "international arrangements to assure that government-supported export credit is developed along rational lines." Other governments should correspond-ingly curtail their own export financing, despite their evolution into creditor status that was enabling them to emulate traditional U.S. credit policies. Having won the first lap of this credit race during the quarter-century since the ending of World War II, the United States tried to call the race to a halt as it watched other nations threatening to overtake it.

U.S. exports were less competitive in world markets as productivity growth trailed that of other industrial nations. Losing the financial as well as commercial strength it had possessed in the early postwar years, America no longer had the means to sell its exports on credit rather than for cash, but other countries now had these means. The U.S. economy was evolving toward what some observers called a post-industrial society, but which seemed simply to be deindustrializing. Seymour Melman blamed matters on a lapse into "Pentagon capitalism" with its cost-plus pricing contracts which bloated costs for America's leading arms manufacturers.

Internationally, The United States was burdened with $6 billion in annual military outlays throughout the world, about to suffer ignominious defeat in Southeast Asia, and unable to withdraw from Europe and other regions without reverting to the status of being just another nation in a world of equals. This it refused to do. America's admittedly immense agricultural powers were constrained by a decaying transport system, and the nation was breaking its export contracts to all areas of the world, prompting them more urgently to seek self-sufficiency in essential foodstuffs.

This was just what U.S. economic planners worked so hard to stave off in 1945 and in the intervening years. Almost the only remaining U.S. advantage lay in military goods. Restoration of a favorable U.S. trade balance therefore seemed conditional upon the rest of the world arming itself rather than developing its own capacity to feed itself by promoting farm investment behind an agricultural protectionism similar to that which America had applied so effectively.

Prospects seemed dim for an underlying improvement in the U.S. payments balance. Devaluation of the dollar by 10 per cent in 1973, over and above the 11 per cent Smithsonian devaluation of December 1971, was calculated to have increased overall military outlays by a reported $300 million annually.[47] The trade deficit meanwhile was widening as a result of increased payments for energy and other raw materials, while the collapsing stock market was discouraging foreign investment inflows.

U.S.–Soviet condominium?

The United States found itself in a position not unlike that of Germany in the 1920s. Unable to compete successfully with its capitalist allies, it could turn only to the Soviet Union for prospective growth in exports. This about-face helped resolve America's Cold War tensions with the Soviet Union. After all, the U.S. and Soviet economies were largely complementary. Russia needed wheat and was a major producer of gold and oil.

Whereas U.S.–Soviet trade had seemed more important to war-torn Russia in 1945, it now appeared to offer equal benefits to the United States. Perception of the new state of affairs led to an ironic turn in the U.S. Cold War economic system. The United States agreed to sell surplus grain to the Soviet Union for cash and, perhaps, gold.

An important byproduct of the Cold War had been to pump dollars into the central banks of America's allies. Now that this process no longer was desired by either the United States or its allied non-Communist nations, U.S. officials sought to draw foreign exchange into the Treasury through the most promising avenue: trade with the Soviet Union and China. The Iron Curtain began to lift.

Already in the election year of 1960 the United States and Soviet Union had seemed near to establishing somewhat normal commercial relations. The United States asked Russia for $800 million to settle its World War II debts, and the Soviet Union offered $300 million. As the National Advisory Council on International Monetary and Financial Policies later described these negotiations, they were broken off when "the United States could not accept the Soviet position that such settlement be accompanied by the simultaneous conclusion of an agreement granting most-favored-nation treatment to the Soviet Union and the extension of long-term U.S. credits to the Soviet Union."[48] Now, in another election year twelve years later, the United States was willing to accept the Soviet conditions. A joint declaration was issued at the conclusion of President Nixon's visit to Moscow in July 1972 asking Congress to grant Soviet Russia most-favored-nation tariff treatment, conditional upon satisfactory settlement of the Lend-Lease debts stemming from World War II. As matters turned out, the United States was soon to sell its grain to Soviet Russia, thereby financing its European troop-support costs by feeding Soviet troops across the NATO border!

The Soviet Union had been making regular payments on that portion of the debt on which it had been able to reach agreement with the U.S. Treasury on October 15, 1945, when it "undertook to pay for 'pipeline' deliveries which ultimately totaled $222.5 million, in twenty-two annual installments, at an interest rate of $2\frac{3}{8}$ per cent per annum. The Soviet Union has been making annual payments on this account and as of December 31, 1970, had paid a total of $187 million." But it had made deductions not recognized by the United States, including $88 million for damage suffered by Soviet commercial vessels in the port of Haiphong during U.S. raids on North Vietnam. In addition, the United States claimed that the Soviet Union owed some $2.6 billion for civilian goods still in use at the end of World War II. These debts finally were to be negotiated as Soviet diplomats arrived in Washington in summer 1972.

The United States began by asking about $1 billion in payment, claiming that some $200 million in interest had accrued since the 1960 discussions. The Soviet Union countered with its 1960 offer to pay $300 million. A midpoint level of $500 million was agreed upon, leaving only the terms of payment to be settled. The Soviet Union asked for the same treatment the British had received after World War II: 2 per cent interest over thirty years. The United States explained that such terms no longer were adequate and suggested 6 per cent interest over the same thirty-year period. Final agreement was reached on October 18, with the Soviet Union paying $722 million over the next twenty-nine years. "In exchange, President Nixon has authorized the Export-Import Bank to extend most-favored-nation treatment to the Soviet Union, which would allow it access to the American market at the lowest possible tariffs."[49]

Russia basically got its way. What it yielded in interest and principal payments in offering to pay $722 million to settle its remaining Lend-Lease debts was gained back indirectly on July 8, when it contracted to buy $750 million worth of U.S. grains over a three-year period. Of this sum, $500 million was financed by the Export-Import Bank. Having secured Soviet Russia and China as grain markets, the United States might mitigate its objections to Britain joining the European Common Market and adhering to the Common Agricultural Policy. Russia might secure a market for U.S. farmers in the event they were shut out of Europe.

A number of U.S. firms announced plans to exploit Siberia's vast natural gas and oil fields. About $10 billion worth of Soviet gas and oil would be exported to the United States in exchange for U.S. development of the Siberian fields and construction of a tanker fleet to transport this output. On November 4, 1972, three U.S. firms – Tenneco, Texas Eastern Transmission Corp. and a Halliburton Company engineering subsidiary – announced that within sixty days they expected to complete a $3.7 billion investment agreement to sell Soviet natural gas in the United States.[50] They would supply and finance $3 billion of American gas transmission equipment, including 1,500 miles of 48-inch steel pipe, plus compressors to liquefy the gas for tanker shipment to the U.S. East Coast. The Soviet Union would sell two billion cubic feet of gas per day to the United States for twenty-five years, using some $8 billion of the total $18.9 billion in export revenues to repay the capital investment loans. Most important of all, it would earmark the $10.8 billion over and above these loan repayments to purchase U.S. goods and service exports. In effect the United

States would pay for its energy imports in blocked dollars – a reversion to similar policies for which its free market diplomats had criticized Germany in the 1930s.

Financing of the energy agreement called for the Soviet Union to put up $700 million in cash, with the Eximbank lending $1.5 billion at 6 per cent interest, and guaranteeing another $1.5 billion in fifteen-year private sector credits at 7 per cent interest. The United States agreed to build twenty oil tankers costing $130 million each (for a total $2.6 billion), over and above its $3.7 billion investment in developing the Siberian oilfields. The construction related to this project was estimated to generate 242,600 man-years of domestic U.S. employment.[51]

On January 12, 1973, the General Electric Company signed a technology exchange pact with the Soviet Union. In April, Occidental Oil announced an $8 billion dollar deal to construct a Soviet fertilizer complex in exchange for deliveries of ammonia, urea and potash.[52] Associated with this project was the construction of various hotels and a trade center in Moscow.

This was a curious turn to the Cold War, which was supposed to guarantee peace within the West and pose the threat of military hostility only vis-à-vis the Communist countries. Peace with the latter was being cemented by the new policy of détente. Indeed, the more America began to lose its hold on its noncommunist allies, the closer America and the Soviet Union drew together, precisely to threaten Europe and Asia with what Henry Kissinger called a new condominium, that is, joint imperialism of America and Russia against their respective satellites.

Largely responsible for this détente was America's balance-of-payments problem stemming from its overseas Cold War spending, and its grain sale to Russia to gain a long-term export market. The U.S. payments deficit was settled by a combination of militarizing its allies and turning to the Soviet Union as a new major export market.

Just as the origin of the U.S. payments deficit was military, so its solution also was becoming increasingly military. Foreign war spending in Southeast Asia and elsewhere was to be balanced by U.S. military sales to America's allies elsewhere in the world. And these sales would only be spurred by growing rapprochement with Russia, potentially at European and Japanese expense.

There was no guarantee that the United States in fact would become the favored industrial supplier of the Soviet Union and China. Just as the USSR had shopped around for credit throughout the world, so it used U.S. offers of investment in its raw materials development as a lever to exact better terms from Japan and Europe. In November 1972, it reached tentative agreement with Japan on a $200 million oil and gas project, and negotiations were underway in other areas.[53]

The United States thus found itself in danger of being played against other capitalist countries on disadvantageous terms. It was obvious that the Soviet Union desired medium- or long-term credits to finance its imports, and nations outside the United States were in a better balance-of-payments position to extend such credits.

The final play came with the Oil War in October 1973. When Egypt and Syria attacked Israel, Arab countries embargoed oil exports to the United States, Holland and Denmark. Oil prices quadrupled, reflecting the pattern of food export prices earlier in 1972–73.

The oil embargo changed the pattern of international payments, restoring surplus to the U.S. balance of payments but driving a wedge between America and Europe. OPEC banks rather than those of Europe and Japan became the major accumulators of dollars. Seeing themselves as Third World countries, they proposed uniting to support raw materials export prices across the board. U.S.–European–Japanese trilateralism was cracking under the balance-of-payments strains imposed by U.S. Cold War spending at home and abroad.

The way the United States chose to resolve these problems was to sell its grain stockpile to the Soviet Union. This tripled or quadrupled world grain and soybean prices, and led to the aforementioned export embargoes which effectively terminated the postwar move toward free trade and investment policies. Led by the United States, the non-Communist countries were becoming more statist. The postwar economic order seemed to be giving way to a new international economic order.

This phase of the postwar world economy, and how the United States achieved its objectives in thwarting the incipient New International Economic Order and European integration to tap the wealth of all foreign central banks accumulating dollars, is described in the sequel to this book, *Global Fracture* (1977).

15 Monetary Imperialism: The Twenty-first Century

Like most individuals, every nation would love to obtain the proverbial free lunch favoring its own interests while other countries passively refrain from promoting their own economies. But few actually have tried to put this kind of double standard into practice. The 1930s showed that when nations press their own self-interest one-sidedly, the international responses tend to degenerate into the zero-sum games of competitive tariff wars and beggar-my-neighbor currency devaluations.

Yet the United States is now able to run trade and payments deficits amounting to hundreds of billions of dollars annually with no audible protest from the rest of the world. Central banks no longer cash in their dollar inflows for gold. Oil-exporting countries no longer seek to buy major U.S. companies, nor do European or Japanese political leaders ask that America finance its payments deficit by selling off its investments in Europe, Asia and other payments-surplus economies. Conditions today are not such that foreign diplomats are willing to take the creditor-oriented stance vis-à-vis the U.S. economy that U.S. officials did from the 1920s through the early years of World War II, when they insisted that Britain sell off its international investments as a condition for obtaining credit.

The sense of shock at the United States' rising trade and payments deficit has been lost as the deficit has been built into the world economic system. The upshot is that almost without anyone really recognizing what has been happening, America's shift into debtor status turned the postwar economy into an exploitative double standard. Since the nation went off gold in 1971, the Treasury bill standard has enabled the United States to draw on the resources of the rest of the world without reciprocation, governing financially through its debtor position, not through its creditor status. As dollar debts have replaced gold as the backing for central bank reserves, and hence for the world's credit supply, the entire system would be threatened if questions into its intrinsic unfairness were reopened.

No nation ever before has been able to invert the classical rules of international finance. Economies that have fallen into deficit have lost not only their world power, but usually also their autonomy to manage their own domestic policies and retain ownership of their public resources and their central bank's financial policy. This is still the financial and political principle they must follow. Yet U.S. diplomats have been able to convince Europe, Asia and the Third World – and since 1991 even the former Soviet Union – to reorient their economies to facilitate America's evolution from payments-surplus to payments-deficit status.

How has America been able to achieve this *quid* without the *quo*, something for nothing, a free subsidy from the world's payments-surplus nations? For one thing, the rationale for acquiescence has shifted from an early postwar faith in American moral leadership and the rhetoric of free markets to the fear that the United States will plunge the world into crisis if it does not get its way.

This book has described the historical path that has led to America's unique position. Rather from using its creditor status as a lever to obtain general international rules that promoted broader long-term economic objectives between World Wars I and II, the United States demanded payment of debts beyond Europe's ability to pay. It chose to "go it alone." But by pursuing essentially autarchic policies it fractured the world economy, and its demand for payments on official credits to foreign governments had helped bring on the Great Depression that engulfed its own economy as much as those of Europe and Asia.

The 1940s saw the United States use its creditor position to create a more unified global economy whose free trade rules promote its interests just as earlier free trade had benefited Britain. The terms of Lend-Lease in 1940–41 and the 1946 British Loan provided the model by obliging Britain to give up its Empire, relinquish its Sterling Area and unblock the wartime balances that Commonwealth countries had accumulated by during the war. British negotiators simply gave in when their interests clashed with those of the United States.

Their acquiescence in these loan conditions reflected the historically unique mood that followed World War II. Believing the very idea of national interest to be ultimately militaristic, many Europeans were willing to subordinate it to what promised to be a cosmopolitan system serving the entire world's welfare. Politicians and diplomats accordingly left it to American planners to draw up the blueprints for such a world system on the principled logic of free trade and ostensibly uniform economic treatment of all countries.

This was not how international diplomacy was supposed to work, much less classical imperialism. Each side was supposed to advocate its own interest, reaching agreement somewhere in the middle or else breaking off relations and possibly even becoming belligerent. But the world had grown weary of such conflict. Most countries were exhausted by the nationalist rivalries that had contributed to the two world wars.

Apart from the moral appeal of a more open world economy, the United States provided Marshall Plan aid to war-torn Europe and offered foreign aid loans to cover the trade deficits anticipated to result from an international economy that everyone recognized would be dominated by U.S. exporters and investors. Such lending was designed to make the postwar system palatable enough for Europe and other regions to adopt relatively free trade and open their doors to U.S. investors as currencies were made freely convertible, and nations agreed not to use devaluation to bolster their international payments at U.S. expense.

The United States insisted as a condition for such aid that it be given veto power in the IMF and World Bank. After all, its diplomats pointed out, America was putting up most of the financing for these institutions. In effect the U.S. proposal was as follows: "We have not demanded reparations from our enemies or war debts from our allies, save for the cost of Lend-Lease transfers that still have a residual economic value to them. Let us develop multilateral organizations to move the world economy toward freer trade without currency controls. Some countries will run trade deficits as they begin to modernize, but we will extend foreign aid to bridge them over this transition period to a new international equilibrium."

"Of course, in order to obtain congressional approval for this funding, certain political realities must be recognized. Although the new multilateral organizations must be internationalist in spirit, Americans would find it intolerable if in practice they infringed on U.S. sovereignty. We cannot abrogate our Agricultural Adjustment Act of 1933, nor can we go along with any Scarce Currency clause for the IMF that would enable countries running deficits to retaliate against U.S. exporters simply for our being so strong an economy. And we think it only fair that in exchange for funding international organizations, we obtain veto power over any decisions they may make. Otherwise, payments deficit countries might vote to make America a tributary to themselves."

The words sounded almost altruistic in comparison to how America had comported itself after World War I. The mood abroad was one of laissez-faire idealism as a general commercial principle, but it was constrained by special concessions demanded by the United States.

The economic implications of the emerging world order were not really grasped. It was not simply that America was the richest nation and largest market, or even that its dollar the currency in which most trade was denominated. This had been the position of sterling already in the nineteenth century, when it was a proxy for gold and Britain's balance of payments normally was in surplus as a result of its industrial and financial leadership. Most important, Britain had sponsored free trade by ending its agricultural protectionism when it repealed its Corn Laws 1846. Opening its food markets was the *quid pro quo* that led other countries to acquiesce in letting it become the workshop of the world and hence consolidating its role as world banker.

By contrast, the U.S.-centered form of interdependence that emerged from World War II was not symmetrical. American diplomats secured as much autonomy as possible for their own domestic and foreign policies, but rejected the idea of foreign influence over the U.S. economy. American agricultural markets and key "national security" sectors remained protected and heavily subsidized by grandfathering into trade agreements the laws and market controls that Roosevelt's New Deal had placed on the books in the 1930s. Also grandfathered in were Britain's sterling debts at an overvalued exchange rate for sterling. This condition laid down for the British loan helped ensure that India, Egypt and Latin American countries would spend their balances on U.S. exports.

Congressional approval for international agreements was simply a fact of American political life. The reason given by Congress for refusing to ratify the United States joining the League of Nations after World War I was to protect U.S. autonomy and prevent foreign countries from imposing policies that might impair U.S. economic interests, including the local vested interests to which Congress always has been mindful. America agreed to join the United Nations, IMF and World Bank after World War II only on the condition that it be given veto power. This enabled it to block any policy deemed not to be in American interests.

Not clearly perceived at the time was the degree to which this condition would enable U.S. representatives to hold these organizations at ransom until they yielded to American policy demands. Diplomatic initiative in these organizations was held by U.S. representatives answerable to Congress and the special interests of its constituencies. In no other country have local politicians had an equivalent ability to reject international agreements reached to by their executive branch, nor have other countries calculated their self-interest on so narrow-minded a basis in negotiating treaties. The upshot has been that the policies of nominally multilateral institutions such as the IMF and World Bank, as well as the Asian Development Bank and other offshoots, reflect an American nationalism writ large.

U.S. "food imperialism" vs. a New International Economic Order

Structural problems were built into the DNA molecules of the World Bank that made its evolution into development lending dysfunctional from the outset. It could lend only dollars and other foreign exchange, not the domestic currency needed for agricultural modernization. And although land reform initially was needed in many former colonial areas of the world, the Bank was not allowed to insist that governments modify their policies along these lines, as that was deemed to be an intrusion into domestic political affairs. By the time the World Bank finally began to insist that governments change their domestic policies in order to qualify for loans, its economic philosophy had become so dysfunctional that instead of promoting policies to make debtor countries more self-reliant, its administrators demanded that loan recipients pursue a policy of economic dependency, above all on the United States as food supplier.

The World Bank has become much more interventionist since 1991, most notoriously in the neoliberal mode epitomized by the Russian "reforms," that is, on the side of kleptocratic oligarchies. The terms of Bank support – on which IMF loans have been made conditional in many cases – have been such as to cripple the long-term viability of governments seeking to finance the modernization of their economies in the way that the United States itself has done. The net result of World Bank and IMF lending programs thus has been to cripple the planning options of economies, leaving them with dollar debts without having put into place the means to generate the foreign exchange to pay, except by selling off more of their public domain. Dependency has been subsidized rather than self-sufficiency being financed.

The World Bank should have advised Russia and other countries to tax natural resource rents and the public domain rather than letting these revenues be taken by insiders and sent abroad as capital flight. Economic rents from public enterprises, and from the land and its mineral wealth, the radio spectrum and other natural monopolies could have saved governments from having to tax labor and capital. But rather than mobilizing resources to enhance national self-sufficiency while funding government policy in this way, the Bank insisted on client governments privatizing their public domain under kleptocratic conditions favoring U.S. investors. The effect was to help impose dependency and oligarchic policies as a condition for aid. The revenues that previously were available to the public sector were paid abroad as dividends, interest, insurance and reinsurance premiums, and management fees by the new private owners of what had been the public domain or had been taken by the government from domestic owners.

Within the IMF its Chicago School monetarists evidently have learned nothing from the failure of their austerity programs in the 1960s and 1970s. (The alternative is to conclude that their crippling programs are deliberate.) Their standard demand is for the governments of debtor countries to tighten the screws by administering high interest rates and levying onerous taxes (on labor and domestic capital, not foreign-owned properties). This austerity stifles the development of domestic market, leaving raw materials to be exported rather than worked up at home. It also keeps domestic wages low, while wrecking government budgets, forcing client regimes to submit to virtual bankruptcy.

Solvency is maintained under such conditions only by selling off national endowments to foreigners, *e.g.* as occurred in the "second" stage of Russian privatizations in the late 1990s. Such sell-offs mean that natural resource rents and monopoly rents cannot be used as the basis for domestic taxes, nor can infrastructure costs be subsidized to keep down the economy's overall cost structure. Monopoly rents are taken by private owners and largely remitted abroad, while those taken by domestic owners also end up abroad through the capital flight forms the counterpart to most IMF "stabilization" loans. What is stabilized is the rate at which domestic financial interests are able to convert domestic revenues into dollars or other hard currencies.

The result is that the hitherto public revenues of privatized enterprises and related kleptocratic takings are being built into the financial systems of North America, Europe and Japan. Collateralizing and pledging these economic rents for bank credit in the world's creditor nations threatens to make the existing world specialization of production and fiscal malstruc-turing irreversible – that is, irreversible without a sharp break occurring, which would involve immediate short-term losses and economic disloca-tions.

However, these losses in the short term pale in comparison with the long-term costs of *not* breaking with the existing system.

For the past half-century U.S. diplomats have discouraged foreign gov-ernments from managing their own economies to achieve self-sufficiency or using foreign aid and loan proceeds to develop the capacity to compete with U.S. exporters. It is mainly America that has been aided, not foreign economies. Especially opposed has been Europe's Common Agricultural Policy (CAP) and Japanese agricultural protectionism to maintain self-suf-ficiency in food. The United States has opposed foreign agricultural subsidies, price supports and import quotas such as America itself has employed for more than three-quarters of a century. Even foreign quality controls on trade in beef and crops have been denounced and remain a thorn in U.S. trade diplomacy with Europe, Asia and the Third World.

Despite these asymmetries in the benefits of today's international trade and investment patterns, pressures to create a New International Economic Order collapsed by the end of the 1970s. The world still seemed to belong to America to make or unmake. The question remained one of just how its diplomats wished to restructure the world economy, and how costly their designs seemed likely to be for Europe and Asia.

The U.S. objective has been to turn foreign economies into a set of residual functions. Foreign demand is to grow smoothly in keeping with U.S. export capacity on a sector-by-sector basis, while foreign production expands to serve U.S. import needs but does not lead to foreign self-sufficiency or displace American products in global markets. Europe, Asia and the Third World are to absorb America's farm surplus, but must not protect their own agricultural sectors in the way that the United States itself has done since 1933. While U.S. agricultural protectionism has been built into the postwar global system at its inception, foreign protectionism is to be nipped in the bud.

The monetary imperialism implicit in the U.S. Treasury bill standard

The U.S. Treasury bill standard's most exploitative feature was an implicit consequence that hardly was perceived at the time the dollar was adopted as a key currency under seemingly objective IMF sponsorship in the financial conditions that existed at the end of World War II. Apart from buying gold, central banks were able to build up their international reserves only by buying U.S. Treasury securities – that is, by the U.S. Government running into debt to foreign governments. Central banks held these interest-bearing dollar IOUs as key-currency reserves on a par with gold, readily convertible at a price of $35 an ounce.

The system began to unravel as America's balance of payments moved into deficit and its gold began to return to Europe – not to private holders who had sent it as flight capital to the United States as the war loomed, but to central banks and hence to governments in France, Germany and other nations. The widening U.S. payments deficit resulted from overseas military spending, not from private sector trade and investment. Starting slowly during the Korean War, and gaining momentum with the onset of the Vietnam War, the gold cover shrank at an accelerating pace, approaching the minimum legal cover of 25 per cent of the currency in circulation.

This military and political coloration of America's balance-of-payments deficit was of critical importance, for the government was now running up debt to finance policies with which most of its European creditors and many Asians disagreed. Under pressure of its military deficit the government intruded increasingly into the realm of international trade and investment, highlighted by the controls it imposed on bank lending abroad and the overseas financing of U.S. companies so as to oblige U.S. companies to buy out foreign firms with foreign-held dollars.

But these controls were not enough, given the time pressures at work. In 1968 the United States began to close the gold window, and in 1971 formally cut the link between the dollar and gold. By the spring of 1973 its officials had developed the strategy that the nation would pursue for nearly two decades. Instead of adhering to the creditor-oriented rules of international finance that it had endorsed in 1945, America used its debtor position to extort more foreign concessions and wealth than it had been able to obtain as a creditor nation. It told payments-surplus economies not to use their dollar holdings to buy into U.S. industry in the way that American investors bought into theirs in the 1950s and 1960s. It obliged European and Asian central banks to extend almost automatic credits via the U.S. Treasury bill standard, while still pursuing a creditor stance vis-à-vis indebted Third World and COMECON countries.

Europe, Asia and other payments-surplus regions were stuck on the horns of a dilemma. If they refrained from absorbing surplus dollars and recycling them to the U.S. Treasury, the dollar would depreciate. At first glance, this would provide U.S. producers with a competitive edge while penalizing exporters in hard-currency economies. Yet the U.S. payments deficit has widened all the more as America's free ride has not helped it restore balance. Or rather, the United States has little interest in doing so. Why should it? After all, it has consistently refused to raise its own interest rates to obtain foreign funds to finance its deficit on the ground that this would slow economic activity at home, even as it demands that other countries running payments deficits sacrifice their economies to pay their foreign debtors.

The Plaza Accords of 1985 obliged Japan to hold down its own interest rates, so that international financial pressures would not lead U.S. rates to rise and deter re-election of the Republican officials who were intent on doing everything they could to destroy Japan's economy. European countries also were pressured in this way. Among the world's debtor economies, they were obliged to submit to austerity programs that U.S. planners refused to adopt for their own economy. Argentina's recent IMF riots which toppled the government in December 2001 are only the most recent example of this double standard.

The result is that even in the face of hundreds of billions of dollars' worth of foreign central bank purchases of U.S. Treasury securities since the gold window was closed in 1971, the dollar declined radically against the Deutschmark, the yen (until 1995) and other hard currencies. Third World dollar users have suffered collateral damage as their oil, copper and other raw materials have remained priced in dollars. Their inability to develop an alternative has helped hold down price levels in Europe and Japan, but much of the value of the U.S. official debt to these creditor economies has been eroded by inflation, which was accelerated accelerated by the quantum leaps that occurred from in the 1973 grain-and-oil shock through the 1979–80 Carter–Volcker inflation.

Unable to obtain more than a marginal competitive edge out of its dollar depreciation, the U.S. Government sought to lock in its share of world markets by negotiating fixed shares. This threatens to turn world trade into a Procrustean bed of managed markets as U.S. officials not only demand that foreign economies guarantee fixed market shares to U.S. exporters, but break world trade rules by imposing import quotas unilaterally.

Elsewhere on the balance-of-payments front, U.S. officials insist that foreign military budgets earmark specific sums for American-made components. West Germany and Japan have been told to pay for the U.S. military presence as part of their own national budgets, while offering them no corresponding control over these troops and weapons. These two nations also have been asked to lend an equivalent amount of dollars to the U.S. Government, with only a hazy idea of when, or even if, the nominal loans are to be repaid.

When central banks are obliged to add dollars to their international reserves, this transfers an equivalent value of resources from their own citizens to finance the U.S. payments deficit – and with it, *pari passu*, America's own federal budget deficit. From $10 billion a year in the early 1970s, the nation's foreign trade and payments deficits grew to nearly $150 billion a year in the late 1980s, and double that amount by the end of the twentieth century.

If deficits of this magnitude no longer inspire crises such as those that occurred in the spring of 1973, it is because the central banks of Europe, Japan, OPEC and other dollar accumulators have acquiesced so thoroughly in what truly may be called a monetary imperialism. The vehicles for this super imperialism are not private international firms or private finance capital, but central banks. Through these international financial maneuverings the United States has tapped the resources of its Dollar Bloc allies. It has not done so in the classic fashion of a creditor extorting debt service, not so much via its international firms and their investment activities, and certainly not any longer through its export competitiveness and free competition. Rather, the technique of exploitation involves an adroit use of central banks, the IMF, World Bank and its associated regional lending institutions to provide forced loans to the U.S. Treasury. This rigged game has enabled the United States to flood the world with dollars without constraint as it has appropriated foreign resources and companies, goods and services for nothing in return except Treasury IOUs of questionable (and certainly shrinking) value.

In sum, the United States is able to rule not through its position as world creditor, but as world debtor. Rather than being the world banker, it makes all other countries the lenders to itself. Thus, rather than its debtor position being an element of weakness, America's seeming weakness has become the foundation of the world's monetary and financial system. To change this system in a way adverse to the United States would bring down the system's creditors to America.

Widespread European and Asian fears of such a breakdown has enabled the United States to dominate the world economy through just the reverse process from that by which Britain ruled in the nineteenth century. Britain governed its Empire not only through its position as world banker, but because as world banker it took responsibility for insuring an international payments mechanism that worked on long-understood lines that were deemed to be equitable to its users. As central banker to the world, Britain took responsibility for keeping the international financial system in working order.

It would have been against what had become a political economy elevated to the status of a veritable civic religion for Britain to have threatened its fellow Commonwealth members that "If you do not let sterling IOUs be issued simply as paper, with no solid assets or willingness to pay to back up these IOUs, your economies will collapse." Other countries would have broken away, perhaps even risking war to become independent of so financially aggressive an economy.

What a contrast the *modus operandi* of Britain's empire provides to that of the United States today! Unwilling to relinquish their nation's position as food exporter to the rest of the world, U.S. officials demand food dependency on U.S. exports on the part of Asia, the former Soviet Union and Third World countries (having lost the fight against Europe's Common Agricultural Policy). Military dependency also is demanded, while the sectors of U.S. industrial dominance are based mainly on electronics and military-related technology which it puts forth as a post-industrial economy as heavy industry and blue-collar employment is being downsized throughout the U.S. economy.

If America is to remain the world banker through the government's Treasury bill standard of international finance, it is as a debtor country, not as a creditor basing its banking position on tangible collateral as did Britain. What began as an *ad hoc* system in 1945 has become a one-sided American ability to tap the resources of its Dollar Bloc allies without their having the ability to stop the process, short of bringing on world financial collapse. Since 1968 the key pressure point has been the readiness of U.S. diplomats to play the role of world wreckers if foreign central banks stop relending their dollar inflows to the U.S. Treasury. This is the monetary equivalent of President Nixon's "mad bomber" threat, metastasized into the financial sphere: If the United States does not get its way, it will act irascibly and quite likely irrationally, and the world will suffer.

In taking this position the United States enjoys an alternative that other countries have not been able to duplicate. Thanks to the large size of its domestic market it can "go it alone." Its financial claims and the super-structure of dollar debts that now permeate the world economy – taken in conjunction with the high levels of direct investment in America by foreigners – mean that a U.S. move towards autarchy would fracture the world financial system.

The specter of bringing on such a collapse has given U.S. diplomats an option not available to nations whose economies are more highly dependent on smoothly functioning international commerce and payments. Foreign trade accounts for only about 5 per cent of America's GNP, compared to some 25 per cent for many European economies. Foreign central banks held over a trillion dollars in U.S. Treasury securities. Until Europe and Asia are able to replace the Dollar standard with a currency system of their own, and until they are willing to run the risk of a trade and investment war as an intermediate step toward achieving their own self-sufficiency, the U.S. economy will have little reason to feel that it needs to live within its means.

What prevents steps from being taken to create a more fair and equitable international economy than is provided by the U.S. Treasury bill standard is the fact that its inherently exploitative character is not more generally recognized. This recognition should become the central premise of global financial diplomacy.

The United States has managed to rule Third World debtor countries through client elites. In the advanced industrial creditor nations it has found that all it needs to represent U.S. interests are central bankers trained in the Chicago School's "monetarism for export" doctrines of financial sub-servience to the United States and IMF. To hold European and Asian politicians and their electorates, American officials loudly and almost incessantly repeat that their economy is the leading practitioner of an objective technocratic wisdom that provides the bulwark for world economic stability.

But the academic doctrinal basis of these claims – their economic theory and even their statistical models – rests on the same dysfunctional monetarist policies that the IMF and World Bank have used to cripple the Third World and formerly Communist economies for the past few decades. And in Japan, when that nation mounted an industrial challenge, U.S. diplomats easily broke its power by getting it to agree to the Plaza and Louvre accords. These economically suicidal agreements committed Japan to inflate its Bubble Economy, leaving it effectively bankrupt after 1990.

Japan has let its economic policies be dictated by U.S. advisors, much as Britain succumbed in the aftermath of World War II, as if American proposals really had foreign interests in mind and put world development above their own national self-interest. It should now be obvious to every nation that such trust in U.S. leadership has been misplaced. Yet how many Japanese are reminded that in 1985–86 their country was asked to lower its rates and create a bubble simply to help promote boom conditions in the United States to help the Republican administration be re-elected?

The equitable world economy based on free markets promised at the close of World War II under U.S. aegis has led instead to an epoch of unprecedented government control. Outside of the United States, central-ized economic planning is promoted via the financial sector, not to increase production or living standards as promised by monetarist economic textbooks, but to squeeze out interest and dividends and transfer them abroad. "Free market economics" of this sort has degenerated into a mere attack on governments intent on protecting their societies from this corrosive exploitation. It pretends to oppose public taxation merely in order to leave a larger economic surplus to be transferred to the United States, either in the form of interest and dividends from debtor countries, or by central bank loans from creditor nations to the U.S. Treasury.

The classical economic world has been turned upside down. It remains for academic economists to incorporate this new reality into their theorizing, and for other nations to incorporate an analysis of the new dynamics into their future foreign policy.

However, the role of vast vested interests in the evolution of post-Bretton Woods monetary arrangements suggests that global financial meltdown rather than mutual diplomacy must precede – indeed, pave the way for – monetary reform at national and international levels. For it has been the threat of such a meltdown that has deterred alternatives from being put forth, as Europe was deterred in 1933 and 1973. It looks like collapse will have to force Europe's hand rather than it taking the lead in protecting its economic self-determination.

*

Parts I and II of this book have traced how the upsweep of U.S. power from World War I through the Korean War reflected its creditor position, augmented by its annual balance of payments surpluses. There were of course two sides to this international diplomacy. Europe (and later, Asia) acquiesced because for centuries these regions had elevated creditor power to the determining crown of global policy-making, even above the goals of national growth and employment. The crisis came in 1933 at the London Economic Conference, when creditor and debtor philosophies met head-on.

What gave the year 1933 a special twist was that while America took a creditor-oriented stance toward Europe, it pursued a debtor-oriented policy at home to help alleviate farm debt, mortgage debt and business debt. Roosevelt's New Deal transformed the financial framework within market forces worked. A second unprecedented twist was the fact that America's creditor position was an expression of government power, not that of private banking and other investor interests. Through 1929 private lending had found a market in facilitating the triangular flow of funds from the U.S. private sector to German municipalities and private borrowers, from them to the European Allies and from these Allies to the U.S. Government to pay war debts. Government debt was paid off by private lenders providing the money that enabled governments to pay. Hence, growth in private debt was what enabled public debt to be wound down, and the wind-down was slow, as most government debt service took the form of interest charges, not amortization credits to work off the balance. In the case of America's S&L collapse, by contrast, governments took over liability for private debt, "socializing the losses." That is the essence of public debt stemming from Moral Hazard, *i.e.*, government bail-outs of "debtors," which really should be called bailouts of bankers, bondholders and other "savers."

When the growing debt superstructure led to economic collapse and Europe's ability to pay was constricted by shrinking production and employment, something had to give. It was at this point that private bankers took a responsible "internationalist" position and asked that inter-governmental debts be waived. Their intention, Roosevelt and his advisors believed, was simply a euphemistic theoretical wrapping for the policy of freeing up the shrinking available debt-paying powers of Europe to pay private sector lenders, not the government. On this logic the United States did not relinquish its debt claims on Europe.

Instead of negotiating the terms on which the U.S. Government would give up its destabilizing claims for interest and amortization by Europe, a sharp break occurred in 1933 at the London Economic Conference. America went its own way, and European countries were forced to "go it alone." Their response at that time was to create rival systems of imperial trade preferences, competitive currency depreciation and tariffs, capital controls and other statist policies along the path leading to World War II.

By 1945, U.S. diplomats took a more enlightened stance, incorporating a global strategy. Foreign debts to the United States, they recognized, would find their counterpart in U.S. payments to foreigners – to import foreign products, to buy out foreign firms and to finance a world military umbrella. America unilaterally put in place a multilateral political structure to serve U.S. policies, and specifically to serve the United States as the world's major creditor power. The postwar years therefore saw U.S. economic, political and military power increase to a degree unprecedented in history for any single nation vis-à-vis others. Its government debt became the interna-tional money used by central banks throughout the world as their means of settling mutual balances amongst themselves. The United States had come to rule not only by gold credit, but by fiat credit.

The final part of this book – Part III – traces how the international financial system was transformed after the U.S. balance of payments moved into deficit during the Korean War, becoming seriously disrupting of international finance. What is so striking is how differently U.S. diplomats comported themselves in their deepening debtor position from the way in which debtor Europe had negotiated in the 1920s, 1930s and early 1940s. Whereas America had insisted that Europe sequester its private capital holdings and sell them off to pay the U.S. Government, Europe made no such demand on America in the 1960s or even in the 1970s – or subsequently, for that matter.

In fact, whereas U.S. domination of the world economy stemmed from 1920 through 1960 from its creditor position, its control since the 1960s has stemmed from its debtor position. Not only have the tables been turned, but U.S. diplomats have found that their leverage as the world's major debtor economy is fully as strong as that which formerly had reflected its net creditor position.

The years 1972–73 is the counterpart to 1932–33, for it was in the latter two years that Europe and the United States, creditor and debtor economies met head to head in a clash. In both cases it was Europe that blinked, not the United States. In both cases it was U.S. Government officials who chose to "go it alone," at the cost of breaking up the international economy. And in both cases, European officials stepped back from shaking up the international structure and entering the institutional no-man's-land in which multilateral structures would have to be built anew. Europe – now joined by Asia, OPEC and the world's raw materials exporting, food-deficit economies (euphemized as the "developing countries") – was willing to sacrifice its idea that international economic institutions should share the gains from international trade and investment equitably, in order to avoid such a restructuring.

Gold and the lack of alternatives deemed to be fair and symmetrical

Gold historically has acted as the abstract "objective" asset, the prize for which national economies have vied. But when it was demonetized in 1971, nothing of equally symmetrical character was developed to put in its place. The absence of such an alternative gave the United States an opportunity to fill the vacuum, and only it sought to fill it, not Europe, Asia or the Third World. Even today, the euro remains little more than a surrogate for dollars, not an international asset providing the services that gold provided for many centuries.

Keynes called gold a "barbarous relic" because it constrained domestic credit creation and hence imposed deflationary conditions that limited markets and employment, and ended by transferring property from debtors to creditors through the foreclosure process. On the international front, gold constrained economies from running balance-of-payments deficits. As most such deficits were historically military in character, gold served as a constraint against war. By the 1970s, the United States was running deficits by buying out European companies and output. Under these conditions a gold standard would have deterred the war in Vietnam, the buy-out of European industry with its own funds, and the free ride enjoyed by America by importing foreign products in exchange for IOUs of the U.S. Government.

Would this have been a bad thing?

Domestic credit has been freed from gold in order to obtain the volume needed to ensure rising employment, production and transactions levels. In the international sphere, it is not needed to finance production, but rather imbalances in international payments. It is a constraint on imbalances, not on production and employment.

The IMF devised SDRs (Special Drawing Rights) as "paper gold" that really were "paper dollars." The purpose was to give countries outside of the United States some kind of freely created IOU that was not a dollar obligation of the U.S. Government. One therefore might say that Europe and Japan abandoned gold prematurely, before developing an alternative to the dollar or dollar-proxy issued by multilateral institutions acting as arms of the U.S. Government.

Recent proposals to give new IMF credit to the world's poorer countries are a euphemism for paying the large bankers by giving debtors who otherwise would default an asset that other countries will accept – not their own IOUs, but those of a super-dollar. The objective of this ploy is to enable the volume of international debt to keep growing exponentially rather than being brought back within the ability to pay by the gold standard constraint.

The reasoning is much the same as when U.S. international bankers in 1933 urged the U.S. Government to forgive the Inter-Ally debts and the allies to forgive German reparations. This would leave the available revenue of these countries free to be pledged to bankers for new loans. These probably would have been of a non-military character, but would just as likely have been military in view of the political forces already carrying Europe toward World War II.

Would it be a bad thing to wipe out bad debts?

Today, in 2002, the euro has not provided the requisite alternative to gold, for it is not a truly political currency as the dollar is. It lacks critical mass, politically speaking. But even more important, there has been no political will for Europe or Asia to take an alternative route. Only America has shown the will to create global international structures and restructure them at will to fit its financial needs as these have evolved from hyper-creditor to hyper-debtor status. It is as if European and Asian society lack some gene for institutional self-programming for their own economic evolution. Like a dancer following the partner's lead, they have acted as the mirror image of America.

Perhaps historians looking back on the modern era from their vantage point a century or two in the future will find it remarkable that neither European, Asian or other countries could devise a New International Economic Order that would have kept economic gains for the national economies producing them, rather than relinquishing them to the U.S. economy. No doubt this era will be seen as one of remarkable asymmetry between the United States and the rest of the world. America has been receiving a free ride, while Europe – even with the history of America's own creditor-oriented strategy before it – has not learned to play the game of international finance with the astuteness of the Americans.

The conclusion most historians will find is a paucity of imagination on the part of Europe and Asia, and of impotence on the part of the Third World economies that made a brief attempt to create a New International Economic Order in the 1970s. American diplomats were able to derail attempts to break free of what has become a tidal wave, a tsunami of deficit dollars.

On the highest plane one may place the blame on economic theory's failure to develop functional categories that would enable politicians, diplomats and the public at large to understand the principles guiding American negotiators in 1932–33 and 1972–73. Without such understanding, no post-dollar world can be created.

Notes

Introduction

1. J. B. Condliffe, "Economic Power as an Instrument of National Policy," *American Economic Review* 34 (Suppl. March 1944), p. 307.
2. Arthur Salz, "The Present Position of Economics," in *ibid.*, pp. 19ff.
3. Jacob Viner, "International Relations between State Controlled National Economies," in *ibid.*, p. 315.
4. John A. Hobson, "The Ethics of Internationalism," *International Journal of Ethics* 27 (1906–7), p. 28, quoted in *ibid.*, p. 321.
5. *Ibid.*, p. 328.
6. Council on Foreign Relations, *The United States in World Affairs, 1945–47* (New York: 1957), pp. 365–8.
7. "Interest Rates and Monetary Growth," Federal Reserve Bank of St. Louis, *Review*, January 1973. See also "Will Capital Reflows Induce Domestic Interest Rate Changes?" in *ibid.*, July 1972.
8. Jacob Burckhardt, *Judgments on History and Historians* (tr. Boston: 1958), p. 171.
9. I elaborate these points in *Trade, Development and Foreign Debt: A History of Theories of Polarization v. Convergence in the World Economy*, 2 vols. (London: 1992) and, more generally, "The Use and Abuse of Mathematical Economics," *Journal of Economic Studies* 27 (2000), pp. 292–315.

Chapter 1

1. Harvey E. Fisk, *The Inter-Ally Debts: An Analysis of War and Post-War Public Finance 1914–1923* (New York: 1924), p. 1.
2. U.S. Department of Commerce, *Historical Statistics of the United States: Colonial Times to 1957* (Washington, D.C.: 1960), p. 565.
3. Quoted in Council on Foreign Relations, *Survey of American Foreign Relations: 1928* (New Haven: 1928), p. 414. (Hereafter referred to as *American Foreign Relations*.)
4. *Ibid.*, p. 422.
5. Philip Snowden, "The Debt Settlement: The Case for Revision," *Atlantic Monthly*, Vol. 138 (September 1926), reprinted in James Thayer Gerould and Laura Shearer Turnbull, *Selected Articles on Interallied Debts and Revision of the Debt Settlements* (New York: 1928), p. 446.
6. *American Foreign Relations*, p. 414.
7. Fisk, *The Inter-Ally Debts*, p. 154.
8. *American Foreign Relations*, p. 410.
9. *Ibid.*, p. 409.
10. *Ibid.*, p. 419.
11. Quoted in Fisk, *The Inter-Ally Debts*, p. 168.
12. Quoted in *ibid.*, p. 162. See also Representative Switzer's comments, *ibid.*, p. 167, and comments of Representatives Rainey and Andrew in Gerould and Turnbull, *Selected Articles*, pp. 306–10.
13. Allen S. Olmsted, 2nd, "Lafayette, We Want Our Money," *The Nation* CXXI (December 23, 1925), p. 723, quoted in Gerould and Turnbull, *Selected Articles*, p. 412.
14. *American Foreign Relations*, p. 412.

15. John Maynard Keynes, *The Economic Consequences of the Peace* (London: 1919), pp. 280–1.
16. Fisk, *The Inter-Ally Debts*, p. 186.
17. National Industrial Conference Board, *The Inter-Ally Debts and the United States. Preliminary Study*, p. 53 (quoted in *American Foreign Relations*, pp. 430ff).
18. Fisk, *The Inter-Ally Debts*, p. 9.
19. Quoted in J. Maurice Clark, Walton H. Hamilton and Harold G. Moulton (eds.), *Readings in the Economics of War* (Chicago: 1918), p. 638.
20. Fisk, *The Inter-Ally Debts*, p. 185.
21. *American Foreign Relations*, pp. 424ff.
22. John Wheeler-Bennett, *The Wreck of Reparations* (London: 1933), p. 160.
23. Council on Foreign Relations, *The United States in World Affairs: 1931* (New York: 1932), pp. 159ff.
24. *American Foreign Relations*, p. 342.
25. George P. Auld, *The Dawes Plan and the New Economics* (New York: 1921–), p. 148.
26. *American Foreign Relations*, p. 183.
27. *Ibid.*, p. 192.
28. On these points see Lloyd George, *The Truth about Reparations and War-Debts* (London: 1932), esp. pp. 11–32 and 110–39. The Council on Foreign Relations observed that "Reparation payments from Hungary were protected by a system of League financial control from injuring [the] Hungarian economy. She was also granted an international loan." (*American Foreign Relations*, p. 342.) In fact, the distinction between domestic capacity to tax, and ability to transform these tax receipts into foreign exchange – later renowned as the basic principle of the Dawes Plan – was first developed in reference to Hungarian reparations, at the urging of Sir Arthur Salter. (See *ibid.*, p. 578.)
29. *American Foreign Relations*, p. 453.
30. R. H. Brind, "The Reparations Problem," *Journal of the Royal Institute of International Affairs* (May 1929) p. 208.
31. Quoted in Gerould and Turnbull, *Selected Articles*, p. 453.
32. On this point, see *ibid.*, p. 301.
33. *Ibid.*, pp. 276ff.
34. Gerhart von Schulze-Gaevernitz, "Amerika's Uberimperialismus," in M. J. Bonn and M. Palyi, (eds.), *Die Wirtschaftswissenschaft nach dem Kriege* (Festgabe fur Lujo Brentano zum 80. Geburtstag) (Munich and Leipzig: 1925), pp. 107–26, p. 109.
35. *Ibid.*, pp. 120ff.

Chapter 2

1. Lloyd George, *The Truth about Reparations and War-Debts* (London: 1932), pp. 116–20.
2. *American Foreign Relations*, pp. 427ff.
3. *Ibid.*, pp. 434ff., quoting the *Combined Annual Reports of the World War Foreign Debt Commission*, p. 597; also, *ibid.*, p. 460.
4. *Ibid.*, pp. 461, 406ff.
5. Mr. Deverall's comments on R. H. Brand's paper, "The Reparations Problem," *Journal of the Royal Institute of International Affairs* (May 1929), p. 226, and Professor Baker's comments, pp. 221ff.
6. *American Foreign Relations*, pp. 462ff.
7. John Maynard Keynes, *The Economic Consequences of the Peace* (London: 1919), p. 281, and *A Revision of the Treaty* (London: 1922), p. 161.

8. "The Interallied Debts," *Atlantic Monthly* 139 (March 1927), quoted in James Thayer Gerould and Laura Shearer Turnbull, *Selected Articles on Interallied Debts and Revision of the Debt Settlements* (New York: 1928), p. 461.
9. U.S. Department of Commerce, "The Balance of International Payments of the United States in 1923," *Trade Information Bulletin*, No. 215 (April 7, 1924). See also the 1924 report, p. 27.
10. See, for instance, the U.S. Tariff Commission's monograph *Depreciated Exchange and International Trade* (2nd edn, Washington: 1922).
11. "The Effect on American Workers of Collecting Allied Debts," *Annals of the American Academy of Political and Social Science* 126 (July 1926), quoted in Gerould and Turnbull, *Selected Articles*, pp. 473ff.
12. *The United States in World Affairs: 1931*, p. 145.
13. Keynes, *The Economic Consequences of the Peace*, p. 284.
14. Frank H. Simonds, "Debt Settlements," *American Review of Reviews* 73 (February 1926), p. 155 quoted in Gerould and Turnbull, *Selected Articles*, pp. 423, 425.
15. Karl Polanyi, *The Great Transformation* [1944] (Boston: 1957), p. 26.
16. George Paish, *The Road to Prosperity* (London: 1927), pp. 17ff., 25, 34–37, quoted in Joseph S. Davis, *The World Between the Wars, 1919–39* (Baltimore: 1975), p. 176.
17. Davis, *ibid.*, pp. 100ff.
18. *The United States in World Affairs: 1933* (New York: 1934), p. xi.
19. Davis, *The World Between the Wars*, pp. 198 and 101, quoting *The Economist*, December 7, 1929 (pp. 1069ff.).
20. Lloyd George, *The Truth*, p. 125.
21. *The United States in World Affairs: 1933*, p. 162.
22. Wheeler-Bennett, *The Wreck of Reparations*, p. 50.
23. *Ibid.*, p. 161.
24. *Ibid.*, p. 53.
25. *Ibid.*, p. 98.
26. *Ibid.*, pp. 103ff.
27. See, for instance, *Verhandlungen der Sozialisierungs-Kommission über die Reparationsfragen*, 2 vols. (Berlin: 1921).
28. Quoted in Carl Bergman, *The History of Reparations* (New York: 1927), p. 200.
29. Quoted in Harold G. Moulton and Leo Pasvolsky, *War Debts and World Prosperity* (Washington, D.C.: 1932), p. 168.
30. *The United States in World Affairs: 1932* (New York. 1933), p. 109.
31. James Harvey Rogers, *America Weighs Her Gold* (New Haven: 1931) p. 201. See also pp. 145, 152. Professor Rogers' book on *The Process of Inflation in France: 1914–1927* (New York: 1929) is definitive.
32. Davis, *The World Between the Wars*, p. 408.
33. Wheeler-Bennett, *The Wreck of Reparations*, p. 163.
34. *The United States in World Affairs: 1932* (New York: 1933), pp. 142ff.
35. Quoted in *ibid.*, p. 168.
36. Wheeler-Bennett, *The Wreck of Reparations*, p. 234.
37. *Ibid.*, p. 169.
38. Department of State, "Report of American Delegates to the Preparatory Committee of Experts on the World Monetary and Economic Conference," p. 7, quoted in Raymond Moley, *The First New Deal* (New York: 1966), p. 39.
39. Moley, *ibid.*, p. 26, citing a memorandum Berle prepared for him on November 15, 1932, in preparation for the meeting between Hoover and Roosevelt described in the next chapter.
40. *Ibid.*, pp. 25ff., citing Rexford Tugwell, *The Democratic Roosevelt* (Garden City: 1957), p. 256.
41. *Ibid.*, pp. 22ff., 43ff., citing Stimson's Diary in the Yale University Library.
42. *Ibid.*

Chapter 3

1. See Simon Patten, *Essays in Economic Theory*, ed. Rexford Tugwell (New York: 1924). For a more general discussion, see my survey of *Economics and Technology in 19th-Century American Thought* (New York: 1975).
2. Cited in Raymond Moley, *The First New Deal* (New York: 1966), p. 25.
3. Raymond Moley, *After Seven Years* (New York: 1939), p. 69. The following discussion follows Moley's 1939 and 1966 narratives, which are the major sources on U.S. debt and financial negotiations with Europe for the year. See also the U.S. Department of State's *Foreign Relations of the United States, 1933*, and the memoirs of Feis, Tugwell, Hoover and Hull.
4. *Ibid.*, p. 70.
5. Moley, *After Seven Years*, pp. 71 and 73. For a later version of this episode see Moley, *The First New Deal*, pp. 23–33.
6. Moley, *After Seven Years*, pp. 71f. See also *The First New Deal*, p. 26. A list of the questions that Roosevelt wrote down on index cards for discussion with Hoover is reproduced in Appendix A of *The First New Deal*.
7. *Ibid.*, p. 74.
8. *The Memoirs of Herbert Hoover*, Vol. III (New York: 1952), p. 179, quoted in Moley, *The First New Deal*, p. 28.
9. Moley, *After Seven Years*, pp. 76ff.
10. *Ibid.*, pp. 78ff.
11. *The United States in World Affairs: 1932* (New York: 1933), p. 189.
12. Moley, *After Seven Years*, p. 84f.
13. *Ibid.*, p. 85, and *The First New Deal*, p. 38.
14. *Ibid.*, p. 86; see also *The First New Deal*, p. 39.
15. *Ibid.*, pp. 95, 87ff.
16. Moley, *The First New Deal*, pp. 39f. See Hoover, *Memoirs*, Vol. III, pp. 185ff.
17. Quoted in *The United States in World Affairs: 1932*, pp. 177, 172.
18. Moley, *After Seven Years*, p. 96.
19. *Ibid.*, pp. 97–100, and *The First New Deal*, pp. 52ff., citing Tugwell, *Notes from a New Deal Diary*, pp. 71ff.
20. Moley, *After Seven Years*, pp. 104ff.
21. Moley, *The First New Deal*, p. 224.
22. *Ibid.*, p. 58.
23. "British Policy on Economic Problems," in *Foreign Relations of the United States, 1933*, I, pp. 465–71. The following summary rests mainly on Moley, *The First New Deal*, p. 412.
24. *The United States in World Affairs: 1933*, pp. xx–xxi, 125.
25. Moley, *After Seven Years*, pp. 199ff.
26. Moley, *The First New Deal*, p. 413.
27. *Ibid.*, p. 414. See also Moley, *After Seven Years*, p. 202.
28. Moley, *After Seven Years*, p. 204.
29. Moley, *The First New Deal*, p. 403.
30. Wheeler-Bennett, *The Wreck of Reparations*, p. 257.
31. Moley, *After Seven Years*, p. 207.
32. *Ibid.*, p. 206.
33. Moley, *The First New Deal*, p. 402.
34. Moley, *After Seven Years*, pp. 210ff.
35. *Ibid.*, pp. 210ff.
36. *Ibid.*, p. 213.
37. *Ibid.*, pp. 215ff.
38. *Ibid.*, pp. 220ff. Moley adds that the $10 million "involved an outlay of only $7,000,000 by them [the British] because they took advantage of the President's authorization (inserted by Key Pittman in the Thomas amendment) to accept up to

$200,000,000 in war-debt payments in silver . . . At the current price of silver in the world market the British could get by on a $10,000,000 payment with approximately $7,000,000."

39. *Ibid.*, p. 182.
40. *Ibid.*, pp. 222ff. See also Moley, *The First New Deal*, p. 26.
41. Quoted in Herbert Feis, *1933: Characters in Crisis* (Boston: 1966), pp. 171ff.
42. *The United States in World Affairs: 1933*, p. 125.
43. *Ibid.*, p. 173.
44. Moley, *After Seven Years*, pp. 217ff.
45. Feis, *1933*, pp. 173, 175.
46. *Ibid.*, p. 180.
47. Moley, *After Seven Years*, pp. 228ff.
48. *Ibid.*, pp. 230, 235ff., 245.
49. *Ibid.*, p. 247.
50. *Ibid.*, p. 249.
51. *Ibid.*, pp. 251, 253.
52. Moley, *The First New Deal*, p. 432.
53. Moley, *After Seven Years*, p. 255.
54. Moley, *The First New Deal*, p. 453.
55. *The United States in World Affairs: 1933*, pp. xx–xxi.
56. Moley, *After Seven Years*, p. 261. See Warburg, *The Money Muddle* (New York: 1934), p. 121.
57. *The United Stares in World Affairs: 1933*, p. 139.
58. William Adams Brown, *The Gold Standard Reinterpreted: 1914–1934* (New York: 1940), p. 1286.
59. Moley, *After Seven Years*, p. 256.
60. *Ibid.*, pp. 270ff, 273.
61. *Ibid.*, pp. 223ff.
62. *Ibid.*, p. 166.
63. Brown, *The Gold Standard*, p. 1287.
64. Feis, *1933*, p. 253.
65. Moley, *The First New Deal*, p. 494, quoting Schlesinger's *Coming of the New Deal*, p. 229, and Jeannette P. Nichols, "Roosevelt's Monetary Diplomacy in 1933," *American Historical Review* 56 (January 1951), p. 317.
66. Hull, *Memoirs*, I, pp. 268ff., and William F. Leuchtenburg, *Franklin D. Roosevelt and the New Deal* (New York: 1963), pp. 202ff., quoted in Moley, *ibid.* p. 495.
67. Polanyi, *The Great Transformation*, p. 27.
68. *The United States in World Affairs: 1934–35*, p. 109.
69. William Diebold, Jr, *New Directions in Our Trade Policy* (New York: 1941), pp. 3, 23ff.
70. Quoted in *The United Stares in World Affairs: 1932*, p. 185.
71. U.S. Department of Commerce, *The Balance of International Payments to the United States in 1938* (Washington, DC: 1939), p. 22.
72. Polanyi, *The Great Transformation*, p. 29.
73. National Advisory Council on International Monetary and Financial Policies, *Annual Report to the President and to the Congress July 1, 1973–June 30, 1974* (Washington: 1975), p. 40.

Chapter 4

1. Edward R. Stettinius, Jr, *Lend-Lease: Weapon for Victory* (New York: 1944), p. 61.
2. Personal letter from John Morton Blum to Robert Skidelsky, cited in Skidelsky, *John Maynard Keynes* Vol. III: *Fighting for Freedom, 1937–1946* (New York 2001), *ibid.*, pp. 260, 99.

3. Skidelsky, *ibid.*, pp. 99 and 102ff., citing *Morgenthau Diaries* 404, p. 86 from the Roosevelt Library in Hyde Park, New York, and Blum, ed., *From the Morgenthau Diaries*, Vol. II: *Years of Urgency 1938–1941* (Boston: 1965), p. 171, that Morgenthau "recognised that the loss of [Britain's overseas] investments would cripple the British economy after the war, but he maintained that England could not afford to worry about this in 1940." Skidelsky adds that Morgenthau's basic assumption was reflected in his admonition to Roosevelt, "Never worry, the British will always find means of paying if they cannot get out of it."

4. *Ibid.*, pp. 102ff.

5. Stettinius, *Lend-Lease*, p. 63.

6. *Ibid.*, p. 73. (Stettinius became Secretary of State in 1945.)

7. Richard N. Gardner, *Sterling–Dollar Diplomacy* (Oxford: 1956), pp. 55ff.

8. Skidelsky, *Keynes*, p. 103.

9. *Ibid.*, p. 104.

10. Council on Foreign Relations, *The United States in World Affairs: 1945–1947* (New York: 1947), p. 344, citing *Statistical Material Presented During the Washington Negotiations*, Cmd. 6706 of 1945, p. 5.

11. Hal Lary and Associates, *The United States in the World Economy* (U.S. Department of Commerce. Economic Series No. 23, Washington, D.C.: 1943), p. 12.

12. Gardner, *Sterling–Dollar Diplomacy*, p. 57.

13. *Ibid.*, p. 60.

14. Warren F. Kimball, "Lend-Lease and the Open Door: The Temptation of British Opulence, 1937–1942," *Political Science Quarterly* 86 (June 1971), pp. 249ff.

15. Gardner, *Sterling–Dollar Diplomacy*, pp. 61ff.

16. Arthur D. Gayer, "Economic Aspects of Lend-Lease," in Jacob Viner et al., *The United States in a Multi-National Economy* (New York: Council of Foreign Relations, 1945), p. 145.

17. *Ibid.*, pp. 141ff.

18. *Extension of the Lend-Lease Act. Hearings on H.R. 1501 Before the Committee on Foreign Affairs*, U.S. House of Representatives, 78th Cong., 1st Sess. (Washington, D.C.: 1943), p. 162, quoted in Gayer "Economic Aspects of Lend-Lease", p. 121.

19. Gayer, *ibid.*, p. 136.

20. *Ibid.* On this reversal see "President Asserts World Will Repay," *The New York Times*, September 8, 1943, and "Roosevelt Revises Lend-Lease Letter," *ibid.*, September 15, 1943.

21. *Ibid.*, p. 134.

22. Stettinius, *Lend-Lease*, pp. 281, 117.

23. Skidelsky, *Keynes*, pp. 322, 546.

24. Gardner, *Sterling–Dollar Diplomacy*, p. 174.

25. Gayer, "Economic Aspects of Lend-Lease", p. 140, referring to *Additional Report of the Special Committee Investigating the National Defense Program*, Senate Report No. 10, Pt. 12, 78th Cong., 1st Sess. (Washington, D.C.: 1943), pp. 13ff.

26. George C. Herring, Jr, "The United States and British Bankruptcy, 1944–45: Responsibilities Deferred," *Political Science Quarterly* 86 (June 1971), pp. 267ff.

27. *Ibid.*

28. Gardner, *Sterling–Dollar Diplomacy*, p. 174.

29. U.S. House of Representatives, Committee on Ways and Means, *Hearings on H.R. 2652, superseded by H.R. 3240, 1945 Extension of the Reciprocal Trade Agreements Act*, 79th Cong., 1st Sess., April–May 1945, p. 37; quoted in Gardner, *Sterling–Dollar Diplomacy*, p. 160.

30. *The United States in World Affairs: 1945–1947*, p. 370.

31. Gardner, *Sterling–Dollar Diplomacy*, p. 208.

32. *The United States in World Affairs: 1945–1947*, p. 359. On these points see also Gardner, *Sterling–Dollar Diplomacy*, pp. 178ff.

33. Gayer, "Economic Aspects of Lend–Lease," p. 134. An identical sentiment was voiced by Eugene Staley in his earlier article on "The Economic Implications of Lend-Lease," *American Economic Review* 33 Suppl. (1943), p. 366.
34. Gardner, "Economic Aspects of Lend–Lease," 170.
35. Skidelsky, *Keynes*, p. 126.
36. *Ibid.*, p. 132.
37. *Ibid.*, p. 451.
38. Alvin H. Hansen, *America's Role in the World Economy* (New York: 1946), pp. 141, 71.
39. See Skidelsky, *Keynes*, pp. 401ff.
40. *Ibid.*, p. 449.
41. *Ibid.*, p. 452, citing Richard Clarke, *Anglo-American Economic Collaboration in War and Peace 1942–49* (1982), p. 57.
42. *Ibid.*, pp. 130ff.

Chapter 5

1. U.S. Department of Commerce, *Historical Statistics of the United States: Colonial Times to 1957* (Washington, D.C.: 1960), p. 565.
2. Among the most important primary materials appeared, in chronological order, "The Fifth *Fortune* Round Table: America's Stake in the Present War and the Future World Order," *Fortune* 21 (January 1940), as well as "The Sixth *Fortune* Round Table: The United States and Foreign Trade," *Fortune* 21 (April 1940); Lewis L. Lorwin, *Economic Consequences of the Second World War* (New York: 1941); Hal Lary and Associates, *The United States in the World Economy* (U.S. Department of Commerce. Economics Series, No. 23: Washington: 1943); U.S. House of Representatives, Committee on Foreign Affairs, *Hearings on Extension of the Lend-Lease Act*, 78th Cong., 1st Sess., 1943, and 79th Cong., 1st Sess., 1945; National Planning Association, *America's New Opportunities in World Trade* (November 1944); U.S. House of Representatives, Special Subcommittee on Post-War Economic Policy and Planning, *Hearings on Post-War Economic Policy and Planning*, 78th Cong., 2nd Sess., 1944; John H. Williams, *Postwar Monetary Plans and Other Essays* (New York: 1944; 2nd edn; 1945). Also, Norman S. Buchanan and Frederich A. Lutz, *Rebuilding the World Economy: America's Role in Foreign Trade and Investment* (New York: 1947). Secondary material on this period includes E. F. Penrose, *Economic Planning for the Peace* (Princeton: 1953), and Gabriel Kolko, *The Politics of War: The World and U.S. Foreign Policy, 1943–1945* (New York: 1968).
3. Lary, *The United States in the World Economy*, p. 13.
4. *Ibid.*, pp. 18ff.
5. *Ibid.*, p. 20.
6. U.S. House of Representatives, Special Committee on Postwar Policy and Planning, *Report*, pp. 1082ff. (1943).
7. Franklin Delano Roosevelt, *Public Papers* 11, p. 492, from his press conference of November 24, 1942, quoted in John Lewis Gaddis, *The United States and the Origins of the Cold War, 1941–1947* (New York: 1972), p. 21.
8. Lary, *The United States in the World Economy*, p. 13.
9. John H. Williams, *Postwar Monetary Plans and Other Essays* (New York: 1944), p. xvi.
10. *Ibid.*, p. 7.
11. U.S. Senate, Committee on Banking and Currency, *Hearings on H.R. 3314, Bretton Woods Agreements Act* (referred to in all subsequent chapter notes as *Senate Hearings*), 79th Cong., 1st Sess., 1945, p. 40; also testimony of Mr Morgenthau, pp. 5–7. See also U.S. House of Representatives, Committee on Banking and Currency, *Hearings on H.R. 2211, Bretton Woods Agreements Act* (referred to in all subsequent chapter notes as *House Hearings*), 79th Cong., 1st Sess., March 9, 1945, testimony of Mr Clayton, pp. 275, 282.

12. *Senate Hearings*, testimony of Imre De Vegh, p. 357.
13. *Ibid.*, p. 164.
14. Mason and Asher, *The World Bank since Bretton Woods*, p. 15.
15. Alvin Hansen, *America's Role in the World Economy*, p. 32.
16. *Ibid.*, p. 6. See also p. 11, as well as the *House Hearings*, pp. 29, 33, 290.
17. *Senate Hearings*, testimony of Edward Brown, Chairman of the Board of the First National Bank, Chicago, pp. 104–5.
18. *Senate Hearings*, p. 37.
19. *Survey of American Foreign Relations: 1928*, p. 218.
20. *Senate Hearings* pp. 168–70. See also *House Hearings*, testimony of Professor Williams, p. 322, and testimony of Mr Clayton, p. 278.
21. U.S. Department of Commerce, *U.S. International Transactions during the War: 1940–45* (Washington, D.C.: 1948), pp. 160ff.
22. *House Hearings*, testimony of Harry A. Bullis, p. 497. See also John H. Williams, *Economic Stability in a Changing World: Essays in Economic Theory and Policy* (New York: 1953), pp. 104, 116–20, 124, 162ff., 173.
23. August Maffry, "Bretton Woods and Foreign Trade," *Foreign Commerce Weekly*, October 7, 1944 (quoted in *House Hearings*, p. 313).
24. Carlyle Morgan, *Bretton Woods: Clues to a Monetary Mystery* (Boston: 1945), p. 78.
25. *House Hearings*, p. 809.
26. *Ibid.*, p. 408. (On Fraser see Matthew Josephson's *New Yorker* article of February 21, 1942.) Related testimony was given by Prof. Kemmerer, p. 869, and Melchior Palyi, p. 901.

Chapter 6

1. J. Keith Horsefield, *The International Monetary Fund: 1945–1965. Twenty Years of International Monetary Cooperation. Vol. I: Chronicle* (Washington, D.C.: 1969), pp. 77ff. On Russia's cooperation in increasing its World Bank quota from $900 million to $1.2 billion as a special friendly gesture toward the United States, see the testimony of Harry Dexter White, *House Hearings*, p. 76.
2. Robert Skidelsky, *John Maynard Keynes, Vol. III: Fighting for Freedom, 1947–1946* (New York: 2001), pp. 259f.
3. *Ibid.*, p. 260.
4. *Ibid.*, p. 351. Skidelsky notes that "When Stepanov the Russian was told [by Morgenthau] that Soviet national income statistics did not justify a quota of $1.2 bn, he replied cheerfully that he would produce new statistics. He got his way," thanks largely to the pro-Soviet bias of the leading Treasury officials.
5. John Gaddis, *The United States and the Origins of the Cold War, 1941–1947* (New York: 1972), p. 174.
6. Quoted in Charles Prince, "The USSR's Role in International Finance," *Harvard Business Review* 25 (Autumn 1946), pp. 118ff. The following analysis leans on Prince's summary of Soviet attitudes toward the Bretton Woods institutions and America's responses.
7. Quoted in *ibid.*, pp. 124ff.
8. Horsefield, *The International Monetary Fund*, p. 117.
9. *Senate Hearings*, testimony of Imre De Vegh, p. 355.
10. *House Hearings*, p. 196.
11. Prince, "The USSR's Role," pp. 122f.
12. George F. Kennan, *Memoirs: 1925–1950* (Boston: 1967), p. 22. Kennan recommended that the loan be cut to $1.5 billion.
13. *Senate Hearings*, testimony of John H. Williams, p. 328. See also Mr Anderson's testimony, *ibid.*, p. 396.

14. Prince, "The USSR's Role," p. 122.
15. *House Hearings*, p. 211.
16. *Ibid.*, p. 196.
17. Thomas G. Paterson, "The Abortive American Loan to Russia and the Origins of the Cold War, 1943–1946," *Journal of American History* 56 (June 1969), pp. 74ff. For a detailed discussion of American thinking on the prospects for postwar US–Soviet trade see Gaddis, *United States*, ch. 6.
18. *Ibid.*, p. 78.
19. Lloyd C. Gardner, "The New Deal, New Frontiers, and the Cold War: A Re-examination of American Expansion, 1933–1945," in David Horowitz et al., *Corporations and the Cold War* (New York: 1969), p.130.
20. Prince, "The USSR's Role," p. 123.
21. *Ibid.*, p. 122.
22. *Ibid.*, p. 127.
23. Hansen, *America's Role in the World Economy*, pp. 5ff.
24. Prince, "The USSR's Role," p. 115.
25. *Ibid.*, p. 118.
26. Quoted in *ibid.*, p. 117.
27. *Problems of Foreign Policy: Speeches and Statements, April 1945–November 1948* (Moscow: 1949), pp. 207–14, quoted in Gardner, "New Deal," p. 129. Skidelsky (*Keynes*, p. 262) dismisses as ideological extremism such works as Gabriel Kolko's *Politics of War*, which viewed Morgenthau and White as seeking to "de-Bolshevising" the Soviet Union by integrating it into the capitalist West on a neo-colonialist basis. It certainly was Russia itself that was pressing for as large a loan as it could get. What the Americans wanted was to maximize postwar markets for their exports, precisely so that they could shift from military arms production to civilian capital goods and consumer goods for export.
28. Herbert Feis, "The Conflict over Trade Ideologies," *Foreign Affairs* 25 (January 1947), p. 220.
29. Prince, "The USSR's Role," p. 125.
30. *Ibid.*, pp. 127ff.
31. *Ibid.*, p. 128. Prince designed such a treaty (*Congressional Record*, June 21, 1946, p. A3856).
32. Skidelsky, *Keynes*, p. 464.
33. William C. Bullitt, *The Great Globe Itself* (New York: 1946), p. 121, quoted in Gardner, "New Deal," p. 132. Gardner remarks that Bullitt "had gone to Moscow full of hopes, but grew disillusioned with the impossibility of dealing profitably with Soviet monopolies in foreign trade or with the Russian government in any way."
34. Horsefield, *International Monetary Fund*, p. 117. For a lengthy treatment of the political aspects of U.S. Lend-Lease credits to Russia and its historical setting, see William Appleton Williams, *The Tragedy of American Diplomacy* (New York: 1962), especially ch. 6, as well as Paterson, "The Abortive American Loan."
35. Gaddis, *United States*, p. 353.
36. Edward S. Mason and Robert E. Asher, *The World Bank since Bretton Woods* (Washington, D.C.: 1973), p. 29n.

Chapter 7

1. *Selected Documents, Board of Governors' Inaugural Meetings*, pp. 29f., quoted in J. Keith Horsefield, *The International Monetary Fund: 1945–1965* (Washington, D.C.: 1969), p. 129.
2. Quoted in Bruce Nissen, "The World Bank: A Political Institution," *Pacific Research & World Empire Telegram* 2 (September–October 1971), p. 15 (quoting a report in *The*

New York Times dated March 24, 1945), and Edward S. Mason and Robert E. Asher, *The World Bank since Bretton Woods* (Washington, D.C.: 1973), p. 34.

3. "Morgenthau 'Shocked' by News Douglas May Head World Bank," *The New York Herald-Tribune*, March 31, 1946. See also Council for Foreign Relations, *The United States in World Affairs, 1945–47*, p. 380.

4. *Ibid.*, p. 38, quoting Fred M. Vinson, "After the Savannah Conference," *Foreign Affairs* 24 (July 1926), p. 626.

5. Quoted in Mason and Asher, *The World Bank since Bretton Woods*, p. 37, and Horsefield, *International Monetary Fund*, pp. 123, 130.

6. Robert Skidelsky, *John Maynard Keynes*, Vol. III: *Fighting for Freedom, 1947–1946* (New York: 2001), p. 465.

7. *The Manchester Guardian*, March 23, 1946, quoted in Mason and Asher, *The World Bank since Bretton Woods*, p. 39.

8. Nissen, "World Bank," p. 16.

9. Mason and Asher, *The World Bank since Bretton Woods*, p. 96, quoting Morton M. Mendels, the first secretary of the Bank, from the Oral History Project of Columbia University, interviews recorded in the summer of 1961 on the IBRD.

10. Council on Foreign Relations, *The United States in World Affairs, 1945–47*, pp. 380ff.

11. *Ibid.*, pp. 370–1, 381.

12. See Nissen, "World Bank," p. 16.

13. *The United States in World Affairs, 1945–47*, p. 381.

14. Nissen, "World Bank," p. 17, quoting *The New York Times* of March 4 and May 27, 1947.

15. *Senate Hearings*, p. 611 (from Morgenthau's article, "Bretton Woods and International Cooperation," *Foreign Affairs*, January 1945)

16. See, for instance, in *House Hearings*, the testimonies of Harry A. Bullis of General Mills, p. 497; Edward O'Neal of the American Farm Bureau Federation, pp. 600f.; Russell Smith of the National Farmers' Union, p. 1036, and the observations of Rep. Baldwin of Maryland, pp. 274ff.

17. *Ibid.*, p. 276.

18. *Ibid.*, p. 286.

19. Hansen, *America's Role in the World Economy*, p. 81.

20. On the former case see, for instance, I. Eshag and R. Thorp, "Economic and Social Consequences of Orthodox Policies in Argentina in the Post-War Years," *Bulletin of the Oxford Institute of Economics and Statistics*, February 1965.

21. J. J. Spengler, "I.B.R.D. Mission Economic Growth Theory," *American Economic Review*, May 1954, p. 583.

22. United Nations, *Measures for the Economic Development of Underdeveloped Countries* (1951), p. 82.

23. *The Failures of the World Bank Missions* (Publication P-1411, June 24, 1958), p. 8.

24. *The Economic Development of Colombia* (Baltimore: 1950), p. 354.

25. John H. Adler, "Fiscal and Monetary Implementation of Development Programs," *American Economic Review*, May 1952.

26. See the published reports of the World Bank missions to *Ceylon*, pp. 108f.; *Nicaragua*, pp. 29, 31; *Syria*, pp. 35ff.; *British Guiana*, pp. 25ff.; *Guatemala*, pp. 23, 27; *Iraq*, p. 4; *Nigeria*, p. 192; *Turkey*, pp. 32, 57; *Tanganyika*, pp. 5ff.; *Jordan*, p. 12; *Uganda*, pp. 15ff.; *Thailand*, p. 4, etc.

27. *Land Reform* (New York: 1951), p. 18.

28. *The Economic Development of Ceylon* (Baltimore: 1953), p. 362. See also *The Economic Development of Tanganyika* (Baltimore: 1962), p. 94.

29. *The Economic Development of Jamaica* (Baltimore: 1952), p. 161.

30. *The Economic Development of Colombia*, p. 63; also p. 360.

31. *Ibid.*, p. 383.

32. *Progress in Land Reform* (New York: 1952), p. 185, which cites many other instances of this dual economic structure. See also the reports of the World Bank missions to *Malaya*, p. 314; *Ceylon*, p. 360; *Syria*, p. 68; *Surinam*, p. 119, etc.
33. Quoted in a review of Catholic opposition to Malthusianism, Eugene K. Culhane's "They'd Rather Decide for Themselves," *America* 120 (May 24, 1969), pp. 621ff. See also Abraham Guillen, "Malthusianism is not for Latin America," *Vispera* (Montevideo, Uruguay), March 1969.
34. Review of *Partners in Development*, SODEPAX (Committee on Society, Development and Peace), (mimeo.; October 8, 1969), p. 11.
35. *Ibid.*, p. 7.
36. "'Lag' in Disbursements. World Bank Criticized On LDCs Operations," *Journal of Commerce*, February 20, 1973.
37. Section 1, paragraph 1, sec. 13(c) (1).
38. *U.S. Congressional Record*, Sept. 14, 1970, p. H8648, during the hearings on H.R.18306.
39. *Partners in Development*, p. 5.
40. "World Bank gets biggest ever loan – from Japan," *The Financial Times*, February 21, 1971.
41. For detailed statistics on debt-servicing costs to the aid-borrowing countries see the World Bank's *Annual Report* for 1969, especially pp. 49–52, 72–79.
42. K. B. Griffin and J. L. Enos, "Foreign Assistance: Objectives and Consequences," *Economic Development and Cultural Change* 18 (April 1970), pp. 317ff.
43. *Ibid.*, p. 326.
44. *Ibid.*, p. 321.
45. *Ibid.*, p. 325.
46. *Senate Hearings*, p. 11.
47. Quoted in Culhane, "They'd Rather Decide for Themselves."

Chapter 8

1. T. W. Schultz, "Value of U.S. Farm Surpluses to Underdeveloped Countries," *Journal of Farm Economics* 42 (December 1960), p. 1026. Reprinted in Gustav Ranis (ed.), *The United States and the Developing Economies* (New York: 1964).
2. U.S. Senate, *Technical Assistance: Final Report of the Committee on Foreign Relations* (Report No. 139, March 12, 1957); 87th Cong., 1st Sess., pp. 18ff. (referred to in all subsequent chapter notes as *Technical Assistance, 1957 Report*).
3. *U.S. Foreign Assistance in the 1970s: A New Approach* (Washington, D.C.: March 4, 1970), p. 16. Referred to in all subsequent chapter notes as the *Peterson Report*.
4. Quoted in *The Report of the Committee on the Working of the Monetary System, Principal Memoranda of Evidence* (London: 1960) 11, p. 105.
5. *Peterson Report*, p. 5.
6. "Congressmen Told of $693-Million Arms Sales under Food for Peace Program," *The New York Times*, January 5, 1971.
7. For an elaboration of this strategy see Lincoln Bloomfield and Amelia C. Leiss, *Controlling Small Wars: A strategy for the 1970's* (New York: 1969).
8. *The Foreign Assistance Program: Annual Report to the Congress for Fiscal Year 1969*, p. 44. Referred to in all subsequent chapter notes as *AID Annual Report*, 1969.
9. Quoted in *The New York Times*, March 8, 1970.
10. For a discussion of the political price exacted for the British loan, see Gabriel Kolko, *The Politics of War: The World and United States Foreign Policy, 1943–45* (New York: 1968), ch. 19, especially pp. 488–95. For Kolko's discussion of U.S. food aid and the political-economic strategy underlying U.S. foreign assistance in the postwar years, see pp. 496–501.

11. Detailed statistics covering the U.S. aid and mutual security programs during 1946–60 by area may be found in the U.S. Department of Commerce's *Balance of Payments: Statistical Supplement* (rev. edn; A Supplement to the *Survey of Current Business*; Washington, D.C.: 1963), pp. 150–71.

12. For a detailed analysis of P.L. 480 activities, see *Food for Peace: Annual Report on Public Law 480*, for the years 1965 through 1970.

13. *Food for Peace: 1965 Annual Report on Public Law 480* (Washington, D.C.: 1966), p. 18.

14. *Ibid.*, p. 17.

15. *The Annual Report on Activities Carried Out under Public Law 480, 83rd Congress, as Amended, during the Period January 1 through December 31, 1969* (mimeo.; Washington, D.C.: June 18, 1970), p. 2. Referred to in all subsequent chapter notes as *1969 Annual Report.*

16. *Ibid.*, p. 23.

17. For a review of the literature on how U.S. food aid has worked to impair foreign agricultural self-sufficiency see Clifford R. Kern, "Looking a Gift Horse in the Mouth: The Economics of Food Aid Programs," *Political Science Quarterly* 83 (March 1968), p. 59.

18. *1969 Annual Report*, pp. 53ff.

19. *Ibid.*, p. 10.

20. *Ibid.*, pp. 24ff.

21. "Fertilizer Group Raps AID Program Change as Harmful to Industry," *Journal of Commerce*, November 9, 1970.

22. *1965 Annual Report*, p. 17.

23. *Peterson Report*, p. 31.

24. *1969 Annual Report*, p. 17.

25. *Ibid.*, p. 1 (parentheses added).

26. *Ibid.*, pp. 2ff.

27. *Ibid.*, p. 85.

28. *Foreign Affairs* 45 (July 1967).

29. *Ibid.*, p. 584.

30. On this and related points concerning the balance-of-payments impact of U.S. foreign aid, see Michael Hudson, "A Financial Payments-Flow Analysis of U.S. International Transactions: 1960–68," New York University, Graduate School of Business Administration, *The Bulletin*, Nos. 61–63 (March 1970), pp. 24–33.

31. *Peterson Report*, p. 32.

32. *AID Annual Report*, 1969, pp. 23ff.

33. Hudson, "A Financial Payments-Flow Analysis," Table 3.

34. *AID Annual Report*, 1969, p. 23.

35. *Ibid.*, p. 6. See also pp. 11ff.

36. *The New York Times*, March 8, 1970.

37. U.S. House of Representatives, Committee on Foreign Affairs, *Hearings on H.R. 10502*, 88th Cong., 2nd Sess., 1964, pp. 83ff. (For an elaboration of this attitude see Mr McNamara's Montreal address of 1967.)

38. *Peterson Report*, p. 7.

39. *Ibid.*, p. 22.

40. *U.S. Congressional Record*, September 14, 1970, p. H8646.

41. *Ibid.*, p. H8649.

42. *Technical Assistance 1957 Report*, p. 28.

43. *Eximbank 1968 Annual Report*, pp. 18ff.

44. *Peterson Report*, p. 14.

45. *Ibid.*, p. 6.

46. *Ibid.*, p. 10.

47. World Bank and International Development Association, *Annual Report: 1970*, Table 9 (p. 48), and *Survey of Current Business*, October 1970, pp. 28ff.

48. *Peterson Report*, p. 33.
49. *Ibid.*, p. 19.
50. Testimony of Frank M. Coffin, December 12, 1962, before the Congressional Subcommittee on International Exchange and Payments, quoted in Ranis (ed.), *The United States and the Developing Economies*, p. 139.
51. "Move by Brazil Stirs U.S. Issue," *The New York Times*, February 22, 1971.
52. "World Bank Used for U.S. Protest. Opposition to Loans Reflects Stand on Compensation of Nationalized Companies," *The New York Times*, June 28, 1971.
53. *Christian Science Monitor*, November 3, 1971, p. 6.
54. Jerome Levinson and Juan de Onis, *A Critical Report on the Alliance for Progress* (Chicago: 1970), quoted in Joseph Page's review in *The New York Times*, January 10, 1971.
55. *Ibid.*

Chapter 9

1. On these points see William Diebold, Jr., "The End of the I.T.O.," Princeton University, *Essays in International Finance*, No. 16 (Princeton: October 1952), especially pp. 14–23. For a compendium of U.S. attitudes, see U.S. House of Representatives, Committee on Foreign Affairs, *Hearings on Membership and Participation by the United States in the International Trade Organization*, 81st Cong., 2nd Sess., 1950.
2. U.S. Senate, Committee on Finance, *Hearings on Trade Agreements System and the ITO*, Pt. I, 80th Cong., 1st Sess., 1947, p. 37.
3. Diebold, "The End of the I.T.O.," p. 23.
4. *Ibid.*, p. 20.
5. *The New York Times*, November 20, 1947, p. 3.
6. Diebold, "The End of the I.T.O.," p. 16.
7. *Ibid.*, p. 31.
8. Council on Foreign Relations, *The United States in World Affairs, 1945–47*, p. 373.
9. Diebold, "The End of the I.T.O.," p. 1.
10. *Ibid.*, p. 34, quoting Jacob Viner's report on *Rearmament and International Commercial Policies*, U.S. State Department, Foreign Service Institute (multigraphed; Washington, D.C.: 1951), p. 9.
11. Raymond Vernon, "America's Foreign Trade Policy and the GATT," Princeton University, International Finance Section, *Essays in International Finance*, No. 21 (October 1954), p. 33.
12. *Ibid.*, p. 29.
13. Oscar Zaglitz, "Agricultural Trade and Trade Policy," in National Advisory Commission in Food and Fiber, Technical Papers (Vol. VI): *Foreign Trade and Agricultural Policy* (August 1967), p. 209.
14. Vernon, "America's Foreign Trade Policy," pp. 10ff.
15. Zaglitz, "Agricultural Trade," p. 213.
16. U.S. Department of Commerce, *Statistical Abstract: 1970*, p. 777.

Chapter 10

1. Council on Foreign Relations, *The United States in World Affairs: 1945–1947*, p. 370.
2. U.S. House of Representatives, Special Subcommittee on Post-War Economic Policy and Planning, *Hearings on H.R. 1205, Economic Reconstruction in Europe*, 79th Cong., 1st Sess., November 12, 1945, p. 13, quoted in Richard N. Gardner, *Sterling–Dollar Diplomacy* (Oxford: 1956), p. 198.
3. Quoted in Gardner, *ibid.*, p. 208.

4. Gabriel Kolko, *The Politics of War: The World and United States Foreign Policy, 1943–1945* (New York: 1968), p. 490.
5. "Inconvertible Again," *The Economist* 53 (1947), p. 306, quoted in Gardner, *Sterling–Dollar Diplomacy*, p. 339.
6. Herbert Feis, *The Changing Pattern of International Economic Affairs* (New York: 1940), p. 58.
7. Joyce and Gabriel Kolko, *The Limits of Power: The World and United States Foreign Policy, 1945–1954* (New York: 1972), pp. 60ff.
8. Quoted in Gardner, *Sterling–Dollar Diplomacy*, p. 242. See also *passim*.
9. *The United States in World Affairs: 1945–1947*, p. 361.
10. *The Economist*, August 1947, quoted in Kolko and Kolko, *The Limits of Power*, p. 367.
11. Quoted in Gardner, *Sterling–Dollar Diplomacy*, p. 247.
12. Quoted in *ibid.*, pp. 227ff.
13. Quoted in *ibid.*, p. 344.
14. Kolko, *The Politics of War*, pp. 490, 493.
15. League of Nations, *International Currency Experience: Lessons of the Inter-War Period* (1944), pp. 226ff.
16. Hal Lary and Associates, *The United States in the World Economy* (U.S. Department of Commerce, Economic Series No. 23, Washington, D.C.: 1943), p. 12.
17. League of Nations, *International Currency Experience*, p. 147.
18. Robert Skidelsky, *John Maynard Keynes*, Vol. III: *Fighting for Freedom, 1947–1946* (New York: 2001), p. 451.
19. Robert Mosse, *Le Système monétaire de Bretton Woods et les grands problèmes de l'après-guerre* (Paris: 1948), p. 48, quoted in J. Keith Horsefield, *The International Monetary Fund. 1945–1965. I: Chronicle* (Washington D.C.: 1969), p. 97.
20. Skidelsky, *Keynes*, p. 351.
21. *Ibid.*, p. 462, quoting Susan Howson and D. E. Moggridge (eds.), *Collected Papers of James Meade, IV: The Cabinet Office Diary 1944–46* (London, 1990), 227.
22. Kolko and Kolko, *The Limits of Power*, p. 633.
23. Horsefield, *The International Monetary Fund*, p. 596.
24. Skidelsky, *Keynes*, pp. 466ff.
25. Horsefield, *The International Monetary Fund*, p. 196.
26. Skidelsky, *Keynes*, pp. 480, 492.

Chapter 11

1. Seymour Melman (ed.), "A Strategy for American Security," *Saturday Review*, May 4, 1963.
2. "The United States Balance of Payments: The Problem and its Solution," in *Factors Affecting the United States Balance of Payments* (87th Cong., 2nd Sess.) (Washington, D.C.: 1963), p. 7.
3. International Monetary Fund, *Summary Proceedings: Annual Meeting, 1963*, pp. 61ff.
4. For a theoretical elaboration of this position see Jacques Rueff, *The Balance of Payments* (New York: 1967).
5. IMF charter, pp. 90ff.
6. *Summary Proceedings: Annual Meeting, 1964*, pp. 53ff.
7. *Ibid.*, p. 64.
8. *Ibid.*, p. 107.
9. *Ibid.*, p. 205.
10. "U.S. Proposes Gold Certificate Plan to Members of the London Pool, Sources Say," *Wall Street Journal*, December 15, 1967.
11. "Le Monde Says U.S. Seeks Gold; Officials Here Ridicule Report," *The New York Times*, December 9, 1967.

12. *U.S. Congressional Record*, December 14, 1967, p. S/18673. See also *ibid.*, Dec. 12, 1967, p. S/18399.
13. "Speaking Out," *Saturday Evening Post*, April 22, 1967.
14. Quoted in the Baltimore *Sun*, January 6, 1968.
15. International Monetary Fund, *Annual Report: 1970*, p. 24.
16. Quoted in the *Wall Street Journal*, April 4, 1968.

Chapter 12

1. M. Barrett and M. L. Greene, "Special Drawing Rights: A Major Step in the Evolution of the World's Monetary System," Federal Reserve Bank of New York, *Monthly Review* 50 (January 1968), p. 12.
2. *England's interest, or the great benefit to trade by banks or offices of credit* (1682), pp. 1ff., quoted in Jacob Viner, *Studies in the Theory of International Trade* (New York: 1937), p. 39.
3. "Debate on SDRs Looms. Fund Hits U.S. Inflation Effort; Holds Payments Status Crucial," *Journal of Commerce*, September 8, 1970.
4. "Dollars Abroad Cause a Problem. Director of Monetary Fund Bids U.S. Settle Balance of Payments with Gold," *The New York Times*, September 22, 1970.
5. Barrett and Greene, "Special Drawing Rights," p. 13.
6. "Rein on Inflation Called 'Crucial,'" *The New York Times*, September 8, 1970.
7. Robert V. Roosa, "Capital Movements and Balance-of-Payments Adjustment," Federal Reserve Bank of Philadelphia, *Business Review*, September 1970, p. 29.
8. H. S. Houthakker and Stephen P. Magee, "Income and Price Elasticities in World Trade," *Review of Economics and Statistics* 51 (May 1969), pp. 121ff.
9. See in particular Walter S. Salant, "Financial Intermediation as an Explanation of Enduring Payments 'Deficits' in the Balance of Payments," National Bureau of Economic Research, Conference on International Mobility and Movement of Capital (mimeo.; January 30–February 1, 1970), as well as Arthur B. Laffer's paper from this same conference, "International Financial Intermediation: Interpretation and Empirical Analysis." The IFI hypothesis was first formulated in its present version by Despres, Kindleberger and Salant, "The Dollar and World Liquidity: A Minority View," *The Economist*, February 5, 1966, pp. 526–29 (reprinted as Brookings Reprint No. 115, April 1966). Also may be mentioned Mr Salant's "Capital Markets and the Balance of Payments of a Financial Center," in W. J. Fellner, F. Machlup and R. Triffin (eds.), *Maintaining and Restoring Balance in International Payments* (Princeton: 1966. Reprinted as Brookings Reprint No. 23, December 1966). All subsequent references refer to Mr Salant's 1970 paper unless otherwise noted.
10. Salant, "Capital Markets," p. 7.
11. Robert Triffin, "The Balance of Payments and the Foreign Investment Position of the United States," Princeton University, International Finance Section, *Essays in International Finance*, No. 55 (September 1966), p. 11.
12. *Ibid.*, p. 19.
13. Laffer, "International Financial Intermediation," p. 1 (mimeo version).
14. Despres, Kindleberger and Salant, "The Dollar and World Liquidity," p. 44.
15. Laffer, "International Financial Intermediation," p. 4.
16. Michael Hudson, "A Payments-Flow Analysis of U.S. International Transactions: 1960–1968," New York University, Graduate School of Business Administration, Institute of Finance, *The Bulletin*, Nos. 61–63 (March 1970), pp. ix–xi.
17. Robert Solomon, "The International Monetary System in the 1970's," *Business Economics* 5 (January 1970), p. 22.
18. Norman S. Fieleke, "Accounting for the Balance of Payments," Federal Reserve Bank of Boston, *New England Economic Review* (May/June 1971), p. 12.

Chapter 13

1. "Trade Bars Abroad Make U.S. Restive: Congress May Well Curtail Imports, Kennedy Says," *The New York Times*, May 21, 1970.
2. "Textile Import Quotas Backed by Administration," *Wall Street Journal*, June 26, 1970.
3. "Europe Maps Retaliation if U.S. Trade Bill Passes," *The New York Times*, November 7, 1970. (Mr Poniatowski's article appeared in the Paris weekly, *L'Economie*.)
4. "Briton Foresees a Rift on Trade: Says Retaliation Is Possible If U.S. Passes Trade Bill," *The New York Times*, November 20, 1970.
5. "Europeans Vexed by U.S. Trade Bill. Warning by Spain," *The New York Times*, November 21, 1970.
6. "Connally Says U.S. Plans No Shift in Money Policy," *The New York Times*, May 8, 1971.
7. "Inside Common Market: Monetary Friction," *The New York Times*, May 11, 1971.
8. "Common Market Drafting a Plan in Money Crisis," *The New York Times*, May 9, 1971. On Mr Schiller's plan, see also "Bonn Revives Idea of 6-Nation Float," *The New York Times*, June 16, 1971.
9. "Monetary Challenge. Currency Crisis Highlights Problems of Rate Flexibility and Trade Policy," *The New York Times*, June 9, 1971.
10. "No U.S. Currency Move Set Now," *The New York Times*, May 11, 1971.
11. *Ibid.*
12. "European Foreign-Exchange Traders Await Trend – U.S. Denies Responsibility," *The New York Times*, May 12, 1971.
13. "Europeans Step up Dollar Pressure. Monetary Inquiry Urged," *The New York Times*, May 13, 1971.
14. "Connally Is Firm on Dollar Policy," *The New York Times*, May 18, 1971.
15. "Monetary Challenge," *The New York Times*, June 9, 1971.
16. "A Special Tariff on Japan Weighed. U.S. Considers a New Duty on All Goods Unless Yen is Revalued Upward," *The New York Times*, May 24, 1971.
17. "Japanese Ponder Trade Imbalance," *The New York Times*, June 19, 1971. See also "Japan Firm on Yen," *ibid.*, May 28, 1971, and "Japan Vows Not to Revalue Yen," *ibid.*, May 18, 1971.
18. Ilse Mintz, *U.S. Import Quotas: Costs and Consequences* (Washington, D.C.: 1973), pp. 1ff.
19. John Lynch, *Toward an Orderly Market: An Intensive Study of Japan's Voluntary Quota in Cotton Textile Exports* (Tokyo: 1968), pp. 77–94, quoted in Mintz, *Import Quotas*, p. 20. See also *ibid.*, pp. 51ff.
20. "U.S. Threat Reported," *The New York Times*, May 12, 1971.
21. "Mansfield Asks 50% Cut in U.S. Forces in Europe," *The New York Times*, May 15, 1971.
22. "Nixon Firm in Fight to Bar U.S. Troop Cut in Europe," *The New York Times*, May 14, 1971.
23. "Economic Analysis: Big Stakes at Issue as Group of 10 Meets," *The New York Times*, September 15, 1971.
24. "Europe Welcomes Move; Dollar Trading Is Mixed," *The New York Times*, August 28, 1971.
25. "13 Billion Gain Sought to Spur Payments to US: Connally Issues Challenge on Improving Balance as Group of Ten Meets. Europeans Skeptical," *The New York Times*, September 16, 1971.
26. "Report on IMF Plan Lifts Currencies," *The New York Times*, September 24, 1971.
27. "Dollar Devaluation: Most Pressing Issue at IMF Talks is Not Whether but How Large it Will Be," *The New York Times*, September 29, 1971.
28. "Group of 10 Fails to Find Accord on Dollar Crisis," *The New York Times*, September 17, 1971.

29. "Summary of the Recommendations of the Commission on Trade," *The New York Times*, September 19, 1971.
30. "Common Market Agrees to Resist U.S. on Dollar. 6 Finance Ministers Ask America to Devalue," *The New York Times*, September 14, 1971.
31. "France Rejects Concession to U.S.," *The New York Times*, September 24, 1971.
32. "Japan Urged to Buy Arms, Help Pay for U.S. Troops," *The New York Times*, September 10, 1971.
33. "U.S. Gives Seoul a Textile Ultimatum," *The New York Times*, September 23, 1971.
34. "South Korea Plans U.S. Pact," *The New York Times*, October 1, 1971.
35. "U.S. Gives Japan Plan on Textiles. Tokyo Told to Accept Curbs or Face Quotas on October 15," *The New York Times*, October 1, 1971.
36. "Textile Makers Defy Tokyo Government," *The New York Times*, October 9, 1971.
37. "Japan Agrees to Restrict Flow of Textiles into U.S.; Surcharge on Them Ends," *The New York Times*, October 16, 1971.
38. "Denmark Plans Surcharge as Protectionist Measure. European Trading Partners Critical – Common Market Retaliation Against U.S. is Said to be a French Goal," *The New York Times*, October 20, 1971.
39. "Import Authority for Nixon Backed," *The New York Times*, November 5, 1971.
40. "Dollar Devaluation: It Could Be Tricky," *The Wall Street Journal*, December 15, 1971.

Chapter 14

1. The Chase Manhattan Bank, *Business in Brief*, April 1967, "Deficits, Dollars and Gold," p. 3.
2. Gottfried Haberler, *U.S. Balance of Payments Policy and the International Monetary System* (American Enterprise Institute for Public Policy Research: January, 1973), pp. 177f, originally published in *Convertibility, Multilateralism and World Economic Policy in the Seventies. Essays in Honor of Reinhard Kamitz* (Vienna: 1972).
3. *Ibid.*, p. 182.
4. "Economic Satellites Plan Gets Under Way," *The Financial Times*, April 5, 1972.
5. "Guiding Light in Dollar Diplomacy," *ibid.*
6. International Economic Policy Association, *The United States Balance of Payments: From Crisis to Controversy* (Washington: 1972), p. 69.
7. *Ibid.*, pp. 67, 87ff.
8. *Ibid.*, p. 83.
9. *Ibid.*, pp. 85, 93.
10. *Ibid.*, p. 16.
11. *Ibid.*, p. 108.
12. *Ibid.*, p. 109.
13. *Economic Report of the President, 1973* (Washington, D.C.: 1973). pp. 124ff. This plan had been put forth initially by Secretary Shultz at the September 1972 IMF–World Bank meetings.
14. *Ibid.*, p. 170.
15. "Texts of Nixon–Tanaka Communiqué and Announcement on Trade in Honolulu," *The New York Times*, September 2, 1972; "Japan's Currency Hoard Rose Last Month to a High as it Took in Masses of Dollars," *Wall Street Journal*, November 1, 1972.
16. President Pompidou's Eighth Press Conference, January 9, 1973 (Ambassade de France, Service de Presse et d'Information).
17. "Mills Sees Need for Dollar Realignment. Declares Exchange Relationship with Other Monies Should be Revised beyond 1971 Action," *The New York Times*, February 8, 1973; "Devaluation Fear Spurs a Renewal of Dollar Sales," *The New York Times*, February 9, 1973.

18. "U.S. Avoided Common Market in Recent Money Crisis Talks," *The New York Times*, February 18, 1973.
19. Norman S. Fieleke, "International Economic Reform," Federal Bank of Boston, *New England Economic Review*, January/February 1973, p. 19.
20. "On Your Mark . . . New Monetary Crisis is Real but Could Aid U.S. Dollar and Trade. Turmoil Eases upward Push on U.S. Interest Rates," *Wall Street Journal*, February 12, 1973.
21. "Surcharge Issue Vexes Europeans. Talk in U.S. of Re-Imposition on Imports Frowned Upon," *The New York Times*, February 10, 1973.
22. "After the Fall," *Wall Street Journal*, February 14, 1973.
23. Economic Report of the President, 1973, p. 128.
24. "Yen Climbs 14% in Hectic Trading; Tanaka Criticized," *The New York Times*, February 15, 1973.
25. "Shultz Says U.S. Seeks New Drop in Dollar Value," *The New York Times*, February 16, 1973.
26. "Assessing the Crisis. U.S. Plan for Revision of Monetary System Worked Well in Crunch," *Wall Street Journal*, February 20, 1973; "Dollar up Sharply Here: Pact Reaction Favorable," *The New York Times*, March 17, 1973.
27. "Devaluation Stirs Anxiety and Dismay in Europe," *The New York Times*, February 16, 1973.
28. "Crisis on Money Is Seen As Just One of a Series," *The New York Times*, February 19, 1973.
29. "Is World Central Bank Needed? International Crises Spark Proposals for S.D.R. Uses," *The New York Times*, February 21, 1973. These remarks were all made at Claremont College in California during an International Monetary Conference held there the preceding week.
30. "Australians Cite Currency Losses," *The New York Times*, February 19, 1973.
31. "Is the Snake about to Hatch a Europa?" *The Economist*, February 24, 1973.
32. "U.S. Pledges Help to Europe In Settling the Monetary Crisis," *The New York Times*, March 10, 1973.
33. "Dollar Advances As Gold Weakens," *The New York Times*, March 14, 1973.
34. "U.S. and 13 Other Nations Adopt Measures to Ease Problem of Excess Dollars," *The New York Times*, March 17, 1973.
35. "The Great Dollar Whodunnit," *Financial Times*, March 21, 1973.
36. "Monetary Officials Divided on Intervention to Prop Dollar in Present Floating System," *Wall Street Journal*, June 11, 1973.
37. "Bonn Increases Official Value of Mark," *The New York Times*, June 30, 1973.
38. "Two-Day Dollar Rally Adds 5% to Value of Battered Currency," *The New York Times*, July 11, 1973.
39. "Reserve Lists Countries Raising Their Credit Lines," *The New York Times*, July 12, 1973; "Dollar Advances 3rd Straight Day," *The New York Times*, July 13, 1973; "Confrontation Avoided by Basel Accord," *ibid*.
40. "Dollar Weakness Aids Export Sales of U.S. Airplanes," *The New York Times*, July 16, 1973.
41. "U.S. Official Backs Claim to Trade Aid in Europe," *The New York Times*, February 22, 1973. See also "Nixon Asks Power to Cut, Raise or Cancel Tariffs and to Set Import Curbs," *The New York Times*, April 12, 1973; "Nixon Asks New Power on Trade. Faster Industry Aid on Import Damage is Also Sought," *The New York Times*, March 23, 1973; "Seoul Weighs Turn To U.S. for Imports," *The New York Times*, April 23, 1973.
42. "Flanigan Backs Nixon Trade Bill. Aide Denies President is Making 'Unprecedented' Bid for Power," *The New York Times*, May 9, 1973; "Shultz Renounces Reciprocity in Trade Negotiations," *The New York Times*, May 10, 1973; "Common Market To Stress Tough Stand in U.S. Talks," *The New York Times*, May 29, 1973.

43. "Farm Bill Stirs Official Concern. Dairy Import Limit is Seen as Threat to Trade Talks," *The New York Times*, June 4, 1973.

44. "Iran Will Buy $2 Billion in U.S. Arms over the Next Several Years," *The New York Times*, February 22, 1973. See also "Pentagon Hoping Iran Will Buy F-14s," *The New York Times*, July 19, 1973.

45. "Nixon Authorizes Jet Fighter Sales to 5 Latin Nations. U.S. Reverses Policy in Bid to Stem Loss of Markets – Chile Placed on List," *The New York Times*, June 6, 1973.

46. National Advisory Council on International Monetary and Financial Policies, *Annual Report to the President and to the Congress: July 1, 1970–June 30, 1971* (Washington, D.C.: February 16, 1972), pp. 3, 57.

47. "Devaluation Said to Cost Pentagon $80-Million," *The New York Times*, February 15, 1973.

48. National Advisory Council on International Monetary and Financial Policies, *Annual Report . . . July 1, 1970–June 30, 1971*, p. 83.

49. "Nixon Trade Plan for Soviet Seeks Debt Repayment," *The New York Times*, July 11, 1972; "Implications of U.S.-Soviet Trade Pact," *The New York Times*, November 22, 1972.

50. "Soviet Gas Deal Help Up as U.S. Studies Cost," *The New York Times*, January 9, 1973. See also "U.S. Concerns and Soviet Sign Big Natural-Gas Deal. 3 Houston Companies to Supply the East Coast from West Siberia," *The New York Times*, June 30, 1973.

51. "Deal is Held Near on Siberia's Gas," *The New York Times*, November 4, 1972.

52. "Soviet and Occidental Oil in Multibillion-Dollar Deal. 20-Year Barter Arrangement Provides for Export of American Technology and Goods for Fertilizer Complex," *The New York Times*, April 13, 1973.

53. "Japan and Soviet Agree on Joint Oil-Gas Project," *The New York Times*, November 25, 1972.

Index

Compiled by Sue Carlton

Moley, Raymond 77, 78, 82–92, 95–6,
    98–106, 108–9
Molotov, V.M. 163, 169–70
Le Monde 304
monetarism 4, 25, 33, 93, 296–7, 388
Moret, Clément 103
Morgenthau, Henry, Jr. 119–20, 216
    and aid to Russia 163, 166, 167
    and Bretton Woods 148, 180–1, 185
    and Lend-Lease system 122, 123, 127
Mosse, Robert 281
Most Favoured Nation (MFN) rule 258–9,
    356, 361, 373, 374
Moulton, Harold 74
Mussolini, Benito 56, 110, 111
Mutual Security Act 229, 232

Nakagama, Sam 362
National Advisory Council on
    International Monetary and
    Financial Policies (NAC) 116–17,
    181, 183, 204, 371, 373
National Labor-Management Council on
    Foreign Trade 250
National Planning Association 140
National Recovery Act (1933) 95
national socialism 6, 56
nationalism xiv, 79, 111, 115
NATO 221, 296, 339
Nearing, Scott 2
Netherlands
    floating currency 336, 337
    and gold standard 104
    and IMF 285
    revaluation 346
New Deal 89, 93, 94, 97, 120, 380, 389
New England Economic Review 359–60
New International Economic Order
    xvi–xviii, 347, 376, 383, 393
New York Federal Reserve Bank 103, 315,
    317, 325, 360, 367
New York Times 221, 304, 318, 335, 362,
    363
New Zealand 280–1
Nixon, Richard 9, 351–2, 355
    and arms aid 371
    and devaluation 361, 362
    and foreign investment 363
    and gold embargo 17, 22, 339–41,
        349–50
    and import quotas 329, 331–2, 369–70
    and import surcharge 345–6
    and Soviet Union 373, 374
    and tax reduction 334
    and tied aid 232

Norman, Montagu 59, 103
North Korea 223, 305
Norway ix, 71, 256

Occidental Oil 375
Ohlin, Bertil 4
oil
    and dollar devaluation 364
    Oil Wars xvii, 376
    prices x, 352
Okinawa 344
Okun, Arthur 334
O'Neill, Paul ix
OPEC countries 307, 352, 364, 371
Open Door policies 10, 12, 25, 140, 143,
    266
Organization for Economic Cooperation
    and Development (OECD) 334, 337
Ottawa Conference 1932 6, 76, 95, 124

Page, Joseph 246–7
Paish, George 67
Pakistan 222
Paley Report 257
paper credit/gold 111, 298, 310, 312–13,
    316, 318, 347, 353, 392
    see also Special Drawing Rights (SDRs)
Patten, Simon 2, 3, 81
Paul VII, Pope 201
Pax Americana 197
Payne-Aldrich Act 1909 65
Peace Corps 238
Pearson Commission/Report 197, 201–6
Penn Central 322
Pentagon Papers xii, xv
Pepper, Claude 180
Perkins Committee 239
Pershing, John J. 51
Peru 235
Peterson Commission/Report 197, 221,
    223, 234, 236, 239–42, 243–4
Peterson, Peter G. 343
Peterson, Rudolf 348–9, 350
Philips, William 110
Phillips, Frederick 120
Pick, Franz 366
Pinochet, Augusto 31
Pittman, Key 102, 104–5, 107
Plaza Accords 1985 xvi, 28, 384, 388
Poincaré, Raymond 71–2
Poland 169, 228
Polanyi, Karl 111, 116
Pompidou, Georges 343–4, 346, 358
Poniatowski, Michel 332